HILDEGARD!

Special Limited Edition

FIRST EDITION

HILDEGARD!

Ann K. Gebuhr

TotalRecall Publications, Inc.

www.totalrecallpress.com

TotalRecall Publications, Inc..
1103 Middlecreek
Friendswood, Texas 77546
281-992-3131 281-482-5390 Fax
www.totalrecallpress.com

Cover Graphic Arp 273, a pair of intersecting galaxies: Hubble Space Telescope.
ISBN: 978-1-59095-128-6
UPC: 6-43977-41290- 4

Printed in the United States of America with simultaneously printings in Australia, Canada, and United Kingdom.
FIRST EDITION
1 2 3 4 5 6 7 8 9 10

To Hildegard, who continues to
awaken, inspire, and touch our souls today.

To four friends who have shared Hildegard's music, message, medicine and vibrant, joyous energy of vision, health and love for all creation –
Rochelle Manske, Teresa Grawunder, Katrin DeBakey, and Carol Nave.

Table of Contents

Introduction

Hildegard von Bingen, an amazing woman of the 12th century
whose energy, wisdom, artistry, spirituality,
and approach to wholeness and healing
speaks loudly to our 21st century souls.

Why?

Hildegard has been the subject of numerous books, videos, movies, and musical performances, especially during the last twenty-five years[1], and many authors have included references to her in articles and books in the areas of theology, medieval art, medieval medicine, music, and literature. So why another book dealing with a nun who has been dead for over eight hundred years?

Three reasons have prompted the writing of this manuscript. The first is that I have discovered that Hildegard is not dead. For the past twenty years of my life, she has been a very energetic, often all-consuming and sometimes irritating presence who has led me into different levels of perception, spiritual health, musical inspiration, and serious questioning. She has been a mentor, a catalyst, a provocateur, an inspiration, a nag, a teacher, an angel, a guide, an open door, and a channel of deep, life-growing energy and love. A brief perusal of the bibliography in Appendix I indicates that she has obviously been alive in like manner for many others in these times. She is not dead…

And so this manuscript is offered, not as some sort of historical tome or authoritative resource about an exceptional historical figure, but as a personal experience of Hildegard in the 20th and 21st centuries. It is written from my perspective as a musician, since that is my particular essence and craft, and it is written much like a gourmet cookbook, including the literary spices and medicinal flavorings and the delicious spiritual beauties with which Hildegard has enriched the main course – music.

And music is the second reason for this manuscript, though it was not the initial means of my introduction to Hildegard. That introduction didn't come in a classroom or through theoretical or musicological study. It happened in the bookstore of the Jung Center in Houston during a 1986 summer browse through resources on spirituality, Jungian archetypes, and books about synchronicity and the like. On a bottom shelf in a dark corner, Hildegard's illumination for the vision about the Trinity leapt out of the darkness and imprinted itself in my soul. It was on the cover of Matthew Fox's book, *Illuminations of Hildegard of Bingen*[2]. Obeying the forceful inner command to pick it up and look through it, I opened to the page containing her self portrait.

---

1 See Appendix 1 for a lengthy though incomplete Bibliography.

2 Fox, Matthew. *Illuminations of Hildegard of Bingen*. Santa Fe, Bear & Company, Inc. 1985

Well. I am a music theorist and composer, who for the past thirty years has specialized in music of the 20th and 21st centuries – living music. I was engrossed in writing a piece based upon some Native American topics, and in the course of that project had been doing a good bit of reading about Native American spirituality and culture. Now here in front of me, riveting my attention, were two figures from the 12th century – not the central figures of the self portrait, Hildegard and Volmar[3], but figures painted on the pillars on either side of them.

Those figures are, as Fox confirmed in the text[4], from the Hopi Indian spiritual tradition, the Corn Man and Corn Woman! They are symbols for new life, for growth, awakening, fertility, and resurrection. And here they were in a 12th century illumination from the German Rhineland!

Hildegard, illumination from *Scivias*, p.5

Hmmm. Well! To that date my knowledge of Hildegard was only that she wrote some music (but I knew nothing about it) and now here in front of me was her self portrait implying mystical communion with God, a 12th century <u>woman</u> writing, and knowledge of powerful American Indian symbols. Amazing. Curious! Intriguing and compelling! I bought the book and began an incredible, delightful, life changing journey.

---

[3] Volmar was Hildegard's secretary and priest for her convent.

[4] Ibid. pp.27-29

Soon followed the purchase of three CDs of Hildegard's music then available[5], and when I heard my first Hildegard chant, the gate to a new path of discovery and wholeness flew wide open. That chant was not like the music from the 12th century which I had spent hours listening to, studying and growing to love in my undergraduate and graduate musicology classes. Hildegard's chants did not employ the rigorous plainchant character of 'liturgical' (i.e. ritual) Gregorian chants and they did not follow the traditional formulae developed through centuries of plainchant writing. There certainly are allusions to those formulae, but she does not rigorously apply them, and as a result, some musicologists have discounted her chants because they don't 'fit'. Well, her chants <u>don't</u> fit! They soar, they leap, they weep, they rejoice, they plead, they praise, they are cosmic. They are alive. They do not emerge from Hildegard's mastery of an established style of writing, but from her love of God and her communion with God. They are an expression of God's love and all of its manifestations transmitted through the openness and love and life of a little abbess who listened. And trusted. And loved. And lived fully! And as a result she has given us a collection of music and other earthly work that has no parallel in history. Music, spirituality, theology, medicine, art, poetry, theater (did you know she wrote the first morality play – really an opera?!) – and she was an administrator, contractor, teacher, dietician, gardner, mineralogist, preacher … the list goes on and on. My goodness! And she continues giving. She is not dead…

Central to all of her work is her belief that it is through music that we best communicate with God. And so that brings this little discourse back to the second reason for writing this manuscript – music. In some small way I hope through a detailed study of several of her chants, to help you experience her spirit and wisdom and the vision which motivated the creation of those chants. Her life, her work and her teaching focused on the deep, elemental connection of mind, body and spirit, and so this manuscript is ordered and compiled in a manner which will hopefully help you experience the chants in a spiritual way through study, understanding, healthy practices, prayer and meditation.

The third reason is pure self indulgence. I love doing this and I love reading about Hildegard and incorporating what I experience from those readings into my own life. I hope that some of that joy and growth moves off of these pages into your life so it becomes a shared experience.

Order

Hildegard lived a very ordered life, framed by practice of the Benedictine Rule and by the hierarchical, societal and political conventions of her time. Those 'orders' are not topics for this manuscript, though the Benedictine Rule will be addressed in a later chapter. But Hildegard lived and created and developed all that she did within those 'orders', offering an exceptional example of the value and the necessity of order for creativity and living well. As a result, this little tome is framed by an 'order'.

Hildegard was very much a user of symbols to carry messages in her illuminations and in her music. Visions were given to her as symbols, and she offers her visions to us through the use of symbols. She even developed a language of her own (the "Lingua ignota"), using newly created symbols as her alphabet. Naturally, numbers were symbolic for her too, as they were and had been for scholars from Plato's era on. And they haven't disappeared in our times either! Numbers which were particularly important to Hildegard as symbols are:

---

[5] The Sequentia CDs, *Sinfonia* and *Ordo Virtutem*, and Gothic Voices' *Feather on the Breath of God*. Please see Discography.

1 (monad) – the Source, the One God, indivisibility, wholeness
2 (dyad) – God and Christ, the duality of the nature of Christ
3 (triad) – the Trinity, the three natures of God; Father, Son, Holy Spirit
-- the three days Christ was in the tomb
-- the three epochs:
1. before the law (Adam to Moses)
2. under the law (Moses to Christ)
3. with grace (Christ and after)
-- the three theological virtues, Faith, Hope, Love
4 (tetrad) -- the four evangelists, Matthew, Mark, Luke, John
-- the four humours, phlegmatic, choleric, sanguine, melancholic
-- the four directions, North, South, East, West
-- the Cross, with its four points
-- Plato's four Cardinal Virtues, prudence, fortitude, temperance, justice
5 (pentad) -- the five wounds of Christ (the Stigmata, two wounds in the hands, two in the feet, and one in the side)
-- the Pentateuch (the Old Testament books Genesis, Exodus, Leviticus, Numbers and Deuteronomy)
-- the pentagram, or pentacle, a symbol for man, the microcosm
7 (heptad) -- days of creation
-- the seven virtues (see Nos. 3 and 4)
-- seven gifts of the Holy Spirit[6]
-- seven petitions in the Lord's Prayer
-- seven sorrows of the Virgin[7]
-- seven joys of the Virgin[8]
-- seven deadly sins (pride, envy, anger, sloth, avarice, gluttony, lust)
-- seven planets (Sun, Moon, Mars, Mercury, Jupiter, Venus, Saturn)
-- seven metals (gold, silver, iron, mercury, tin, copper, lead)
-- seven days
-- seven liberal arts:
Grammar, Rhetoric, Logic for a Bachelor's degree
Arithmetic, Music, Geometry, Astronomy for a Master's degree

This list could continue, but that is not the purpose here. Instead, know that this book is 'ordered' around the richness of the number seven, for the sake of convenience and because it is my favorite and personal number (self indulgence again). And so there are seven chapters after this introduction, each with seven parts:

a. introduction of a particular aspect of Hildegard's multifaceted gifts
b. introduction of a Hildegard illumination and chant

---

[6] Wisdom, Understanding, Knowledge, Counsel, Courage, Piety, and the Wonder and Awe of God.

[7] A series of meditations on the seven sorrows of Christ's mother, Mary: Simeon's prophecy for the infant, the flight into Egypt, the three days Jesus was 'lost' as a child, meeting Christ on the 'way of the cross', watching the crucifixion, receiving Christ's body from the cross, watching Christ's entombment.

[8] Conception by the Holy Spirit, Pregnancy during visit to Elizabeth, the birth of Jesus, Adoration of the Magi, finding the child Jesus in the temple, seeing Christ after his resurrection, being received by Christ in heaven.

c. commentary on the relationship of Hildegard's chant and illumination
d. presentation of a Hubble image in response to Hildegard with a suggested meditation
e. presentation of a new flute solo composed in response to Hildegard's chant
f. a suggested physical exercise to follow the meditation
g. recipes for Breakfast, Lunch and Dinner based upon Hildegard's diet and recipes

The seven chapters also lead a structured experience of the selected chants and visions based upon the order of seven parts of the Creed:

I. God the Father
II. God the Son
III. God the Holy Spirit
IV. the Church
V. the Communion of Saints
VI. Forgiveness of Sins
VII. Eternal Life.

Additionally, within the context of the seven chapters, four different musical forms used in medieval liturgies will be presented as created by Hildegard: Antiphon, Sequence, Hymn, and Responsory. As well, after an introductory chapter offering some history and context of Hildegard's life, five of the different 'disciplines' enjoyed by Hildegard will receive some commentary pertaining to the illumination and/or the chant presented for each chapter: Music, Theology, Poetry with Mysticism, Medicine with Healing, and Art (Illumination).

Hildegard was, in her thinking, teaching and understanding of the universe and the presence of God in the universe, cosmic and mystical. The concept of the human being a microcosm within the macrocosm was not new with Hildegard[9], but it is reaffirmed and investigated in everything she wrote. Numerous illuminations carry the symbol of the circle, as do many of her prayers and poems.

One of her earliest illuminations is now quite well known – the image of an egg, representing the universe and everything in the universe which is visible and known as well as invisible and unknown. As was the case with Hildegard's concept of macrocosm/microcosm, her vision of the universe as an egg was not new. The earliest references to the universe as an 'egg' come from ancient Sanskrit sources, where the universe, or cosmos, is called the 'Brahmanda'. "Brahm means 'Cosmos' or 'expanding', anda means 'Egg'.[10] Other references to a 'cosmic egg' are found in ancient Egyptian, Chinese, and Finnish mythology. This particular illumination bears closer examination as it is essential to the core of Hildegard's way of life and belief and spirituality.

---

[9] See Pythagorus, Socrates, Plato, etc., particularly The Dictionary of the History of Ideas , Electronic Text Center, Charlottesville VA

[10] Wikipedia contributors. "World Egg". *Wikipedia, The Free Encyclopedia.* 30 June 2007. Page Version ID: 141652302. <http://en.wikipedia.org/w/index.php?title=World_egg&oldid=141652302>

Scivias, Part One, Vision 3

What a remarkable and wonderful vision of God's universe! And such a lesson for us in what perhaps is the basic foundation of Hildegard's spirituality: the universe is a unity, and everything in the universe is interconnected and purposeful for the well-being of the whole. This is really a 12th century representation of the 20th century structuralist theorem: "the whole is equal to more than the sum of its parts"!

Hildegard's 'more' is certainly the belief that everything is interconnected, that humanity is part and parcel of that interconnectedness. And the richness of the cosmos, of life, of growth, of creativity, of joy lies in the 'viriditas', the greenness, the cosmic food of that interrelatedness, not in separate, individual elements of the cosmos. Furthermore, abuse, misuse, overindulgence, starvation, or any type of imbalance affects the whole, from the tiniest particle, cell, or living 'thing' right on up to the entire cosmos.

The vision is described and discussed by Hildegard in her first book, *Scivias*[11]. The following list identifies the symbols in the illumination with corresponding numbers on the monochromatic sketch.

1 – the outer ring of flame, God's divine goodness which permeates the cosmos.
2 – the four winds, all constantly active:
  a - the North winds on the left just inside the ring of fire
  b - the West winds on the bottom
  c - the South winds on the right
  d - the East winds at the top of the innermost circle
3 – the planets known at that time:
  a - Saturn, Jupiter and Mars are the three torches at the top of the Egg
  b - Venus and Mercury are the two torches inside the ring of fire at the top
4 – the Sun, Christ
5 – the Moon, the Church
6 – a "gloomy" ring "full of sounds, storms and the sharpest stones large and small"
7 – the pure sky inside the 'gloomy' layer, containing stars
8 – the inner center, earth
  a - surrounded by clouds
  b - with air full of water
  c - the globe of the earth (notice, it is round!)
  d - containing a mountain which separates light from dark

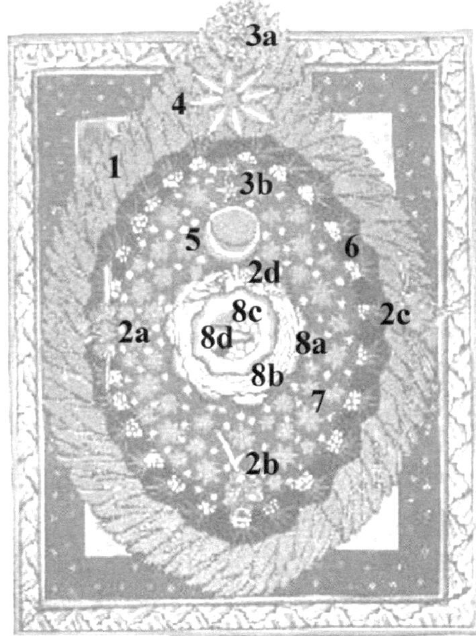

[11] Hildegard von Bingen, tr. Bruce Hozeski. *Scivias*. (Santa Fe, Bear & Co.) 1984, pp.27-36

These elements have symbolic meanings. The outer ring of fire is the divine goodness of God which engulfs and energizes the whole cosmos. The sun symbolizes Christ, “the son of justice who has the light of burning love. The Son exists in such glory that every creature is illuminated by the brightness of the Word’s light.”[12] The three torches (Saturn, Jupiter and Mars) above the Son “kept the fire from falling down upon the globe itself. These torches giving their help clearly signifies that the Word of God, descending from heaven to earth and leaving the angels behind in heaven, also gave help by showing heavenly things to people while they were in their souls and bodies.”[13]

The ring of gloomy fire symbolizes the action of bad energies, murderous deeds, plots, plans, and activities. The pure air beneath this gloomy fire is the serenity of faith dependent on Christ. The stars present in the circle of pure air are the ‘fruits’ of faith, the good works generated by faith. The two torches just inside the ring of ‘gloomy fire’ (Venus and Mercury) are symbols for the Old and New Testaments which “guide the church so that it does not overextend itself in a variety of diverse ways, for the Old and New Testaments show the church the blessedness of its heavenly heredity”.[14] The moon is a symbol for the church, “shining white in the innocent brightness of faith”.[15]

The four winds are symbols for preaching the good news (Word) and the sacrament of Baptism. One of the winds lies in each of the four main circles of the ‘egg’ – the South wind within the ring of God’s fire, the West wind in the pure air, the North wind in the gloomy ring of fire, and the East wind in the ring of air full of water. Hildegard says that “occasionally the various kinds of air would shake themselves…and they would make this dry globe [earth] move a little with their strength. This signifies that at the proper time the creatures of God embrace the fame of the miracles of the one who created them. As a result, miracle is woven to miracle with the great thundering of words. A person struck by the greatness of miracles shakes in mind and body, and when the person has been stunned by this shaking, the person then thinks about his or her own weakness.[16]

The mountain represents the ‘great fall of humanity’, and as the separation of light from dark, Hildegard states that humanity "holds the misery of damnation in those who were disgraced through the worst deception of the devil, and it holds the happiness of redemption in those who were chosen through their desire for salvation.”[17] Light and dark, for Hildegard, are absolutely separate. She ends her explanation of the vision by saying:

> “Whence whoever has knowledge in the Holy Spirit and wings in faith, let that person not pass over my warning, but let that person lay hold of it by embracing it in the enjoyment of the soul.”[18]

---

[12] Hildegard. *Scivias.* Tr. Bruce Hozeski. Santa Fe. Bear & Company. 1986. p.29

[13] Ibid.

[14] Ibid., p.32

[15] Ibid.

[16] Ibid. p.35

[17] Ibid.

[18] Ibid. p.36

The concept of the universe as an egg has many, many symbolic implications, as does Hildegard's placing of the earth in the position of the yolk. As stated earlier, this symbolic construct of the universe had been around for awhile.[19] For us, this symbol identifies Hildegard with what has been termed "creation-centered" theology, an approach which had a different emphasis than the "cross and redemption" theology that emerged as the predominant emphasis of theology and Christian teaching after the medieval period. Hildegard regarded all of creation as God's blessing and humanity's role in creation as guardian. She also sees those relationships as the life-blood of the universe, and any damage done to those relationships, on any level, constitutes true 'sin'. And 'sin' (imbalance or breaking of the relationships) is the cause of all disease, misfortune, suffering, and misery.

In this time of ecological and spiritual malaise, Hildegard's concept of the universe and humanity's place and role speaks loudly. I offer a quote from Matthew Fox's preface for the first book containing Hildegard's words in the English Language, *Meditations With Hildegard of Bingen*, by Gabriele Uhlein[20]

> ...If creation is a cosmic blessing, then true sin represents a rupture in the cosmos, a rupture in relationships. "Creation blooms and flourishes when it remains in right relationship and keeps to its assigned tasks" she declares. The breaking of right relationship is injustice and all injustice represents a rupture in the cosmos itself. "Without nature, humankind cannot survive" she warns us—a particularly timely warning for our times of nuclear threat. The following lament sounds like Hildegard might have been present in Hiroshima or Nagasaki. Or at Three Mile Island. Or at Love Canal.
>
> Now in the people that were meant to be green, there is no more life of any kind. There is only shriveled barrenness. The winds are burdened by the utterly awful stink of evil, selfish goings-on. Thunderstorms menace.
>
> The air belches out the filthy uncleanliness of the peoples. There pours forth an unnatural, a loathsome darkness, that withers the green, and wizens the fruit that was to serve as food for the people.
>
> Sometimes this layer of air is full, full of a fog that is the source of many destructive and barren creatures that destroy and damage the earth, rendering it incapable of sustaining humanity.

---

[19] References to a 'world egg' exist in ancient Chinese and Egyptian mythology. The 'Cosmic Egg' appears in Hindu tradition, and, interestingly enough, in recent astrophysical studies about the nature of the universe and the 'Big Bang' theory.

[20] Gabriele Uhlein. *Meditations With Hildegard of Bingen*. Santa Fe. Bear & Company, 1983.

> The ultimate sin, Hildegard recognizes, is ecological: a sin against the earth, against the air, against the waters, against God's creation—for in injuring creation's interdependent balance we are destroying all life including our own. Hildegard shouts to us through eight centuries of silence: "The earth should not be injured. The earth should not be destroyed." And she warns humankind of the result—not that individuals ought to be afraid of a private hell but because creation itself seeks a balance and keeps a record of how it is treated that no human power can cover up. "If the elements of the world are violated by ill-treatment," she warns, "God will cleanse them through the sufferings and the hardships of humankind." If we misuse the "privilege" that creation is, then "God's justice permits creation to punish humanity."[21]

Uhlein's book was published in 1983, over twenty years ago, and the issues mentioned by Matthew Fox had not yet been amplified by Chernobyl, much less the current threats of 'dirty bombs' or global warming. And what about the current extraordinary experiences of 'Mother Nature' – devastating hurricanes, floods, drought, fires? Might Hildegard be warning us today about creation's response to the yearly extinction of thousands of species, pollution of the air and waters, and other injuries done to creation and to each other by our human disuse of gifts and abilities? How might this small planet change, and creation and the cosmos rejoice, if we employed our gifts and abilities in the service of goodness and peace instead of war, weapons of death, and self-serving greed? Hildegard's visions – her prophecies, if you will – are not apocalyptic. They certainly carry the language of her times, and the imagery of her times, but they are full of hope and joy and delight which is the message of the third epoch – God's limitless and unconditional love for his creation – which includes humanity…

This book (Uhlein) was the second Hildegard book to come into my possession, and for ten years or so I glibly passed over the preface and foreword to dig into the meditations. And so I deprived myself of fully experiencing the core of the meditations, using the texts within my own sphere of understanding and experience – and I gained a great deal from using them that way! But when I happened to become curious about the fact that there was both a preface and a forward to the book, which also contained an introduction, I really began to wake up and grow. And purchase more books. And CDs. And videos.[22]

Then began more frequent trips to the beach and to the mountains, and fuller appreciation of the beauty of God's grand landscapes. But it really wasn't until two or three years ago that, through the grace of a friend and spiritual mentor, I began to really see and touch and smell and hear God's creation as personal and interior experiences – and connections. What a magnificent gift and change to rather uninteresting patterns of exercise by walking in a forested park instead of on a treadmill looking at TV. To see flowers, bees, trees, birds, even snakes and spiders, instead of marching in place with other people, watching TV and counting steps or heartbeats and going nowhere with the greatest effort. To breathe deeply and feel the warm kiss of sunlight or the cool caress of a breeze – and the healthy moisture of honest sweat soon to be followed by the bracing cleanliness of a cold then hot shower! Or to sit quietly in the backyard and watch the busy-ness of the birds, the play of the squirrels, the intricate, amazing geometric progress of a

---

[21] Ibid. p.10

[22] See appendices 1 and 2 if you would care to indulge yourself further! Most books, recordings and videos are still available, and more appear each year.

spider building a web, the splashing of patterns of shade on the colors of grass and flowers. And to feel the peace and grace and gratitude of those experiences. Why do we break our connections to creation?

Hildegard has so much to offer to us. She lived to the ripe old age of 81, never slowing down in her energy and creativity. She began writing when she was in her 40s, so we have forty years' worth of material from her. Certainly we could read everything available in a few years' time, but to really connect with it, to begin to understand it, and to gain in experience from it is a lifelong journey! So let's begin, you and me, with just a miniscule portion of her gift, hoping to heal some 'ruptures' in our own lives, to listen to Hildegard, and to enjoy the process. Uhlein offers one of Hildegard's prayers:[23]

O Holy Spirit,
Clear fountain,
In you we perceive God,
how he gathers the perplexed
and seeks the lost.
Bulwark of life,
you are the hope of oneness for that which is separate.
you are the girdle of propriety,
you are holy salvation.
Shelter those caught in evil,
free those in bondage,
for the divine power wills it.
You are the mighty way in which every thing
that is in the heavens,
on the earth,
and under the earth,
is penetrated with connectedness,
is penetrated with relatedness.

---

[23] Ibid. p.41

I.
Hildegard in History

A number of books have been written about Hildegard's life. The purpose here is not to replicate the work of those authors, but to place Hildegard in the context of her time as regards the numerous areas of her curiosity and contributions. As an introduction, the following brief history of her life is offered, primarily drawn from the three sources indicated.[24]

Hildegard was born in 1098 CE and lived to the remarkable age of eighty-one, passing out of this world in 1179 CE. She was born in Bermersheim, Germany, the tenth child of Hildebert von Bermersheim and Mechtild of Merxheim. Seven of her siblings are known:

Drutwin, eldest brother
Hugo, choirmaster of the Mainz Cathedral
Roricus, canon at Tholey in the Saar
Sisters Irmengard, Odilia, Jutta, and
Clementia, who became a nun in Hildegard's convent

The manor house in Bermersheim and a small church next to it were deeded to Hildegard by her oldest brother, and the nuns of the convent at Rupertsburg and later Eibingen controlled the property until the left bank of the Rhine became part of France. All that remains on the property today is the small church, of which it is believed that only the steeple remains from Hildegard's time. Hildegard was probably baptized in this small church.

From early childhood Hildegard was identified as an unusually intelligent and intuitive child, and it is believed that as early as age three, she had experienced visions. At that age, she had described some unusual markings on an unborn calf, and the calf did indeed have those unusual markings when it was born. As she grew older she kept her visions as secret as possible, realizing that no one else saw what was visible to her.

---

[24]See especially Flanagan, Sabina. *Hildegard of Bingen: A Visionary Life*; Newman, Barbara. *Voice of the Living Light: Hildegard of Bingen and Her World*; and Schipperges, Heinrich. *The World of Hildegard of Bingen: Her Life, Times and Visions*. These are listed with full bibliographic notation in Appendix One.

The practice of 'tithing' a child to the church, called an 'oblation', was common in the medieval era. This was the case with Hildegard who was tithed to the church at age eight by her parents as she was their tenth child. Some children entered monasteries at even younger ages than Hildegard, who possibly was sent to the monastery at Disibodenberg at age eight. The Venerable Bede[25], for instance, went at age seven. Another mystic -- Gertrude of Helfta[26] -- went at age five, as did Thomas Aquinas[27] nearly a century later. As a matter of fact, it is not certain that Hildegard entered the monastery and become 'enclosed' with the anchoress Jutta[28] at age eight as Jutta was only six years older than Hildegard. There is some speculation based upon a recently discovered medieval biography of Jutta that Hildegard might first have spent some time at Sponheim with Jutta's family, entering the monastery as a teenager when Jutta was about twenty years old.

For the next thirty years, Hildegard was in the care and tutelage of Jutta in the monastery at Disibodenberg. She learned to read and write in Latin, she was taught music -- singing, reading music, notating music and possibly how to play the ten-string psaltery. She lived by the Rule of Benedict[29], learned to sew, to create illuminated manuscripts, and she studied medieval theology. Jutta and Hildegard became well known in the area, and as more and more young women of nobility came to Disibodenberg to join their group, eventually a convent was formed with Jutta as Abbess.[30]

[25] The Venerable Bede (c.672-735), a historian and Doctor of the Church, author of the classic *Ecclisiastical History of the English People.*

[26] Gertrude of Helfta (1256-1302), who was born more than a half century after Hildegard's death, entered the Cistercian abbey of Helfta in Eisleben at age five. Her writings are still in print today.

[27] Thomas Aquinas (c.1225-1274) was a philosopher, theologian, Doctor of the Church, and patron of Catholic universities. Born into a royal family of Naples, he was sent to the Benedictine Monastery of Monte Cassion at age five.

[28] Countess Jutta von Sponheim (1091-1136) became an anchoress (symbol for an 'anchor' for the world to God) and later Abbess at the Benedictine convent in Disibodenberg. It is believed that Hildegard came to her at age 14 on All Saints, 1 November 1112.

[29] St. Benedict of Nursia (c.480-543) was the founder of western monasticism. The Benedictine Order continues to be very strong and international in scope today. *Hildegard was a Benedictine.*

[30] Pictures are of the ruins of the Disibodenberg Convent and of its 'ground plan,' taken during a visit there in 2009.

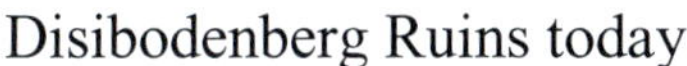

Disibodenberg Ruins today

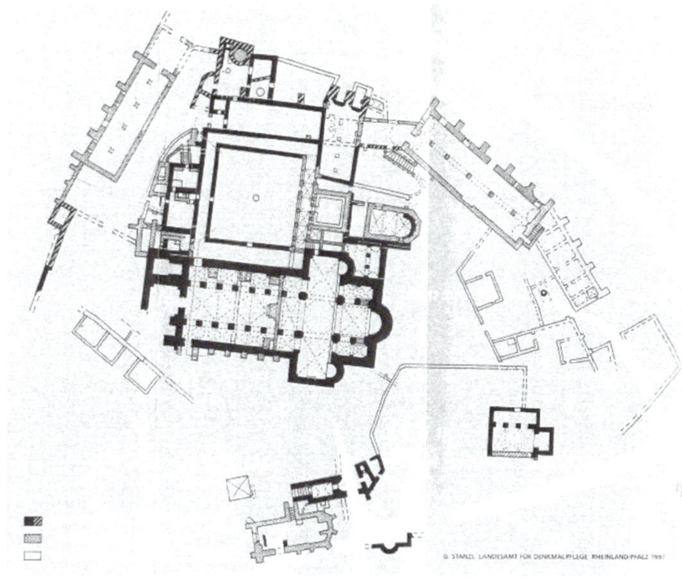

Diagram of the Disibodenberg double monastery during Hildegard's time

When Jutta died in 1136, Hildegard was elected 'Magistra', or abbess of the convent at Disibodenberg. Five years later, at age 42, she had a remarkable and intense vision in which she was told (in her own words),

O weak person, ashes of ashes, and decaying of the decaying, speak and write what you see and hear. Because you are timid about speaking and simple about explaining and unskilled about writing those things, speak and write those things not according to the mouth of a person nor according to the perception of human inventiveness nor according to the wishes of human arrangement. But according to the extent that you see and hear those things in the heavens above in the marvelousness of God, bring to light those things by way of explanation, just as even a listener, understanding the words of a teacher, explains those things according to the course of the teacher's speech – willingly, plainly, and instructively. So therefore even you, o person, speak those things which you see and hear; and write those things not according to yourself nor according to another person, but according to the will of the one knowing, see and arrange all things in the secrets of the divinity's own mysteries.[31]

This vision began the recording of Hildegard's visions and led to the legacy of her work which is available to us today:

Scivias (Know the Ways) -- 1141-51
Physica (Book of Simple Medicine) -- 1151-58
Causae et curae (Book of Compound Medicine) -- 1151-58
Symphonia harmoniae celestium revelationum (Symphony of the Harmony of Celestial Revelations -- before 1158

---

[31] Hildegard. *Scivias*. Hozeski, tr. p.1

Liber vitae meritorum (Book of Life's Merits) -- 1158-63
Liber divinorum operum (Book of the Divine Works -- *De operatione Dei* -- On the Activities of God) -- 1163-74
*Epistolae (*Letters) -- 1147-79

Minor works:
Vita Sancti Disibodi (The Life of Saint Disibod)
Vita Sancti Ruperti (The Life of Saint Rupert)
Expositio Evangeliorum (commentary on the Gospels)
Explanatio Symboli S. Athanasii (Commentary on the Athanasian Creed)
Explantio Regulae S. Benedicti (Commentary on the Benedictine Rule)
Lingua ignota: Litterae ignotae (Unknown Language, Unknown Writing)

Bernard of Clairvaux

After this commanding vision, what had been fairly constant illness for Hildegard nearly disappeared, leading her to believe that the illnesses were caused by hiding and denying the gifts given to her by God. When she began to use those gifts, her health improved. Through the support and influence of Bernard of Clairvaux, her visions and writing were affirmed by Pope Eugenius III at the Synod of Trier in 1147-48. She was ordered by Pope Eugenius to write down her visions, and her first book was *Scivias*, or "Know the Ways".

In the first illumination for this work, Hildegard shows herself receiving visions with the flames of the Holy Spirit descending on her.

She wrote the visions on a wax tablet balanced on her knee, and Volmar of Disibodenberg transcribed her words from the wax tablets to parchment. In addition to Jutta, Volmar had been her teacher, and he was also the provost of her convent as well as her secretary.

Within a short time after her affirmation by Eugenius III at the Synod at Trier, Hildegard became quite famous throughout the Rhineland and many people came to consult with her – nobles, government officials, and even international figures. Her intuition and clairvoyance allowed her to know what was in a person's mind and heart before they spoke. As well, with true Benedictine hospitality, she and her nuns nursed the sick, advised the spiritually infirm, and welcomed all, regardless of need. In so doing, she brought fame – and wealth – to the monastery at Disibodenberg.

After another vision, Hildegard believed she was to take her growing convent of nuns from the double monastery at Disibodenberg to establish their own single convent at Rupertsberg. There was considerable discussion and foment about this proposed move among the monks at Disibodenberg and with the Archbishop of Mainz. As well, a number of well-born nuns who were accustomed to a certain degree of comfort in their lives at

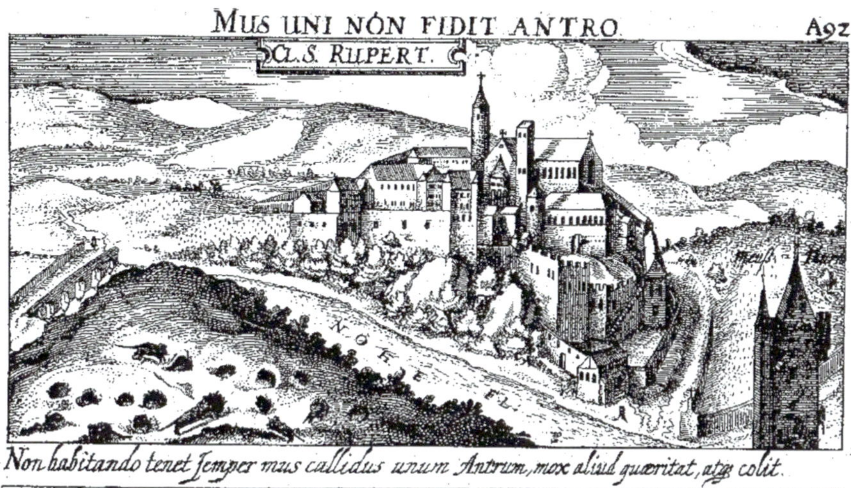

Disibodenberg were opposed to the idea, as they would be faced with a move from a well-built, comfortable monastery to a monastic ruin on a small mountain above the Rhine which was badly in need of rebuilding. But finally in 1148 Hildegard was given permission to leave – eventually taking her twenty nuns' dowries with her – to establish a new convent. Some of the more disgruntled nuns left her for other convents, but those who went with her were quickly and enthusiastically welcomed by the peasants and nobles of nearby villages. The Rupertsberg was rededicated on 1 May 1151, just three years after Hildegard moved there and began its renovation.[32]

In 1158 she began her first preaching tour along the river Main, publicly preaching in Würzburg and Bamberg. She was welcomed as a prophet, and in her preaching she urged the people to repentance, conversion and penance. At this time a schism in the church began, which was to last eighteen years. The elector Frederick Barbarossa named the first of three antipopes, and Hildegard, though much in disagreement with the move, at this time refrained from saying anything. Frederick had become King of Germany after the emperor Conrad III died, and Pope Hadrian IV, the only Englishman to ascend to the papacy, crowned Frederick Holy Roman Emperor in 1155. When Hadrian died in 1159, the schism began. Hildegard had held Frederick in high esteem just after his election as King, and he also held Hildegard in high esteem and probably a bit of fear too.[33]

In 1160, she made a second preaching tour, this time along the river Mosel including public preaching in the cities of Metz and Trier. The next year she took a third tour, preaching in Cologne and as far north along the Rhine as Werden. Her fame as a preacher, prophetess, musician and healer was considerable throughout the Rhineland

---

[32] Convent of Rupertsberg at the time of the Thirty Years' War from: Rheinhessen in seiner Vergangenheit (Herausgeber G. Behrens), Bd. 5: Alt-Bingen, Teil 2 von J. Como, Schneider, Mainz 1926

[33] Art Resource/Bridgeman Art Library, London/New YorkBridgeman/Art Resource, NY, from <http://encarta.msn.com/media_121618358/Frederick_I_and_His_Sons.html >

by this time, and in 1163 Barbarossa granted imperial protection for the Rupertsberg convent.[34] The following map shows the paths of her preaching tours.

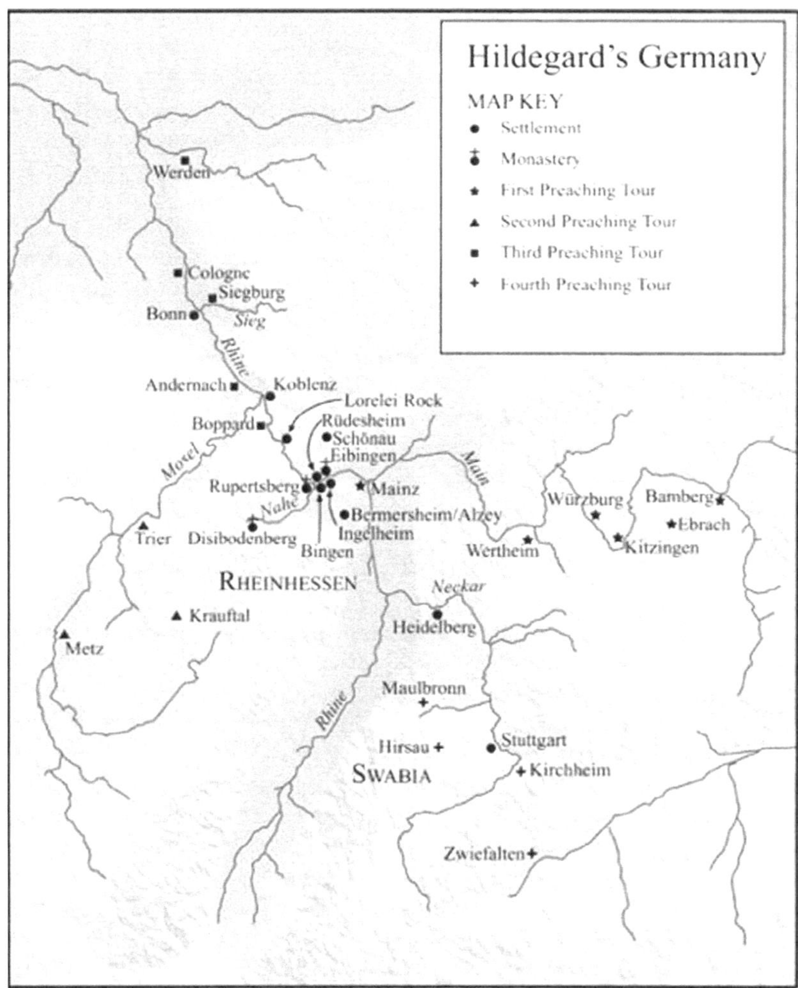

In 1164, the second antipope was elected, and this time Hildegard sent a scathing letter to Barbarossa:

O King, it is imperative for you to have foresight in all your affairs. For in a mystic vision I see you like a little boy or some madman living before Living Eyes. Yet you still have time for ruling over worldly matters. Beware, therefore, that the almighty King does not lay you low because of the blindness of your eyes, which fail to see correctly how to hold the rod of proper governance in your hand. See to it that you do not act in such a way that you lose the grace of God.[35]

---

[34] Map used in *Hildegard of Bingen: A Spiritual Reader* by Carmen Butcher, published by Paraclete Press. |Date=November 6, 2006 |Author=Sean Butcher |Permission= Creative) Creative Commons CC-BY-SA-2.5

[35] The date of this letter is in question, with Peter Dronke speculating its date as 1164, and the current source dating it before Pentecost, 1153. Baird, Joseph L. and Radd K. Ehrmann, tr. *The Letters of Hildegard of Bingen, Vol. III.* Oxford University Press. 2004. p.113

Barbarossa must have feared Hildegard's power of prophecy not enough to change his course of action, but enough to continue protection of her convent.

In 1165, at age 67, Hildegard began to build a third convent with eighteen of her nuns, this time across the Rhine from Rupertsberg in Eibingen. For the rest of her life, she would travel across the Rhine at least twice each week to visit the new convent. The Eibingen convent is the only one of the three which remains today, although the buildings are not the original buildings. It sits on the hills above Rudesheim, in the vineyards.

Then in 1169, after the election of a third antipope, she wrote to Barbarossa:

He Who Is says: By My own power, I do away with the obstinacy and rebellion of those who scorn Me. Woe, O woe to the evil of those wicked ones who spurn Me. Hear this, O king, if you wish to live. Otherwise, My sword will pierce you.[36]

Hildegard was quite weak at this time, but she continued to work, writing the *Life of St. Disibod* and making a fourth preaching tour to Swabia. This preaching tour occurred after she received a vision in which she was told to make the journey, visiting and preaching at monasteries. At her last stop, Kirchheim, she delivered a sermon publicly to a gathering of priests. This sermon was written and survives, and in it she offers an allegorical image of the church, Ecclesia, which is beset and besieged without the care of loyal and worthy priests and servants of God. After this sermon, Hildegard returned home to Rupertsberg, never to leave again.

In 1173 her Provost and secretary Volmar died, and she asked for a replacement. The Abbot of Disibodenburg, who had sent Volmar to her, did not cooperate, and it was necessary to go to the Archbishop of Mainz for mediation. Finally the monk Gottfried was appointed, and Hildegard finished her book *De operatione Dei.* But in 1176 Gottfried, who had started to write a biography of Hildegard, died. He was replaced by a French monk, Guibert of Gembloux, a great admirer of Hildegard, but he was called back to Gembloux in 1180, leaving Hildegard's biography incomplete. A monk from Echternach, near Trier, saw to the eventual completion of the biography of Hildegard in 1187, a remarkable work about a remarkable woman of those times.[37]

---

[36] Ibid. p.114

[37] Maddocks, Fiona. *Hildegard of Bingen: The Woman of Her Age.* New York. Doubleday, 2001. p.254

In 1178, a young nobleman who had been excommunicated from the church and who was running from the authorities came to Hildegard's abbey in Rupertsberg. He had been severely wounded, and Hildegard and her nuns took him in and cared for him. Hildegard, of course, cared for him not only physically, but also spiritually, and just before he died he confessed and received absolution. Hildegard had him buried in the convent grounds. The Archbishop heard about this and demanded that Hildegard 'dig him up' and throw his body off the sanctified grounds of the Rupertsberg convent. Hildegard refused, saying he had been reconciled to God and the church before he died. The Archbishop, furious with Hildegard, sent his men to do the task, but Hildegard and her nuns concealed all evidence of the grave, so there was no way to tell where he was buried. The Archbishop then placed Rupertsberg under interdiction, an action which rendered the convent unable to celebrate Mass. Additionally, the nuns could not sing the Divine Office as a community, but each nun must pray the office individually in a whisper behind closed doors. This interdict disrupted the community which was the lifeblood of the convent, and it denied the nuns the Eucharist, which was their life-giving communion with Christ. The fact that her nuns supported her in this 'disobedience' attests to their loyalty to Hildegard, and more importantly to their belief in the divine source of her visions, for Hildegard embarked on this path of disobedience only after receiving visions concerning the young nobleman.

The interdict continued for nearly a year, and finally, after much correspondence, it was lifted in March, 1179. Hildegard died just six months after the interdict was lifted, on 17 September -- the date which is observed as her name day to the present time.

Before moving to the chant and illumination, a chronological list of events in Hildegard's life is offered for your study.

	World Events	**Hildegard**
1066	Norman Conquest	
1079	Peter Abélard born	
1088-1130	Abbey of Cluny reconstructed	
1090	Bernard of Clairvaux born	
1095	First Crusade	
1098	Seige of Antioch	Hildegard born, Bermersheim, Rhinehessen
1099	Crusaders capture Jerusalem	
1100	*Chanson de Roland* notated	
1106	Henry IV, German emperor, dies in 1105. Henry V, German emperor (1111-1125)	Hildegard taken to Jutta, probably at the Sponheim estate
1112	Disibodenberg Monastery flourishes and builds	Hildegard and Jutta enclosed in Disibodenberg
1112-1115		Hildegard makes profession of vows and becomes a Benedictine nun
1120	*Rubáiyát of Omar Khayyám*	
1122	Eleanor of Aquitaine born	
1123	Frederick Barbarossa born	
1136		Jutta dies. Hildegard elected 'Magistra'
1140	Peter Abélard condemned for heresy	
1141		Hildegard receives a vision from God commanding her to write her visions. Volmar, a monk from Disibodenberg, is her secretary, as is the nun Richardis von Stade. She begins to write *Scivias*
1142	Peter Abélard dies. First Latin translation of the *Qur'an*	

1146		Hildegard corresponds with Bernard of Clairvaux. They never met personally.
1147-9	The second crusade.	Synod of Trier -- Pope Eugenius III reads Hildegard's work aloud on the recommendation of Bernard. Hildegard receives official affirmation and is ordered to continue to write down her visions.
1148		Hildegard received a vision to begin her own convent, and runs into difficulty with the Abbot. Odo, a professor in Soissons, writes of Hildegard's music, showing the chants are already widely known and admired.
1149	Church of the Holy Sepulchre in Jerusalem dedicated.	Hildegard takes 18 nuns to begin building at Rupertsberg after two years of difficulty with the Disibodenberg Abbot.
1151		Hildegard completes *Scivias* and begins *Physica* and *Causae et curae.*
1152 1152-cont.	Frederick Barbarossa becomes king of Germany. Henry II marries Eleanor of Aquitaine.	Hildegard sends a letter paying respects to Frederick. Certification and re-sanctification of the church at Rupertsberg.
1153	Bernard of Clairvaux dies	
1154-5	Frederick crowned Emperor	Hildegard meets with Frederick at Ingleheim. He grants her exclusive and free rights to the Rupertsberg property.
1158	Frederick grants a charter for the University of Bologna	Hildegard begins the first preaching tour, despite illness
1159	Beginning of 18-year schism -- election of the first anti-pope, Victor IV	
1160		Hildegard undertakes second preaching tour. She preaches openly in Trier on Pentecost Sunday.
1161		Hildegard's third preaching tour, preaching in public in Cologne.
1163	Frederick grants the Rupertsberg imperial protection, addressing her as 'Abbess'	Hildegard begins writing *De operatione Dei*
1164	Second anti-pope elected, Pascal III	Hildegard writes a stern letter to Frederick, taking the side of Pope Alexander III.
1165		Founding of the 'daughter' convent at Eibingen. Hildegard writes to Henry and Eleanor of Aquitaine.
1167		Hildegard becomes severely ill.
1168	Third anti-pope, Callistus III	Hildegard writes a threatening letter to Frederick about the anti-pope. She is still ill.
1170	Thomas Becket murdered in Canterbury. Fibonacci born. Earliest known version of the *Tristan und Isolde* legend written.	Still ill, Hildegard writes the *Life of St. Disibod* and undertakes the fourth preaching tour.
1173-74	Leaning tower of Pisa started.	Volmar dies. After much trouble, Gottfried is appointed. Hildegard finishes *De operatione Dei*. Book I of *Hildegard-Vita* is started by Gottfried.
1176		Gottfried dies. Guibert of Gembloux becomes Hildegard's secretary.

1178		Rupertsberg placed under interdict. Hildegard writes to Mainz Archbishop (who is in Rome).
1179	Lateran Council, Pope Alexander III against the Albigensians (Cathars)	Interdict lifted in March. Hildegard dies in September (the 17th).
1181	St. Francis of Assisi is born.	
1187	Jerusalem is recaptured by Saladin	
1189-92	Third crusade	Books II and III of *Hildegard-Vita* completed by monks and the teacher, Theodoric.

Hildegard's Chant

Music and text

Any discussion of Hildegard's music must begin with the musical forms used in worship during the 12th century. Already for over one hundred years, musicians in the schools at St. Martiale and Notre Dame (in Paris) had been 'experimenting' with polyphony[38], a bold new style invading the centuries' old practice of monophonic[39] plainchant (also called 'Gregorian' chant). The use of organum[40] with its 'avant garde' compositional practice of adding one or more voices to the traditional chant melody was firmly based upon the collection of worship chants accumulated and ordered into a complex system of liturgical rites at the direction of Pope Gregory in the seventh century[41]. These new polyphonic innovations were usually limited in use to serving as embellishments for specific portions of the mass liturgy, primarily for special festival celebrations.

Those new 'experiments' were known to Hildegard, and she was acquainted with the pedagogical practice of solmization offered by Guido d'Arezzo (the 'Guidonian Hand').[42] There are no indications in the manuscripts of her chants that she experimented with more than one melodic line at a time, but it is within the realm of possibility. The practice of improvisation was common, and might it not be possible that some of Hildegard's chants emerged from that practice? And if so, possibly two singers improvising at the same time might have initiated a type of improvisatory polyphony much like improvisatory jazz, or the improvisatory instrumental accompaniments to the repetitive songs of today's Taize community[43]. As well,

---

38 Polyphony – two or more individual melodic lines sounding at the same time.

39 Monophonic – one melodic line

40 Organum – the earliest form of polyphony, based upon a cantus firmus (chant melody) with a second and third melodic line decorating the slowly moving chant line. There were several specific types of organum, dependent upon the intervallic and rhythmic relationships to the cantus firmus.

41 Liturgical rites which were 'universal' in their use. The chants for the Mass and the Divine Office were found in collections copied and distributed from Rome and used throughout the western Church. More information on these two particular rites will follow in Chapters Two and Seven.

42 It is interesting to note that the first two identified composers of this new polyphony were also two of the first composers whose names were formally 'attached' to their music: Leoninus (c.1135-1201) and Perotinus (c.1165-1220). Ha. Look at those dates. Our Hildegard is old enough to be their mother! And she is the first composer (male or female!) to have had an autobiography written about her life and her many contributions! And there are manuscripts available with notated music identified as her compositions, dating from the 1170s.

43 The Taize community was established for inter-denominational worship by two Catholic monks after World War Two. Their worship community has grown tremendously, and the style of music is repetitive and improvisatory,

Hildegard speaks in her correspondence of the use of instruments, and given the intense spirituality of worship at her monasteries which was so remarkable and well known during her time there might very well have been some instrumental accompaniment to her chants. But the fact remains that what we have available from Hildegard for examination today is strictly monophonic.

Hildegard did not consider herself to be a 'composer', and she continually emphasized her lack of education and preparation for any of the work she accomplished. But the legacy she left in words, music, thought, and vision certainly show that she was a composer of beauty and inspiration, and her many books, letters, poetry, and indeed her life attest to her intellectual capabilities. Her modest demeanor and abnegation of self are, I believe, signs of her total love for God and belief in her role as 'servant of the Living Light' rather than false modesty on her part or any indication of a bad case of medieval 'academic intimidation' or patriarchal subjection.

Hildegard's musical milieu was centered in plainchant as the means for worship. She grew up in the enclosure with Jutta hearing the monks sing not only the daily Mass, but also the Divine Office, which was the spiritual 'backbone' of the monastery. So she knew the chants and the prescribed liturgy for each day and for special feast days and she and Jutta might very well have sung in their enclosure along with the monks in the adjacent chapel. After moving out of the enclosure into their own 'half' of the newly double monastery, they taught those chants to the other women who came to join them. The chants were the lifeblood of the monastery, the order of their universe. A fuller discussion of the Benedictine Rule and the order of the Divine Office will follow in another chapter, but suffice it to say here, in this historical context, that plainchant was as familiar and useful to Hildegard and her nuns as the hymns and liturgies of our present day churches have been to our parents, grandparents and to us. Perhaps more so!

Hildegard did not attempt to 'rewrite' the Mass. The collection of her chants which are available for study – and performance! – show that she wrote new works for the Propers of the Mass and the Divine Office. The 'propers' are texts which change to correspond with particular days of the church year. The 'ordinary' texts are those which remain the same in all Mass celebrations, forming the 'backbone' of the liturgy[44]. Furthermore, Hildegard does not create new chants for any of the scriptural texts of the Divine Office or the Mass. This marks a very pronounced difference in the creation of her music as compared to other music being written for worship during her lifetime. All of Hildegard's chants are musical settings of her own texts.[45]

Hildegard's new chants were certainly intended to be sung at Mass or within the context of the Divine Office, and they followed (sometimes loosely) four traditional formulaic patterns that had been in use for several centuries – antiphons, hymns, responsories, and sequences. Each of these forms will be explained in much more detail in later chapters

But now as an introduction to her music, her prayers, and her visions, a consideration of the illumination from the second vision of *Liber Divinorum Operum* is offered.

---

using texts from all over the globe.

[44] There are five ordinary texts – Kyrie, Gloria, Credo, Sanctus, and Agnus Dei.

[45] Pierre Abelard (1079-1142), an almost exact contemporary of Hildegard and a famous French poet and philosopher, also composed music and wrote a hymnal for his beloved Heloise's congregation. There were apparently several hymn texts which might be sung to the same melodies in that hymnal. These were newly composed texts and tunes, but like Hildegard's, did not attempt to change or 'reset' any portion of the Divine Office or Mass liturgies.

Liber divinorum operum

Book of Divine Works Vision Two: On the Construction of the World

Symbology of the illumination[46]

On the construction of the world is the illumination from the second vision in Hildegard's book, *Liber divinorum operum*, or *The Book of Divine Works*.[47] This vision (dated 1163) is compared by Hildegard to that of the vision from *Scivias* of the universe as an egg (discussed in the Introduction), completed twelve years earlier in 1151. The fundamental concept of the universe as a unity of all created things remains in this second illumination, but here humanity is portrayed as the central image – the microcosm of the macrocosm. The following list is a guide to the rich symbology of this vision.

---

46 *Liber divinorum operam*. Ed. Matthew Fox. Santa Fe (Bear & Co.) 1987. pp.22ff.

47 Ibid.

1 – God the Father
2 – God the Son
3 – Circle of bright fire, a symbol of God's power, giving light to all things. On the right there is a lion's head, the symbol of the south wind, and on either side of the lion's head, the heads of a serpent and a lamb. These are auxiliary winds and not as powerful as the major wind. The lion symbolizes God as judge of the world. The serpent is cunning and the lamb is patience.
4 – circle of black fire (half wide as 3), under the power of God's power, a judgement fire, containing lightening and ice, cold and hail. This circle is united with the first, showing a unity of God's might and judgement to form a single justice. In the circle on the left is the head of a bear, the powerful north wind which "forces us to inner meekness, causing us to walk along the right path by exercising patience like a lamb and avoiding evil by behaving cleverly as a serpent."[48]

[48] Ibid. p.44

5 – circle of pure ether (as wide as 3+4), emerging out of the first two circles, symbolizing the pure atonement of sinners either by God's grace (bright circle) or fear of God's judgement (dark circle). The dimension (density) of this circle restrains the circles above as well as the zones below. In the east (below the heads of God the Father and the Son and the five planets and the sun) is the head of a leopard, symbolizing the 'fear' of God, or repentance. To the left of the leopard is the head of a crab (trust) with two pincers (hope and doubt), and the crab is breathing out constancy. To the right is the head of a stag (faith), and out of the stag's mouth is the breath of holiness.[49]

6 – air full of moisture, same density as circle of bright fire, symbolizing the holy works of "exemplary and just individuals" whose works are pure as water. In the west (under the human's feet) there is a wolf's head "which is hidden in the woods and grows ravenous whenever it looks for food."[50] It is the west wind which bursts out of its hiding place and causes the plants to grow, but it also causes them to dry up and wither.

7 – strong, white and clear air, hard as sinew in the human body, same density as circle of black, holding back possible floods from the circle above. Discretion strengthens holy works by moderation.

8 – thin air carrying high, thin clouds but also dark, low clouds. This is the 'lung' of the universe, the breath drawing in and breathing out the Holy Spirit. It symbolizes longing and steadfastness, at times strong and vibrant, and at other times weak and tremulous.

9 – a line extended from East to north and then to the western part. The part which this line separates from the circle (the north, with the bear's head) does not receive the warmth of the sun. "The sun is simply opposed to the north wind in the orbit in which the wind rages fearfully…because [there] the Devil displays his wickedness in the struggle against God."[51]

10 – a ball is in the center, with a diameter equal to the width of the first four circles, and to the width of the distance from the outermost clouds to the 'altitude' of the ball. This is earth, exiting in the center of all matter in order to receive proper guidance from all sides.
"It is maintained on all sides by these circles, is tied to them, and receives constantly from them the greening freshness of life and the fertility needed for the Earth's support."[52] The earth is the center of all activity.

11 – a human figure touches the circumference of the circle of strong, white and clear air (7) with its head, feet and the fingertips of both hands. The human has a soul which is powerful, and the human can place into motion both higher and lower things. Whatever humanity does (right and left hands) permeates the entire universe, and as the soul constantly directs human aspirations toward God in spiritual and worldly endeavors, the human then knows God in every creature, always looking in faith at God with their physical eyes.

---

[49] Ibid. pp. 37-38

[50] Ibid. p40

[51] Ibid. p.45

[52] Ibid. p.33

Hildegard says that believers who trust in God and strive to do good works "will also honor the stability of the world: the orbits of the sun and the moon, winds and air, earth and water, everything God has created for the honor and protection of humanity. We have no other foothold. If we give up this world, we shall be destroyed by demons and deprived of the angels' protection."[53]

12 – at the top, in the ring of bright fire, and extending in a line through the dark fire, are the seven planets (the same as in the 'egg', Mars, Jupiter, Saturn, the Sun, Venus, Mercury, and the Moon). Rays from the sun touch three of the animal heads (not the bear in the north), warming and strengthening the entire universe. The sun also sends rays to the moon and to the brain and heels of the human. It thus "moderates with its powers all our limbs, just as it keeps alive the rest of creation."[54]

A ray falls from the moon to the eyebrows and to the ankles of the human, balancing the human body, and with the sun, brings "either health or illness according to the mixture of atmosphere and aura".[55]

The seven planets symbolize the seven gifts of the Holy Spirit which have been present through all three epochs of history.

13 – in the outer circle of bright fire, there are sixteen major stars sending their radiation into the circle of thin air. Hildegard likens them to human blood vessels, strengthening the entire universe in the same way our circulatory system strengthens the entire body.

14 – all of the stars in the rest of the circles (the sky) carry the message that nothing in the universe can exist without God's power. They send their cosmic power to the wind which carries it to the clouds which then bring that power to humanity.[56]

Hildegard's explanation of the vision continues on a second level, in a discussion of relationships. All six circles are connected without gaps, and the Light of the uppermost circle flows through all others while the moisture from the fourth circle dampens all others. This is interpreted as the powers of virtue which are strong and implanted in believers by the 'infusion' of the Holy Spirit, allowing them to accomplish good works in harmony with the rest of the cosmos.

The sixteen major stars are symbols for the greatest teachers who have taught and are teaching the perfection of the ten commandments. And the other stars and the clouds represent the eight beatitudes.

And finally, out of the mouth of the figure of God streams the brightest light, true love, from which comes all goodness. Everything in the world shows and teaches humanity that we are bound body and soul to God, and every cosmic power in the universe is "directed and curbed by another power, just as a strong man may fall into the arms of an enemy to avoid killing himself or others. Thus every creature is linked to another, and every essence is constrained by another."[57]

---

53 Ibid. p.41

54 Ibid. pp.45-46

55 Ibid. p.47

56 Ibid. p.50-51

57 Ibid. p.45

Such a brief outline of the vision received by Hildegard does not do justice to the content and richness of her explanation in *Liber divinorum operum*[58]. It would certainly be worthwhile to read the vision in its totality, perhaps with the above outline of the symbols as a helpful additional resource.

I have chosen the antiphon[59] *O eterne Deus* to accompany the content of Hildegard's vision of the universe for several reasons. Hildegard's antiphon embraces and is embraced by so much of the content of the vision, even though it is fairly certain that the antiphon was composed before this vision was recorded. Her collection of chants, *Symphonia Harmonie celestium revelationum* (Symphony of the Harmony of Celestial Revelations) was part of her first book, *Scivias* (know the Ways),[60] completed by 1151 (1158 was the year she began to write the *Liber divinorum operum*). It is not known whether any of her chants were written as a result of a specific vision, or even if any of her music was 'given' to her in a vision, but the content of her chant texts corresponds wonderfully with the content of her visions, so it is appropriate to hear her music as an expression of her experience with the visions.

O eterne Deus

O eternal God

O eterne Deus,	O eternal God,
nunc tibi placeat	now may it please you
ut in amore illo ardeas	so in love to burn
ut membra illa simus	that limbs we may become
que fecisti in codem amore,	which were made in the same love
cum Filium tuum genuisti	with which you made your Son
in prima aurora	in the primal dawn
ante omnem creaturam,	before all creation.
et inspice necessitatem hanc	Look on this need
que super nos cadit,	that upon us falls,
et abstrahe eam a nobis	and lift it from us
propter Filium tuum,	for the sake of your Son,
et perduc nos	and lead us
in leticiam salutis.	into delight of salvation.[61]

In *O eterne Deus* we immediately are embraced by the bright burning fire of love, the Living Light which created all things, as well as the Word, God's Son, who embraces all of creation as well. In Hildegard's illumination, God's Son is the bright ring of burning fire that encircles the universe, and he is the universe which is in the breast of the Father. In her poems addressing the creator, Hildegard asks for the grace of salvation to become the limbs of Christ, doing good works and holy deeds for the good and benefit of all creation. In the illumination, Christ embraces the cosmos, so Hildegard's petition in this antiphon addresses the belief that Christ is in humanity, and humanity is to be Christ on earth. The text ends with prayer for protection and

[58] Ibid. pp. 22-55

[59] See the following discussion for a definition of the term "antiphon".

[60] Newman, Barbara. *Symphonia.* Cornell University Press. 1988. p.8

[61] Apologies are in order for the cumbersome and 'unpoetic' nature of the translation, but for these purposes a rather literal, word for word translation is most suitable.

rescue from need, which in her illumination would probably have blown in on the breath of the north wind (the bear), where the Devil and all evil, disease, and other imbalances reside.

As an antiphon, *O eterne Deus* was probably not intended to be sung before and/or after a Psalm. Psalms were sung throughout the day as part of the Divine Office – in fact, all one hundred fifty Psalms were sung each week during the Divine Office. Not all were sung with antiphons (even in the longer offices of Matins, Lauds, Vespers or Compline) nor was the Psalm prayed during Mass each day always preceded or followed by an antiphon. The function of this antiphon has not been specifically discovered, but it was possibly used more than once each year. Certainly Psalm 8 would be a likely candidate for the use of this antiphon if it was used with a Psalm.

Antiphon

O eternal God, now may it please you
so to burn in love that we might become
limbs which were made in the same love
with which you made your Son in the
primal dawn before all creation.
Look upon our needs and difficulties
and for the sake of your Son,
lift them from us and lead us to the
joy of your salvation.

Psalm 8[62]

Yahweh our Lord, how majestic is your
name throughout the world!
Whoever keeps singing of your majesty
higher than the heavens, even through the
mouths of children or of babes in arms,
you make him a fortress, firm against your
foes, to subdue the enemy and the rebel.
I look up at your heavens, shaped by your
fingers, at the moon and the stars you set
firm—what are human beings that you
spare a thought for them, or the child of
Adam that you care for him?
Yet you have made him little less than a
god, you have crowned him with glory and
beauty, made him lord of the works of your
hands, put all things under his feet, sheep
and cattle, all of them, and even the wild
beasts, birds in the sky, fish in the sea,
when he makes his way across the ocean.
Yahweh our Lord, how majestic your name
throughout the world!

Forty-three of Hildegard's chants are antiphons, comprising the majority of her work. There are three categories of antiphons: Psalm antiphons, Votive antiphons, and Gospel antiphons. *O eterne Deus* may be either a Psalm antiphon or a Votive antiphon. Psalm antiphons are most often followed by a short grouping of neumes[63] called a 'differentia', which connects the end of the antiphon musically to the beginning of the Psalm chant (found in one of the collections of chant prepared by the Church). *O eterne Deus* does not have a differentia following its notation in the Dendermonde manuscript, so Hildegard might have used it as a Votive antiphon[64] which

[62] *The New Jerusalem Bible*. 1985. Doubleday. pp. 821-822

[63] Neumes are symbols used to indicate a specific pitch or pitches on a musical staff. They are the precursor of our current notational symbols – 'notes'.

[64] Votive antiphons were longer than Psalm antiphons, and often used nonscriptural texts. During the late 14th and

might have been sung at the beginning of the Mass, during the Communio, or at the end of the Mass[65]. Another reason *O eterne Deus* is most likely a votive antiphon is that it lasts over two minutes in length of performance, and Psalm antiphons were much shorter.

The scribe who notated Hildegard's music used a notational system called 'Hufnagelschrift'[66], or 'hobnail writing'. The system received its name because of its appearance; the symbols for the neumes resembled the shape of the nails used to shoe horses in the middle ages. Someone had a sense of humor – and the name 'stuck'. If the word is 'googled', it is apparent that Hufnagel was or became a family trade name, initially appended to a family of blacksmiths or cobblers – who have since the twelfth century become medical doctors, scientists, professional football players and skateboarders!

Hildegard's manuscript for this antiphon is found in the Dendermonde (Rupertsberg) Codex as the second antiphon in the *Symphonia*[67].

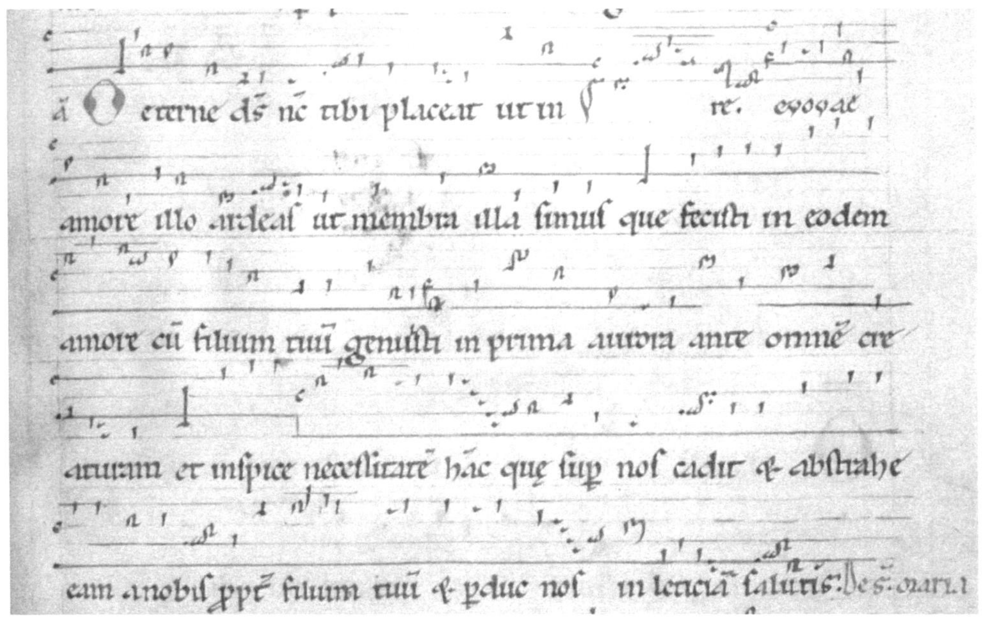

Musical notation has always and continues to be a complex and difficult problem for composers and musicians. How is it best possible to notate in a static medium sounds which contain so many different levels of richness and proportion? Anything that is used to record the living, breathing, energy of organized sound limits it and falls short in so many ways. And any type of notation of sound is, of course, symbolic. Our notational systems are much like a written language, with 'neumes' and 'notes' serving as words and letters. Beyond textual symbols though, melodic notation also indicates inflections of pitch, ascending and descending sounds and the directional relationships of those sounds to each other.

---

early 15th century they became the 'anthem' of the English church.

65 The structure of the Mass and of the Divine Office are discussed in some detail in chapter seven.

66 Hufnagelschrift was used in Germany during roughly the 10th through the 13th centuries, although manuscripts from as late as the 15th century exist.

67 Hildegard of Bingen. *Symphonia harmoniae caelestium revelationum.* Dendermonde St.-Pieters & Paulusabdij Ms. Cod. 9. Peer: Alimire, 1991. f.153

Well, the purpose here is not to provide a history of musical notation, tuning, or compositional practice, but to understand a bit of the musical milieu in which Hildegard lived and worked. So an abbreviated examination of the manuscript of her antiphon is in order, leaving the history and exposition of the development of the notational system to other sources.

The Dendermonde Codex[68] is copied on heavy parchment, an involved and lengthy process, and one undertaken with great care by a person of considerable experience and skill. There were no erasers or 'delete' buttons in the twelfth century. The parchment was made with considerable effort and skill, so nothing was wasted including space on a page. The first line of *O eterne Deus* ends with the words "ut in", and the remainder of that system contains the end of the preceding antiphon, *O magne Pater* – a melisma[69], the terminatio[70] neumes on the syllable 're', and the closing acclamation "in saeculo saeculorum, amen" (euouae). It is curious that the scribe would conclude one antiphon after the next had been initiated in this manner, as this practice does not appear again in the manuscript. Perhaps this instance was a way of correcting a mistaken omission resulting from interrupted copying sessions.

Hufnagelschrift notation uses red lines for the musical staff and black ink for the neumes and text. In typical Gregorian notation, the staff and neumes are black, and the staff uses only four lines throughout with the text appearing below the staff. Here we see four lines consistently, but occasionally a fifth briefly appears. The four lines are equidistant from each other, and the added fifth line is inserted between or above the continuous lines (see the third line of text, 'amore'; at the beginning of the line a short line appears at the top). There is always one line which is darker than the other three – the 'f' line, upon which the pitch 'f' is notated.

At the beginning of each staff (the four continuous lines) there is a small letter 'c' which identifies the location of the pitch 'c' on that staff. There is also a 'dot' at the beginning of the 'f' line. The designation of which line is 'c' or 'f' may change in the course of a chant, and that is the case in this antiphon. The antiphon begins with 'f' as the second line and 'c' as the fourth (reading from the bottom to the top line) until the third system, where the 'f' is the lowest line – as well as the inserted 'half-line' at the top, with 'c' as the third line. Then at the end of the word 'genuisti', the 'f' moves to the second line and the 'c' to the fourth line, remaining there until the word 'necessitatem', where the 'f' and 'c' move once more to the first and third lines. The staves used in Hildegard's antiphon are:

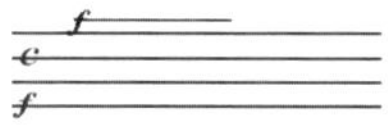

or: 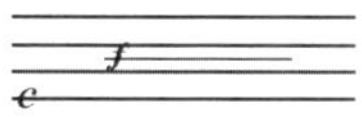 or: 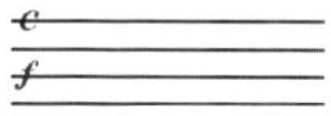 or: .

The 'c' is always on one of the lines, and only the 'f' is indicated with a 'half-line'. These correspond to what became commonly known as 'c clefs'.

A neume is placed on the staff lines and indicates the specific pattern of pitch to be sung for the accompanying syllable of text . Neumes are used like pieces of colored glass or porcelain in the creation of a beautiful mosaic, specifying one to three or sometimes more pitches for each syllable. They may occur in any order or at any pitch level. Some combinations of neumes were used in specific manners, especially to create ceasura (terminatio: a figuration used to end a musical phrase), or to begin musical phrases (initio).

---

[68] One of the primary sources of Hildegard's work dating from the 12th-13th centuries.

[69] Melisma – many (six or more) notes for one syllable of text.

[70] Terminatio – a pattern of notes (2-5) which ends a musical phrase.

Several persons have developed software programs to aid in the transcription of chant and even of Hufnagelschrift. One very generous scholar has made the symbols available on the internet[71], and so they are shared below with you. Other handwritten neumes from the Virginia Tech Musical Dictionary[72] (also available on-line) and the nuemes in Gregorian Chant notation, appear in columns three and four, and the fifth provides a current notation for the neume.

	Neume Name	**Computer Hufnagel**	**Handwritten**	**Gregorian Notation**	**Current**
One note	Punctum				
	Virga				
Two notes	Stropha (repeated note)				
	Oriscus (descent to a repeated note)				
	Pes				
	Clivis				
	Pressus				
	Quilisma				
	Epiphonus (liquiscent)				
	Cephalicus (liquiscent)				
Three notes	Torculus				
	Porrectus				

71 <http://www.blindchicken.com/~ali/> Ali Corbin's homepage

72 <http://www.music.vt.edu/musicdictionary/appendix/notation/Neumes.html>

Compound neumes	Pressus subpunctus				
	Pressus liquescens				
	Pes-porrectus				
	Pes-pressus subpunctis				
	Quilisma-cephalicus				
	Quilisma-porrectus				

With these neumes identified, it is possible to transcribe Hildegard's antiphon into our modern notation, as has been done by several persons.[73] To indicate how this is done, the first phrase of the chant appears below with the original manuscript on top, the neumes as offered in the computer generated form is indicated immediately below, and then modern notation is shown below that. In the example of modern notation, slurs (⁀) have been added to connect pitches of the neumes used.

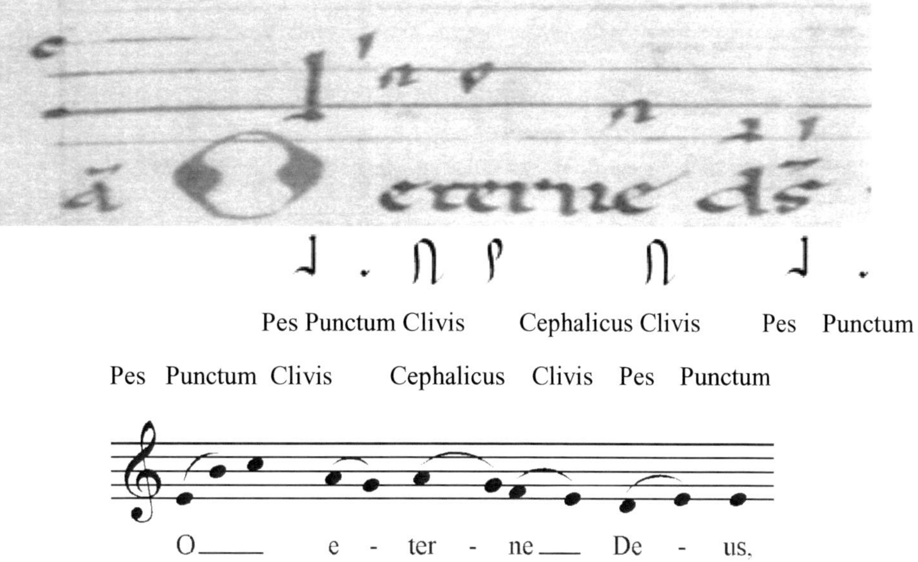

[73] See particularly for this antiphon and for a thorough discussion of the relationship between Hildegard's text and music, Jeffreys, Catherine Mary. *Melodia et rhetorica:* The Devotional-Song Repertory of Hildegard of Bingen. Ph.D Thesis, University of Melbourne, 2000. Published on the internet at <eprints.unimelb.edu.au/ADT/adt-VU2000.0422/index.html>

The rhythm of the chant, or indications of how long the duration of each note should be, was not indicated (rhythmic notation and the development of rhythmic modes was in the beginning stage during Hildegard's time), though there were some basic conventions:

a. the use of the stropha (bistropha and tristropha) on the same syllable indicated a lengthening of that pitch
b. the liquiscent neumes implied a shortening of the last pitch indicated
c. use of a horizontal episema above a syllable or a neume indicated a longer duration (see the word 'Deus' above – the last syllable has an episema)

In the example of modern notation, proportional notation has been used to indicate the lengthening or shortening of certain pitches:

a. the third pitch of the syllable 'O' is lengthened to equal approximately the same duration as the preceding pes (also called a podatus)
b. the cephalicus on the syllable '-ter-' is a liquiscent neume, indicating a shorter, lighter sounding of the second pitch (serving as what we call today a 'passing tone', connecting one important pitch to another)
c. both of the clivis neumes show equal emphasis on both pitches, as do both of the pes neumes and each of the puncti.
d. the final punctum, because of the episema over the text syllable, would receive a longer duration, ending the first phrase

A complete transcription of the antiphon with slurs identifying pitches contained within the Hufnagelschrift neumes follows. There are small 'ticks' on the top line of the modern staff which parallel Hildegard's use of both horizontal and vertical episemae, which shape her chant into musical phrases.

The chant is set in a 'neumatic' fashion, meaning that each syllable of text receives 2-5 pitches. Other chant settings might be syllabic (one note for each syllable) or melismatic (many notes for a syllable of text). There are two instances of melisma in *O eterne Deus*, on the words 'hanc' and 'nos', and there are several instances of single punctae for single syllables.

O eterne Deus

Dendermonde 9 fol. 153

Hildegard von Bingen

Hildegard's text offers fourteen phrases with which she creates a remarkable unity and shaping in sound. The images of the 'Egg of the Universe' and 'The Construction of the World' are appropriate in a microcosmic sense when observing the construction of her antiphon.

a	O eterne Deus,	1	O eternal God,
b	nunc tibi placeat	2	now may it please you
a^1	ut in amore illo ardeas	3	so in love to burn
b^1	ut membra illa simus	4	that limbs we may become
c	que fecisti in codem amore,	5	which were made in the same love
d	cum Filium tuum genuisti	6	with which you made your Son
a^2	in prima aurora	7	in the primal dawn
a^3	ante omnem creaturam,	8	before all creation,
c^1	et inspice necessitatem hanc	9 (GS)	and look on this need
e	que super nos cadit,	10	that upon us falls,
c^2	et abstrahe eam a nobis	11	and lift it from us
c^3	propter Filium tuum,	12	for the sake of your Son,
d^1	et perduc nos	13	and lead us
a^4	in leticiam salutis.	14	into the delight of salvation.

In this graph, each phrase of text is assigned a letter to show the musical relationships among the phrases, indicating that there are five different melodic configurations of the neumes upon which the fourteen phrases are based (a,b,c,d,e). The superscript numbers identify variants of the primary phrase structure and the indication 'GS' identifies the phrase of the Golden Section[74] of the text.

The text is separated into the three sections:

1-8: initial address and praise	(a ternary form of aba^1b^1 cd a^2a^3)
9-12: petition	(four phrases based on 'c' material)
13-14: closing resolution	(ending with a return to A material)

Hildegard sets these sections in a very unified and rounded ternary form (A B A'). She introduces all of her thematic material in the eight phrases of the A section, in which she praises the creative work of God who has created all things and who created his Son before anything else. Then she uses to the material introduced in phrase 5 (c) for the B section, reminding God of his love for his Son who was both divine and human. She offers a strong petition in that love, for the sake of the Son. Then in the A' section and with the material from phrase 6 (a reminder again of the love for the Son and for his sake), she asks that humanity be led to the eternal (phrase 1) delight of salvation (which is eternity).

A closer examination of how Hildegard creates the mosaic that carries the circular shape of the antiphon is in order. First, all of the varied phrases can be lined up beneath the initial phrase, showing what variations occur.

[74] Golden Section – see discussion on page 28.

A Phrase Variations

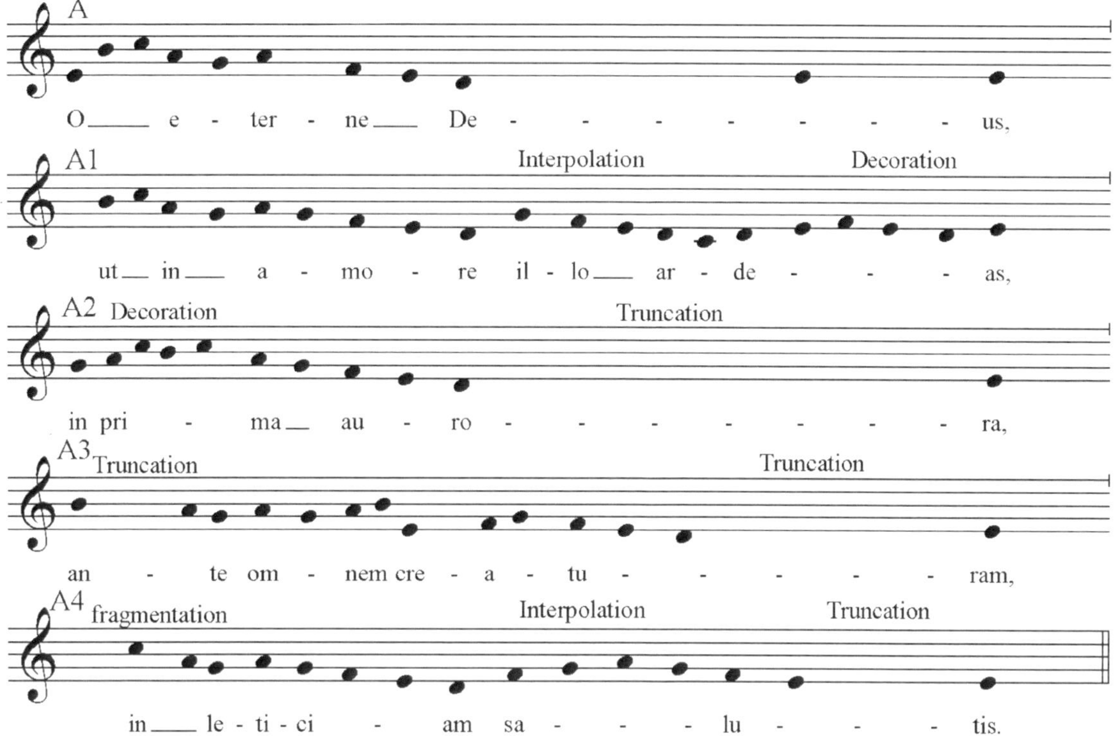

There is no repetition of the sequence of neumes found in A in any of the varied phrases.

The points of greatest variation occur in the opening neumes, beginning on, rising to, or centering around the dominant pitch b, and as decorations of the terminatio pattern of d to e.

None of the varied phrases use the initial pes of the A phrase (e rising to b).

All of the phrases descend from the dominant pitch b or its upper neighbor c to the finalis e.

a^1 includes an interpolation, or interior addition , as well as a circular decoration of the word ‘burn’.

In a^2 there is a slight variation of the initium, ‘prima’.

a^3 is the most varied, related most closely to a1.

a^4 does not have the opening pes from e to b, but then follows closely the shape of the initial ‘a’ until a new interpolation occurs on the word ‘salutis’.

B Phrase Variations

The two b phrases are quite straightforward in use of the same pitches, though they result from the use of different neumes.

Other than different pitch repetitions, the b phrases are identical.
The phrases are very narrow in range, using only four pitches.
The only leaps in the phrases are part of the very common 2-7-1 finalis pattern.
Both phrases are an extended 7 – 1 pattern, and as such, both serve as consequent phrases for the preceding a and a^1 phrases. In fact, they are more nearly 'cadential' extensions for the a phrases.

The first two a phrases describe or address God the creator, and the two b phrases form a petition on the behalf of humanity, which might be interpreted:

O eternal God, [may you] burn so in love	(a, a^1)
[that it] please you [to make us] become limbs	(b, b^1)

All four of the first phrases (a b a^1 b^1) end on the finalis of the mode[75] Hildegard employs for this chant, the Phrygian mode based on e. This certainly helps to establish e as the focal point, the initial pitch and the goal of the chant. It also gives her the dominant pitch b as the second most important structural pitch, and indeed, the second pitch of the chant is b. All of the A phrases move essentially in a descending manner from b to e, with the exceptions:

- a: the initium is a dramatic leap of a fifth from e up to b, an ascent to the eternal God in prayer
- a^2: beginning on the mediant g and hovering around the b before descending to the finalis
- a^4: begins on the pitch above the dominant, and never touches the dominant as it descends to the delight of eternity

Even though the exceptions occur, the basic motion perceived in all a phrases is from b down to e with stretches to the note above (c) and below (d).

The a and b phrases are 'tame', resembling the traditional Gregorian chant formulations which had been in use for centuries. It is in the c phrases that Hildegard soars and sings in her own unique style, the style for which she became so well known and which distinguishes and personalizes her chant. Most Gregorian chant floats within the range of an octave with occasional pitches occurring a step below the lower finalis. That is a broad generalization in describing chant – often motion from one basic mode to the 'hypo' mode is common, but once the chant is centered in either the basic mode or the hypo mode, its range usually stays within the interval of a sixth.

---

[75] Modes will be discussed in more detail in the next chapter.

Hildegard does not follow that pattern at all times, and in this particular antiphon, we see her spiritual exuberance demonstrated in the c phrases.

C Phrase Variations

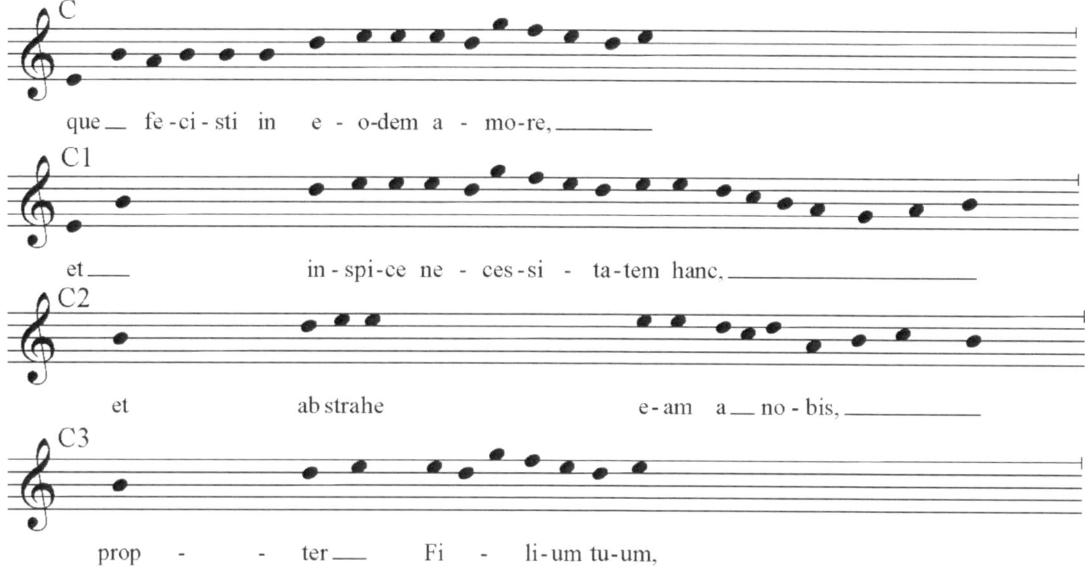

The c and c^1 phrases extend beyond the range of an octave. They are flung to the highest pitches from the lower finalis e through the strong dominant b.
c^2 and c^3 remain in the upper registers, hovering and insisting on the b.
With the exception of the two initial pitches of e in phrases c and c^1, all melody occurs above the dominant pitch in these four phrases.

And what do these phrases say?

c: [the limbs] which were made in the same love
c^1: and look on this need
c^2: and lift it from us
c^3: for the sake of your Son

Hildegard reaches into the cosmos, reminding God that he made humanity with the same love as his Son, so for his Son's sake may it please God to care for the earthly needs of humanity. She was not a timid woman in any sense, though she would certainly protest and say so. And this prayer petition is not made from a polite, reserved, humble or groveling attitude. She is asking the maker of the macrocosm to care for and help his creation, the microcosm! The first ascent to the cosmos occurs in the c phrase, in the first section of the prayer, where Hildegard claims God's love for humanity. She not only rises to the upper mediant, the highest pitch in the antiphon, but she elaborates the word "amore" with seven pitches, ending the phrase with multiple pitches on one syllable. This is the first time she has done that, and she also ends on the upper finalis in the highest register used to that point. Instead of the descending figures of the A and B phrases, she flings her petition into the cosmos. And she asks by taking the same care for proportion and unity that is expressed through her vision.

The c^1 phrase occurs at the golden mean of the text, a proportion that is considered to be 'perfect'. This relation had been known for millenia prior to Hildegard, and had been employed by the ancient Egyptians in the building of the pyramids, and by the ancient Greeks. It is a ratio based upon the use of the number *Phi* (1.61803...) where if A is 1.618 (*Phi*) and B is 1, A is to B as B is to the remainder of the whole line, C.

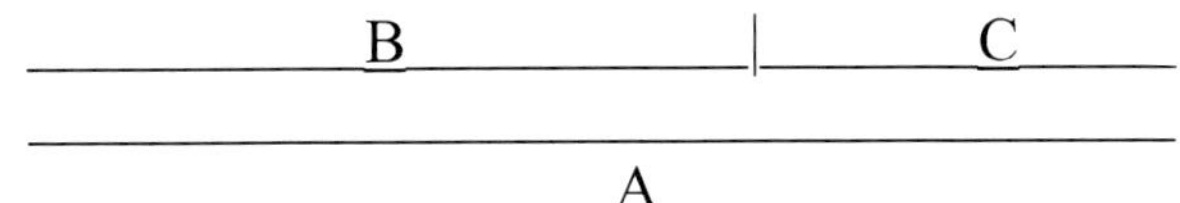

In Hildegard's prayer, the ninth line of text (c^1) contains the golden mean, or golden section which is .618 of the way through the entire text. This line of text (c^1) is also that which contains the first true melisma of the chant, eight pitches within the context of one compound neume and a closing pes.

The c^2 phrase lifts the prayer back to the upper finalis once more, and the c^3 phrase elevates it back to the highest pitch on the word 'Son', referring once more to God's love.

D Phrase Variations

Both of the d phrases serve the same purpose – they are a 'celestial ladder', returning to the earthly stratum of the universe after flying in the cosmos!

Phrase d, "with which you made your Son" returns to the lowest pitch, back to earth so to speak, with a reference to Christ's human nature. This phrase is also that which would form the 'reverse' golden mean, with the division of a line of the entire text at .382.

d^1 ("and lead us") leads us out of the cosmos back to the dominant pitch, remaining there at a higher level than the low pitch ending the longer d. d^1 prepares us for a return to the ethos of the opening salutation, the closing a^4. It also contains a melisma, a repetition of the melisma ending c^1, reiterating and emphasizing humanity's ("nos", us) needs ("hanc", this [need]).

E Phrase

The e phrase is given here in two versions, the first as it appears in the Dendermonde manuscript, and the second as it is performed by several different excellent performers.

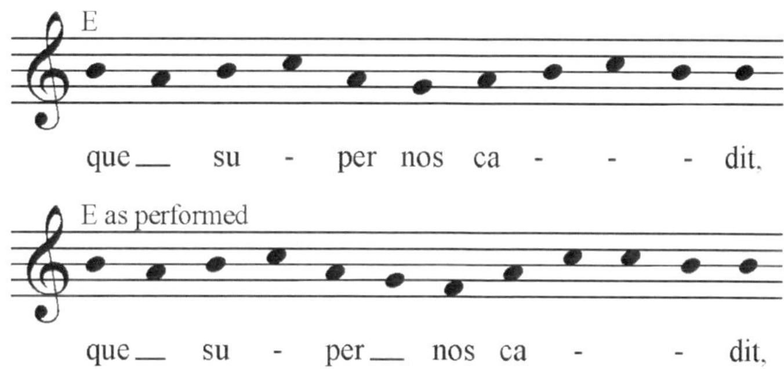

This phrase is really an extension of the Golden section phrase, the c^1. The line in the Dendermonde Codex circles around the dominant pitch, in a sense continuing the melisma at the end of c^1 (the aforementioned "hanc" duplicated in d^1's "nos"), identifying the need as one which falls upon us as humans. The limited range of a Perfect fourth is the smallest of any phrase in the antiphon, pointing to its descriptive nature.

The second notation is certainly more interesting and possibly has more emphasis and meaning as it 'falls' to the pitch f, a tritone away from the initial and final pitch of b. The tritone was an unusual and even 'dangerous' interval in the medieval era, carrying the moniker of 'Diabolus in musicus', or the 'devil of music'. In fact, the first 'accidental', or 'musica ficta' in Western music was the b-flat, introduced to avoid this very interval of the tritone between f and b. The text here certainly would carry the 'diabolus' well, lamenting the trials and tribulations which 'fall' on humanity. This rendition does avoid a 'direct' tritone, falling to the f from its dominant, c and then rising back to that c again, forming a 'neighboring' motion (c a f a c) to the e b e of the preceding phrase. But nowhere else in the antiphon does such a relationship occur, and the original Dendermonde manuscript does not support this transcription.

Hildegard's Antiphon Today!

The preceding discussion about Hildegard's *O eterne Deus* draws on centuries old analytical practice, identifying neumes, phrases, variation processes, and the overall shaping process, or form, of the antiphon. Well, over nine hundred years have passed since her birth, and hopefully we have developed some during those years! I don't think Hildegard would mind one bit if some current means of examining her antiphon were employed.

It is interesting to examine relationships in Hildegard's antiphon in light of her deep conviction and belief in the unity of all things in the cosmos. Her visions of the 'cosmic egg' from *Scivias* and that of the circular nature of the universe embedded in the breast of the Creator from her later work, *Liber divinorum operum,* are certainly evidence of that, so why not look at the antiphon from that perspective?

In both illuminations, Hildegard deals with enormous, cosmic elements. In her accounts of what the "voice of the Living Light" told her of those visual images, the implication is that such unifying relationships reside on many different levels. Each of the visions moves from relationships between universal elements to individual human relationships, human to human and God to human. And the smaller individual relationships are seen within the context of the enormous, cosmic relationships between all elements of the universe. The human body is shown to have the same sort of physical and metaphysical makeup as the entire universe, and the health and spiritual well-being of the human 'microcosm' depends upon the health and well-being of the universal 'macrocosm'.

Is this a Medieval 'general systems theory'?! Hildegard is certainly making the point that the whole (the cosmos) is 'equal to more than the sum of its parts' – all must be in good relationship and balance for the 'whole' to live in a healthy and vital manner. That paradigm works on all levels too, not only on the cosmic level. Any pairing or grouping of individual elements becomes more because of that pairing or grouping. And once those relationships have been made, any change to one or more of the elements profoundly affects the whole.

Her description of humanity as a 'microcosm' may not be unique for her time, but it forms one of the basic principles of her theology. And it certainly predates contemporary perceptions of humans as being mere 'elements' of the physical makeup of the earth. Hmmm. Personally I enjoy thinking of myself as a microcosm of the universe much more than being a mere carbon unit…

Hildegard's 'system' is hierarchical of course, and she shows this clearly in her illuminations. The Creator and his Son – and then the microcosm! All interrelated and embraced and sustained by the Holy Spirit. The Psalmists have identified humanity as being created only 'a little less than the angels', being given dominion over all created things. So again, humanity's relationships with everything in creation is crucial to the well-being of all of creation.

Is this concept so far removed from the musical concept of the musical 'grundgestalt', or Heinrich Schenker's offering of the Ursatz, or Eugene Narmour's implication-realization model? All of those systems are based upon relationships of 'microcosms', to the 'macrocosm'. The interrelationships within a single work are perceived not in a linear fashion, but in a wholistic, multidirectional, multidimensional global manner, where the richness of the whole resides in those interrelationships and not in the number or ordering of the individual elements. The 'whole' musical work can perhaps best be perceived as a 'globe', with height and breadth and depth, with motion, fluidity, light, darkness, activity, respite, emotion, meaning, and on and on. It exists in a musical universe, surrounded and connected by relationships to epochs, to locations, to societies, to national cultures, to families. And every time it is performed, it lives and breathes again with some new interrelationships. This is music.

With that in mind, and sensing Hildegard's gaze over my shoulder, I offer the following model for her antiphon.

Reading the diagram in a clockwise manner from the bottom, the three sections are labeled and then portrayed in colors: green for A, blue for B, and blue/green for A^1. Green was a special color for Hildegard, and she used a term for her special understanding of 'greenness', "viriditas". Viriditas is a rich, vibrant, earthy, verdant greenness full of life, birth, growth, breath, and health. And so green is used in this diagram as a symbol for viriditas, creation.

Blue is for God's action in the cosmos and among the community of 'microcosms' – humanity. Blue has been a color symbolizing the Holy Spirit, God's 'Ruach', or breath, for centuries. Hildegard has called herself, in typical holy modesty, a 'feather on the breath of God'.

The final segment of the circle is a blue/green color, symbolizing the growth in the lives of the microcosm through a 'breathing' relationship with God in the Holy Spirit.

The red circle is, of course, eternity, and more specifically the eternal energy of God's power and love.

The lines of interconnection form a pentagram, a five-pointed star within the wheel of God's energy. And the pentagram appears within the confines of a pentagon. The relationship to

Hildegard's illumination from the *Liber divinorum operum*[76] is obvious. The four points of her 'tetragram' within a circle are the God-head (plus the head of the human figure), the two hands, and the feet of the human microcosm, creating the symbol of the cross. The typical pentagram from ancient Greek philosophy gives, instead of one point for the feet as in Hildegard's tetragram, two points, resulting in the five-pointed star. In Christian practice, the pentagram is a symbol for the five wounds of Christ or for the five senses, and if the letters S A L U S are appended to each point, it symbolized good health. During Hildegard's time, the pentagram symbol was believed to be able to protect believers against the powers of the devil. Sadly, in the 20th century the symbol was largely discarded by the Christian church as it had been appropriated by neopagan and wicca cults.

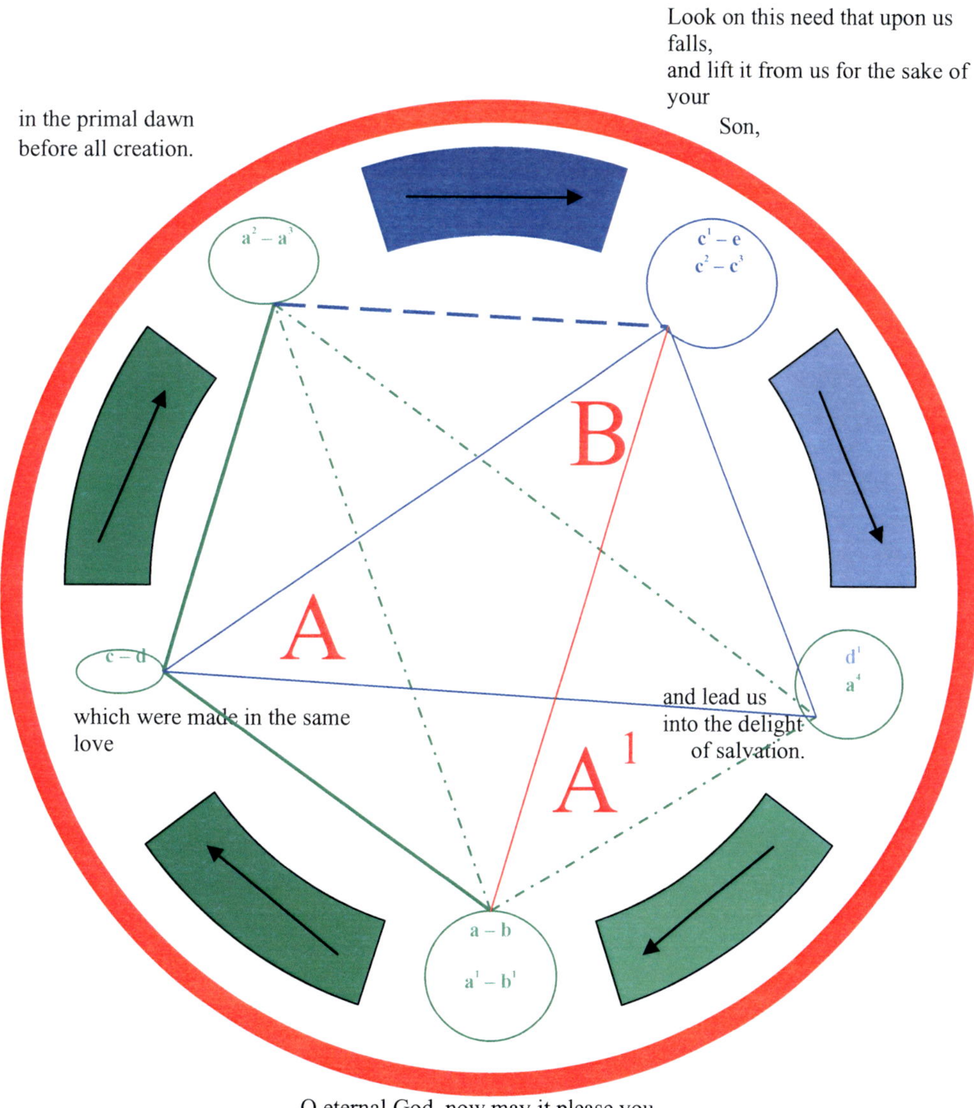

[76] See p.13.

The lines of interconnection in the model were not 'contrived' in order to generate the pentagram. But there it is, and, I believe, rightly so, since all of the lines bisect each other at the point of the Golden Mean! In her antiphon, Hildegard's text and melodic range reach their highest points at the Golden Mean. In the model, there are 'oodles' of Golden Means, as each interior line is bisected twice (at .618 and .382), and each triangle is composed of a line 'bent' at the Golden Mean whether read from one longer line or the other. In the middle, a smaller pentagram is formed – a microcosm of the macrocosm on a middleground level?

So, what leads to the generation of the lines of connection? The list below explains.

1. The red line from a-b, a^1-b^1 to c^1-e, c^2-c^3 represents the trust in God's love, expressed in the opening acclamation, that through love for his Son who was both divine and human, he will help humanity. Four of the five different phrase structures occur in these two areas of connection.
2. The green lines also connect four of the five phrase structures.
   a. the heavy green lines connect the a and b phrases to the c and d phrases: a-b, a^1-b^1 and a^2-a^3 are God's action of creation c-d is the Son, created before all things
   b. the dotted green lines connect phrases of creation and eternity (all a phrases)
3. The blue lines connect phrases of action by God in the cosmos (c phrases)
   a. the heavy dashed blue line symbolizes Hildegard hurling her petition into the cosmos (and the Golden Mean)
   b. one lighter blue line connects the limbs of c-d to the need of energy from God (c^1-c^3)
   c. the other light blue line connects the limbs (microcosm) to attainment of eternity through the Son (d^1)

Thus from Hildegard's antiphon emerges a pentagram within a circle, a unity of text and music reflecting her belief that our earthly music is more than a mirror of the celestial music – it too is a microcosmic creation in sound of the universe created by the loving energy of an all-powerful God.

Meditation

Well.... after all of this thinking, it is perhaps time to settle down and meditate for a few minutes. Our days become so full of so many things and thoughts and perceived problems and difficulties. We most likely take time for ourselves, our bodies, our spirits, and our minds only when everything else has been 'taken care of'. Which means we seldom take time for ourselves. Most Americans have two to four weeks of 'unfettered' time each year. Those weeks are so anticipated and planned, that they often become more 'fettered' than the normal months of employment. We've all probably heard ourselves or a friend say that it was a relief to return to work from a hectic, intense 'vacation'. Taking at least fifteen minutes a day to meditate as a spiritual discipline has been shown to equal, if not surpass, the benefits of several hours of fitful, nervous sleep. Building up the time of meditation over weeks and months to half an hour, forty-five minutes, or an hour multiplies the benefits ten-fold!

Hildegard (as well as thousands of her sisters and brothers in the Benedictine order) has demonstrated a very strict and wonderful discipline of prayer and meditation called the 'Divine Office'. That order of prayer and meditation will be covered in much more detail in a later chapter, but at the moment, the following brief meditation, a guided meditation, is offered, one which will take probably fifteen minutes, and one which you can duplicate using any object of nature as a focal point. It does not matter what time of day or night you choose, or where you are. What the meditation should do is take your mind off of the matters of the moment and of the place where you are, and guide you to an experience of the majesty of God's creation, whether it be the image offered below, a beautiful flower or leaf, a remarkable insect, the wonder of a raindrop, the possibility of a seed, or anything which presents itself to you. You will return to your daily schedule refreshed and renewed, having been somewhere else in the presence of beauty and wonder for fifteen minutes or more. At first, it might take fifteen minutes to remove the hustle and bustle from your attention. But continue to practice centering on the image, and interior silence will come more and more quickly. If you are distracted, gently bring your attention back to the image again – and again!

Find a comfortable, quiet space and sit or lie down, relaxing your body bit by bit, from your toes to the very top of your head. Breathe in slowly and deeply, holding your deep breath for at least five seconds before exhaling equally slowly and as completely as possible. Repeat this three or four times. Then slowly read and follow the meditation.

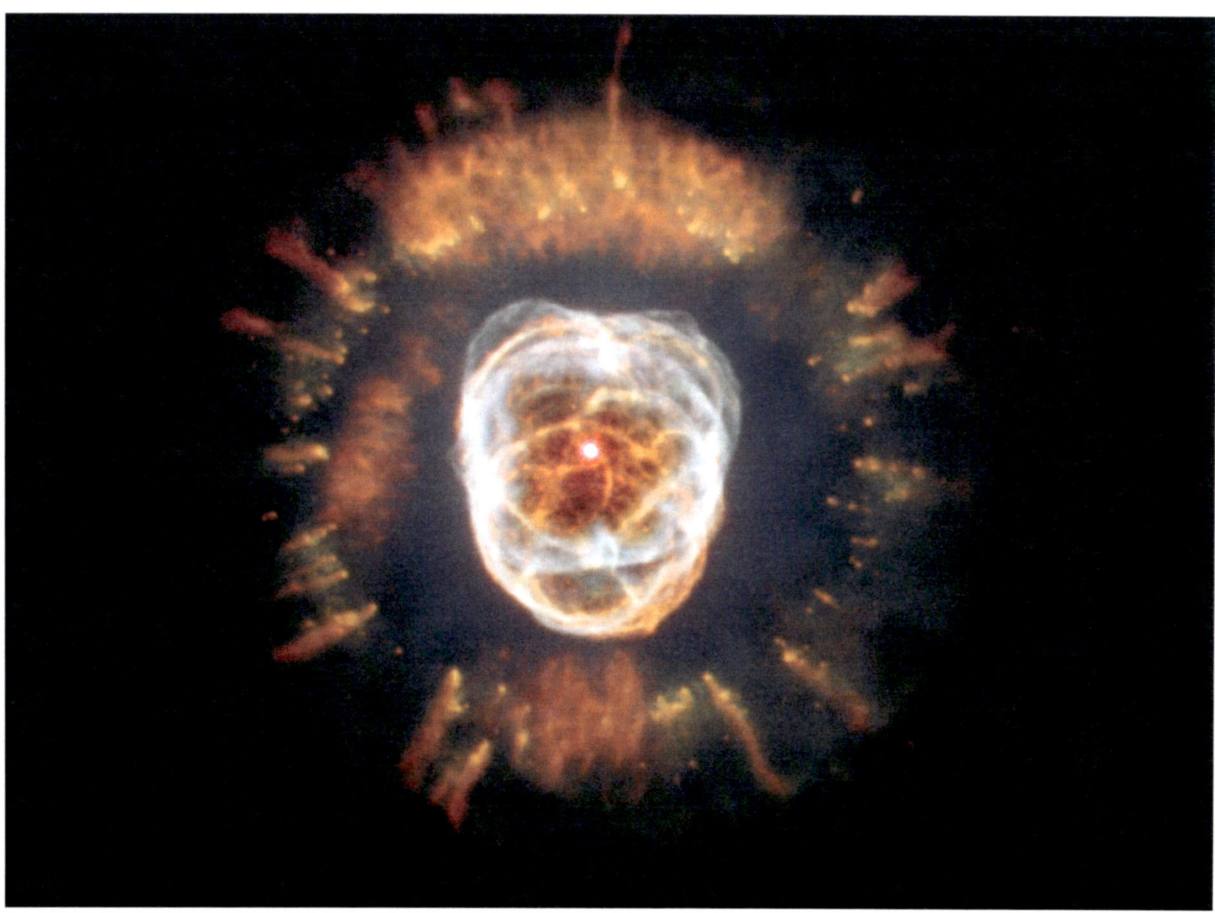

The Eskimo Nebula (NGC 2392)

Spend a few minutes comparing this image[77] to your memory of Hildegard's illumination of the Creation of the Universe. Do not look at Hildegard's illumination again! Search for similarities from your memory.

Close your eyes and see this image in your mind's eye.
    Move closer to it, slowly entering the center of the image.
    What new things do you see?
    What do you hear?
    What do you feel?
Gradually withdraw from the image.
    Sense the chair or floor beneath you.
    Open your eyes and look at the image again, thinking about your experience.
    Thank God for the universe.
    Thank God for creating you as part of the universe.
    Think of one thing you will do every day for the next week to deepen your awareness of and love for creation.
Breathe deeply as at the beginning of the meditation.

Some persons find it helpful to meditate with music. In this age of Ipods and MP3 players, everyone can probably have their favorite music available anywhere and at any time. If you would like to use music with this meditation, you might use the CD which accompanies this book. The first track is intended particularly for this image: a new contemplation of Hildegard's antiphon *O eterne Deus* for solo flute with a rainstick.

---

77 The image is one made in 2000 by the Hubble Telescope. NASA provides the following information about the nebula:

In its first glimpse of the heavens following the successful December 1999 servicing mission, NASA's Hubble Space Telescope has captured a majestic view of a planetary nebula, the glowing remains of a dying, Sun-like star. This stellar relic, first spied by William Herschel in 1787, is nicknamed the "Eskimo" Nebula (NGC 2392) because, when viewed through ground-based telescopes, it resembles a face surrounded by a fur parka. In this Hubble telescope image, the "parka" is really a disk of material embellished with a ring of comet-shaped objects, with their tails streaming away from the central, dying star. The Eskimo's "face" also contains some fascinating details. Although this bright central region resembles a ball of twine, it is, in reality, a bubble of material being blown into space by the central star's intense "wind" of high-speed material.

The planetary nebula began forming about 10,000 years ago, when the dying star began flinging material into space. The nebula is composed of two elliptically shaped lobes of matter streaming above and below the dying star. In this photo, one bubble lies in front of the other, obscuring part of the second lobe.

Scientists believe that a ring of dense material around the star's equator, ejected during its red giant phase, created the nebula's shape. This dense waist of material is plodding along at 72,000 miles per hour (115,000 kilometers per hour), preventing high-velocity stellar winds from pushing matter along the equator. Instead, the 900,000-mile-per-hour (1.5-million-kilometer-per-hour) winds are sweeping the material above and below the star, creating the elongated bubbles. The bubbles are not smooth like balloons but have filaments of denser matter. Each bubble is about 1 light-year long and about half a light-year wide. Scientists are still puzzled about the origin of the comet-shaped features in the "parka." One possible explanation is that these objects formed from a collision of slow- and fast-moving gases.

The Eskimo Nebula is about 5,000 light-years from Earth in the constellation Gemini. The picture was taken Jan. 10 and 11, 2000, with the Wide Field and Planetary Camera 2. The nebula's glowing gases produce the colors in this image: nitrogen (red), hydrogen (green), oxygen (blue), and helium (violet).

Object Names: Eskimo Nebula, NGC 2392

Image Type: Astronomical

Credit: NASA, Andrew Fruchter and the ERO Team [Sylvia Baggett (STScI), Richard Hook (ST-ECF), Zoltan Levay (STScI)] http://hubblesite.org/newscenter/archive/releases/2000/07/image/a/

O eterne Deus

Ann K. Gebuhr

All durations are proportionate indications, and are not intended to be metered.

O eternal God, now may it please you so in love to burn
that limbs we may become, which were made in the same love
with which you made your Son in the primal dawn before all creation.
Look on this need that upon us falls,
and lift it from us for the sake of your Son,
and lead us into delight of salvation.
-- Hildegard

Houston, 1 October 2007
Abtei St. Hildegard,
Rudesheim, 12 July 2009

Exercise

Physical exercise is always part of balanced, healthy living style, and it is often the last thing we make time for in our 21st century lives. These last three portions of each chapter, the meditation, exercise, and recipes, are designed in such a way as to help you change or enhance your healthy lifestyle as you read through the book. The world with its beauty and nurturing environment contain more than what we need to help to maintain our body, mind and spirit in a healthy balance.

The above meditation began with some breathing practice, and this first exercise builds on that, adding some very basic stretching to the breathing. It is an exercise that can be used as a warmup for any activity, as a relaxation moment in the middle of an intense day, as a way to awaken your body first thing in the morning, or, as given here, as a means to reactivate your systems after a period of meditation.

Stand with your feet slightly apart, placed directly beneath your shoulders. Slowly bend down, starting from your head and neck, through each vertebrae of your back, until you bend from your hips, slightly flexing your knees so they are not locked, letting your arms fall loosely from the shoulders until they are hanging as low as you can bend without straining. As you bend slowly down, exhale all of the air in your lungs and hold that position for a slow count of three. Then slowly straighten up, reversing the bone-by-bone bend, keeping your arms straight and raising them straight over your head. Reach as high as you can, standing on your toes. As you slowly straighten up and stretch, inhale equally slowly, holding your breath in the highest stretched position to the slow count of three. Then begin a slow exhalation as you slowly bend over again, slowly exhaling all of your breath down to the lowest bending position.

You might want to start with two or three of these, being careful to not hyperventilate or become light-headed. This deep breathing will reoxygenate your entire body and bring 'fresh air' to all of your organs, including your brain! I have used this in my music theory classes that meet at 8 AM – full of students in their late teens and early twenties. All of a sudden, after doing this deep breathing, they begin to discuss, ask questions, and connect concepts. Over the years, several have told me that they continue to do this in the morning, and it has helped quiet their need for caffeine!

After completing one more breath than what is comfortable for you, always drink some good, 'room temperature' water. In fact, you should drink a lot of water every day, and that is water, not 'liquid'. Our bodies are made up of over 70% water, and that includes our brains! Bodies need to be rehydrated regularly, and rehydration doesn't occur with 'fizz' or caffeine, mocha caramel ooey gooey, or any other type of liquid. If those types of drinks are necessary for you, go ahead and have them, but drink eight ounces of water before and another eight ounces after drinking them! It is amazing what we clog up our bodily systems with, and how our incredible body deals with all of it for years and years. We can help it a lot by drinking water!

The meditations and exercises are presented throughout this book in an order which might help you to change or modify your lifestyle to become integrated and balanced in a healthy, wholesome manner. They aren't intended as a 'cure' or as the 'end all and be all' for that purpose, but as aids on a path to wholeness with Hildegard as the inspiration and teacher.

Recipes

In addition to water, what we give to our body as food is important. I just saw an ad for a new, bigger, better burger that was amazing…over a half pound of ground beef and over 1,000 calories (without the accompanying french fries or soft drink), dripping with fat and bacon grease, surrounded by a white-flour bun (which turns into sugar immediately…). Just the size of the thing was overwhelming! And we are encouraged to spend money to gift our bodies with that as nutrition. I wonder how many of us, if we were to eat that thing, would bother to follow the advice to 'chew everything at least fourteen times' before swallowing, thereby helping our soon to be overworked stomach to begin to try and digest that mountain of carbohydrates, grease, sugar and possibly very fatty, poor quality meat. Perhaps a meditation on our own stomach as it is stuffed with such a meal would give some insight into what we do to our bodies.

Our bodies. The microcosms, the temples of the soul, the incredible living 'machines' that we still don't understand completely. We have become a generation of body abusers, resulting in all-time high incidences of heart disease, cancer, diabetes, obesity, and a myriad of other problems caused by body abuse. It would be interesting, and perhaps a bit frightening to hear what Hildegard would have to say about our eating habits…

What she does have to say is perhaps first, MODERATION! One of her strongest messages in everything she wrote was moderation. And she also recommended food that nourished the body – not food that gratified the tastebuds or some other need or longing. We eat to nourish our body and mind. Any food consumed for pleasure is all right, but in moderation. She extolled the healthful benefits of good wine, and she offered many recipes for desserts and cookies and breads – everything we enjoy today (that is not synthetic or chemical). The emphasis is on wholesome eating and drinking, with moderation! One of her basic ingredients which is so excellent for our digestion is spelt grain. Spelt is an ancient wheat grain that has not been hybridized, and its gluten is much more easily digested than the gluten from whole wheat flour or white flour. It also contains numerous vitamins and minerals as well as excellent fiber content. So a number of the recipes to follow use Spelt.

The recipes offered below take no longer than 30 minutes preparation/cooking time, and use whole foods, not the very available 'fast' foods or processed foods that are so popular and fattening. Each chapter will offer one recipe for breakfast, one for lunch, and one for dinner. The recipes are for one serving, since so often we must eat alone or on our own schedule. They may be doubled, tripled, and quadrupled for small groups. I have no idea what the calorie count is, or what the daily per centage of basic food categories are for these recipes! They are recipes of good, basic, whole food in moderate proportions, and if prepared with delight and care and eaten in moderation, your bodies will be wholesomely nourished. Oh – drink at least eight ounces of water with each meal too…!

Breakfast

Spelt Wheat Breakfast Biscuits (makes 12 biscuits)

eat no more than two each meal!

Dry ingredients:

2½ C whole spelt flour
1/3C Sucanat (organic, unprocessed brown sugar) or brown sugar
1Tbs.baking powder
½ Tsp. sea salt or 2/3 Tsp. Himalayan salt

Wet ingredients:

1¼ C organic whole milk
3 organic cage-free eggs, beaten
1 Tbs. olive oil or coconut oil

Optional ingredients:

½ C blueberries, craisins, chopped dates, raisins or any mixture of small fruits.

Preparation:

Preheat the oven to 425°F.

Prepare a muffin tin by greasing and flouring (with spelt flour!) the individual cups, or use one of the new silicone muffin tins, which need no preparation.

1. Combine all dry ingredients and mix them well.
2. Combine all wet ingredients and mix them well.
3. Add the wet to the dry, lightly stirring until all is moist.
4. If desired, add the optional fruits to the mixture, mixing well.
5. Fill the muffin containers 2/3rds full.
6. Bake for 15 minutes or until done.
7. Cool slightly and pop out of muffin tin. Enjoy (only two or three!)

Lunch

Fresh Mozzarella and Tomato Salad with Spaghetti and Zucchini (serves 1)

Dry ingredients:

10-15 pieces of dry spaghetti noodles
1 Tsp. salt
2 Tsp. chopped fresh basil
3 fresh basil leaves
Sea salt, fresh ground pepper to taste
½ C grated Pecorino or Parmesan cheese

Wet ingredients:

3 ¼-inch round slices of fresh Mozzarella
1 ripe tomato, sliced into ¼-inch thick rounds
extra virgin olive oil
1 Tsp. minced garlic
1 small zucchini, sliced
juice from ½ lemon

Preparation:

1. Bring a pot of water to a boil, add the spaghetti, stir and cover. When the water comes to a boil again, uncover the pot.
2. Heat 1 Tsp. of olive oil in a small skillet. Add the garlic and zucchini and sauté on medium until the zucchini begins to brown.
3. Add salt and pepper to the zucchini, then the lemon juice and strips of basil. Stir, then remove from heat.
4. Spread the Mozzarella slices on the edge of a dinner plate, slightly touching or overlapping.
5. Place the tomato slices on top of the Mozzarella, add the chopped basil on top, and salt and pepper to taste.
6. Drizzle a very thin line of olive oil through the center of the row of tomatoes.
7. Drain the spaghetti and place it on the dinner plate with the Mozzarella salad. Sprinkle the Pecorino or Parmesan cheese on top.
8. Add the zucchini on top of the spaghetti, and enjoy your lunch.

Dinner

Baked Salmon with Vegetables (serves 1)

Preheat the oven to 375°F

Ingredients:

One small wild salmon fillet (4-6 oz) (any other fish may be substituted)
juice from ½ lemon
Olive oil or coconut oil (preferred)
2 Small golden potatoes, cubed or wedged
½ onion, sliced
½ carrot, sliced
¼ bell pepper (green, yellow or red), sliced small portions of any other vegetables in your refrigerator Sea salt and freshly ground pepper

Preparation:

1. Lightly, very lightly cover the bottom of a baking dish with the oil.
2. Place the fish at one end of the dish and squeeze the lemon juice on it.
3. Arrange the vegetables in a single layer in the rest of the dish, turning them over once to cover them lightly with the oil.
4. Add salt and pepper to taste.
5. Bake in the oven for 20 minutes or until fish is done.

Serve: with a nice glass of red or white wine, and one or two slices of fennel, a big, round radish, and a small slice of goat cheese for a side salad. If you desire a dessert, slice a piece of fruit and add a half-cup of flavored kefir milk for a ‘smoothie’ topping.

II.
Hildegard the Musician I

Music is at the heart of everything by and about Hildegard, for she believed that through music we come the closest to eternal paradise, the "heavenly kingdom". She says that music is the highest form of praise to God and through music we participate in the worship of the heavenly kingdom as in a mirror, reflecting the praise of the heavenly choirs – no, more than that – actively mirroring the praise of the heavenly musicians here on earth, joining heaven and earth in stereophonic surround-sound worship! And we also best express our unity with all of God's creation when making music, filling the universe and the earth in all dimensions and directions with praise and worship.

Hildegard's music is unique for her time, for the entire Medieval age, and certainly for her location. In fact, her music was overlooked and largely ignored until the last quarter of a century or so, most likely due to its individuality and unique qualities. It simply 'did not fit' into the general style of northern European Medieval music in the 11th and 12th centuries. And why might that be? Before we can understand Hildegard's individuality, we should look at what was happening musically during her lifetime.

Before her enclosure with Jutta at age fourteen, it is very likely that Hildegard heard and probably sang some of the childhood songs of her time and location, and she certainly must have heard many performances of some of the secular tunes brought to her parents home and to the von Sponheim estate by traveling musicians. There is no record of her musical experiences prior to her enclosure at the monastery of Disibodenberg, but it seems reasonable to assume that music was a love of her whole life, including early childhood experiences.

Jutta von Sponheim presenting the eight-year-old Hildegard to sisters at Disibodenberg, from the Rochus Kapell altar.

Medieval music was based upon a system of modes (what we now commonly call scales) generated out of ancient Greek musical theory. Hildegard's modal system had been in use for centuries, and it was the basis for plainchant, or "Gregorian Chant" – music with which Hildegard was very familiar. Both sacred and secular music of her time was based on the same system of modes, so her early childhood musical experiences and those encountered after entering the monastery enclosure were not differentiated as far as musical language was concerned. Understanding a bit about the modes and some of the compositional techniques used to 'activate' the modes into melodies will help to explain the uniqueness of Hildegard's compositional craft.

The graph below lists the modes as they were defined in early centuries (the older terminology of "Ancient Music"), during Hildegard's time in the middle of the Medieval age (the 10th-11th centuries, time of the Crusades) and as they have been identified since Hildegard's time to the present. Also provided on the graph are the specific 'tunings' of the modes, the pitches upon which they were formed. The 'finalis' was the focal pitch of the mode, generally corresponding to what we today call a 'tonic' pitch. The 'confinalis' was the second most prominent and important pitch, but it only corresponds to our current 'dominant' pitch in the case of the Dorian, Phrygian, Lydian, and Mixolydian modes. The 'Hypo' modes have a confinalis that is in a 'third relationship' to the finalis, in two instances the interval of a minor third above the finalis, once a major third above, and once a minor third below.

Older Terminology	10th-11th Century Terminology	Current Terminology	Number of Mode	Finalis, Confinalis	Ambitus
Protus authenticus	Primus tonus	Dorian	1	d, a	d-d
Protus plagius	Secundus tonus	Hypodorian	2	d,f	a-a
Deuterus authenticus	Tertius tonus	Phrygian	3	e,b	e-e
Deuterus plagius	Quartus tonus	Hypophrygian	4	e,g	b-b
Tritus authenticus	Quintus tonus	Lydian	5	f,c	f-f
Tritus plagius	Sextus tonus	Hypolydian	6	f,a	c-c
Tetradus Authenticus	Septimus tonus	Mixolydian	7	g,d	g-g
Tetradus plagius	Octavus tonus	Hypomixolydian	8	g,e	d-d

Each of the modes consists of a particular pentachord (five-note ascending series) and tetrachord (four-note ascending series), and they are identified by the finalis and the corresponding confinalis. Modes with the ambitus (range) extending above the finalis are based upon a pentachord. Those with the ambitus of a tetrachord extending up to the finalis are 'Hypo-modes'. The pentachords and tetrachords are called 'species' of fifths and fourths, and they serve as basic melodic sets.

Modes and Species

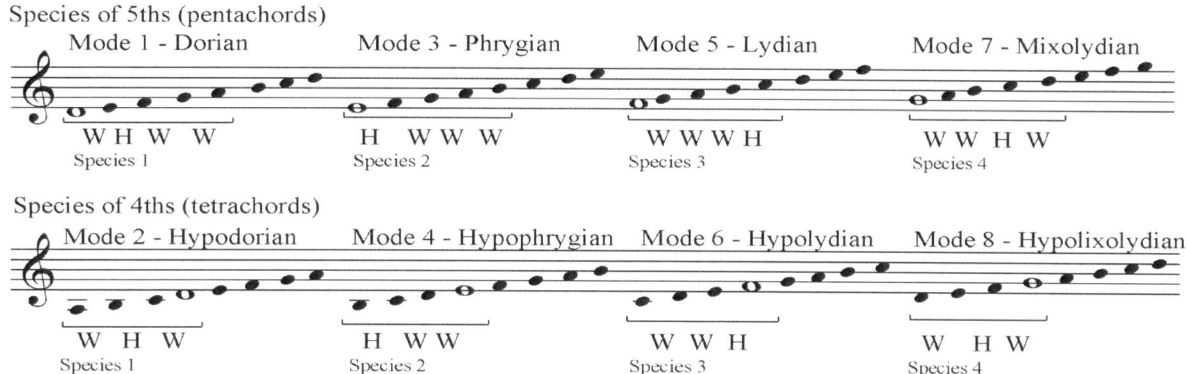

In the graph above, the 'finalis' for each mode is shown as a whole note (). These are only the pitches d, e, f, and g for both species.

The letters "W" and "H" identify the arrangement of whole steps (M2) and half steps (m2) within each pentachord or tetrachord, arrangements which give each mode a specific configuration, or 'sound'.

What we today call 'major' scales begin with a pentachord or tetrachord containing two consecutive whole steps (Lydian, Hypolydian, and Mixolydian modes), and 'minor' scales begin with a pentachord or tetrachord containing one whole step and one half step (all of the other modes listed above).

The modes and species were combined much like the combination of neumes, creating a delightful and varied 'commixture'. An example using one of Hildegard's favorite modes and beginning with one of her favorite initial intervals is given below.

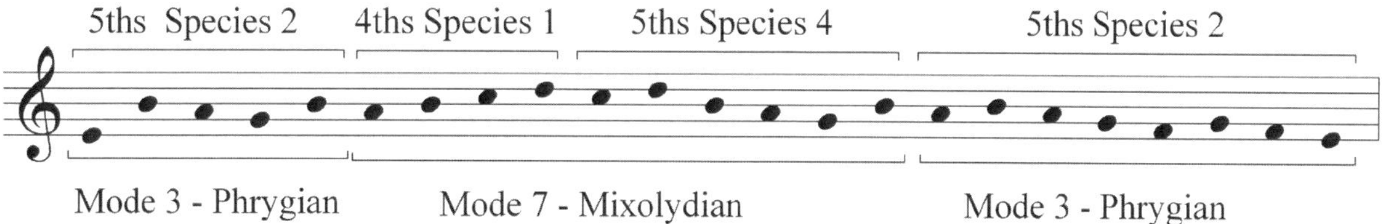

In this example the opening gesture uses the second species of 5ths, establishing the finalis 'e' and the Phrygian mode with the use of the diapente (5th pitch in the series above 'e' – 'b') -- also called the 'confinalis'. A Medieval 'modulation[78]' follows, with the tetrachordal species 1 ascending to 'd', becoming the diapente of species 4 of the pentachords. The combination of those two segments create an internal emphasis on the 7th mode, the Mixolydian mode. The final segment of the example returns to the Phrygian mode, using Species 2 of the pentachords.

As indicated earlier, the initial interval of the rising 5th is one of Hildegard's 'signature' motives, and she often follows that rather dramatic interval with an immediate ascending leap to the diapason (the finalis at the interval of an octave). In the above example, the inner portion of

[78] The term modulation refers to a portion of music where the tonic pitch has been changed, in modal terms, where the 'finalis' has been changed.

the chant moves to a focus on G Mixolydian precisely because it does not ascend to the octave 'e', articulating instead the 'd' (diapente of G) twice as the apex of the melodic line. The return to E Phrygian is then smoothly accomplished through the centrally located mediant of the G Mixolydian mode, 'b', which is, of course, the diapente of 'e'.

In modern notation, the chant would include 'slurs' to identify the neumes used, and the neumes are seen as melodic elaborations of the syllables of the text. No neumes with multiple pitches are shared by two or more syllables, clearly showing the use of the pentachord and tetrachord structure.[79]

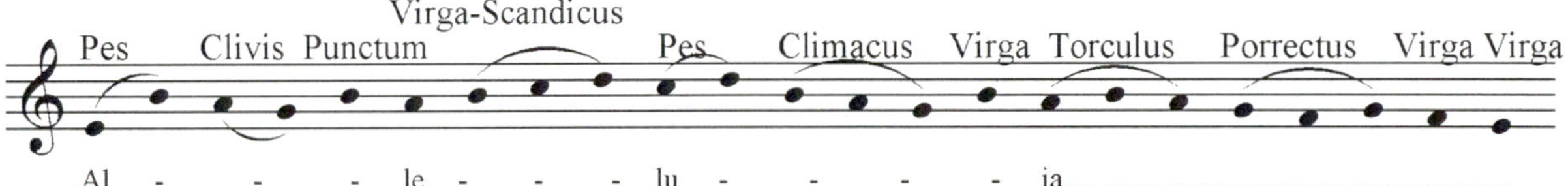

Other composers of her time

Until the 12th Century, it was unusual to know the composer of a sacred musical work. Hildegard's work represents one of the earliest collections of musical compositions clearly identified. Her chants were included in her literary works, showing once again that music was an intrinsic element of her life and that she included music as an essential and normal part of the life of her community.

Only two composers of sacred works are identified prior to Hildegard's time, and a third immediately precedes her life span. The two earlier composers are Notker Balbulus (d.912) and Tuotilo (d.c.915). Both of these men were associated with the famous and influential Swiss monastery of St. Gall, and both were influential in the development of new musical forms for plainchant.

Tuotilo was Notker's teacher at St. Gall, and he was the originator of 'tropes', interpolations of additional texts into authorized Gregorian Chant texts. It is thought that these texts were originally added to lengthy passages of melisma, and that eventually the texts became longer and new music was written for them. One of the earliest examples of Tuotilo's work shows this practice clearly.[80]

Notker Balbulus

79 See the chart of neumes in Chapter One.

80 *Liber Usualis*, p.25

IV. — Aux Fêtes Doubles. 1.

(Cunctipotens Genitor Deus)

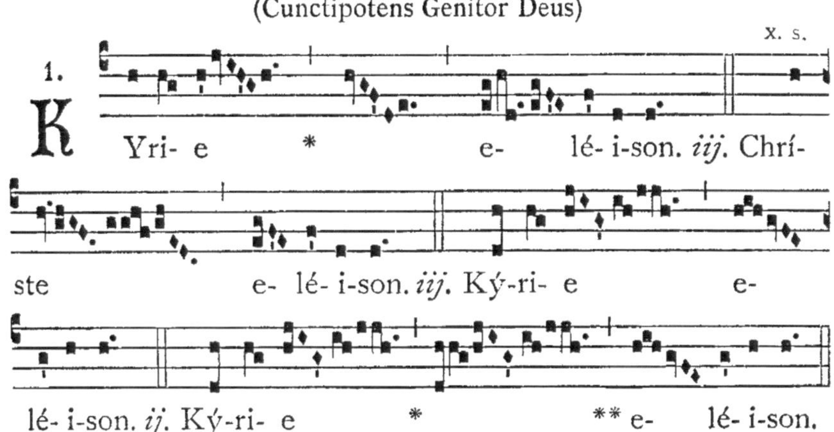

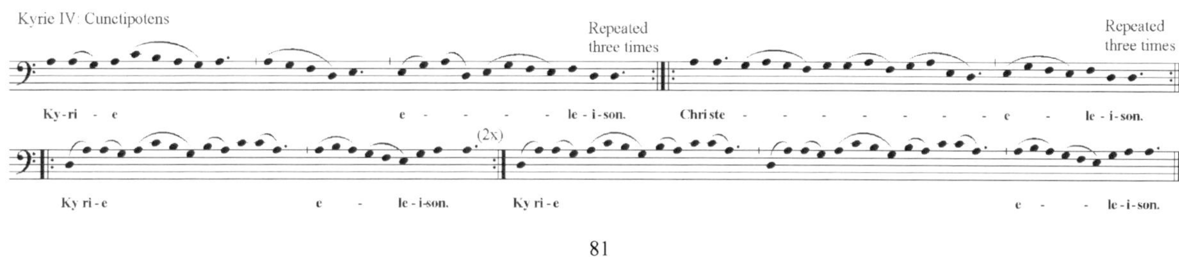

81

To this traditional Mass chant, Tuotilo added text to the melismae for the first Kyrie (a verse text for each of the three repetitions of the phrase), to that of the Christe (again three verses), and to the final Kyrie (three more verses). An example of the Kyrie with its troped text is:[82]

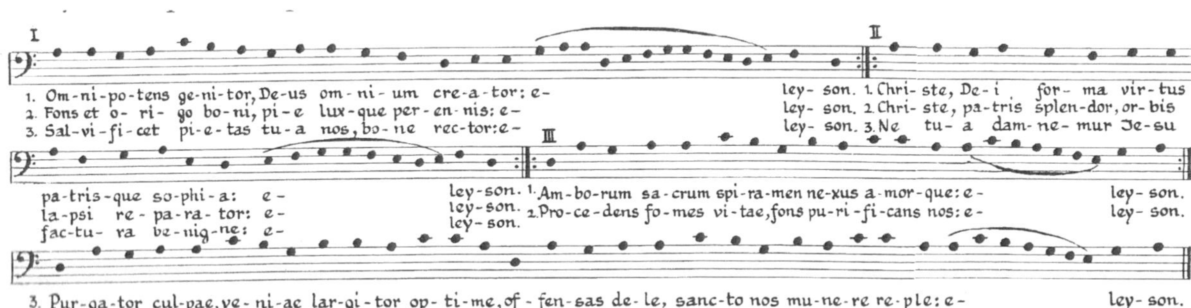

The text is Trinitarian, with the first Kyrie addressing the Omnipotent Father, the Christe of course addressing the Son, and the final Kyrie addressing the Spirit.

Tuotilo (c.850-915) was, like Hildegard, multi-talented. He was born in Ireland and educated at the Abbey of St. Gall (now in Switzerland). In addition to his musical gifts, he was an artist. Several of his paintings survive to this day, and the Library at St. Gall holds a manuscript for which Tuotilo created the binding from two ivory plates he acquired from the St. Alban's Benedictine abbey in Mainz (very close to Hildegard's home) around 900 CE. A glimpse of the

---

81 Apel, *Historical Anthology of Music*. Cambridge, MA (Harvard University Press, 1966) p. 13

82 *Ibid.*

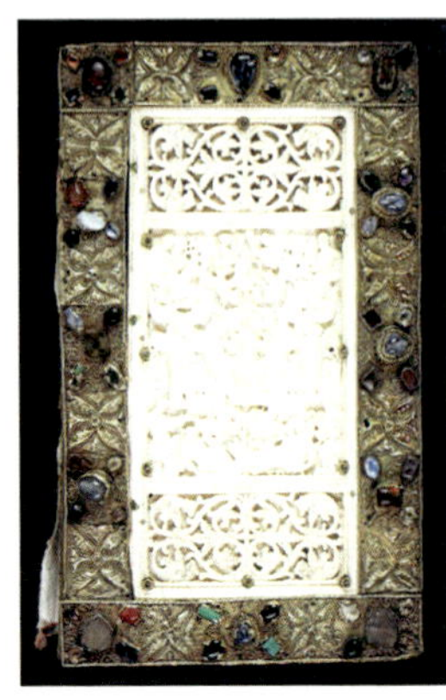

cover binding for the manuscript, *Evangelium longum* (text by the monk Sintram) shows the level of artistry employed by Tuotilo.

Notker Balbulus continued Tuotilo's practice of 'troping' text to the melismae of the Kyrie and other Gregorian chants, focusing particularly on the melismae associated with the 'Alleluia' which immediately preceded the Gospel in the Mass. He fit text to the melisma (called the 'jubilation'), and developed the troped verses into what became the 'Sequence'. It has long been thought that Notker was the 'inventor' of the Sequence, but recent scholarship has indicated its earliest origins were French. Certainly Notker can be credited with considerable influence on the development and spread of the Sequence to Germany and to Eastern Europe.

Notker Balbulus

One of the most famous sequences remaining in use today, the sequence *Victimae Paschali Laudes*, is attributed to Wipo of Burgundy (c.1000-1050), a monk and composer who just precedes Hildegard's lifetime.[83]

This sequence has remained a favorite Easter hymn for over a millenium now, and has been rhythmicized for congregational use, quoted in instrumental works (symphonies, tone poems, etc.), arranged as a chorale prelude probably hundreds of times, and it continues to be used in its original chant setting. *Victimae paschali laudes* was one of several thousand sequences that were written between the late 900s and the Council of Trent (1543-1563), when all but four sequences were eliminated from common usage and inclusion in the *Liber Usualis*.[84] Hildegard wrote seven sequences.

Before taking a peek at Hildegard's compositional style, may I offer another of her visions to serve as a companion to a closer study of her musical creativity? The first vision in her book *Liber divinorum operum* is a remarkable illumination, *On the Origin of Life*.[85]

---

[83] *Liber Usualis*, p.780

[84] *Victimae paschali laudes* (Easter sequence from the 11th C.), *Veni Sancte Spiritus* (Pentecost, from the 12th C.), *Lauda Sion Salvatorum* (Corpus Christi, 12th C.), *Dies Irae* (All Souls Day and the Mass for the Dead, 13th C.).

[85] *Liber divinorum operum*, Codex 1942, Biblioteca Governativa at Lucca

Hildegard writes that the 'Voice of the Living Light' proclaims about this vision:

"I, the highest and fiery power, have kindled every spark of life, and I emit nothing that is deadly. I decide on all reality. With my lofty wings I fly above the globe: With wisdom I have rightly put the universe in order. I, the fiery life of divine essence, am aflame beyond the beauty of the meadows. I gleam in the waters, and I burn in the sun, moon, and stars. With every breeze, as with invisible life that contains everything, I awaken everything to life. The air lives by turning green and being in bloom. The waters flow as if they were alive. The sun lives in its light, and the moon is enkindled, after its disappearance, once again by the light of the sun so that the moon is again revived...

God, who created everything, has formed humanity according to the divine image and likeness, and marked in human beings both the higher and the lower creatures. God loved humanity so much that God designated for it the place from which the fallen angel was ejected, intending for human beings all the splendor and honor which that angel lost along with his bliss. The countenance you are gazing at is an indication of this fact.

For what you see as a marvelously beautiful figure in God's mystery and in the midst of southern breezes -- a figure similar to a human being -- signifies the Love of our heavenly Father. It is Love -- in the power of the everlasting Godhead, full of exquisite beauty, marvelous in its mysterious gifts."[86]

---

[86] *Ibid., pp.9-11*

Beneath the illumination is one of Hildegard's self-portraits, emphasizing the fact that the vision was just that – a vision given to her by the 'Living Light'. In this self portrait, she is receiving the vision, writing it on a wax tablet. Volmar is transcribing the vision to parchment in the cell to her left, and another nun, probably Richardis, is observing the event. A closer look:

This illumination is powerful, and Hildegard's description and interpretation deserves a long and thoughtful reading and meditation. This is not the place for that, but it is highly recommended.[87] This vision is titled "The Origin of Life", and should have the subtitle "Held by Love". Pardon the brevity of the following summary of Hildegard's interpretation.

The vision begins with the voice of the Living Light describing itself as the highest and fiery power kindling the spark of life in everything. In poetic language, we hear of God's presence in the universe, in all celestial matter, in everything on the earth. The "fiery life of divine essence" is aflame, gleams, burns, awakens, revives, establishes, breathes.

> "For I am life. I am also Reason, which bears within itself the breath of the resounding Word, through which the whole of creation is made. I breathe life into everything so that nothing is mortal in respect to its species. For I am life.. whole and entire (vita integra) – not struck from stones, not blooming out of twigs, not rooted in a man's power to beget children. Rather all life has its roots in me. Reason is the root, the resounding Word blooms out of it.[88]

Hildegard 'defines' the Trinity in this vision too, stating that the power of creation, of life, is threefold, and that, as a microcosm, God has marked humanity, giving us body, reason (mind), and soul, formed out of the earth. She goes on to connect the soul with water, in which God is illuminated, and the mind (reason) with fire (sun, moon and stars), and the body with air and wind, which enlivens and supports us as we grow and mature.[89] In her description of the Trinity,

---

[87] See pp. 8-21, Matthew Fox, ed. Hildegard. *Book of Divine Works* (Santa Fe: Bear & Company, 1987)

[88] *Liber divinorum operum*,. p.10

[89] *Ibid.* p.11

"eternity is called the "Father," the Word is called the "Son," and the breath that binds both of them together is called the "Holy Spirit."[90]

The voice from heaven continues to speak to Hildegard, saying that being created in the divine image marks humanity with the higher and lower creatures also, and that God loves humanity so much, humanity was intended for the splendor and honor lost by the fallen angel. This vision is the vision of Love, appearing in human form "because God's Son, when he put on flesh, redeemed our lost humanity in the service of Love."[91]

As in the previous chapters, a list of symbols follows, attached to corresponding numbers on the illumination.

1. A golden ring, signifying faith through which the abundance of Love can be known.
2. A second head above the golden ring, an 'elderly man' signifying the over-powering loving-kindness of the 'Godhead for all eternity. God's Son, Love, leads humanity directly to the heavenly kingdom, the eternal Godhead.
3. The two wings signify the love of God and love of our neighbor, joined together at the top with 'the greatest longing'. They are joined through divine Love in the unity of faith.
4. On the right wing, an eagle's head with fiery eyes. Spiritual people who gaze at God are marked with an eagle; they continually praise God, and in this image, they are reflected in the eyes of the eagle as in a mirror.[92]
5. A human face is at the top of the left wing. This represents those who protect and defend the Creator among and within "earthly things that…attack us…"[93] "God gave to us human beings the place and honor of the fallen angels so that we might complete God's glory, which is something those angels had refused to do."[94]
6. Wings extend down from each shoulder, symbolizing Christ's attraction, through his love, for the just (carried on his shoulders) and sinners (carried on his knees) who he has called back from the path of error.[95]
7. A radiant garment clothes the Son. He lived in human form (the garment) in purity and love.
8. Christ carries a lamb, also radiant in color. "For love has revealed in the deeds of the Son of God the gentleness of a true faith that outshines everything else.[96]
9. A dark, horrible figure (injustice) is trampled by the Son of God, Love. The serpent is Satan, who "fastens his jaws in strife" and causes conflict. The different colors of the serpent's skin symbolize cunning and insinuating evil. He also has been cast down and is overcome by Love.

---

[90] *Ibid.* p.11
[91] *Ibid.* p.12
[92] *Ibid.* p.13
[93] *Ibid.* p.15
[94] *Ibid,* p.16
[95] *Ibid.*
[96] *Ibid,* p.17

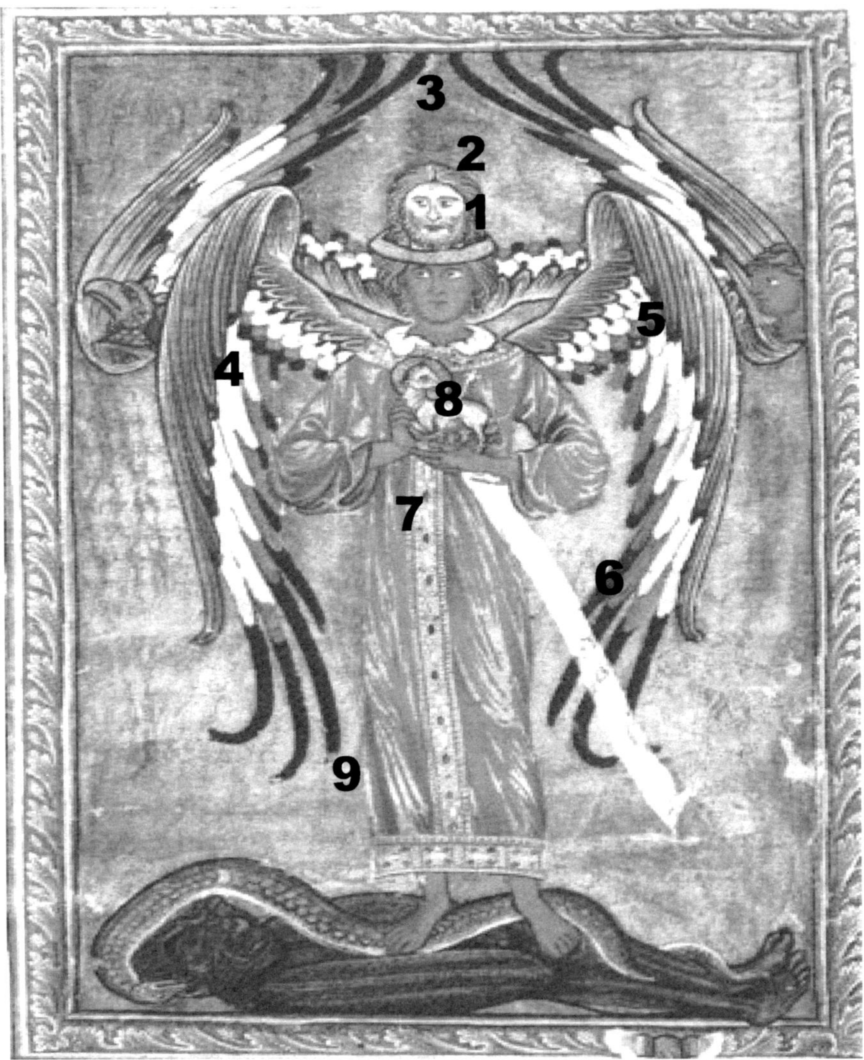

What a wondrous, beautiful, inspiring image. It is inspiring and a bit unnerving too, as we are being shown and told that God intends for us to take the place of the fallen angel, Satan, intending for us all of the honor and splendor he lost. But we are carried in Christ's arms[97] and he (Love) conquers injustice and evil. How unfortunate that our language affords us words associated with conflict and violence to describe acts of ultimate love and being...conquers, triumphs, victory, etc....are we not capable of understanding or experiencing unconditional love and peace and beauty without the opposite extremes generating a yearning for them?

Hildegard's Music

To review a bit, Hildegard's chants are of four types, all appropriate for singing as part of the Divine Office. They are antiphons (psalm antiphons), responsories (great and small), sequences (between the Alleluia and the Gospel), and hymns. Hildegard was a whole, holistic person in her lifestyle, and she loved beautiful colors, sounds, scents or fragrances, gems, flowers, -- for her, everything beautiful in God's creation. This love for creation coupled with her intensity as a

[97] the sheep is a 'Janus-faced' symbol of Christ's care for us and also of Christ's sacrifice

personality was forcefully expressed in her music. Music and text were, for her, in a symbiotic relationship, united completely in her response to what she had seen, experienced, and wished to express from her soul. Her lack of formal education (which is somewhat questionable[98]) perhaps freed her to express herself without the restrictions and inhibitions often imposed by 'formal academic' training. In any case, her music was not cast in the mold of music being written at Notre Dame, St. Martial, or other musical 'hot spots' of her times.

To demonstrate some of Hildegard's unique, individualistic manner of composition, let's take a look at a relatively short but profound Antiphon – *O pastor animarum*. The text of this antiphon was written by Hildegard and addresses Christ, the Shepherd of souls. It also reflects the core of the vision presented above.

O pastor animarum
O shepherd of souls

O pastor animarum et o prima vox	1	*O shepherd of souls and first voice*
per quam omnes creati sumus	2	*through which we are all created*
nunc tibi, tibi placeat ut digneris	3	*now you, if it pleases you and you deem it worthy*
nos liberare de miseriis	4	*free us from our miseries*
et languoribus nostris.	5	*and our languor.*

Hildegard's prayer is cast in five lines in a three-part textual form very common for liturgical prayer. The first part (lines 1-2) addresses Christ as shepherd and creator. In the vision, Christ is joined with God the Creator-Father in a very profound and specific imagery with a ring of faith. He is also identified as a shepherd, carrying a lamb next to his heart that is also a symbol of his divine, sacrificial love.

The second part (line 3) is a 'polite' petition, a transition from praise to request, identifying our human relationship to the shepherd as the lost who wish to be found. In the vision, we are placed at the top of his left wing, a position of honor. We are carried on his shoulder, and also on his knee, a burden balanced by shoulders and knees, lifted from the abyss so to speak.

The final part (lines 4-5) is the direct request, identifying our state of misery which is perpetual without Christ's intercession and love.

The musical form of the antiphon is also cast in three parts, but not of three equal lengths: A^1 B^1 A^{m1}-B^{m2} A^2 B^2. The first part offers the musical materials to be used throughout the antiphon, the melodic patterns, the modes and the character of the two contrasting lines, A and B.

The second part, a combination of A and B, is more like a development of the first part rather than a full pairing such as that used in the first and last parts. In this shorter almost parenthetical phrase, Hildegard includes all of the material introduced in the first part! It is the most active and inclusive line in the antiphon.

The third part, occurring at the Golden Section of the antiphon, is a direct reflection of the first part. But it has been altered, textually and musically, to reflect once more the human condition for which we hope and pray for change. The following graph indicates several observations and classifications of materials used by Hildegard in this antiphon. And a copy of the modern notation for the antiphon follows with the phrases and motives identified on the score.

---

[98] Certainly hers was not a 'university' or formal school education, but under the tutelage of Jutta, Volmar, and probably other monks trained classically in their own areas of specialty, Hildegard received the most current and thorough training in numerous areas of study. And there was the large library at Disibodenberg too.

Phrase	Mode	Ambitus	No. of pitches	Line
A^1	Dorian -- Mode 1	C4-D5	23	1
B^1	Hypodorian -- Mode 2	A3-A4	24	2
A^{m1}-B^{m2}	Dorian - Hypodorian	D4-D5/A3-A4	10-12 (22)	3
A^2	Dorian	C4-D5	(GS)[99] 20	4
B^2	Hypodorian	A3-A4	25	5

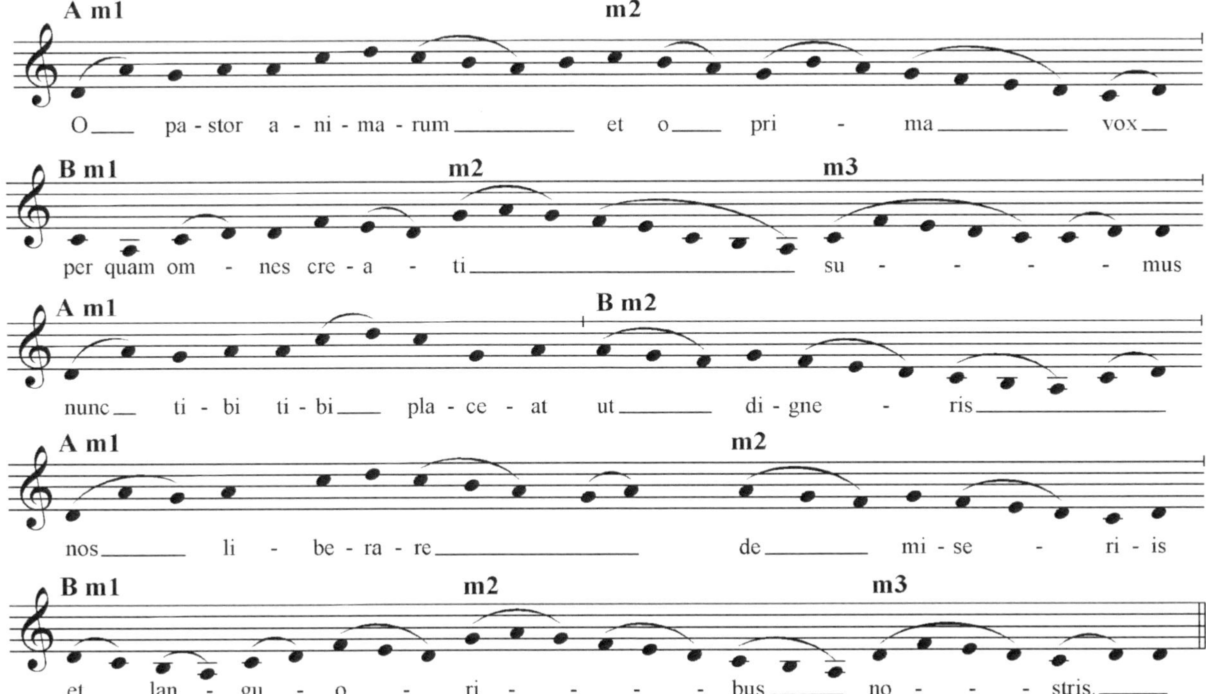

The antiphon is set in the Dorian mode, centered on the pitch d. Its confinalis is a, and a scan of the first line shows Hildegard's 'signature' serving as an underlying structure for the opening address:

-- a rising P5 on the opening 'O pastor'

-- completion of her 'signature' with an ascent to the octave d on 'animarum'.

In *O pastor animarum* we find a less exuberant antiphon which is more of a supplication than a Medieval 'praise chorus'. Here her signature 1-5-1 or finalis-confinalis-finalis motive is completed gently, perhaps with hesitancy or difficulty. The upper finalis occurs in only once in each of the three 'A' phrases. She does not fling her song into the heavens, but quietly approaches the height of the line through the subtonic pitch C5. The line moves immediately away from the finalis, returning back to a prolonged confinalis A4 and at the end of each phrase, to the finalis D4. Both complete A phrases (lines 1 and 4) exhibit an arched contour, reaching the apex early, and then slowly returning to the starting point.

Hildegard constantly moves from the heights to the depths, from heaven to earth, with the A phrases flowing from the finalis D up to the higher octave, and the B phrases descending to the lower dominant A and working within the ambitus of its upper octave A.

[99] The Golden Section of the antiphon (.618) occurs on the second pitch (within the first neume)

Our bond with earth is reflected in the 'B' phrases, initially with the employment of the hypodorian mode. The contour revolves from the finalis D4 down to the lower A3 and then all of the way up to the A4, followed by the melismatic descent of an octave back to the A3.

There are two contoural accents on the pitch f̲ (the first syllable of 'creati' and the second pitch of 'sumus'), the confinalis of the hypodorian mode. The same ambitus, indeed nearly the same exact line is used at the end, which concentrates on our state of languor, lack of direction, sluggishness, poor energy, even melancholia that can lead to all kinds of even more unhappy states. Perhaps the message here is that without the love and care of the shepherd, we 'creatures', even though created in the image of God, languish and 'float' if left to our own devices.

Line 3, the second part, contains a conjoining of phrases A and B using the first motive of A (m1) and the second motive of B (m2). Perhaps here Hildegard is symbolically joining heaven and earth in a polite reminder to the shepherd of his care and promises to us?! What Hildegard does not say in words, she dares to shout in music! Everything in the antiphon appears in this one phrase, the microcosm within the macrocosm, reaching out in prayer with a reminder of earthly need, the highs and lows, both modes, and all three characteristic patterns (Hildegard's 'signature', a hypodorian descent of an octave, and the terminatio figure).

All five phrases end with a terminatio to the finalis. There is always danger of 'over-analyzing', but it might be understood from this unusual occurrence of successive closures that Hildegard was returning humanity at the end of each phrase of the prayer to the fairly miserable and stagnant (languorous?) state from which the prayer arose.

A diagram of structural pitches illuminates some observations about the character of this antiphon.

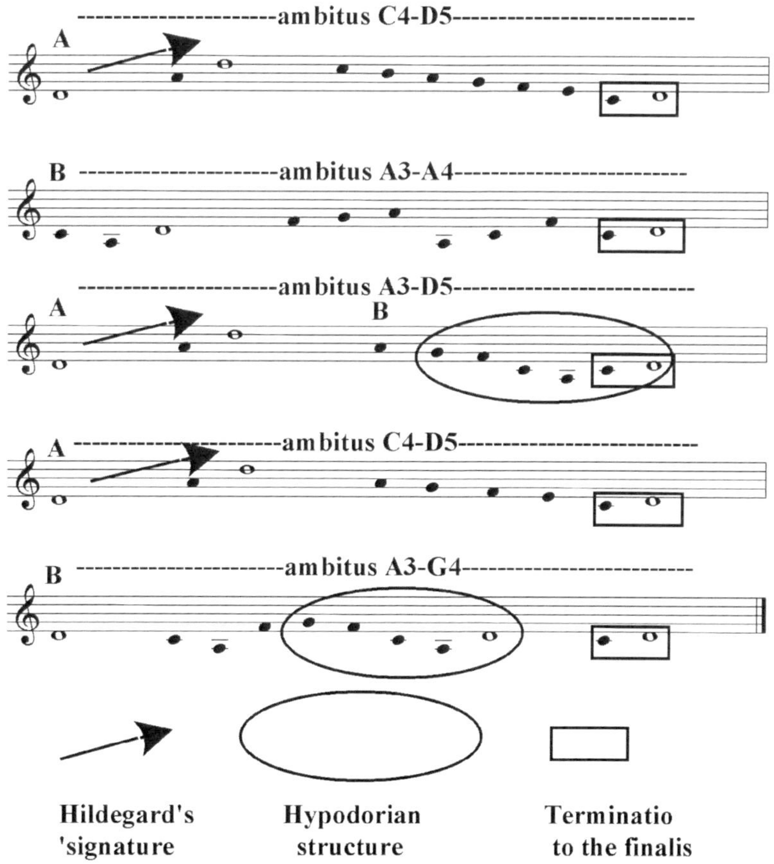

To sum up the above observations:

-- the A phrases are arch contours, petitions, reaching 'up' to the shepherd before returning to our earthly state.

-- the B phrases are reflective of our human condition, set in a wave contour in the hypodorian mode -- really a very low register.

Text painting is certainly present on the melismatic passages for:

Line 2, "creati" and "sumus"-- "we are all created". Use of the hypodorian mode and the lengthy descent from a to its lower octave, the lowest pitch in the antiphon, brings God's breath of life from heaven into the 'mud of earth' (a favorite Hildegardian term), giving humans life.
The word "sumus" ("we are all") is a melismatic terminatio figure, beginning on the subtonic C4, re-emphasizing the hypodorian with a leap to the confinalis D4, and returning to an emphasis on the subtonic C4 before the cadence to D4.

Line 4, "liberare" -- "free". Here Hildegard rises to the diapason on the accented syllable of the word, and then gently moves by step back to the position of momentary pause on the confinalis. Freedom is requested and then 'longed for'.

Line 5, "languoribus" -- "languor". Whoa. Sixteen pitches! This is certainly an example of 'languishing' on a word! She also descends to the lowest pitch A3 twice, climbs out of the depths to the higher A4 and then sinks back to the A3, outlining again the hypodorian before the very slightly decorated terminatio on D4.

A closer look at Hildegard's use of neumes shows craftsmanship ('craftsnunship'?) in use of the neumes to create specific musical patterns to set different words of text. As in all good melodic writing, changes of direction, high and low pitches, beginnings and endings must correspond with text accents or else the lines sound awkward and out of balance. So it is not always possible to assign different words to the same music (or vice versa) and have it 'work'. In this antiphon, Hildegard does use the same melodic ideas to set different text, but she must employ different neumes to 'get it right', to have musical and textual accents correspond with each other. The following example shows the neumes used for the antiphon.

O pastor animarum

Reisenkodex fol. 466va

Hildegard von Bingen

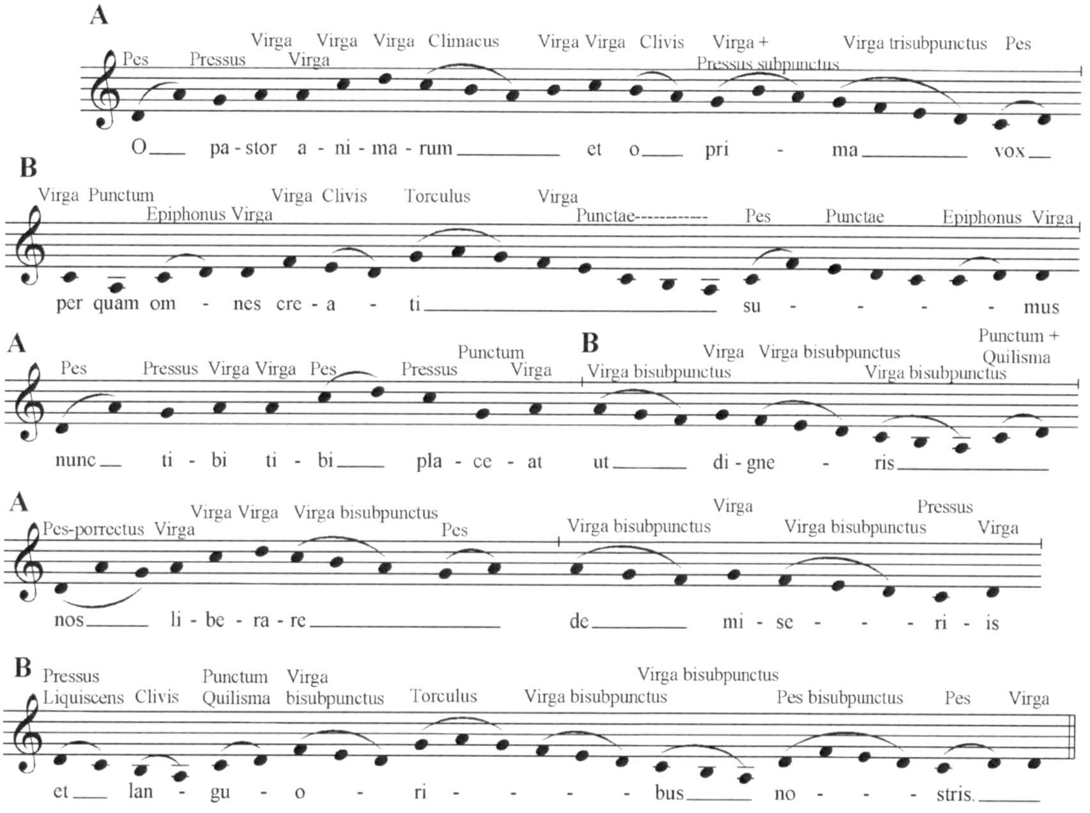

A
Pes Pressus Virga Virga Virga Virga Virga Climacus Virga Virga Clivis Virga + Pressus subpunctus Virga trisubpunctus Pes
O___ pa - stor a - ni - ma - rum_______ et o___ pri - ma_______ vox___

B
Virga Punctum Epiphonus Virga Virga Clivis Torculus Virga Punctae----------- Pes Punctae Epiphonus Virga
per quam om - nes cre - a - ti_______ su - - - - - mus

A
Pes Pressus Virga Virga Pes Pressus Punctum Virga
nunc___ ti - bi ti - bi___ pla - ce - at

B
Virga bisubpunctus Virga Virga bisubpunctus Virga bisubpunctus Punctum + Quilisma
ut_____ di - gne - ris_______

A
Pes-porrectus Virga Virga Virga Virga bisubpunctus Pes Virga bisubpunctus Virga Virga bisubpunctus Pressus Virga
nos_____ li - be - ra - re_______ de_____ mi - se - - - ri - is

B
Pressus Liquiscens Clivis Punctum Quilisma Virga bisubpunctus Torculus Virga bisubpunctus Virga bisubpunctus Pes bisubpunctus Pes Virga
et___ lan - gu - o - ri - - - - - bus_____ no - - - stris._____

Looking at the first eight pitches of each of the 'A' phrases show Hildegard's manipulation of neumes to set the different lines of text. There is no repetition of text, so clearly Hildegard created musical repetition to shape the musical effect of the antiphon. The first two 'A' lines are the most similar with one slight change on pitches 7-8, necessary to place the contoural accent on the accented syllable of 'animarum' in the first phrase, and to de-emphasize the highest pitch on the repeated word 'tibi' with emphasis instead on the subtonic C5 with its repetition on 'placeat' in the second phrase. The third A phrase begins with a durational emphasis of three pitches on the word 'nos' (us), and a contoural accent again on the D5 preceding the melisma on the word 'free'.

Similar employment of different neumes is apparent in the first and last B phrases, the last beginning with a 'decoration' of the first. The melismae at the end of 'creati' in the first B and the end of 'languoribus' in the last B are interesting too. Hildegard used an incomplete scale pattern from A4 down to A3 in the first B -- perhaps to imply that we 'creatures' are incomplete? We are the microcosm, but we are not God... And in the last phrase, the scale from A4 to A3 is complete -- we do languish without our shepherd's help.

The final terminatio is intriguing also. Hildegard has just completed a rather dramatic fall outlining the entire hypodorian scale, and she finishes on the finalis of the dorian mode. But she precedes the finalis with the confinalis of the hypodorian...more or less leaving us hanging...waiting for an answer? It is time to meditate on these things.

Meditation

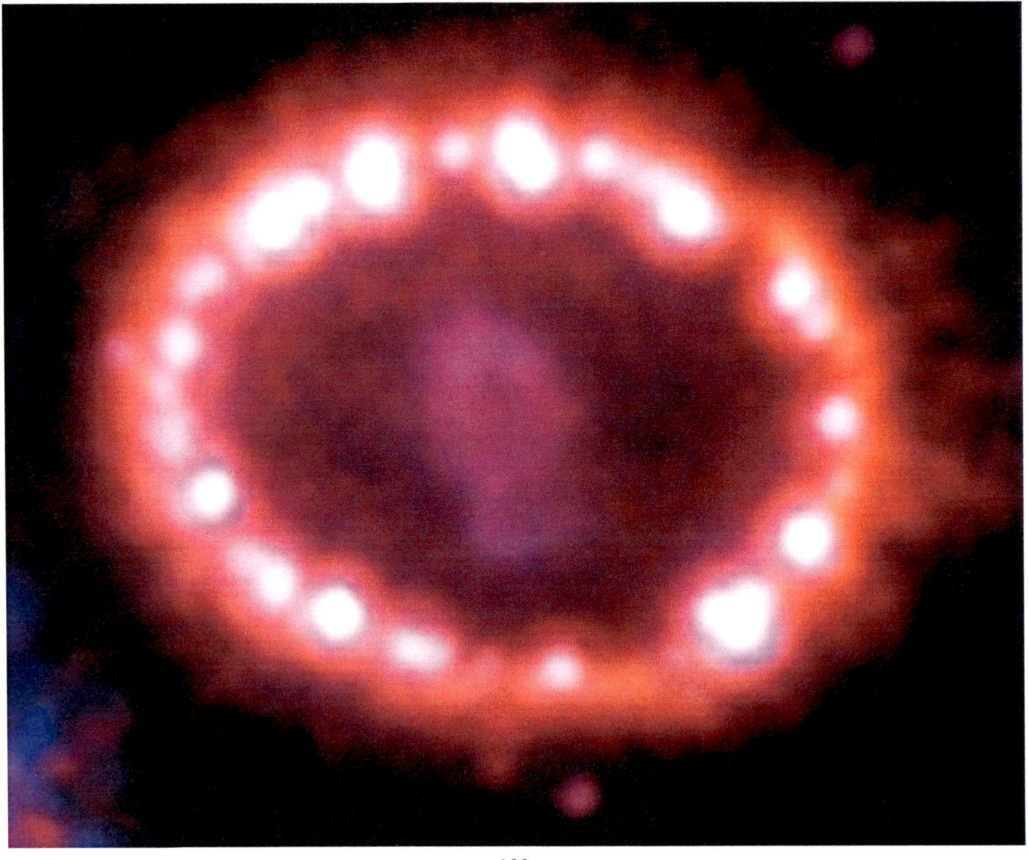

100

Reflection on Hildegard's Words

For what you see as a marvelously beautiful figure in God's mystery...--a figure similar to a human being--signifies the Love of our heavenly Father. It is Love--in the power of the everlasting Godhead, full of exquisite beauty, marvelous in its mysterious gifts. Love appears in a human form because God's Son, when he put on flesh, redeemed our lost humanity in the service of Love.[101]

The following contemplation on Hildegard's antiphon is offered for use during the meditation.

---

[100] Years ago, astronomers spotted the brightest stellar explosion ever seen since the one observed by Johannes Kepler 400 years ago. Called SN 1987A, the titanic supernova explosion blazed with the power of 100,000,000 suns for several months following its discovery on Feb. 23, 1987. Although the supernova itself is now a million times fainter than 17 years ago, a new light show in the space surrounding it is just beginning. This image, taken Nov. 28, 2003 by the Advanced Camera for Surveys aboard NASA's Hubble Space Telescope, shows many bright spots along a ring of gas, like pearls on a necklace. These cosmic "pearls" are being produced as a supersonic shock wave unleashed during the explosion slams into the ring at more than a million miles per hour. The collision is heating the gas ring, causing its innermost regions to glow. Astronomers detected the first "hot spot" in 1996, but now they see dozens of them all around the ring. The temperature of the flares surges from a few thousand degrees to a million degrees Fahrenheit. Individual hot spots cannot be seen from ground-based telescopes. Only Hubble can resolve them. Object Name: SN1987A
Credit: NASA, P. Challis, R. Kirshner (Harvard-Smithsonian Center for Astrophysics) and B. Sugerman (STScI)

[101] *Liber divinorum operum*. Op.Cit., pp.11-12.

O pastor animarum

(after an antiphon by Hildegard von Bingen)

Ann K. Gebuhr

37
mf
mf
mf
47
mp
p
57
mp
mp
p
65
p
pp
n
O shepherd of souls and first voice
through which we are all created
now you, if it pleases you and you deem it worthy
free us from our miseries
and our languor.
--Hildegard
Houston, 21 July 2009

Meditation Experience

Look at the image attentively. Lose yourself in the center.

Read Hildegard's words slowly. Stop when you come to a word that captures your imagination or attention. Draw it into the center of the ring with you. Take time do continue this process through the entire reading.

Draw someone you know who is suffering in some way into the ring with you. What do you experience with him/her? Together with God?

Move back slowly into your current reality. Decide what to do together with the person who shared this experience with you.

Say a prayer of thanksgiving.

Exercise

Okay, this has been a long chapter to read...it's time to get up and move! Stand up and do the deep breathing exercise from Chapter One (you have been doing this at least once daily, haven't you?). While breathing and stretching, decide where you are going to walk -- outside! Choose a park nearby, or choose your neighborhood, somewhere with trees and plants and blue (or cloudy) skies, but with fresh, unconditioned air!

Wear comfortable shoes and don't carry anything with you. If you bring a water bottle, put it in a pocket or leave it somewhere until you finish walking.

If you haven't been exercising regularly, begin with a fifteen minute walk. Walk, not a saunter. Set a walking pace for yourself just slightly faster than what is a comfortable 'saunter', and maintain that pace for fifteen minutes. I find that using a repetitive phrase that matches my stride is very helpful. Listening to music is possible, but not recommended -- your attention should be on your body, your stride, and on what your eyes are drinking in around you. You should be noticing the sounds of your environment and creating your own 'beat'. March to your own drummer, not someone else's!

Keep your brisk pace steady, and let your arms swing freely. Consciously release tension in your neck and shoulders, and then in the rest of your body, so your motions become loose and fluid. Think up variations on the repetitive phrase -- make up a poem or limerick about what you see and hear. Fifteen minutes will fly by! So go for thirty, then forty-five, then an hour. Don't think about distance, only time. Be conscious of your body -- it will tell you when you are taking it too far or fast.

Breathe deeply, from your abdomen as you walk -- no shallow chest breathing allowed! We do that too much when we sit and are sedentary, leaving dirty old air in the bottoms of our lungs for long periods of time. Deap breathing, with shoulders flung back and arms extended cleans it out and reoxygenates our minds and bodies Yay! Have fun! Enjoy the beauty and surprises of God's creation. Don't 'languor' in an airconditioned environment in front of the computer or TV -- lift your eyes to the treetops and relish the color and life of creation!

Recipes

Hmmm. What we do to ourselves with our diet! I just learned that my very favorite hot and sour soup, one I thought would be healthy and 'safe', was one of the worst 'salt-carriers' on the planet! Close to 7,000mg per bowl!!! That is nearly four days of the maximum intake of salt recommended. And I would drive ten miles out of my way just to have that soup...

Salt is a necessary component of our diet, but not that much. And the type of salt we consume is important too. Iodized NACL table salt is probably what most of us have used since early childhood, and that is what we are served in public restaurants and probably at most of our friends' homes. It is not poisonous for us, but it isn't the best salt to use. Sea salt or Himalayan salt are natural salts, and they are absorbed better and nourish our cells with the minerals needed for good health. Manufactured salt, the iodized variety, can serve too, but not as well.

In any event, 7,000mg is too much... It has been shown that curbing our salt intake (in other words, MODERATION in salt intake) is a very healthy practice. We have become so addicted to the taste of salt, it has lost its special taste for us. Three months without salt, or with very little salt, can return the special quality and also balance our bodies in a healthy manner.

The following recipes use little, if any salt, and they are delicious!

Breakfast

Habermus (an original recipe of Hildegard, a healthy way to begin the day!)

1 C cracked spelt berries (available from several online companies)
2 C water
1 cut up apple, in chunks
Juice from half a lemon
1 pinch of each of the following:
- Galangal (a form of Thailand Ginger, highly revered by Hildegard, who called it "The spice of life", invaluable for a variety of ailments, particularly heart disease)
- Cinnamon
- Bertram (Pellitory, or *Anacyclus officinalis*)

1 tsp honey or agave nectar
several peeled, soaked almonds
1 tsp Psyllium

Pour the cracked spelt into a pot with the water and bring to a boil. Stir constantly. Add the spices and lemon listed above and cook for 5-10 minutes. During the last minute or two, add the apple (or any other fruit you might have on hand -- mango is wonderful), and sprinkle the almonds and Psyllium on the porridge after serving it. Squeeze the lemon juice over it before eating.

Lunch

Lentil soup (a hearty soup that yields good protein)

2 Tbs	Olive oil
1	Chopped onion
3 Tbs	Minced garlic
1 Tbs	Chopped oregano
1 Tbs	Chopped basil
2 C	Lentils
10 C	Water or organic vegetable broth (or a combination)
3 C	Chopped carrots, bite-sized

Heat the oil and add onions, garlic, oregano and basil. Cook for about 5 minutes. Then add the liquid and carrots. Bring to a boil and then reduce heat to simmer for at least one hour.

Serve with crackers or a small garden salad.

Dinner

Carraba's Pasta (a recipe harvested from a local talk show, easy and delicious with many possible variations on the ingredients of the sauce).

1 C	Olive oil
8	garlic cloves, sliced
2	large cans of diced tomatoes, salt free if possible
1 Tb	Sea salt
1 Tb	Freshly ground black pepper
12	leaves of fresh Basil, roughly chopped
1 pkg	Spelt rotini pasta, or Conchiglie pasta

Bring sufficient water seasoned with the sea salt to a boil. Add the pasta and cook for 12-13 minutes. While it is cooking, prepare the sauce. Heat the oil and add the garlic for 2 minutes. Add the tomatoes, pepper and basil, heating all thoroughly. When the pasta is done to your liking, drain it (do not rinse it) and serve it with the sauce.

I have doubled and tripled this recipe very successfully, and have added other vegetables, shrimp, scallops and even other meats to it. Usually the canned tomatoes contain more than sufficient salt, but if you use fresh tomatoes instead, you might want to add some sea salt to the sauce.

Serve with a nice red wine and fresh fruit for dessert.

III.
Hildegard the Musician II

We will spend two full chapters on Hildegard's music, with this second chapter taking a look at one of her sequences in considerable depth. If it has been some time since you last picked up this tome, you might go back and reread the beginning of Chapter Two, as it serves as an excellent introduction to the chant considered in this chapter, *O ignis spiritus paracliti*, a prayer to the Holy Spirit. Before getting into a considerable discussion of the sequence, let's spend some time with a vision and illumination that is probably one of the best known of Hildegard's works. This illumination was the one on the cover of Matthew Fox's book that first drew me to Hildegard, and it has remained a favorite of mine for nearly a quarter of a century now.[102]

Numerous sources have named this image "The Man in Sapphire Blue" for obvious reasons. Hildegard called it "The Trinity in the Unity", and it accompanies the second vision in book two of *Scivias*. Hildegard describes this vision:

> "Therefore you see *a bright light*, which without any flaw of illusion, deficiency or deception designates the Father; *and in this light the figure of a man the color of a sapphire,* which without any flaw of obstinacy, envy or iniquity designates the Son, Who was begotten of the Father in Divinity before time began, and then within time was incarnate in the world in Humanity; *which is all blazing with a gentle glowing fire,* which fire without any flaw of aridity, mortality or darkness designates the Holy Spirit, by Whom the Only-Begotten of God was conceived in the flesh and born of the Virgin within time and poured the true light into the world. And that bright light bathes the whole of the glowing fire, and the glowing fire bathes the bright light; and the bright light and the glowing fire pour over the whole human figure, so that the three are one light in one power of potential."[103]

The recurring themes of light, energy, and unity are beautifully encapsulated in this image, and Hildegard's description as well as the basic shape of the image are circular -- without beginning or ending. There are many psychological, spiritual

[102] Public Domain image *Die wahre Dreiheit in der wahren Einheit* (The true Trinity in the true Unity) from the Scivias Codex

[103] Hildegard. *Scivias*. Mother Columba Hart and Jane Bishop, Tr. New York, The Paulist Press, 1990. p. 161

affects emanating from the image too; hope, warmth, energy, light, comfort, love, clarity... The list could go on and on. But, as Matthew Fox points out in his essay about this image[104], the primary message here (other than the unity of the Trinity) is compassion. The choice of the colors, blue for the figure representing Christ who is embraced and surrounded by the fiery gold of the Holy Spirit and energized by the white light of the Creator (that light also surrounds and embraces the figure), are different than the more 'traditional' colors assigned to members of the Trinity. Usually God the Creator/King/Father is portrayed in gold, the Son/Paschal Lamb/Redeemer in white, and the Holy Spirit/Paraclete in blue.

In Hildegard's image, the blue Christ figure holds his hands in an unusual position. The figure is iconic, and the hands are raised in a gesture of healing, almost as if he was ready to lay his hands on humanity. And the Holy Spirit is represented by a ring of fire, carefully portrayed in a fiery color and made of loops, or ropes of energy. Those ropes are paralleled in gold in the outer ring of white light, perhaps symbolizing the binding together of the three persons of the Trinity. Energy, energy, energy sending the God-man to the microcosm in compassion and love.

Hildegard's sequence, *O ignis spiritus paracliti*, is a prayer to the Holy Spirit, the fiery energy which permeates and touches everything in existence. It circles and encircles, it burns and inspires, and it comforts and heals.

Hildegard's Music in Context

Since the late 1990's Hildegard's music has come under close scrutiny from a number of sources -- in fact from a number of continents[105]. The general tone of these commentaries is certainly one of interest and admiration, but there seems to be a hint of apology, or excuse, running in the background. This is, I think, due to applying a comparative approach to the study of Hildegard, using the then current 'standards' of music composition as presented by a few treatises or codexes about music (primarily plainchant) of the 12th century. Hildegard doesn't 'fit'.

The apologetic, veiled critical tone is possibly fueled by Hildegard's repeated statements about her lack of formal training -- in music, Latin, or any subject of medieval academic study. Her repeated comments of self-abnegation -- even self-derision -- offer a platform for critical comment and, for some academic musicologists, dismissal without any acknowledgement whatsoever of Hildegard or her musical works. There is a question (which will never be answered with certainty) as to whether or not she notated her songs herself. If she didn't, the works we have to examine from the Dendermonde and Reisencodex manuscripts are not authentically Hildegard, but edited transcriptions of her oral performances. If this is so, slight changes might have been made to her original work by the scribes who notated them and some changes might have been done to 'fit' the chants into common practice for the time, the practice with which the scribes were familiar. Or such changes might add to unique aspects of Hildegard's music, causing some of the criticism.

Well, my approach to Hildegard's music varies from the above in that yes, she must be understood in the context of her time and environment, but no, she does not need to be compared critically only with the compositional conventions of her time or place. Hildegard was an

---

[104] Matthew Fox. *Illuminations of Hildegard of Bingen.* Santa Fe. Bear and Company, Inc. 1985. p.24

[105] Dissertations and books have come from the US, Australia, and Europe, focusing on Hildegard's music in a variety of contexts: music and rhetoric, music and theology, music as a feminist expression, etc. Please see bibliography.

incredibly gifted and intuitive woman, open to God (first and foremost) and to the experiences of life in her monasteries and country, fully and thoughtfully! Her music was intrinsically a part of her life and her relationship to the cosmic God of her visions and her heart. She wrote eloquently[106] about the role of music as creating and carrying the 'essence' of the word much more than 'merely' the literal fact of the text. For her, music and text were united as one within the unity of the whole created universe. She states in *Scivias*:

> And so the Word designates the body, the symphony indeed manifests the spirit: because celestial harmony also announces divinity and the Word spreads the humanity of the Son of God. (*Scivias* III; 13:12, p.631)[107]

For Hildegard, music was beyond craft and convention. Music was a connection with the Celestial Hierarchy, a means of praising God here on earth to reflect the praise of the celestial voices. In her music she used what she knew, what she practiced, what she literally grew up with in the monastery, and she took those elements of plainchant beyond the current convention. Her song is not a mere 'doodling around' with sound, or an improvisation on well-known patterns or 'maneria'. She was not 'copying' convention, or 'imitating' one of the 'guys' famous for his music at that time[108]. No, Hildegard thoughtfully and ecstatically established her own 'style', a style which is recognizable today for its spiritual depth, its individuality and certainly for its beauty. It is a style which is unique to Hildegard.

The previous chapters contain much information about chant, its history, its notation, and its basic character. And a later chapter will discuss in detail Hildegard's daily worship discipline, the *Opus Dei* of the Benedictine Order. For our purposes here, the point must be made (again) that Hildegard's music was part of the fabric of her being, of her prayer life, her administerial responsibilities, her worship, her healing -- her breathing. She did not compose for an 'audience', she did not compose for a particular performer, and she certainly did not compose for any self-interest or praise. She composed for worship and expression -- because she was commanded to do so! She wrote her texts as expressions of worship, and the combinations of text with music were the most profound and deeply felt experiences with eternity and her God that were possible. They were connections with the universe and everything in the universe. And they came from a very humble -- very brilliant! -- mind (soul) and heart. Hmm. Hildegard wrote the contemporary Christian music of her day, and it is still speaking to us and through us today!

One might question her 'humility' in that her chants were notated and preserved for posterity. This was an unusual occurrence in her time, and nearly unthinkable for a woman[109]. The simple, and I trust not 'simplistic', response to that question is 'simply' that she was told to do so. In her vision of authority, the 'voice of the Living Light' commanded her to write all that she saw and heard, and to make it available to the world. As a result, her songs and her morality play, *Ordo virtutem* were included in her first book, *Scivias*. Thanks be to God that she was an obediant Benedictine!

---

[106] See her letter to the Archbishop of Mainz after the interdict was placed on Rupertsberg: Baird, Joseph L. and Radd K. Ehrman.*The Letters of Hildegard of Bingen*, Vol. I. Oxford University Press, 1994. pp.76-79.

[107] Quoted in Catharine Mary Jeffreys. *Melodia et rhetorica: The Devotional-Song Repertory of Hildegard of Bingen.*
Unpublished doctoral thesis, University of Melbourne, 2000. p. 89.

[108] Bernard of Clairvaux or Pierre Abelard, to name two of the few from the 12th century with whom Hildegard was acquainted.

[109] Hildegard is the first composer in Western music history to be named with a complete record of her compositions.

A leaf from the manuscript of *Scivias*, with the well-known illumination showing Hildegard receiving a vision and writing it on a wax tablet, with Volmar observing.[110]

One of Hildegard's sequences will serve our purposes to search for characteristics which help to identify Hildegard's musical voice. *O ignis spiritus paracliti* is one of several sequences composed by Hildegard. In a time of burgeoning sequences - a very 'popular' genre - Hildegard wrote only seven (that we know of), contained in the *Symphonia*. The sequence, as mentioned in a previous chapter, rose out of the practice of adding newly written text (not scriptural quotations) to the final 'jubilation', or melisma, of the Alleluia in the Mass (the Alleluia immediately preceded the reading (chanting) of the Gospel text, and in practice, it often included a long melisma at the end). Somewhere in France, it is believed, toward the end of the 10th and through the 11th century, it became common to add a textual 'trope', probably to aid in singing the jubilation. For a time, it was thought that Notker was the inventor, but earlier French sequences have been discovered.

By Hildegard's day, it was customary to create the troped text in rhymed couplets, using the same music for both parts of the couplet. This works very well if the lines of the couplet correspond with the same number of syllables. Well...Hildegard is a poet, but she was not a poet in the manner of 12th century poets. In fact, her image-filled, expansive, non-rhymed phrases are similar more to current 21st century free, unrhymed, allegorical poetry than to the poetry being written in her day!

[110] Photo © Erich Lessing/Art Resource, NY.
From a facsimile of the *Codex Rupertsberg*, lost during World War II.

The text for *O ignis spiritus paracliti* is offered as an example.[111]

1a O ignis spiritus paracliti,
vita vite omnis creature,
sanctus es vivificando formas.
1b Sanctus es unguendo periculose fractos,
sanctus es tergendo fetida vulnera.

O spirit of fire, bringer of comfort,
Life of the life of every creature,
you are holy, giving life to forms (i.e. living creatures).
You are holy, anointing those perilously broken;
you are holy, cleansing festering wounds.

2a O spiraculum sanctitatis,
o ignis caritatis,
o dulcis gustus in pectoribus,
et infusio cordium in bono odore virtutum.

O breath of holiness,
o fire of love,
o sweet savor in our breasts,
infusing hearts with the scent of virtue.

2b O fons purissime,
in quo consideratur
quod deus alienos colligit
et perditos requirit.

O clearest fountain,
in which we see
how God gathers the alienated
and finds the lost.

3a O lorica vite
et spes compaginis membrorum omnium
et o cingulum honestatis, salva beatos.

O breastplate of life
and hope of the whole human body,
o belt of honor :save the fortunate.

3b Custodi eos qui carcerati sunt ab inimico
et solve ligatos
quos divina vis salvare vult.

Guard those imprisoned by the enemy
and free those who are bound
whom the divine power wishes to save.

4a O iter fortissimum
quod penetravit omnia
in altissimis et in terrenis
et in omnibus abyssis,
tu omnes componis et colligis.

O mightiest course
that has penetrated all things
in the heavens and on earth
and in every abyss –
you reconcile and draw all humanity together.

4b De te nubes fluunt, ether volat,
lapides humorem habent,
aque rivulos educunt
et terra viriditatem sudat.

From you clouds flow, wind flies,
stones produce moisture,
water flows in streams,
and the earth exudes living greenness.

5 Tu etiam semper educis doctos
per inspirationem
sapientie letificatos.

You are always teaching the learned,
who, through wisdom's inspiration,
are made joyful.

6 Unde laus tibit sit qui es sonus laudis
et gaudium vite
spes et honor fortissimus
dans premia lucis.

Thence praise be to you who are the sound of praise,
the joy of life,
the hope and greatest honor,
granting the prize of light.[112]

O ignis spiritus paracliti is a prayer to the Holy Spirit, Hildegard's "Light of the Living Voice", the fire which settled upon her to impart knowledge of God's word and will in her visions. In her own nonmetrical, unrhymed manner, Hildegard creates a wonderfully expansive, even cosmic image of the Holy Spirit. Barbara Newman, in her critical edition of Hildegard's *Symphonia*, describes Hildegard's poetic style in the following manner:

---

[111] This Sequence is chant number 28 in Hildegard's *Symphonia harmoniae caelestium revelationum.*

[112] An excellent ranslation by Susan Hellauer in the insert booklet for the CD: Anonymous 4. *The Origin of Fire; Music and Visions of Hildegard von Bingen.* harmonia mundi usa, HMU 907327. 2004.

> In style they [Hildegard's chant texts] are much closer to *Kunstprosa*, a highly wrought figurative language that resembles poetry in its density and musicality, yet with no semblance of meter or regular form...Before the advent of the rhymed sequence, liturgical chants other than hymns were generally nonmetrical, influenced primarily by the Vulgate Psalms. Hildegard's originality, then, lies less in the invention of new forms than in the audacious and luxuriant elaboration of old ones.[113]

The Holy Spirit is the third member of the Trinity, for Hildegard the completion of the "Trinity in unity".[114] Reference to the Holy Spirit occurs throughout both the Old Testament[115] and New Testament, and the Spirit is described with the particular term used in this sequence in the gospel of John, as part of Christ's discourse during the Passover supper (the 'Last Supper) the night he was arrested.

> Anyone who loves me will keep my word,
> and my Father will love him,
> and we shall come to him
> and make a home in him.
> Anyone who does not love me does not keep my words.
> And the word that you hear is not my own:
> it is the word of the Father who sent me.
> I have said these things to you
> while still with you;
> but the Paraclete, the Holy Spirit,
> whom the Father will send in my name,
> will teach you everything
> and remind you of all I have said to you.[116]

This New Testament passage must have been much loved by Hildegard, and I recommend the entire discourse to you. You will see many of the themes and images employed by Hildegard in this prayer offered by Jesus for his disciples -- John 13-17.

In her text, Hildegard identifies and names the Holy Spirit in twelve beautiful ways:

1a O spirit of fire
2a O breath of holiness
O fire of love
O sweet taste in the breast
2b O purest fountain
3a O breastplate of life
Hope (of unity)
O belt of honor
4a O mightiest course (as in a river)

---

113 Newman, Barbara. *Hildegard of Bingen: Symphonia*. 2nd Ed. Cornell University Press.1998. pp.32-33.

114 Hildegard. *Scivias* I; 4:31, p.91

115 See particularly Proberbs 8 and the Book of Wisdom.

116 John 14:22-26. *The New Jerusalem Bible.*Darton, Longman & Todd, Ltd. and Doubleday.p.1777

6 The sound of praise
The joy of life
Hope and greatest honor

Even though she has arranged the text into couplets (supported by her musical composition), none of the pairs have rhyming endings, and the last two (labeled 5 and 6) are not coupled together musically, standing alone as individual verses. Furthermore, none of the coupled verses share the same number of syllables:

Couplet	Syllables	Final word
1a	30	Formas
1b	25	vulnera
2a	43	Virtutum
2b	30	Requirit
3a	32	Beatos
3b	31	Vult
4a	43	Colligis
4b	36	Sudat
5	28	Letificatos
6	32	lucis

Some characteristics of her poetic writing style may be observed in this table.

1. In her arrangement of couplets, the second half is always shorter than the first half, lending a larger rhythmic pattern to the couplet of 'long-short'. The only exception to this is in the third couplet, where both parts are nearly equal in length. The greatest difference in length is obviously in the second couplet.
2. Sections 1, 3, and the combination of 5 and 6 are of similar lengths (55-63 syllables), with sections 2 and 4 being of considerably longer length (73-79 syllables).
3. None of the final words rhyme with each other.

The first two couplets 'identify' and describe the Paraclete's attributes and actions. The third couplet is a prayer, a petition, first describing particular attributes which would make granting of the petition possible; to save the fortunate (who are not captured...by Satan?), to guard those who have been captured, and to free those whom the Paraclete wishes to save. Then the fourth couplet and the final two free phrases return to descriptive praise, assigning more allegorical symbols to the Holy Spirit.

The poem is thus shaped into a ternary form, with descriptive praise in the first and last sections, and a fervent prayer in the middle section. The first section contains couplets of two phrases each, and the last section has a couplet of two phrases and two final phrases which are separate from each other. The middle section (B), the prayer petition, is shorter in that it has only one couplet, but each of its phrases has three clauses that are longer than those in the other couplets. Its total length of syllables roughly equal those of couplet 1 and the combination of 5 & 6. The diagram below demonstrates:

A (descriptive praise)	B (prayer)	A' (descriptive praise)
5 'identities'	3 'identities'	4 'identities'
Couplets 1 and 2	Couplet 3	Couplets 4, 5 & 6
55 syl.	63 syl.	79 syl.
73 syl.		60 syl.

It is also interesting to note that in shaping the couplets into the larger form, there are clauses in couplets 2 and 4 that share the same number of syllables:

2a	O spiraculum sanctitatis,	
	o ignis caritatis,	7 syllables
	o dulcis gustus in pectoribus,	10 syllables
	et infusio cordium in bono odore virtutum.	
2b	O fons purissime,	
	in quo consideratur	7 syllables
	quod deus alienos colligit	10 syllables
	et perditos requirit.	
4a	O iter fortissimum	
	quod penetravit omnia	8 syllables
	in altissimis et in terrenis	
	et in omnibus abyssis,	
	tu omnes componis et colligis.	10 syllables
4b	De te nubes fluunt, ether volat,	
	lapides humorem habent,	8 syllables
	aque rivulos educunt	
	et terra viriditatem sudat.	10 syllables

A more detailed graph of the form of the text now shows:

A (descriptive praise)	B (prayer)	A' (descriptive praise)
5 'identities'	3 'identities'	4 'identities'
Couplets 1, 2	Couplet 3	Couplets 4, 5 and 6
55 syl.	63 syl.	60 syl.
73 syl.		79 syl.
shaped lines		shaped lines
(2 & 3 = 2 & 3)		(2 & 4 = 2 & 4)

It is interesting to note that the Golden Section of the text (applied to the total number of syllables used) falls on the word 'omnia' in couplet 4a. Omnia -- all. Hah...! There is absolutely no indication anywhere that Hildegard had any knowledge of the ancient Golden Section, Phi. But I reiterate...Hah!

What the diagram above does show is a formal structure underpinning Hildegard's free verse, one which is based firmly in the liturgical practice of forming prayers in three parts (the number three referring time and again to the Trinity). And here we have a three-part sequence addressing the third person of the Trinity, with the twelve (4x3) 'identities' or 'descriptors' of the Paraclete presented in a balanced fashion throughout the poem.

It also shows that in a larger shaping process Hildegard is quite symmetrical. She alternates shorter sections with longer, and within the longer sections she shapes specific lines into lengths which reflect each other. The format creates a palindromic, or 'rondo-like' structure. I suggest that her poem was not created through a 'stream-of-consciousness' experience, but through careful and always symbolic thought coupled with the inspiration (breathing in) of her visions.

Hildegard composed the text in Latin, but as noted by Marsha Genensky (for the recording of this sequence by Anonymous 4), what we hear performed today is likely quite different from the sound of the chant as sung in Hildegard's monastery.[117] Likewise, Hufnagel notation offers opportunities for interpretation, so transcriptions are probably not exactly what was heard either. The beginning of *O ignis spiritus*, as notated in the Dendermonde Codex[118], reminds us again of the difficulties inherent in transcribing Hufnagelschrift into current notation.

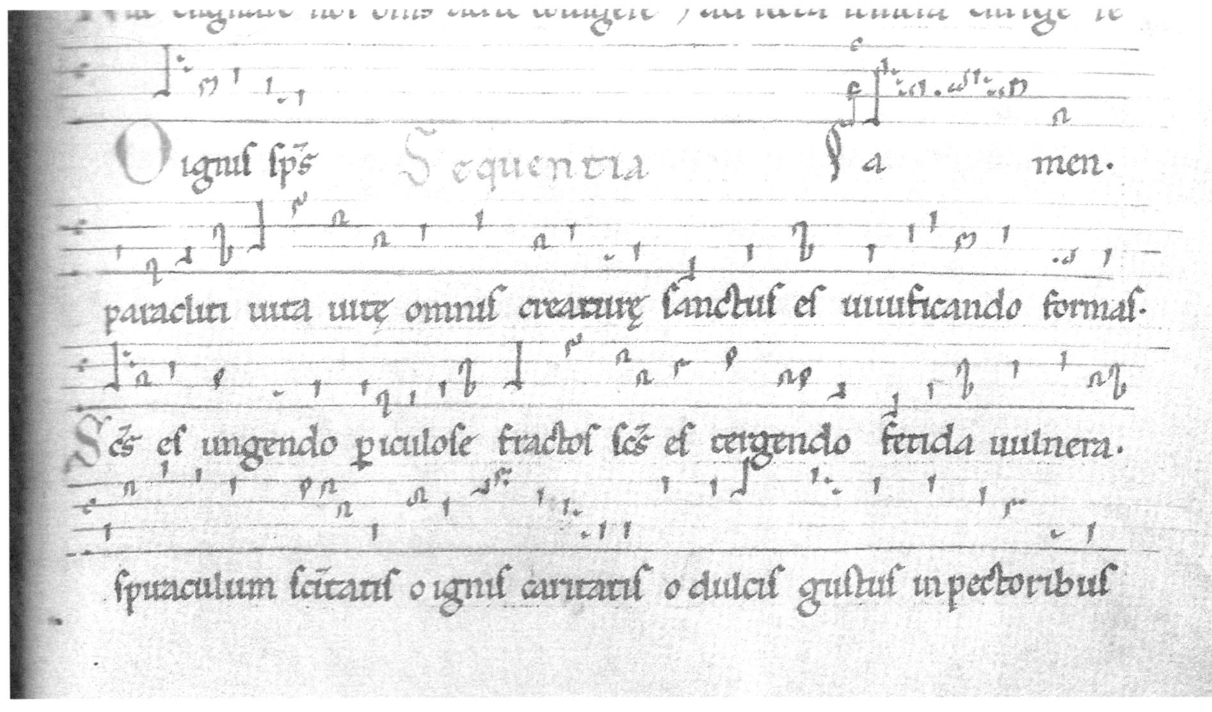

The opening invocation, "O ignis spiritus", appears on the staff above the term "Sequentia", and then continues on the staff below (the "amen" belongs to the preceding chant). 'C' and 'F' lines are clearly marked, and there are no 'half lines' in this excerpt, though they do occur later. The following transcription is from the facsimile of the Dendermonde manuscript.[119]

---

117 Anonymous 4, *Op. Cit. p.9* "Perhaps because it was a second language for everyone who used it, medieval Latin took on many elements of pronunciation of the vernacular dialect or language of each region or country. In Germany, the pronunciation of Latin was very much influenced by the sounds of German as it was spoken in the Middle Ages."

118 Hildegard von Bingen. *Symphonia harmoniae caelestium revelationum.* Facsimile editions, Alamire. 1991. Leaves 158-159.

119 Hildegard of Bingen. *Symphonia Harmoniae Caelestium Revelationum.* Dendermonde, St.-Pieters & Paulusabdij MS. Cod. 9. Alamire Peer 1991. Leaves 158-159. Transcription by Ann Gebuhr.

A

O ignis spiritus

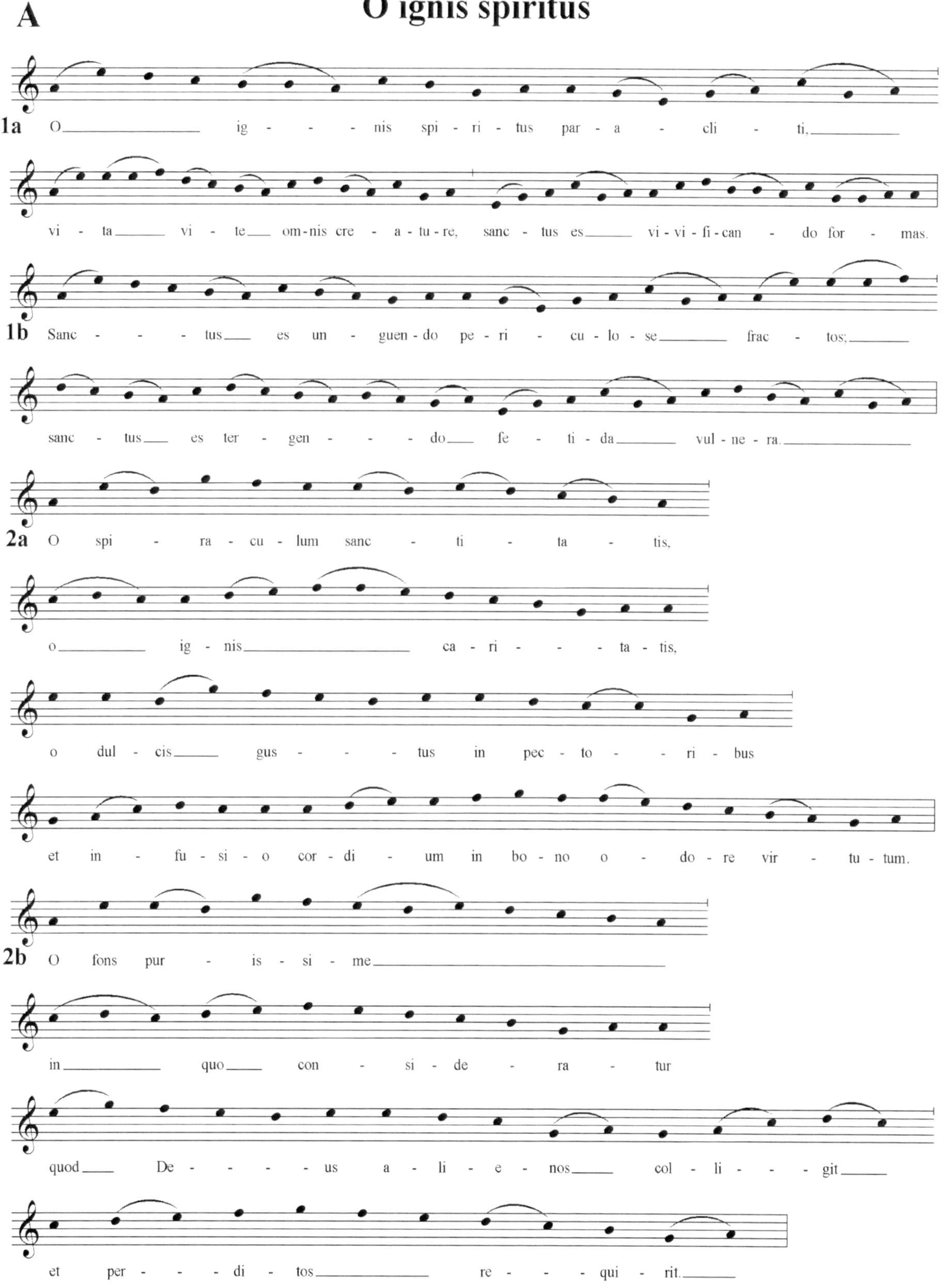

B
3a O lo - ri - ca vi - te
et spes com - pa - gi - nis mem - bro - rum om - ni - um
et o cin - - gu - lum ho - ne - sta - tis sal - va be - a - tos.
3b Cu - sto - di e - os qui car - ce - ra - ti - sunt ab i - ni - mi - cos
et sol - - - ve li - ga - - - tos
quos di - vi - na vis sal - va - re vult.
A'
4a O i - - - ter for - tis - si - mum
quod pe - ne - tra - vit om - ni - - - - - - - - a
in al - tis - si - - - - - mis et in ter - re - - - nis
et in om - ni - bus a - bys - - - - - - - - sis
tu om - - - nes com - po - - - - - nis et col - li - gis.

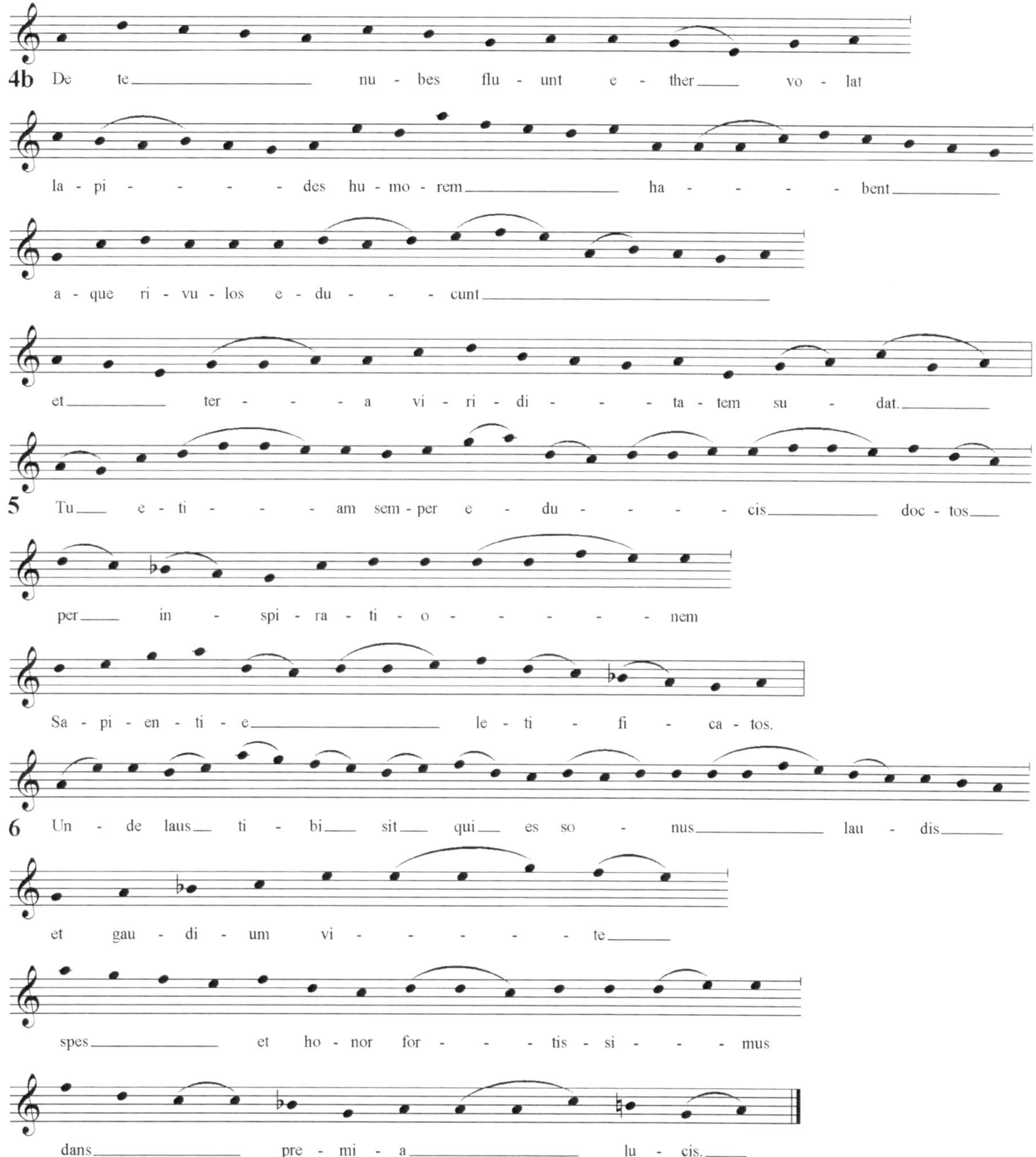

The transcription includes slurs over pitches contained in Hufnagelschrift neumes and virga or punctum neumes appear as individual notes. The word extension lines identify neumatic or melismatic combinations of neumes used to set one syllable of text.

I compared my transcription to two other excellent transcriptions, and was delighted to see that the above rendition is very similar to both of them. Where I discovered differences, I chose to use what appeared to be closest to the original notation in the facsimile.[120]

---

[120] Page, Christopher, ed. *Abbess Hildegard of Bingen: Sequences and Hymns.* "O ignis spiritus". Antico Edition, 1983. pp. 4-5 and Pfau, Marianne Richert, ed. *Hildegard von Bingen: Symphonia armonie celestium revelationum.* Vol. III, "O ignis Spiritus paracliti". Hildegard Publishing Company, 1997. pp.11-14.

In the transcription I have included formal descriptors showing the ternary shaping of the text (A, B, A') and the individual phrases as arranged into couplets (1a, 1b, etc.). The phrases which form the couplets are made up of several clauses (1a1, 1a2, 1a3 etc.) each, so the phrases are notated with one clause on each staff, separated by a small 'tick' on the upper line. These 'ticks' and the full bar line at the end of each phrase are mine, and do not appear on the facsimile manuscript.

Hildegard's Music: Harmony

What do we do with Hildegard's use of the word 'harmony'? We use the term today quite differently than it was used and understood during Hildegard's time. Medieval 'harmony' was an expression of unity, a framework of sound structures. The framework is more than the order of phrases and more than the occurrence of successive pitches. It certainly was not what we today commonly refer to as 'harmony' -- the application of chords or progressions of chords within a specific 'key' to support a melody or texture. Hildegard's chants are monophonic (a single unaccompanied melodic line), so the melody is all that we have to examine and perform. In order to see the framework, the 'harmony', of *O ignis Spiritus*, we must see how she establishes the foundation of her structure, what we today call the 'mode' ('key') and the 'finalis' ('tonic').

Mode

A considerable discussion about the use and application of medieval modes can be found in chapter one. To refresh your memory, there are eight modes based upon the formation of pentachords and tetrachords. There were four commonly used finalis pitches, d,e,f and g, and based upon the ambitus of pitches, these finalis pitches were established as the lowest pitch of a rising pentachord or the highest pitch of a rising tetrachord. Within a chant, these formations could vary, creating a 'commixture' of modes. As well, the use and formations of pentachords and/or tetrachords could be based upon a finalis other than d,e,f or g.

In addition to the four modes (Dorian, Phrygian, Lydian and Mixolydian -- finalis of d,e,f and g) and their plagal representations (the 'hypo' modes), two other modes were frequently employed by Hildegard. These modes are the Ionian mode with c as a finalis (g as the confinalis) and the Aeolian mode with a as the finalis (e as the confinalis). C Ionian uses the pentachord pattern (species 4) of the G Mixolydian mode and the tetrachord pattern (Species 3) of the F Hypolydian (Plagal) mode. The Aeolian mode uses the pentachord pattern (species 1) of D Dorian and the tetrachord pattern (species 2) of the E Hypophrygian (Plagal) mode. (These modes are related to but are not the plagal Hypolydian or Hypodorian modes with f or d finalis pitches.)

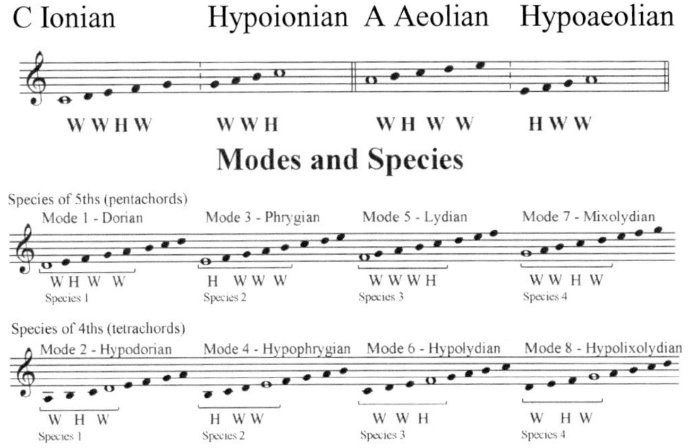

O ignis spiritus is 'set' in the Aeolian mode based on the pitch a. Hildegard establishes this 'home' through the use of patterns that begin and end each of the clauses of text. The middle portions of each clause revolve around or repeat on a pitch which is part of the elemental framework of each clause. In the table below, I have shown the first (initium) and last (terminatio) patterns, and the internal pitch(es) (recitation) around which the melody is centered.

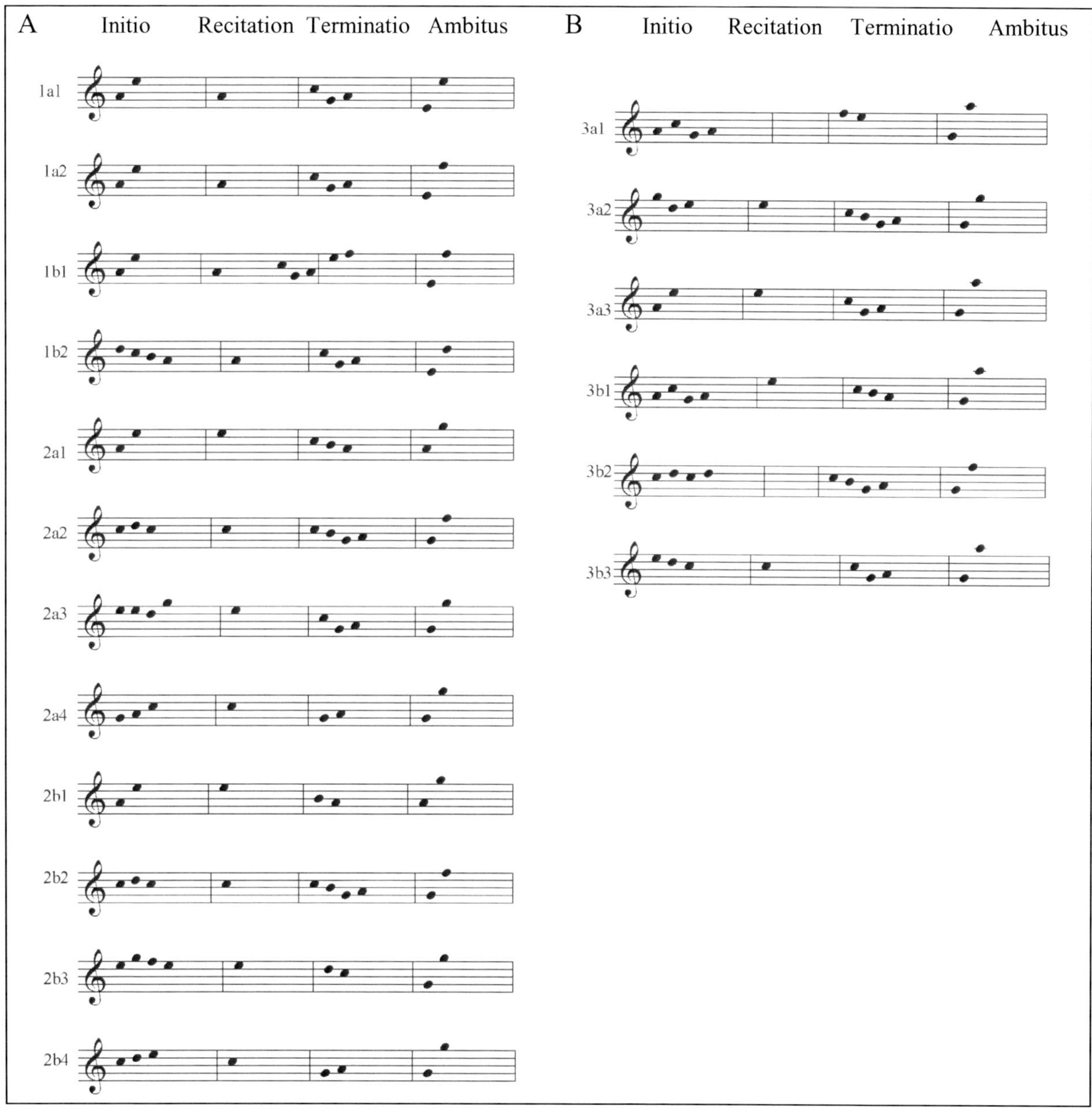

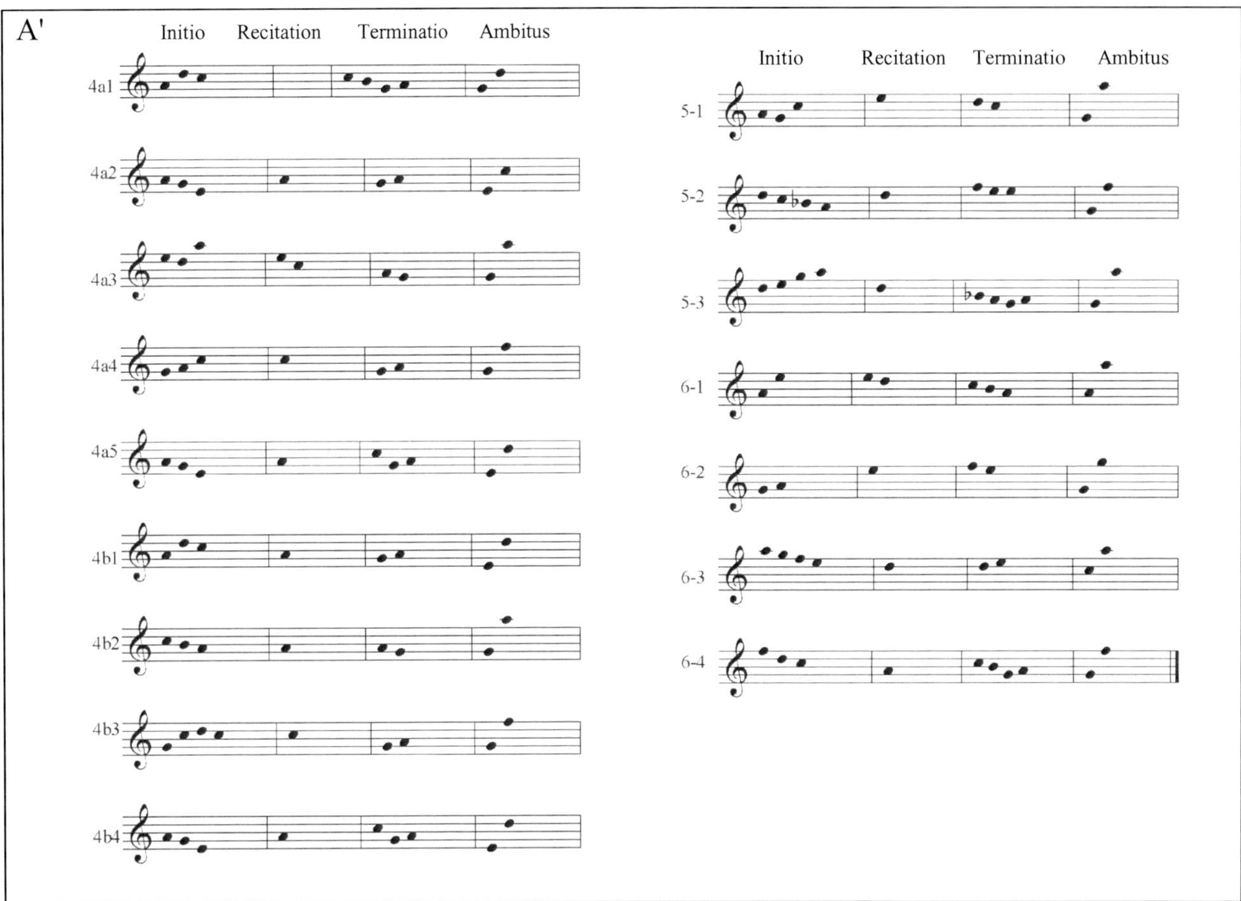

The fourth indication, the 'ambitus', shows the range of each clause, the lowest and highest pitches.

A first observation shows that there are only eight terminatio figures that do not end on the pitch A. As well, the recitation pitches all are related to a triad formed on A (a,c,e) except in the last part of A', phrases 5 and 6. And the initio figures all focus on A, C, or E. These clause frameworks thus support A as the finalis, with the structural mode, or scale, being the Aeolian mode. There is some use of musica ficta[121] in phrases 5 and 6 which will be discussed later.

Exploring the initio patterns (especially in conjunction with the ambitus indications) shows a secondary emphasis on C, due to the presence of g-c motion and the ambitus ranging from G4-G5 (e.g. 2a2, 2a3, 2a4 and 2b2, 2b3, 2b4). This is especially true in the clauses that have a recitation on C5. The important placement of the pitch e in those same clauses strengthens the hint of a commixture with C Ionian (a mode based on the confinal of the plagal A Hypodorian). However, an actual shift to the C Ionian mode never takes place, as the terminatio figures of those clauses end with the finalis A.

---

[121] Musica ficta is the use of pitches not contained in the diatonic mode, primarily b-flat and f-sharp, in order to avoid awkward leaps or outlines of awkward intervals such as the tritone, or 'Diabolus musicus'.

The point of furthest departure from the Aeolian mode occurs in 5-2 and 5-3. At the end of 5-1[122] the terminatio is not, for only the fifth time in the sequence, the finalis or confinalis[123]. The recitation for this clause has changed from the confinalis e to the pitch d, and d is maintained as the reciting tone for the remainder of 5-2 and 5-3. Musica ficta (b^b) is used first to soften the descent from f on "doctos" and later within the descending line on "letificatos", avoiding a 'diabolus musicus' (diminished 5th) pattern. Furthermore, Hildegard 'de-emphasizes' the finalis pitch a, using it only four times before the terminatio of 5-3:

-- in 5-1 it is the first pitch of the phrase, part of a retrograded terminatio figure (c-g-a, now a-g-c)

-- in 5-1 as the apex, but de-emphasized as an 'escape tone' which is not the first pitch of the word "educis". It then drops to d, a falling Perfect 5th (an unusual motion in chant) to the new recitation pitch.

-- in 5-2 a is part of a descent from d down to g, a passing tone

-- in 5-3 on "Sapientie" it is the apex, and part of a strong outline of the d-a rising and falling Perfect 5th. D remains the recitation pitch until the termination at the end of the phrase.

This diversion from a strong a as finalis takes the sequence into a region of D Aeolian. Creating d as a finalis with a confinalis of a, Hildegard's return to A Aeolian at the end of 5-3 (the Phrygian terminatio figure) and the beginning of 6-1 (a structural 'signature' motive) is very smooth. Hildegard reminds us again of this diversion in 6-3 and 6-4, returning to the d recitation and another long descent from f-g with the musica ficta b^b. There is no musica ficta indicated for the final terminatio.

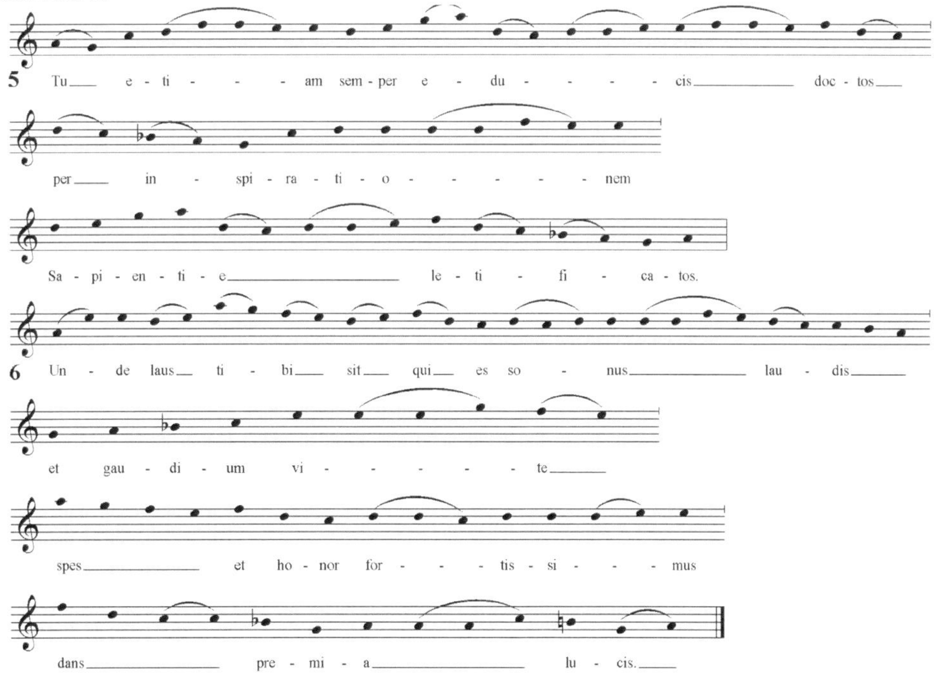

[122] There is some confusion about the transcription of the end of 5-1. In Dendermonde there is an f half-line inserted that would raise the pitches a third from the syllable "-du" in "educis" to the end of the clause, terminating on the confinal e. The Page and Pfau transcriptions make note of this discrepancy (the Reisencodex does not include the f half-line) and transcribe the line as indicated above.

[123] The other four instances were 1b1, 2b3, 4a3, and 4b2, ends of interior clauses which may or may not be sung with a pause.

The ambitus indications offer another observation about the manner in which Hildegard shapes her sound-space framework in this sequence. The highest pitches in the opening A section move from:

1a1	1a2	1b1	1b2	2a1	2a2	2a3	2a4	2b1	2b2	2b3	2b4
e ↗	f →	f	(d) ↗	g	(f)	g →	g →	g	(f)	g →	g

The structural line formed by highest pitches moves up by step from e (the confinalis) to f and then to a long prolongation on g (the confinalis of C Ionian...). Clause 1b2 'retreats' to an apex of d, giving a strong motion to the next apex of g (a structural rising Perfect 4th). When g is attained, in clause 2a1, the recitation pitches no longer include the finalis a, but are members of a triad built on C. There are two 'retreats' in 2a2 and 2b2 to apex pitches of f, but the structural prolongation of g continues throughout the rest of the A section.

In the B section, the prayer petition, Hildegard carries the structural line to its apex, the octave a. The rise to A5 is accomplished with her 'signature' motive, A4-E5-A5, the first time it has appeared in this sequence. The text is "O lorica vite" (O breastplate of life)", with the highest pitch A5 occurring on the first syllable of 'life'. The 'signature' motive is initiated out of the now familiar terminatio figure introduced in clause 1a1, preceded by the finalis pitch. What a strong, unified emphasis on the image of the Holy Spirit as the breastplate of life!

Finalis Terminatio 'Signature" ------

Okay, time for a brief digression. What is this 'breastplate' Hildegard is using as an image? The simplest and most universally known definition is that of a plate of armor made out of one of a variety of strong materials worn to protect the upper torso from injury. In biblical times, a Hebrew High Priest wore a 'breastplate' made of woven fabric that was inlaid with twelve precious stones signifying the twelve tribes of Israel. There is a description in Exodus:

'From among the Israelites, summon your brother Aaron and his sons to be priests in my service: Aaron and Aaron's sons Nadab, Abihu, Eleazar and Ithamar. For your brother Aaron you will make sacred vestments to give dignity and magnificence. You will instruct all the skilled men, whom I have endowed with skill, to make Aaron's vestments for his consecration to my priesthood. These are the vestments which they must make: a pectoral, an *ephod*, a robe, an embroidered tunic, a turban and a belt. They must make sacred vestments for your brother Aaron and his sons, for them to be priests in my service. They will use gold and violet material, red-purple and crimson, and finely woven linen.

'They will make the *ephod* of finely woven linen embroidered with gold, violet-purple, red-purple and crimson. It will have two shoulder-straps joined to it; it will be joined to them by its two edges. The waistband on the *ephod* to hold it in position must be of the same workmanship and be of a piece with it: of gold, violet-purple, red-purple and crimson materials and finely woven linen. You will then take two cornelians and engrave them with the names of the sons of Israel, six of their names on one stone, the remaining six names on the other, in the order of their birth. By the stone-carver's art--seal engraving--you will engrave the two stones with the names of the sons of Israel. You will have them mounted in gold settings and will put the two stones on the shoulder-straps of the *ephod*, to commemorate the sons of Israel. In this way Aaron will bear their names on his two shoulders, before Yahweh, as a reminder. You will also make golden rosettes, and two chains of pure gold twisted like cord, and will attach the cord-like chains to the rosettes.

'You will make the breastplate of judgement of the same embroidered work as the *ephod*; you will make it of gold, violet-purple and crimson materials and finely woven linen. It must be square and doubled over, a span in length and a span in width. In it you will set four rows of stones: a sard, topaz and emerald for the first row; for the second row, a garnet, sapphire and diamond; for the third row, a hyacinth, a ruby and an amethyst; and for the fourth row, a beryl, a cornelian and a jasper. These must be mounted in gold settings. The stones will correspond to the names of the sons of Israel, twelve like their names, engraved like seals, each with the name of one of the twelve tribes. For the breastplate you will make chains of pure gold twisted like cords, and on the breastplate you will make two gold rings, putting the two rings on the two outside edges of the breastplate and fastening the two gold cords to the two rings on the outside edges of the breastplate. The other two ends of the cords you will fasten to the two rosettes, putting these on the shoulder-straps of the *ephod*, on the front. You will also make two gold rings and put them on the two edges of the breastplate, on the inner side, against the *ephod*; and you will make two gold rings and put them low down on the front of the two shoulder-pieces of the *ephod*, close to the join, above the waistband of the *ephod*. The breastplate will be secured by a violet-purple cord passed through its rings and those of the *ephod*, so that the breastplate will sit above the waistband and not come apart from the *ephod.* Thus Aaron will bear the names of the sons of Israel on the breastplate of judgement, on his heart, when he enters the sanctuary, as a reminder, before Yahweh, always. To the breastplate of judgement you will add the *urim* and the *thummim*, and these will be on Aaron's heart when he goes into Yahweh's presence, and Aaron will bear the Israelites' judgement on his heart, in Yahweh's presence, always.[124]

This biblical breastplate is described with many repetitions and precise descriptions. Today, replicas of the breastplate are used to protect the Torah. The breastplate has been a symbolic part of Christian practice too, and perhaps the most famous reference in Christian literature is 'St. Patrick's Breastplate' -- another prayer that has been set to music.

Well, back to the B section of Hildegard's sequence. She describes the Holy Spirit as the breastplate of life, followed quickly with a clause hoping that the Holy Spirit will unite all bodily limbs (a reference to the Christian image of the Body of Christ, the Church). In the late 12th century, with Barbarossa appointing antipopes, a schism in the church, and the ongoing Crusades, this certainly would be a fervent prayer, and one to be flung into God's heaven, rising to the highest melodic apex!

---

[124] *The New Jerusalem Bible.* Darton, Longman & Todd, Ltd. and Doubleday. 1985. pp116-117. Picture from Holstein, Joanne. "Ephod. " *Becker Bible Studies* Jan 2006. Retrieved 2 June 2009 from: http://www.guidedbiblestudies.com/topics/ephod.htm.

There is no 'tick' or pause indicated in the manuscript after the word vite, but I chose to divide the very long phrase at this point for several reasons:

1. it ends a clause, an invocation
2. it is followed by a conjunction (et) leading to a definition of the subject
3. the third clause also begins with a conjunction (et) which defines the subject
4. the third clause ends with the verb applied to all of the foregoing ('save the blessed'):

    O breastplate of life....save the blessed,
    [and] hope of [unity]....save the blessed,
    [and] belt of honor...save the blessed.

Furthermore, the 'signature' offered in the first clause (A4-E5-A5) serves as a framework for the rest of the section, creating a larger structure. It does not appear again in such a straightforward way, but, in Hildegard's manner, it is decorated and varied in 3a3, 3b1, and 3b3.

Similar structural uses of this signature motive appear in 4b2, 5-1, and 6-1. All uses of this motive, melodic and structural, appear toward the beginning of the clauses, followed by a gradual descent to the confinal or the finalis after the dramatic rise to A5. So in her sound space, Hildegard uses contour as a means of creating a rhythmic perception of 'short-long', an energetic acclamation (quick rise of an octave) followed by a more meditative, descending return to the source.

To summarize, the diagram shows clearly the use of the Aeolian mode on a as the sound focus, the 'tonality', of this sequence. It also points to phrases and clauses where there is some digression from a as the primary focus, particularly to c and its Ionian mode. To show Hildegard's modal (i.e. harmonic) structure for the sequence, we can return to the diagram offered earlier:

A (descriptive praise)	B (prayer)	A' (descriptive praise)
5 'identities'	3 'identities'	4 'identities'
Couplets 1, 2	Couplet 3	Couplets 4, 5 and 6
55 syl.	63 syl.	79 syl.
73 syl.		60 syl.
shaped lines (2 & 3 = 2 & 3)		shaped lines (2 & 4 = 2 & 4)
(128 syllables total)	(63 syllables total)	(139 syllables total)

A Aeolian ------------------------------A Aeolian--A Aeolian
Hints of C Ionian D Aeolian

Hildegard's Melody

Twelfth Century chant had been formulated and refined over the centuries, and there are several 'conventions' of which we should be aware in order to understand and appreciate Hildegard's creativity and unique style of expression. The following list is by no means exhaustive, but it will be helpful.[125]

Plainchant Characteristics

Ambitus: usually not beyond A3 - G5 (the lowest and highest pitches of the eight modes. There are, of course, exceptions to be found.)

Contour: phrases are most frequently arch-forms, with a rising initio, a recitation on the and a descent to the terminatio. These arches are often 'wavy', with some changes of direction.
Occasionally shorter phrases might be only ascending or only descending.
Some few examples of inverted arch contours may be found.

Cadences: most cadences (terminatio patterns) are approached by ascending or descending seconds or descending thirds.

Accents: the creation of accents for specific syllables are by:
- a dynamic accent (>) placed over the neume
- an agogic accent (two successive identical neumes on a single syllable, or other marking such as an episema indicating a longer duration on a single syllable)
- a contoural accent, usually a higher pitch on the syllable to be accented, followed by pitches a step lower for the other syllables in the word (also called 'tonic' accent).
- melismatic or neumatic accents, related to the agogic accent, in that they prolong a single syllable of text through a number of pitches.

---

[125] Please see Apel, Willi. *Gregorian Chant*. Indiana University Press, 1958, pp. 247-304 for much more information.

Melodic Progressions: the predominant progression from one pitch or neume to the next is by step.

Unison repetitions on the reciting tone are common.

Leaps (intervals larger than the second) are limited to primarily thirds. Ascending Perfect Fourths (and descending) are somewhat frequent.

Ascending Perfect Fifths are more rare, occuring at the beginning of a phrase.

Descending fifths are very rare. They are most often a-d (descending) or g-d (ascending). Others are found, but often involve the third also (f-a-c).

Leaps larger than the fifth are very rare. And "The octave occurs only as a dead interval in some very late chants which have no connection to the Gregorian repertory"[126].

Two leaps in succession are limited primarily to thirds in the same direction (i.e. outlining a triad). An ascending fifth followed by a third is fairly common as is an ascending fourth followed by another fourth.

Very rarely, one finds a succession of a fifth and a fourth, or the span of an octave connected by two intervening pitches.

Motivic Repetition: many instances of repetition of a melodic motive are found:

-- immediate repetition on the same pitch level

-- sequential repetition (on a different pitch level)

-- repetition at different places in the chant Musical rhyme: use of similar or the same motives in specific places, particularly as initio or terminatio motives.

"Reiterative style"[127]: a practice of reiterating a pattern with additional pitches andneumes interpolated among the initial pitches. This practice was called "oriental", and "our vocabulary has only more or less derogatory terms to indicate it: pleonasm, prolixity, diffuseness, etc., all indicative or suggestive of a lack of conciseness."[128] Since the publication of *Gregorian Chant*, we have developed terms to identify this practice (decoration, ornamentation, interpolation, etc.). Apel does indicate that this was a common and pervasive character of Gregorian Chant.

The above categories of investigation provide oppoertunity for a comprehensive and organized look at Hildegard's melodic style in this sequence, and should yield some observations about how she moved beyond the conventions of her time.

---

[126] Apel. *Op. Cit.*, p.253.
[127] Apel. *Op. Cit.*, p.262
[128] Apel. *Op. Cit.*, p.262

Hildegard: O ignis spiritus

Ambitus: The ambitus for each clause in Hildegard's sequence is indicated in the diagram on pages 81-82. The following diagram is a summary showing the ambitus for each phrase.

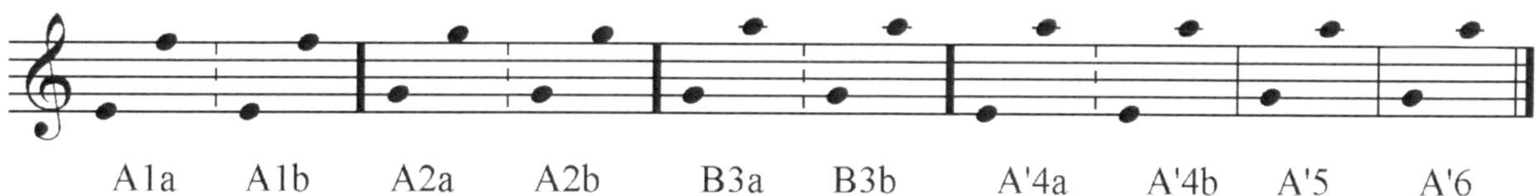

Hildegard is very consistent in the ambitus for each couplet, even though the pitch succession (melodic progression) for each phrase is varied. The ambitus for the entire sequence only slightly exceeds that indicated as the most common for plainchant, here rising to A5 (instead of G5). So the ambitus for O ignis spiritus is not unique or exceptional.

The diagram does show and support the earlier commentary about the structural, or framework, progression of highest pitches, leading to the highest point in section B, where the prayer petition occurs in the text. Considering the lower pitches too, it also shows the 'return' to A materials in A'4 and A'5-6. Thus the 'return' includes the entire gamut of pitches.

Contour: A graph showing the framework of Hildegard's phrases also demonstrates the contour of each phrase. It also shows the craft of composition through the use of very similar, if not identical, frameworks used for each clause in the couplets.

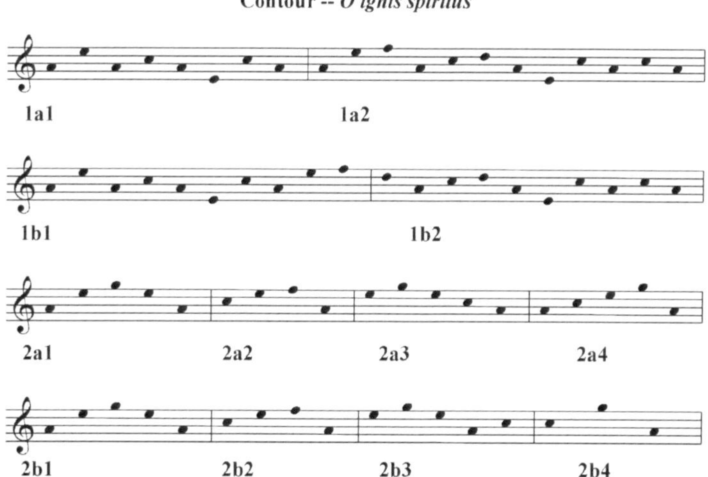

In the A section, comparing the phrases of the first couplet, 1a-1b, yields wave contours with identical frameworks but for one point, the connection of 1b1 with 1b2. Hildegard maintains the structure of the whole phrase 1a in 1b, but ends the first clause of 1b (1b1) with an incomplete closure on F5 -- the third structural pitch of 1a2. 1b2 then completes the framework of 1a2 with the initio being the only change.

The second couplet is also nearly identical in the framework, but now showing arch contours in the clauses of the couplet. The entire phrases are, of course, wave forms. The only deviation in the repetition occurs at the end of 2b3 through 2b4, where the same type of overlapping seen in 1b1-1b2 occurs.

The B section shows similar application of melodic frameworks, once again wave forms for clauses and complete phrases. The signature A4-E5-A5 is seen here as a structural pattern.

Overlap is seen in the first two clauses of the second verse of the couplet.
More diversity in contoural frameworks is used in the final section, A'.

The fourth couplet (4a,4b) uses a combination of arch contours (4a1,4a4,4b3) and wave contours. And phrases 5 and 6 include even more diversity, with 'wavy' arch forms (5-1, 6-1), an inverted arch (6-3), and a descending wave (6-4). There is no attempt to 'pair' the last two phrases (5-6) as closely as the other couplets were paired, though an even more basic 'background' similarity in contour can be traced between 5-1,2 with 6-1,2 and 5-3 with 6-3,4.

Interestingly, the signature A4-E5-A5 motive appears in each of these frameworks, serving as a unifying element for the final section (4a2-3, 4b2, 5-1, 6-1).

If these frameworks are compared to the diagram of initio-recitation-terminatio on pages 81-82, it is obvious that Hildegard's melodies are much more active than typical plainchant, using more activity and deviating much further above and below the recitation pitch in the interior portions of phrases.

Cadences: Throughout the sequence, the terminatio patterns all approach the cadence pitch in good modal fashion by step. As mentioned earlier, all but eight terminate on the finalis A. The patterns themselves show a remarkable unity, with fourteen of the thirty-four employing a c-g-a motion (or an elaboration with an interpolated b), forming a familiar and well-used cambiata figure.

or

This cambiata is a variation of the descending third terminatio mentioned by Dr. Apel (see p. 87), combining that motion with the more common ascending second motion to the finalis.

Accents: Syllables of text are accented in this sequence in seven different ways. There are no dynamic accents indicated in the manuscript of this sequence. The following details refer to accents which coincide with a change of syllable, not accents which occur within a melismatic or neumatic figuration of a single syllable. Thus the accent is both musical and textual.

There are several places where Hildegard emphasizes a syllable of text with the use of two or more identical neumes (repetitious neumes) in succession, in contemporary terminology named an agogic accent (accentuation by means of longer duration):

A:	1a1	ignis (fire)
		vita (life)
		vivificando (life-giving)
		formas (forms)
	1b1	fractos (broken)
	2a3	pectoribus (breasts)
B:	3a3	cingulum (belt)
		honestatis (honor)
		beatos (fortunate)
	3b3	salvare (to save)
A':	4b2	habent (produce)
	5-1	etiam (are)
		edu-cis (teaching)
	5-2	inspirationem (inspiration)
	5-3	Sapientie (Wisdom)
	6-1	sonus (sound)
	6-2	vite (life)
	6-3	dans (granting)
		premia (prize)

With the exception of 5-1 "etiam", the words accented with the agogic accents are active nouns or verbs, leading to the conclusion that these repetitious neumes were used for emphasis on the text, and not for compositional purposes (i.e. to lengthen a phrase, to create unity of motivic ideas, to balance 'rhythm' patterns, etc.).

Contoural accents are by far the most frequent accents, and they are responsible in large part for the perception of rhythmic pulse in chant. Those that are approached by ascending leap and followed by descending step motion are the most ‘dramatic’, and in Hildegard’s sequence they are less frequently used, thus adding to their ‘dramatic’ effect.

Contoural-a:

A:	2a1/2b1	spiraculum/purissime (breath/clearest)
B:	3a1/3b1	vite/qui (life/who)
	3a2	omnium (whole)
A':	4a1/4b1	iter/te (course/you)
	4a2	omnia (all things)
	6	Unde (Thence)

Contoural accents approached by ascending step followed by descending step motion are more frequent (only accents which coincide with a new syllable of text are indicated).

Contoural-b:

A:	2a4	infusio (infusing)
		bono (good)
	2b2	consideratur (we see)
	2b4	perditos (lost)
B:	3b1	inimico (enemy)
A':	4a3	terrenis (on the earth)
	4a4	omnibus (every)
	4b3	rivulos (streams)
		educunt (flows)

Contoural accents which are approached by ascending step and followed by descending leap also occur with some frequency.

Contoural-c:

A:	1a2	vivificando (giving life) Note: the syllable '-can-' is emphasized with an agogic accent. Even though '-fi-' is set with a contoural accent, the agogic accent on '-can-' receives more weight.
	1b2	vulnera (wounds)
B:	3a3	honestatis (honor) Note: this contoural accent is also followed by a neumatic setting of the final syllable containing an agogic accent, thus giving the last syllable more weight.
	3b3	salvare (to save) Note: this is the corresponding place in the second part of the couplet, so treatment of the last two syllables of 'salvare' is identical to that found in 'honestatis'.
A':	4a5	componis (reconcile) Note: this contoural accent is followed by a neumatic figure.
	4b3	viriditatem (greenness)
	5-3	Sapientie (Wisdom) Note: again, the contoural accent is followed by a neumatic setting containing an agogic accent.
		letificatos (made joyful)
	6-1	qui (who)

The use of the above contoural accents places more emphasis on the syllable following than on the syllable receiving the accent. Leaps, especially in chant, are more dramatic movements than step motion, and reaching an apex in a line followed by a descending leap is really quite dramatic. Hildegard reinforces the drama in the majority of instances noted above by emphasizing the next syllable of text with neumatic embellishment and/or an agogic accent.

Contoural accents approached by ascending leap and followed by descending leap are the least frequent, but also the most dramatic.

<u>Contoural-d:</u>

(The most frequent pattern is the approach to the terminatio figure c-g-a)

A:	1a1	paracli<u>ti</u> (Paraclete)
	1a2	crea<u>ture</u>
		vivifican<u>do</u> (giving life)
	1b2	feti<u>da</u> (festering)
B:	3a3	<u>be</u>atos (fortunate)
A'	4a5	colli<u>gis</u> (draw together)
	4b4	su<u>dat</u> (exudes)

By far the most rare contoural accents are approached and left by leap:

A'	4a3	al<u>tis</u>simis (heavens)
	4b2	humo<u>rem</u> (moisture)

Neumatic accents create slight emphasis on syllables by the use of neumes containing three or four different pitches. Technically, neumes containing two pitches may be counted as "accentual", but for our purposes here, only those containing three and no more than four different pitches will be considered. These accents are closely related to the agogic accent in that they prolong the expression of a syllable, but here they also involve change of pitch, placing even more emphasis on the syllable than an agogic accent. The terminatio figure c-g-a is not included in this list

A:	1a1	O
	1a2	es (this uses the terminatio figure) (you are)
	1b1	<u>Sanc</u>tus (holy)
		periculo<u>se</u> (this uses the terminatio figure) (perilously)
	1b2	ter<u>gen</u>do (cleansing)
		vulner<u>a</u> (wounds)
	2a2	O
		ig<u>nis</u> (fire)
	2a3	<u>gus</u>tus (savor)
	2b2	in
	2b3	<u>De</u>us (God)
	2b4	perdi<u>tos</u> (lost)
B:	3a2	mem<u>bro-rum</u> (human body)
	3a3	honesta<u>tis</u> (honor)
		sal<u>va</u> (save)
	3b2	<u>sol</u>ve (free)
	3b3	salva<u>re</u> (to save)
A':	4a3	altis<u>si</u>mis (heavens)
	4a5	com<u>po</u>nis (reconcile)
	4b1	te (You)
	4b2	<u>ha</u>bent (produce)
	4b3	e<u>du</u>cunt (flows)
	4b4	et (and)
		viri<u>di</u>tatem (living greenness)

5-1	etiam (are)
	edu-cis (teaching)
5-2	inspirationem (inspiration)
6-1	so-nus (sound)
6-3	spes (hope)
6-4	dans (granting)

Melismatic accents place emphasis on a syllable of text by prolonging the syllable through many (more than four) different pitches. They are commonly acknowledged to be used for text painting and most often occur either at the beginning or at the end of a clause:

A:	2b1	purissime (clearest)
B:	3b3	vult (wishes)
A':	4a2	omnia (all things)
	4a4	abys-sis (abyss)
	4b2	humorem (moisture)
	4b3	educunt (flows)

The following table shows the seven different types of accents enumerated above and the frequency of their use within the ternary form of the chant.

Accent	Agogic	Contoural a	Contoural b	Contoural c	Contoural d	Neumatic	Melismatic	Total
A	6	2	4	2	4	12	1	31
B	4	3	1	2	1	5	1	17
A'	9	4	4	5	4	13	4	43
Total	19	9	9	9	9	30	6	91

Several observations leading to some conclusions about Hildegard's writing style may be made based upon the table above.

1. The nature and form of the text is supported by the number and type of accents employed in the musical setting. The final, longer section is accented proportionately slightly more than the first two sections.

Section	No. of Syllables (340 total)	Per Centage Of Total Syllables	Number of Accents (91 total)	Per Centage Of Total Accents	Per Centage of Syllables receiving an accent
A	128	38%	31	34%	24%
B	63	18%	17	19%	27%
A'	149	44%	43	47%	29%

2. The per centage of syllables receiving musical accents is quite consistent, growing only slightly with each section. This consistency would be expected in a syllabic or neumatic setting of a text.
3. The more dramatic accents, the agogic, and especially the melismatic accents, are used much more sparingly than contoural and neumatic accents, and as a result, they carry more emphasis.

Well, the above was a rather lengthy and probably somewhat boring listing of minutiae. And some of the details may be interpreted differently from what I have offered. But if these details are usable to gain a fuller understanding of how Hildegard creates a living, breathing sound structure which connects us to the heavens and the source of all being, they are valuable little things for us to have and use...!

The manners in which Hildegard accents her text musically are coupled with the manners with which she creates a musical line, the melody. To begin our study of Hildegard's melodic process, we'll use the list from Willi Apel's book, *Gregorian Chant*, found on pp. 81-82 earlier.

Melodic Progression

Apel uses this term to refer to the manner in which successive pitches or neumes in a melody are connected. Naturally connection by ascending or descending step motion is the predominant manner of creating melody. Skips, or leaps, are less common, and in traditional chant they are handled carefully, most often preceded and followed by step motion moving in the opposite direction of the leap. Hildegard's sequence, *O ignis spiritus paracliti* offers some examples of how she expanded the conventions (in italics below) of melodic writing current during her time.

Ascending Perfect Fifths are...rare, occurring at the beginning of a phrase.[129]

This progression is very prominent and frequent in Hildegard's music. It is the initial motion of her 'signature' motive, and in this sequence it appears at the beginning of seven clauses, and at least once in each of the three sections (all instances are the rising P5 from A4-E5).[130] She also uses it three times within clauses, an even more unusual occurrence.[131] And she uses a rising P5 from D5-A5 two times in the final, A' section.[132]

Descending fifths are very rare. They are most often d-a...[133]

Hildegard breaks with tradition here, using descending fifths ten times. She does not use any descending fifths in the first section of the sequence, the section of praise, so they begin to appear in the middle section, bringing the prayer petitions back down to earth from their apex pitches.[134] The last section contains six instances of descending fifths.[135] There are only two types, six descents from the confinalis E5 to the finalis A4 and four from the diapente A5 to D5, two of which help to create the emphasis on D Dorian in 5-1 through 5-3 (there are no descending fifths of the first type in this verse).

Two leaps in succession are limited primarily to thirds in the same direction.. Very rarely, one finds a succession of a fifth and a fourth, or the span of an octave connected by two intervening pitches..[136]

---

129 Apel, *Op. Cit.,* p.253

130 1a1, 1a2, 1b1, 2a1, 2b1, 3a3, 6-1

131 1b1, 3b1, 4b2

132 4a3 on "altissimis" and 4b2 on "humorem"

133 Apel, *Op. Cit.,* p.253

134 See clauses 3a2 (e ↘ a), 3a3 (a ↘ d), 3b2 (e ↘ a), 3b3 (a ↘ d).

135 See clauses 4a3 (e ↘ a), 4a4 (e ↘ a), 4b2 (e ↘ a), 4b3 (e ↘ a), 5-1 (a ↘ d), 5-3 (a ↘ d)

136 *Ibid.*p. 262

Hildegard does not use two leaps in succession in this sequence -- EXCEPT -- for her signature motive![137] As noted earlier, the signature motive (first appearing in 3a1) serves as the framework for several passages:

The example from 3a3 is the first 'framework' use of the signature motive. There is a long 'prolongation' on the confinalis E5, with the belt (cingulum) circling around before connecting to the diapente A5 by ascending step. The falling P5 which follows "cinches" it, and again it circles back to the confinalis E5, but only after an agogic accent on D5! Hildegard knew what she was doing here...

The example from 4b2 is particularly rich, as it contains two ascending fifths. The first (A4-E5) initiates the structural signature motive, is balanced with descending step motion, and then leaps a P5 again to the diapente, followed by descending motion of a third before resting on the confinalis. Moisture was important to Hildegard!

6-1 resembles 3a3, but without so much decoration. Praise is offered to the Spirit, who is the sound of praise. Earthly praise hovers around the confinalis E5 and is lofted to the Spirit (tibi), the diapente A5.

Motivic Repetition

One of Hildegard's admonitions for us is to "use discretion in all things". Her craftsmanship as a composer is a primary exhibit of this! It also is an example of unity, of interconnection and of creativity. This sequence, *O ignis spiritus paracliti,* is created from four basic melodic motives, motives which we have seen before in *O eterne Deus* and *O pastor animarum*. Those two works studied in chapters one and two were antiphons, and *O ignis spiritus paracliti* is a sequence, but they all three were created by one heart and mind as gifts of praise to the one Creator. The similarities are elements of Hildegard's musical style that are unique to Hildegard, and her manipulations of musical motives help to define that unique style.

Apel lists immediate repetition, sequence, and reiteration as three basic repetitive techniques[138] common to plainchant, and he defines 'musical rhyme' as being the use of similar or identical motives as initio or terminatio figures. Hildegard's music is replete with these motivic uses, and she takes them a bit further, applying what we today call 'developmental

---

137 "Very rarely, one finds a succession of a fifth and a fourth, or the span of an octave connected by two intervening pitches." p.262. Hildegard uses her signature motive of A4-E5-A5 in 3a1.

138 *Ibid*. p.262

processes' to the foundational motives. Indeed, we might even go so far as to look at her signature motive as being a 'grundgestalt', or foundational pattern serving on many levels as a 'framework' motive. Now, that's a 20th Century view of Hildegard's craftsmanship!

To see this 'mosaic' creation of melody, we can identify four elemental motives and their most frequent variations:

The signature motive has been presented at some length in this and the previous chapters. Here two forms are presented, the first (x) showing the ascending Perfect fifth followed by descending step motion back to the finalis. It is the very first melodic gesture in the sequence. The second form (x-full) shows the ascending Perfect fifth followed by the ascending Perfect fourth, and a stepwise descent back to the confinalis.

The palindrome motive is just that -- a palindrome, reading the same forward and backward. Again we see a framework involving the finalis (first and last pitches) and the confinalis (central pitch), here connected by descending step-third motion and then ascending third-step motion. The Aeolian mode is identified -- repetition of the finalis (beginning and ending pitches), contoural accent on the confinalis, and approach to the finalis through the subtonic (not the leading tone) pitch.

The finalis motive was presented earlier in the first two formats (z, and z-full) shown above. The retrograde (↘ M2 ↗ P4) is used at the beginnings of clauses and in the interior portions of clauses, but not as a finalis motive, often at this pitch level, but occasionally beginning on other pitches.

The torculus motive is a 'neighbor-tone' motive, used in both ascending and descending fashion. It is shown here as it first appears, on the mediant pitch C5, but it occurs on a number of pitches, serving clearly as a decorative figure ('torculus' is the name of the neume giving this pattern).

To see how Hildegard uses these motives, we will take each separately and trace its appearance through the sequence. The signature motive appears in two forms, incomplete (with opening fifth but no rise to the diapente) and full.

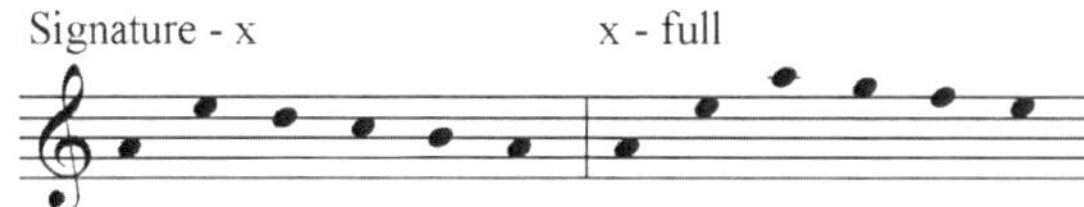

The incomplete or basic 'x' motive appears eight times in the sequence, most frequently decorated.

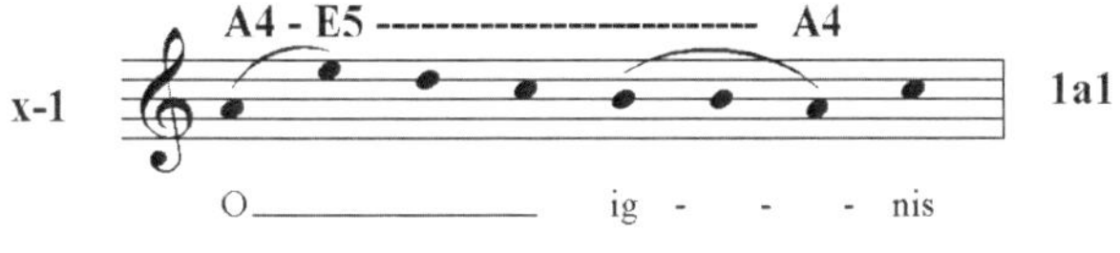

--the opening gesture decorated with an agogic accent and followed with a m3 rise to C5.

--the complete motive with an agogic accent at the beginning, decorated with an F5 escape tone before the descent to A4.

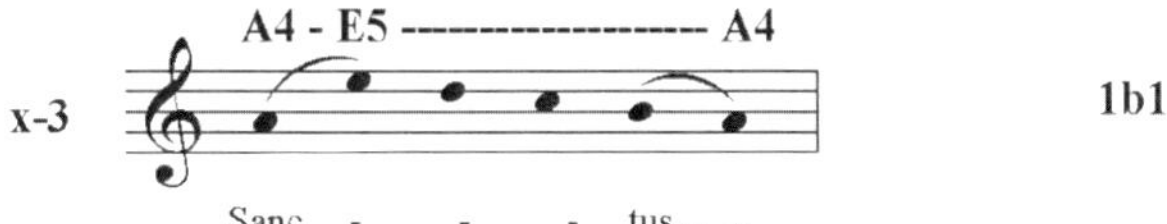

--a 'pure' form of the motive without decoration.

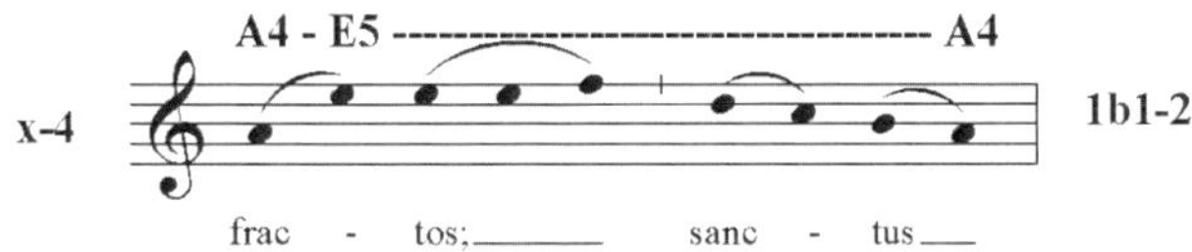

--an 'elided' form, beginning at the end of one clause and completed in the following clause. This elided form is identical to that in x-2.

--this motive is decorated with a clivis followed by a rise to G5 (the z-R motive), then a prolongation of E5 through a repeated clivis before the final descent.

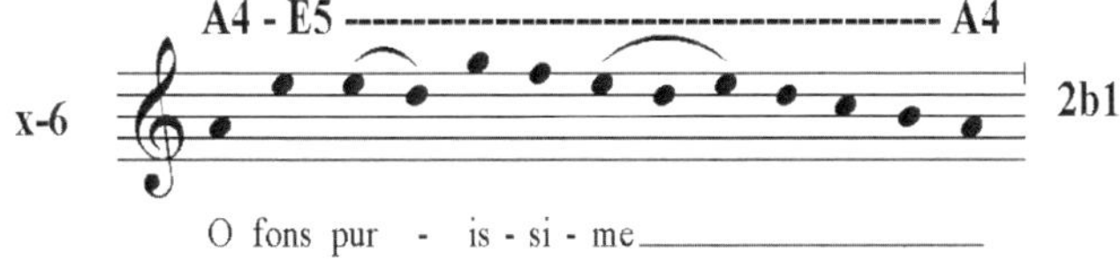

--nearly identical to x-5, this motive sets fewer syllables and ends with a torculus and a melisma.

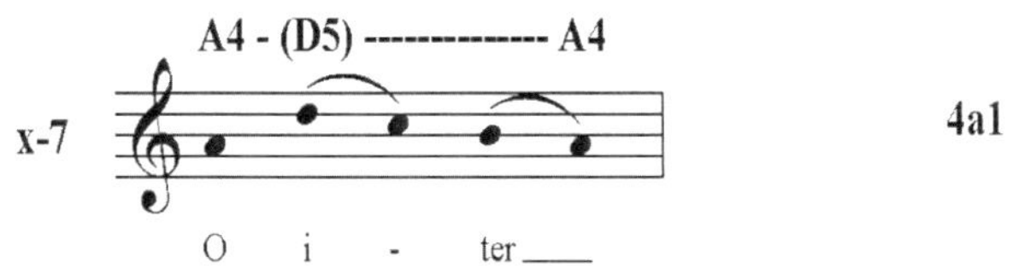

--an intervallic contraction of the x motive, the opening leap is a P4 to D5, followed by two clivis neumes descending to A4. The E5 was omitted.

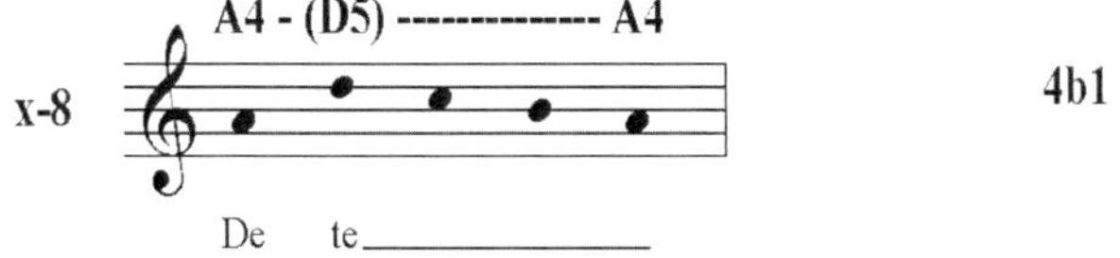

--identical to x-7, but formed with individual punctae.

The x-full motive appears six times, serving as a pitch framework for the clauses in which it is used.

--the first appearance is introduced by the finalis and the z-motive ("O lo-").

--here the initial rise to E5 is prolonged, followed by a m3 leap to G and then a step to the apex A5. The return to E5 is dramatic, with a falling P5 and an agogic accent.

--similar to z-full 1, with an added P4 rise preceding the A5 and creating a palindrome decoration of the return to E5 (using z-R and z!).

--a framework in the middle of the clause, preceded by a descending m3 from C5. The rise to A5 uses two ascending P5ths (on A and D), and the descent to E5 includes a falling m3 and a Torculus.

--a 'summary' figuration, using an opening Pes, repetition of E5, and interpolation of D5 on 'laus' and 'sit'.

--a phrygian elided s-full motive, connecting two clauses. It begins on A4 and rises a third through the musica ficta B^b to a prolongation of E5. The prolongation contains a rising m3 to G5 and its descending return before leaping to the A5 at the beginning of the next clause, returning quickly to the E5.

The palindrome motive ('y') occurs nine times, often initiating a clause or preceding a terminatio and always on the same pitch level. There are several appearances in the interior portions of clauses as well. It begins with the finalis and descends to the lower confinalis before returning to the finalis, creating a momentary use of the plagal, or hypoaeolian mode.

This motive does not appear in a pure, decorated or framework manner in the second half of A (2a or 2b), in the B section, or in the last two verses of A' (5 or 6). Those verses do not use the plagal form of the mode, never descending to the lower confinalis, so the observation can be made that the 'y' motive is employed to move to the plagal confinalis and return to the pentachord. The plagal range of the sequence is characterized by the use of the 'y' motive, and the color of verses 1 and 4 is therefore deeper and fuller than 2, 3, 5 and 6.

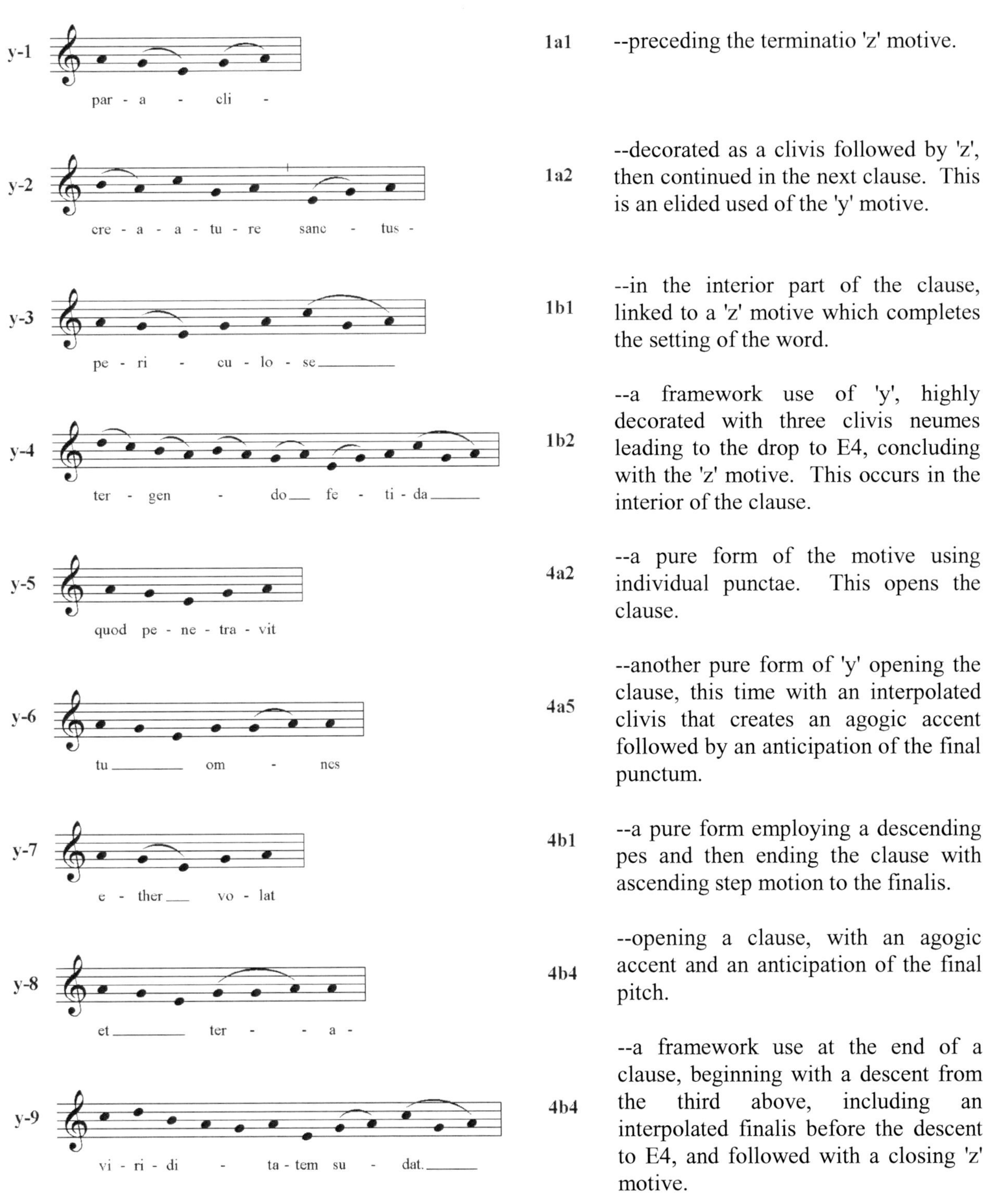

As indicated earlier, the 'z' motive, or the 'Finalis' motive appears in three forms. The first two ('z' and 'z-full') end with the finalis pitch and are most often found at the ends of clauses. The third, 'z-retrograde', appears most often at the pitch level indicated above, facilitating a motion from the confinalis E5 to the m3 above, G5. It is a retrograde of the 'z', though it does not serve in a terminatio pattern. As is obvious from the examples below, the 'z' is not limited to terminatio patterns either, and the motives with their ascending and descending leaps provide a great deal of the motion and 'drama' for Hildegard's melody. There are fifteen appearances of 'z'.

z-1	ti.	**1a1**	--terminatio
z-2	a - tu - re,	**1a2**	--terminatio
z-3	es	**1a2**	--used in an interior part of the clause
z-4	do for - mas.	**1a2**	--terminatio
z-5	se	**1b1**	--used in an interior part of the clause
z-6	da	**1b2**	--used in an interior part of the clause
z-7	vul - ne - ra.	**1b2**	--terminatio with closing neumatic gesture
z-8	pec - to - - ri - bus	**2a3**	--terminatio with agogic accent
z-9	a - li - e - nos	**2b3**	--used in an interior part of the clause
z-10	et spes	**3a2**	--used at the beginning of a clause
z-11	be - a - tos.	**3a3**	--terminatio
z-12	ti - sunt	**3b1**	--used in an interior part of the clause
z-13	vult.	**3b3**	--terminatio, as part of a melisma
z-14	gis.	**4a5**	--terminatio
z-15	su - dat.	**4b4**	--terminatio

There are ten uses of the z-full motive. Most serve as terminatio figures, though two follow an opening 'x' and precede a 'y' motive.

z-full-1	nis spi - ri - tus	**1a1**	--first appearance, after an 'x' motive and before a 'y'
z-full-2	ca - ri - - - ta - tis,	**2a2**	--terminatio
z-full-3	de - ra - tur	**2b2**	--terminatio
z-full-4	re - - - qui - rit.	**2b4**	--terminatio
z-full-5	om - ni - um	**3a2**	--terminatio
z-full-6	li - ga - - - tos	**3b2**	--terminatio
z-full-7	for - tis - si - mum	**4a1**	--terminatio
z-full-8	nu - bes flu - unt	**4b1**	--as in 1a1, after the altered 'x' and before a 'y'
z-full-9,10	dans pre - mi - a lu - cis.	**6-4**	--a phrygian form elided with an agogic accent on C5, then the aeolian terminatio.

The 'z-R' motive, 'z' reversed, appears ten times, most frequently in the interior parts of clauses.

z-R-1	spi - ra -	**2a1**	--after a rising P5, at the beginning of a clause
z-R-2	dul - cis	**2a3**	--after an initial confinalis, at the beginning of a clause
z-R-3	pur - is -	**2b1**	--a decorative figure within an 'x' motive at the beginning of a clause
z-R-4	om - ni - um	**3a2**	--preceding and elided with a terminatio z-full motive
z-R-5	car - ce - ra - ti - sunt	**3b1**	--a decorative figure within an 'x-full' motive in the middle of a clause
z-R-6	li - ga - - - tos	**3b2**	--preceding and elided with a z-full terminatio motive

z-4-7	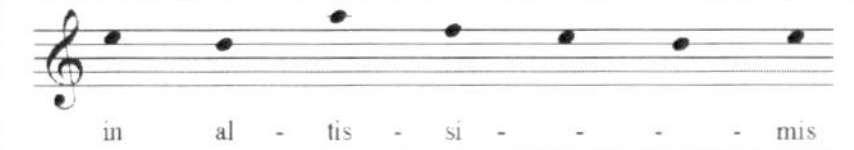 in al - tis - si - - - - mis	**4a3**	--with an interval expansion to a P5, rising from the confinalis E5 to the diapente A5
z-R-8	 hu - mo - rem	**4b2**	--within a highly decorated 'x-full' motive
z-R-9	 Tu e	**5-1**	--beginning a clause
z-R-10	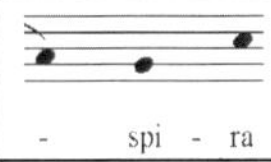 - spi - ra	**5-2**	--within a clause

Now for the 'Torculus' motive ('t'). The term 'torculus' is the name of a neume containing three pitches. The middle pitch is either a step above or below the first and last pitches, which are the same (in current terminology, it is called a neighbor note pattern). In Hildegard's sequence, I have identified motives as 't' motives if they exhibit that intervallic pattern, not only if they are notated as the 'torculus' neume, but if they result from the combination of two neumes or three consecutive punctae. The motive is used to set one syllable or it is part of a neumatic or melismatic pattern, so it is not 'shared' by two syllables. I do not include any 'framework' motives here, as its nature and purpose is decorative. It is the most frequent of all four motives, occurring twenty-four times in the sequence in all sections (though not in the first couplet).

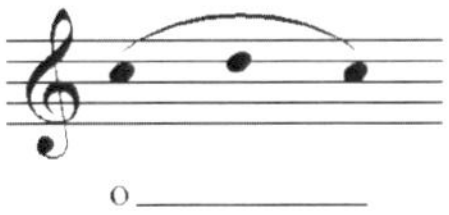 o t-1	**2a2** -- notated as a torculus.
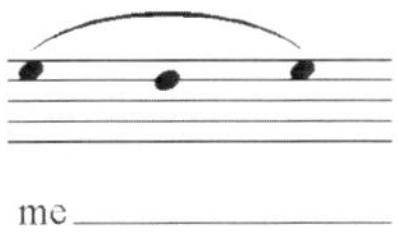 me t-2	**2b1** -- notated as a torculus, continued as a melisma with four punctae following.
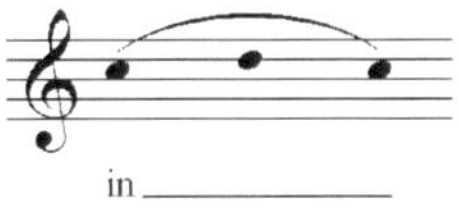 in t-3	**2b2** -- notated as a torculus.
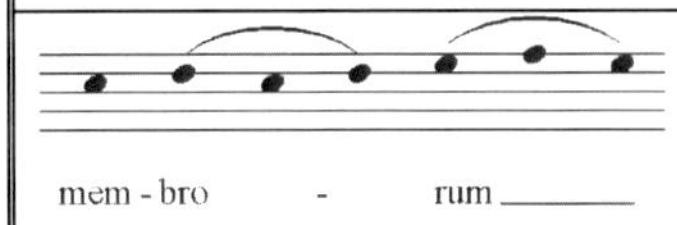 mem - bro - rum t-4 t-5	**3a1** -- notated as torculae, both descending and ascending.
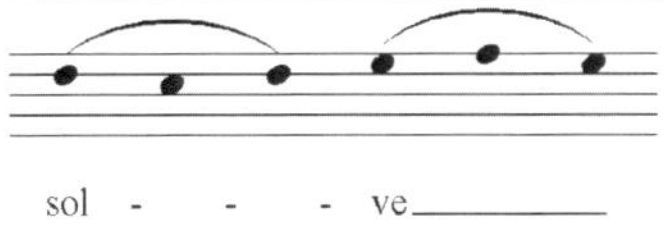 sol - - - ve t-6 t-7	**3b2** -- notated as torculae.
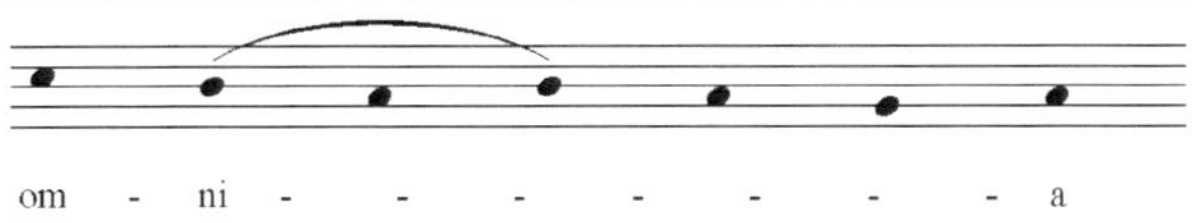 om - ni - - - - - - - a t-8 t-9	**4a2** -- the first notated as a torculae, the second as three punctae.

et in om - ni - bus a - bys - - - - - - - - sis t-10 t-11 t-12 t-13	**4a4** -- the first 't' as three punctae on 'omnibus', followed by two torculae and a final 't' as a Clivis + punctum.
com - po - - - - nis t-14	**4a5** -- part of a neumatic gesture, composed of three punctae.
la - pi - - - - des t-15 t-16	**4b2** -- at the beginning of a clause, a torculus and three punctae, making up a small melismatic gesture.
hu - mo - rem t-17	**4b2** -- three punctae ending a small melisma.
e - du - - - cunt t-18 t-19 t-20	**4b3** -- two torculae followed by a combination of a clivis + punctum.
e - du - - - - cis t-21 t-22	**5-1** -- the most veiled use of 't', a descending clivis + ascending clivis, followed by a torculus with an agogic accent.
Sa - pi - en - ti - e t-23	**5-3** -- an identical formation to t-21.
so - nus t-24	**6-1** -- a torculus.

Seeing these motives indicated on the full score shows how unified and economic Hildegard is in constructing her melodies. The following symbols are used in identification:

Torculus

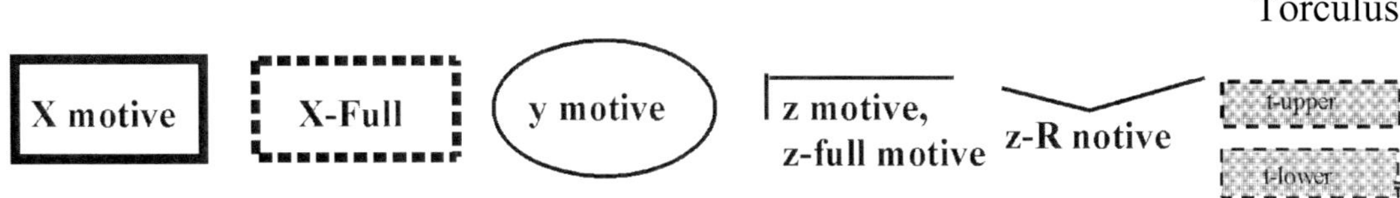

O ignis spiritus

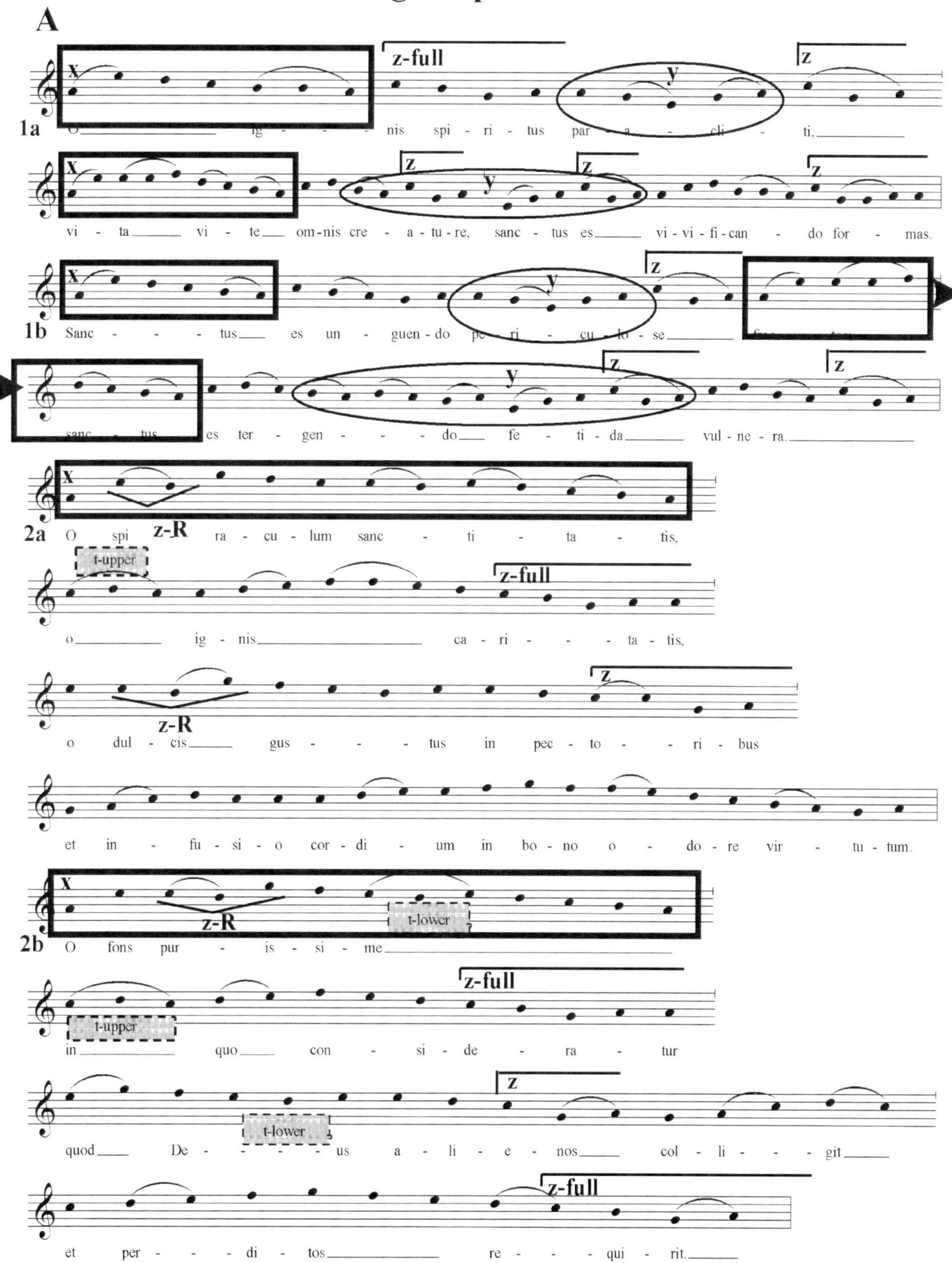

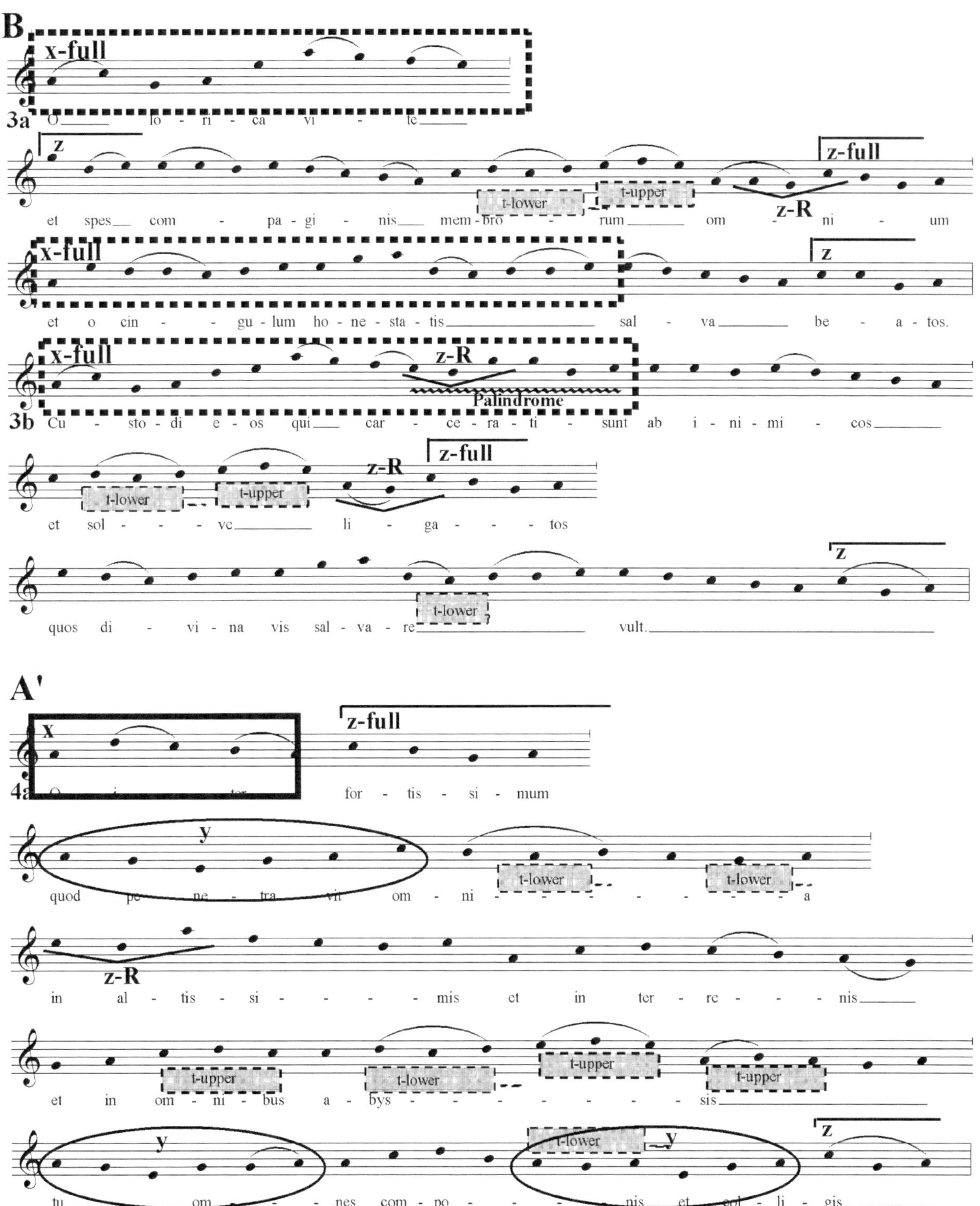
B
x-full
3a
O lo - ri - ca vi - te
z
t-lower
t-upper
z-full
z-R
et spes com - pa - gi - nis mem - bro - rum om - ni - um
x-full
z
et o cin - - gu - lum ho - ne - sta - tis sal - va be - a - tos.
x-full
z-R
Palindrome
3b
Cu - sto - di e - os qui car - ce - ra - ti - sunt ab i - ni - mi - cos
t-lower
t-upper
z-R
z-full
et sol - - - ve li - ga - - tos
t-lower
z
quos di - vi - na vis sal - va - re vult.
A'
x
z-full
4a
for - tis - si - mum
y
t-lower
t-lower
quod pe ne tra vit om - ni - - - a
z-R
in al - tis - si - - - mis et in ter - re - - - nis
t-upper
t-lower
t-upper
t-upper
et in om - ni - bus a - bys - - - sis
y
t-lower
y
z
tu om - - - nes com - po - - - nis et col - li - gis.

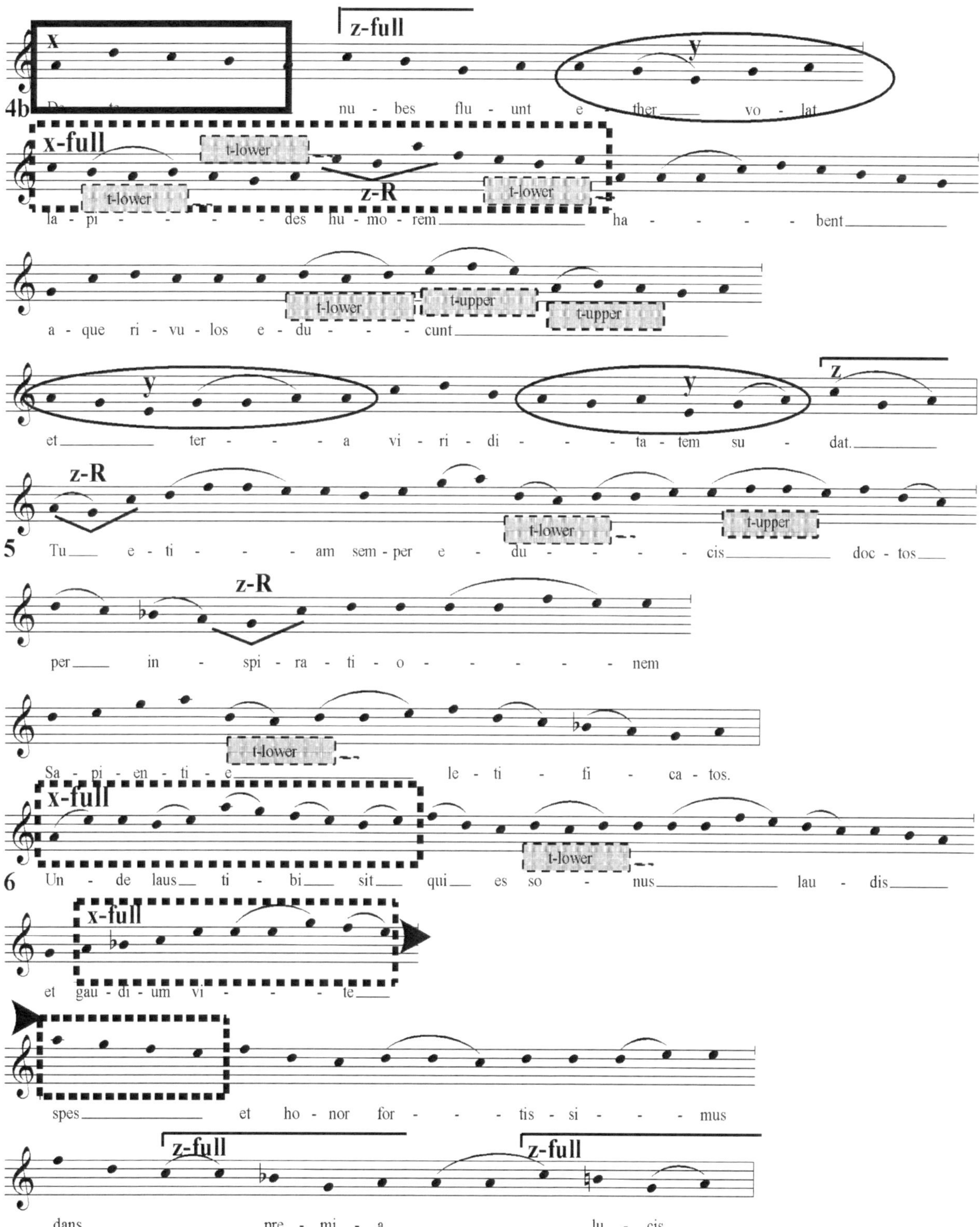

Reiterative style

The last category listed by Willi Apel in *Gregorian Chant* is that of reiterating a pattern of chant with interpolations of neumes or, conversely, of omitting neumes. It would seem probable that this practice would be used by Hildegard in the sequence, since she composes her poetry in free verse containing different numbers of syllables in each of the couplet lines. Indeed we do find it. As Apel indicated, this practice was not looked upon with favor by the theoreticians and established composers of the day, but the practice is found in numerous medieval chants, including, of course, Hildegard's chants.

A somewhat thorough discussion of this practice may be found in chapter one, pages 35-38, pertaining to the antiphon *O eterne Deus*. In the sequence *O ignis spiritus paracliti,* comparison of the opening clauses of each of the paired couplets shows Hildegard's variation process, necessitated by her free verse. Pitches have been lined up to show the similarities.

Clauses 1a1 and 1b1:

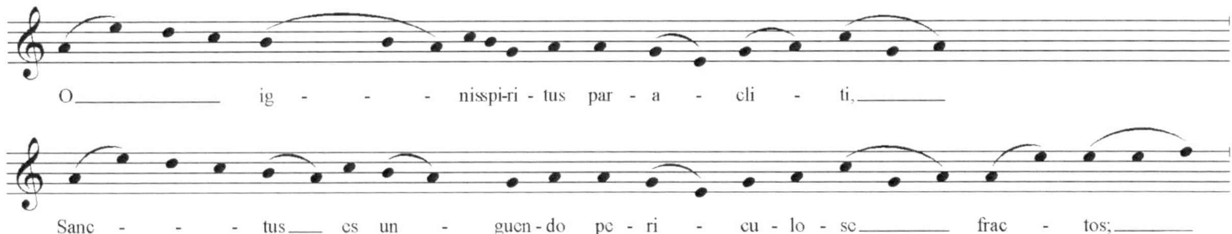

-- Clause 1b1 interpolates two pitches on "-tus es"
-- Clause 1b1 omits (truncates) two pitches on "unguendo"
-- Clause 1b1 adds two neumes to finish the text of the clause (extension), "fractos"

Clauses 2a1 and 2b1:

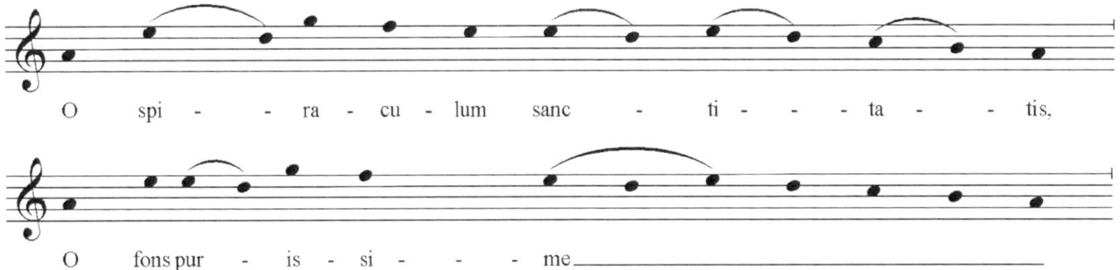

-- Clause 2b1 interpolates one additional punctum for the word "fons"
-- Clause 2b1 omits (truncates) one E5 found in 2a1 on "saeculum"

Clauses 3a1-2 and 3b1-2

Two clauses are combined for each part of the couplet to show the length of the nearly identical reiteration:

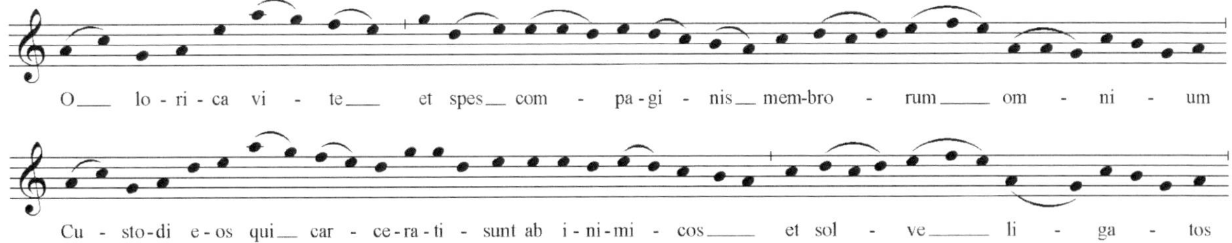

-- Clause 3b2 adds a G5 on "carcerati"
-- Clause 3b3 omits an agogic accent on A4 on "ligatos"

Clauses 4a1-2 and 4b1-2

Again, two clauses are shown for each part of the couplet, here showing elision and considerable extension in 4b1 and 4b2.

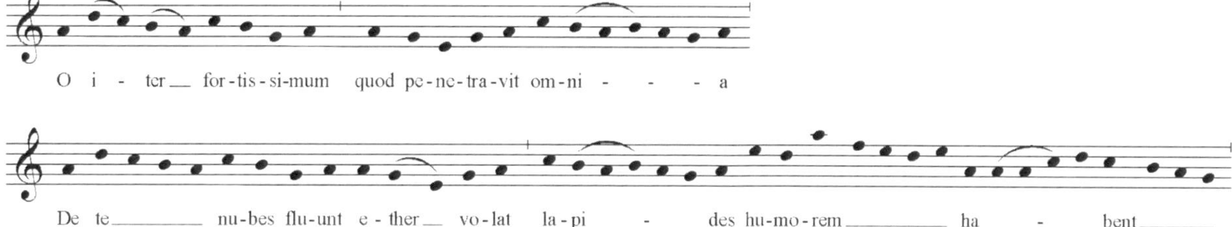

-- Clause 4b1 is identical to 4a1 and the beginning of 4a2, eliding the pitches from the first two 4a clauses to complete the 4b1 clause

-- Clause 4b2 (after the 'tick') uses the continuation of 4a2 and then extends the melodic line for a considerable length to finish the clause of text

There is no reiteration in 5-1, 5-2 though numerous instances of motive repetition occur.

Clause 2b1 is quite similar to clause 6-1:

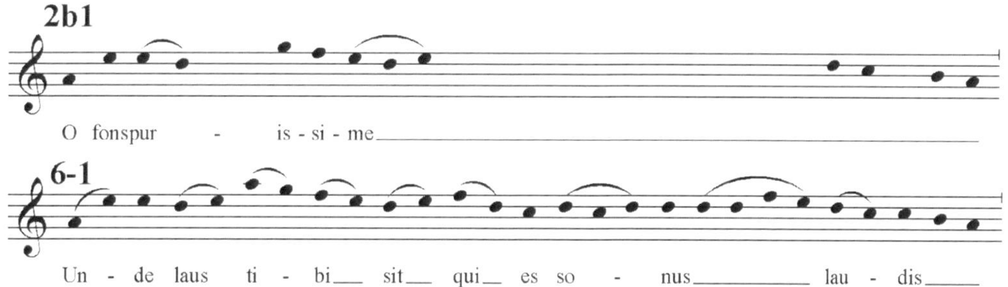

-- a rise from E5 to A5 is interpolated in 6-1

-- a considerable interpolation, due to additional syllables in the clause, occurs before the terminatio (which also has one additional C5 interpolated)

This last example is questionable as an example of reiteration. There are extensive differences and the length of the two clauses is not at all proportionate. The example does, however, show the unity with which Hildegard crafted her chants, and it also supports the effect of 'return' in the A' section.

Summary: Hildegard's Compositional Style

Well, it's time to bring all of the details and observations together and see what we have discovered about Hildegard's compositional style. I will use an orderly method of discussion introduced in the 1970's by Jan LaRue, in his book *Guidelines for Style Analysis*[139] abbreviated as "SHMRG" -- Sound, Harmony, Melody, Rhythm, and Growth. The discussion of rhythm and growth will occur in later chapters, and there will be a final summary at the end of this tome...

---

139 LaRue, Jan. *Guidelines for Style Analysis, 2nd Ed.* (Michigan: Harmonie Park Press, 1993)

Sound

1. Timbre

Since Hildegard's music was written for use in worship by the nuns in her monasteries, it is safe to assume that the primary, if not the only, timbre was that of the female voice. There is some speculation that instruments accompanied the singers (in unison or as a drone finalis of confinalis pitch), and those might be:

--the psaltery
--small drums
--the lyre
--the cithara (similar to the lyre, but larger)

All of the instruments were tuned to one specific diatonic mode.

2. Texture

Hildegard's chants are monophonic, containing only one melodic line. If instruments were used, they probably accompanied the chant line as described above, and did not have melodic figurations that sounded with the chant melody.

Texture might vary in the following ways:

a. a solo voice
b. unison choir
c. alternation of solo and choir (solo and ripieno)
d. alternation of choir and use of instruments

3. Dynamics

Again, we can only speculate as there were no symbols used to indicate dynamic levels. Dynamics, or intensity, may be changed through changes in tessitura (higher ranges are often perceived as being louder). Thus fluctuation in melodic contour would create a natural ebb and flow of dynamic level, subtle but nonetheless present.

Also, alternation between solo and chorus would create dynamic contrast.

4. Acoustics

Hildegard's churches were stone and they had no pews, so the reverberation would have been considerable. The height of the ceiling and the gabling would have added to the reverberation, possibly yielding anywhere from three to eight seconds of time for a sound to disappear. Singing in such an acoustical space very nearly creates a sense of polyphony, as the overlapping sounds decay over such a long period of time. The blend of tones creates a 'celestial harmony'!

Another element of sound affecting the end result of singing Hildegard's chants would be the Germanic pronunciation of the Latin texts. Well-enunciated 'church' Latin is not punctuated with strong consonants...the 'colloquial' Latin of Hildegard's medieval time would probably have contained many strong consonant sounds as well as exaggerated dark or light vowels.

5. Notation

Mention should be made again of the manner in which Hildegard's manuscripts were notated -- in Hufnagelschrift, a medieval German system of notation that bore many resemblances to plainsong notation, but which looked quite different (please see pp. 29-32). Hufnagelschrift is a bit more open to interpretation than traditional plainsong notation, and it is not unreasonable to assume that there might be some errors made by the scribes, so there are places where different editions of Hildegard's works might not agree. Hmmm. It does give musicologists and theorists something to argue about!

Harmony

1. Definition

The term 'harmony' does NOT refer here to the sounds made by combinations of different tones. Medieval use of the term refers to 'how' tones are grouped and organized to create a unified structure or 'framework'. It refers to the use of mode, to repeated or reiterated motives, to the unity of text and melody, and the shaping of all of these into a meaningful, 'harmonious' structure.

2. Pitch basis

Hildegard uses the modes:

O ignis spiritus paracliti -- A Aeolian and Hypoaeolian, hints of C Ionian and D Aeolian

She freely uses commixture of modes, particularly the initial mode and its plagal counterpart. There are interior instances of momentary emphasis on a 'new' finalis, but the terminatio figures of those clauses usually return to the original finalis or confinalis.

3. Harmonic structural framework

Harmonic structure is united with textual form (please see diagram on p.87)

a. the first and last sections (A and A') are similar in a retrograded fashion

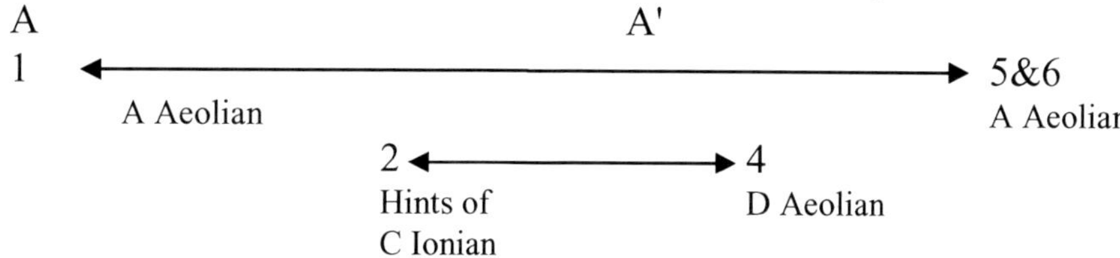

b. the middle section (B) is different from both the A and A'
- -- B has the highest consistent tessitura of the three sections
- -- B remains in A Aeolian and Hypoaeolian throughout
- -- B describes the Holy Spirit in three different ways, all protective

c. the structural framework of each section helps to delineate the form

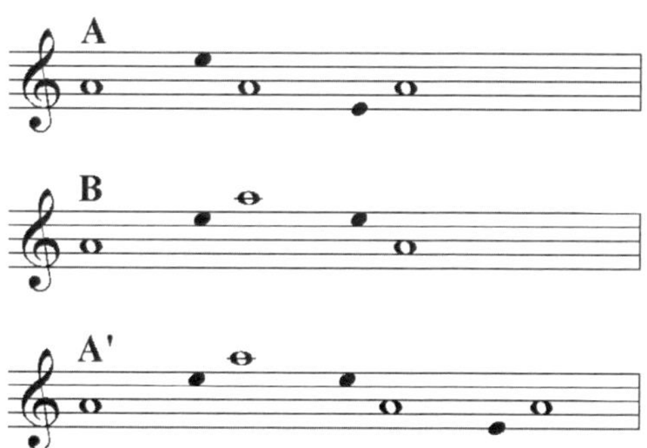

A uses primarily the species 1 pentachord, but dips to the plagal tetrachord.

B introduces the complete 'signature' P5-P4, but does not use the plagal tetrachord, maintaining a higher tessitura than A.

A' uses the entire gamut of the frameworks employed in A and B.

Thus the poetic structure of Invocation (A), Prayer (B) and Praise (A') is reflected in the growth of the structural frameworks:

-- Introduction with the incomplete 'signature' (A),
-- raising the prayer petition to the heavens (B),
-- and praising to the fullest with everything possible (A').

4. Cadence structures

Hildegard's cadences are traditional for the style of plainchant in that all cadence pitches are approached by ascending or descending step motion.

a. the majority of terminatio motives end on the finalis (25/34) -- 74%
b. four end on the confinalis (4/34) -- 12%
c. two end on the mediant C5 (one in the C Ionian region) (2/34) -- 6%
d. two end on G4 and one on F5, unusual cadences ending interior clauses of couplets, so they are not particularly strong or remarkable -- 6%, 2%

Melody

1. Ambitus

In this sequence, the ambitus extends from the lower confinalis to the diapente finalis. This yields a range that has a higher tessitura than most plainchant and is also slightly larger than most plainchant (mainly confined to an octave range).

2. Contour

Most of the clauses in this sequence employ a wave contour. These waves are more active than traditional plainchant (which uses more arch forms, rising to the recitation tone and then returning to the starting pitch).

3. Accents

Melodic accents are of three types:

-- durational, or agogic, accents created by repeated punctae, elongating a syllable

-- pitch accents, or contoural accents:

a. the strongest are approached by leap, followed by step motion
b. gentler accents are approached and left by step motion
c. frequent accents are approached by ascending step and left by descending leaps
d. the least frequent but most dramatic are those approached by ascending leap and left by descending leap

-- gestural accents, extending a syllable with several pitches:

a. neumatic accents, containing 3-4 pitches
b. melismatic accents, containing 5 or more pitches

4. Melodic Progression

Use of P5 leaps:

-- the ascending P5 is part of Hildegard's signature though it is not a common occurrence in plainchant. The rising fifths leap to the confinalis and to the finalis in this sequence.

-- descending P5ths are also more frequently used by Hildegard than they are in plainchant, both from the confinalis and from the finalis. This allows for a smooth transition from A Aeolian to D Dorian in the final section.

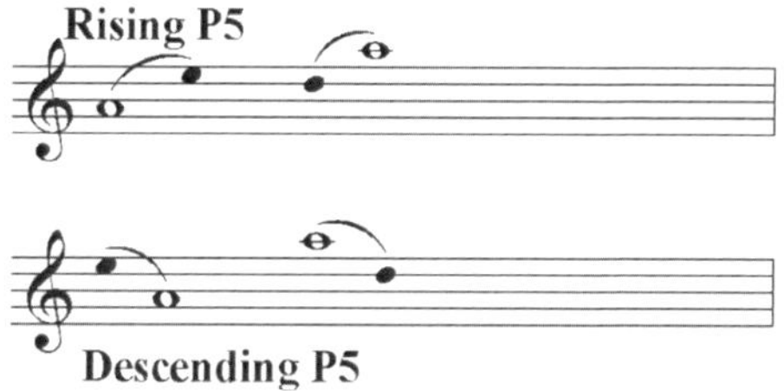

Leaps in succession:

-- two leaps in succession are used only in conjunction with the signature motive. She does not outline triads in this sequence with four exceptions

1 -- on the word 'altissimis' in verse 4a3. The outline (a d minor triad) after an ascending d-a fifth (part of a z-R motive) when she descends a m3

2 -- in the same clause immediately after the preceding outline, descending a fifth from e-a, followed by an ascending m3 to C5 (an a minor triad)

3 -- in the elided x-full motive of 4b2 on the word 'humorem', the same pattern as occurred on 'altissimis' appears.

-- and corresponding to the line described in 2 above, the connection of 'humorem' and 'habent' contains the a minor triad.

The unity of sound is obvious here, with the outlining of triads framed by the rising and falling P5ths.

Individual leaps of thirds or fourths:

-- individual leaps of thirds or fourths are most often part of one of the identified melodic motives

-- individual leaps in one direction are often balanced fairly quickly by a leap in the opposite direction

Step motion is the most common melodic progression.

Leaving the order of SHMRG for this chapter, I'm going to 'skip' the 'R' (rhythm), which is a large and speculative topic. We'll have a look at that in the next chapter. Instead, let's move on to 'G', or growth, to see Hildegard's unity in craftsmanship.

Growth

The above summary of sound, harmony and melody have given us a surface view of Hildegard's music in this sequence. The real 'meat and potatoes' (Fleisch und Kartoffelen) of Hildegard's musical language lie in the methods with which she uses pitch patterns to reflect and set the text -- and her philosophical beliefs about...everything! Particularly the relationship between God and his realm, the macrocosm, and his creation, the microcosm. Okay, this goes a bit beyond meat and potatoes... It also goes beyond simplistic composition, the application of given principles to create music which follows the rules and is performable (and often not particularly 'inspired'), music which solely serves the text or 'sets' the text. For Hildegard, text and music were one, a unity.

Hildegard didn't sit down one night and say to herself, "I think I'll write a sequence", followed by some hours spent creating the text and then figuring out how to set it to music. No, Hildegard had a vision, and in the vision she experienced the fire and passion and love and power of the Holy Spirit, something which was far beyond her own power to approach or recreate! In response to her vision, the words flowed, accompanied by interior music that must be notated, and in the process of notation, must go through the crucible of her heart and soul and mind, emerging as the very best that she had to give. Her music is a microcosm of what she experienced during her visions, a reflection of the celestial choirs -- a joining with the celestial choirs in praise, supplication and worship.

So her composition is not just 'a little night music', but something which was elemental and at the root of her belief, her being and her life. We don't know if Hildegard could write music in Hufnagelschrift herself. Her frequent comments about her own lack of education leads to the speculation that she probably did not. We also don't know if she was taught to sing using written manuscripts or if she learned the chants of the Opus Dei 'by ear'. And so we also do not know with any certainty how she offered her own chants to the scribes for permanent inscription in *Scivias* and later works. She must have sung the chants in bits and pieces numerous times so the scribes could notate what she sang. And the scribes must have sung what they notated back to Hildegard -- an aural proofreading! This was not a simple process, but one which would require and allow much fine tuning, so to speak. The scribes, who would certainly have been musicians well-versed in music and Hufnagelschrift notation, would probably question and suggest as they notated, and then sung their notation back to Hildegard for corrections and approval. So what we have in the manuscripts available are chants very likely carefully edited and approved by Hildegard <u>and</u> her scribes, works of art that have gone through rigorous compositional process and refinement, created in response to a command from the Creator.

And how do we summarize the growth patterns in this sequence, this work of art, *O ignis spiritus paracliti*? Jan LaRue offers the following investigative list to which I have inserted summative findings regarding information recorded in detail earlier in this chapter.

1. **the background, or large-scale framework**
   a. sectional construction/connections
   b. foundational harmonic framework

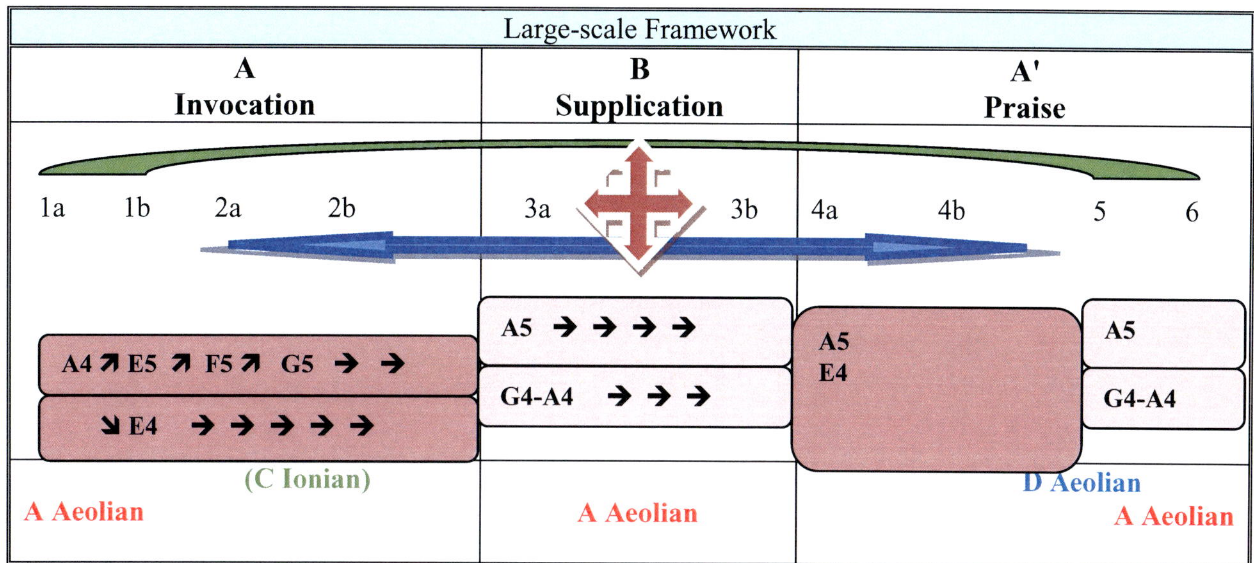

Hildegard's large-scale framework is a circular palindrome, founded on the Aeolian mode. It contains three sections reflecting the common prayer form of Invocation, Supplication, Praise (faith, hope, love). The last section contains elements of the first two sections, so the growth pattern of the whole sequence moves to the beginning of the A',

-- where Hildegard uses all of her motives,

-- where the Golden Section occurs on 'omnia' (preceded by the first palindrome motive 'y' used since the 1b verse)

-- where she uses triad outlines on A and D ('altissimis)

-- where she uses the full ambitus of pitches for the first time, E4 up to A5.

2. **the delineation of musical form**
   a. sectional harmonic framework (shown in the table above)
   b. repetition and reiteration

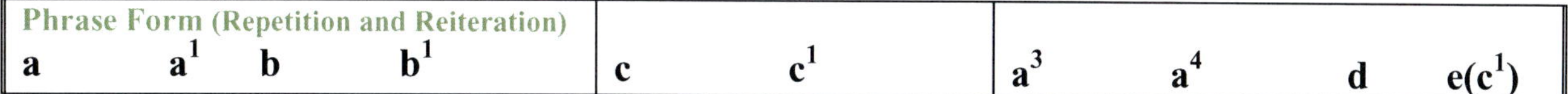

Phrase Form (Repetition and Reiteration)									
a	a^1	b	b^1	c	c^1	a^3	a^4	d	$e(c^1)$

A graph of the phrase form for the sequence further supports the Large-scale Framework and shows Hildegard's respect for the established form of the sequence, at least in her musical writing (the poetic text does not rhyme or share meter). Her musical repetition is always varied repetition. It also shows:

-- Hildegard's individuality in leaving the established form of the sequence after using three contrasting musically paired couplets by reiterating a varied form of the first couplet -- a return!

-- introducing new melodic elements in the fifth verse (and a new finalis!)

-- creating a second 'return' in the sixth verse, bringing back the full 'x' motive in a phrase quite similar to c^1 (3a3). This is most unusual for chant (please refer to the score).

c. changes of range (shown in the table above)
d. hierarchies of stress (closure and non-closure)

Terminatio motives for verses 1 & 2	**Terminatio motives for v. 3**	**Terminatio motives for verses 4, 5 & 6**
1a1, z 1b1, open 2a1, 2↘1 2b1, 2↘1 1a2, z 1b2, z 2a2, z-full 2b2, z-full 2a3, z 2b3, open 2a4, 7↗1 2b4, z-full	3a1, 6 ↘ 5 3b1, 2↘1 3a2, z-full 3b2, z-full 3a3, z 3b3, z	4a1, z-full 4b1, 7↗1 5-1, open 6-1, 2↘1 4a2, 7↗1 4b2, open 5-2, 6↘5 6-2, 6↘5 4a3, open 4b3, 7↗1 5-3. 7↗1 6-3, 4↗5 4a4, 7↗1 4b4, z 6-4, z-full 4a5, z

The table above shows all thirty-four cadences, or closures in the sequence. Full closures are those ending on the finalis (including 'z' and 'z-full' as well as those ending on '1').

Half closures end on the confinalis ('5'). The 'open' ends of phrases are those mentioned earlier (please see p. 112 "Cadences").

-- the A section is very stable, with only two clauses ending on something other than the finalis.
-- the B section opens with a question, and then all clauses end on the finalis.
-- the A' section is not only the longest section, it has the most active motion, with six clauses ending on the confinalis or pitches other than the finalis. Most of the non-closures occur in verses 5 and 6.

Adding the above 'middleground' elements to the diagram gives more information:

Large-scale Framework		
A **Invocation**	**B** **Supplication**	**A'** **Praise**
1a 1b 2a 2b	3a 3b	4a 4b 5 6
A4 ↗ E5 ↗ F5 ↗ G5 → → **↘ E4 → → → → →**	**A5 → → → →** **G4-A4 → → → →**	**A5** **E4** **A5** **G4-A4**
(C Ionian) **A Aeolian**	**A Aeolian**	**D Aeolian** **A Aeolian**
Middleground Elements		
Phrase Form (Repetition and Reiteration) **a a^{1} b b^{1}**	**c c^{1}**	**a^{3} a^{4} d e(c^{1})**

Terminatio motives for verses 1 & 2	**Terminatio motives for v. 3**	**Terminatio motives for verses 4, 5 & 6**
1a1, z 1b1, open 2a1, 2↘1 2b1, 2↘1 1a2, z 1b2, z 2a2, z-full 2b2, z-full 2a3, z 2b3, open 2a4, 7↗1 2b4, z-full	3a1, 6 ↘ 5 3b1, 2↘1 3a2, z-full 3b2, z-full 3a3, z 3b3, z	4a1, z-full 4b1, 7↗1 5-1, open 6-1, 2↘1 4a2, 7↗1 4b2, open 5-2, 6↘5 6-2, 6↘5 4a3, open 4b3, 7↗1 5-3. 7↗1 6-3, 4↗5 4a4, 7↗1 4b4, z 6-4, z-full 4a5, z

3. compositional practice

a. elasticity, or variation within repetition and reiteration

-- motives and motivic development Hildegard uses four repeated or reiterated motives in the sequence, and four identifiable variations of those motives, for a total of eight:

x -- an incomplete signature motive, used at the beginning of clauses. There is one occurrence within a clause, in 1b1 (the result of elision)

x-full -- the complete signature motive followed by descent to the confinalis

y -- a palindrome figure descending from the finalis to the lower confinalis

z -- a 3-note terminatio figure, also transposed and used within clauses

z-full -- a 4-note terminatio used within clauses as well as at the end

z-R -- the retrograde of the 3-note z, used within clauses and to begin clauses on different pitch levels

t -- a neighbor tone motive, the torculus neume, used ascending and descending. This motive is sometimes elongated with an agogic accent on the first pitch

Use and Frequency of Motives

a	**a^1**	**b**	**b^1**	**c**	**c^1**	**a^3**	**a^4**	**d**	**$e(c^1)$**
x - 2	x - 2	x - 1	x - 1			x - 1	x - 1		
				x-full - 2	x-full - 1		x-full - 1		x-full - 2
y - 2	y - 2					y - 3	y - 3		
z - 4	z - 3	z - 1	z - 1	z - 2	z - 1	z - 1	z - 1		
z-full - 1		z-full - 1	z-full - 2	z-full - 1	z-full - 1	z-full - 1	z-full - 1		z-full - 2
		z-R - 2	z-R - 1	z-R - 1	z-R - 2	z-R - 1	z-R - 1	z-R - 2	
		t↑ - 1	t↑ - 1	t↑ - 1	t↑ - 1	t↑ - 3	t↑ - 2	t↑ - 1	
			t↓ - 2	t↓ - 1	t↓ - 2	t↓ - 4	t↓ - 4	t↓ - 2	t↓ - 1

By studying the graph, some practices become readily apparent:

-- the sequence is unified through the use of the eight motives

-- growth is evident in the additive process applied to the use of the different motives:

a,a1 = 4, b1 = 5, b2 = 6 c,c1 = 6 a3 = 7, a4 = 8 → d,e = 5 →

-- Hildegard always varies her repetitions and reiterations. No two phrases contain the same number or pattern of motives.

-- thematic development.

Please see pp. 101-103 for a discussion of Hildegard's practice of elision and interpolated reiteration. The extent to which Hildegard employs these techniques was unusual for her time, something which distinguishes her compositional style from plainchant and from other composers.

-- destabilization of mode, use of musica ficta.

The Aeolian mode on A is destabilized slightly in the second verse, 2a, 2b. The recitation tones become C and E, with rises to G apex notes. The terminatio all return to the A finalis, though, so there is only a 'hint' of C Ionian.

Hildegard uses musica ficta sparingly, and in this sequence only in the last section. It does not appear until verse five, where there is a subtle movement to D Aeolian. The end of the phrase returns to A, but with a Phrygian cadence, thanks to the musica ficta B^b.

The final phrase uses a commixture of A Aeolian (B natural) and A Phrygian (B^b), concluding with an extended termination of two z-full patterns, the first Phrygian and the second Aeolian!

-- rhetoric (word painting)

Hildegard does not 'paint' certain words, though she does emphasize them:

-- applying melismatic elongations
-- using high or low contoural accents
-- reiteration of important motives

4. melodic and harmonic growth based upon the above observations

The diagram developed throughout this summary serves as the final summation of Hildegard's architecture for this sequence. Adding a final graphing of the structural high and low pitches yields the final diagram of the growth of the sequence.

-- there is a gradual rise in the melodic line from the confinalis to the diapente. The melodic line never exceeds that apex pitch. Though it retreats from it, there are returns to it for the remainder of the sequence.

-- after the initial descent to the lower confinalis in 1a and 1b, the lower range of the sequence does not return to that pitch until the final section's 4a and 4b. The ambitus then remains G4-A5 through verses five and six.

-- the structural melodic line, ambitus, and additive process of motives all lead to thereturn of the 'a' phrases in the last section.

-- "omnia" is the Golden Section of the prayer text
-- "altissimis" is the apex of the return phrase 4a. It contains the two triad outlines on D and A.
-- three appearances of 'y' bring back the lower tetrachord E4-A4.
-- Hildegard uses seven of the eight motives in 4a, and brings in the eighth motive in 4b

-- a fairly quick 'retreat' follows the arrival in 4a-4b.

-- no 'x' motives are used in verse 5
-- musica ficta is introduced in verse 5, as is the D Aeolian mode
-- fewer motives are used, lightening the density of reiteration found in 4a and 4b
-- phrase 6 acts as a final return, bringing back the 'x-full' motive and summing up the final section with the double termination figure using both the Phrygian and Aeolian forms.

The final diagram with the growth graph at the bottom:

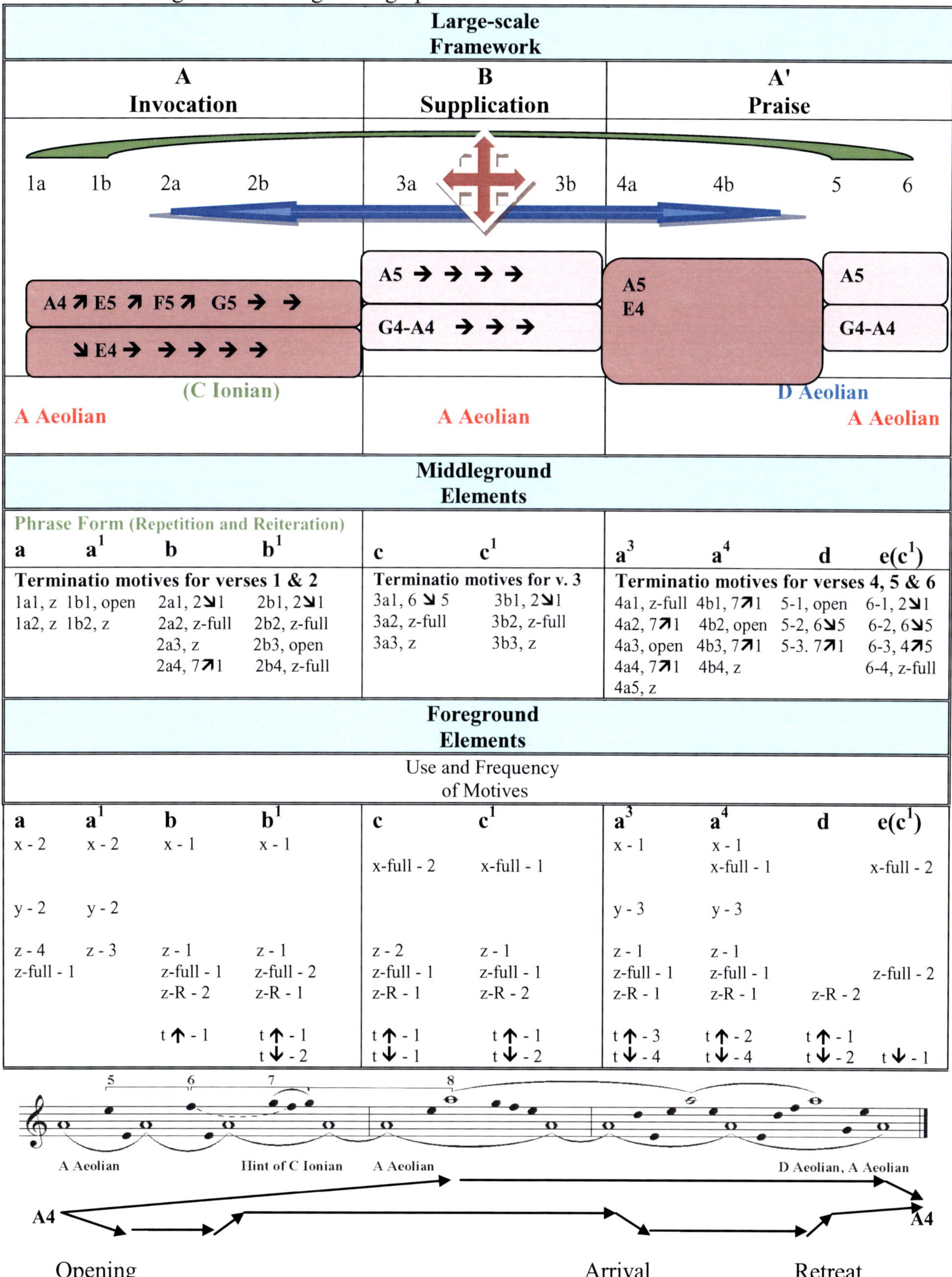

Well...WooHoo! Woot![140] You've just been 'SHMGed'! Hopefully you can appreciate and grow to love -- and use -- this sequence on a deeper, more intimate and personal level. We can also speculate about some things too, always an enjoyable rumination!

Perhaps Hildegard used repetition and reiteration of motives so much as a means to help her sisters learn and remember the chant. Her melodies flow so beautifully and naturally, largely in part due to this varied repetition and reiteration. It is really remarkable how she creates such unity of sound within a work which has no exact repetition (unlike the more rigorously trained composers in the major musical centers of the time). She successfully creates 'freedom within boundaries', predating Debussy and Stravinsky by nearly a thousand years with her 'mosaic' melodic construction. Her music 'works' because of the boundaries she chooses and then uses so well, her large-scale formal structure and her use of reiterated and varied melodic patterns. The melodic frameworks that govern her phrase structures, coupled with the growth toward a jubilant, all-inclusive spiritual shout of praise take this sequence far beyond the utilitarian or 'normal' musical setting of text! Hildegard breathes and lives the thoughts, emotions, and beauty of the text as she melds it to music -- a unity that is truly unique, remarkable and God-given. Let's meditate on this fiery spirit!

Meditation

O spirit of fire, bringer of comfort, life of the life of every creature,
you are holy...[141]

Sit quietly and sink into the image.

This image contains a blue heart in the center. How does this image reflect Hildegard's vision of the 'Man in Sapphire Blue'?

Recall the first time you were aware of the activity of the Holy Spirit in your life.

How has the fiery spirit affected your life as:

-- as the bringer of comfort
-- as the life of your life
-- as a breath of holiness
-- as the fire of love
-- as a sweet savor in your heart
-- as a clear fountain
-- as a breastplate
-- as hope
-- as a belt of honor
-- as a reconciler and unifier

Read Hildegard's poem slowly as a prayer, reflecting on how each phrase relates to your life.

---

[140] Terms learned from Facebook...

[141] From Hildegard von Bingen, *O ignis spiritus paracliti*. Translation by Susan Hellauer, *Op. Cit.*

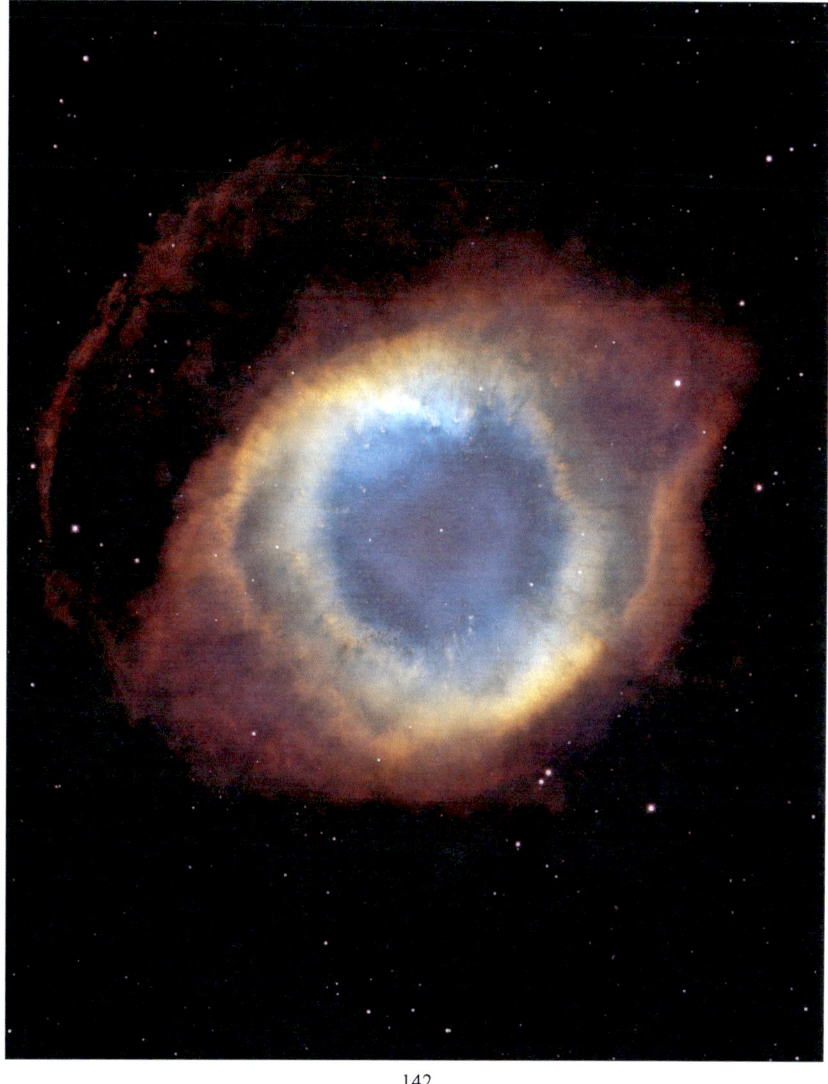

142

I offer an older work for this meditation, one written in response to the discovery of some of the oldest parts of the universe through the COBE space telescope. 2.73 was the kelvin temperature of the background matter spread throughout the new universe shortly after the 'big bang', and it is an active imagination work – what it might be like to be with the Holy Spirit watching creation happening.

---

[142] This composite image is a view of the colorful Helix Nebula taken with the Advanced Camera for Surveys aboard NASA's Hubble Space Telescope and the Mosaic II Camera on the 4-meter telescope at Cerro Tololo Inter-American Observatory in Chile. The object is so large that both telescopes were needed to capture a complete view. The Helix is a planetary nebula, the glowing gaseous envelope expelled by a dying, sun-like star. The Helix resembles a simple doughnut as seen from Earth. But looks can be deceiving. New evidence suggests that the Helix consists of two gaseous disks nearly perpendicular to each other. One possible scenario for the Helix's complex structure is that the dying star has a companion star. One disk may be perpendicular to the dying star's spin axis, while the other may lie in the orbital plane of the two stars. The Helix, located 690 light-years away, is one of the closest planetary nebulas to Earth. The Hubble images were taken on November 19, 2002; the Cerro Tololo images on Sept. 17-18, 2003.
Credit: NASA, ESA, C.R. O'Dell (Vanderbilt University), M. Meixner and P. McCullough (STScI)
http://hubblesite.org/newscenter/archive/releases/2004/32/image/d/

for Teresa Hrachovy Grawunder

2.73

Ann K. Gebuhr

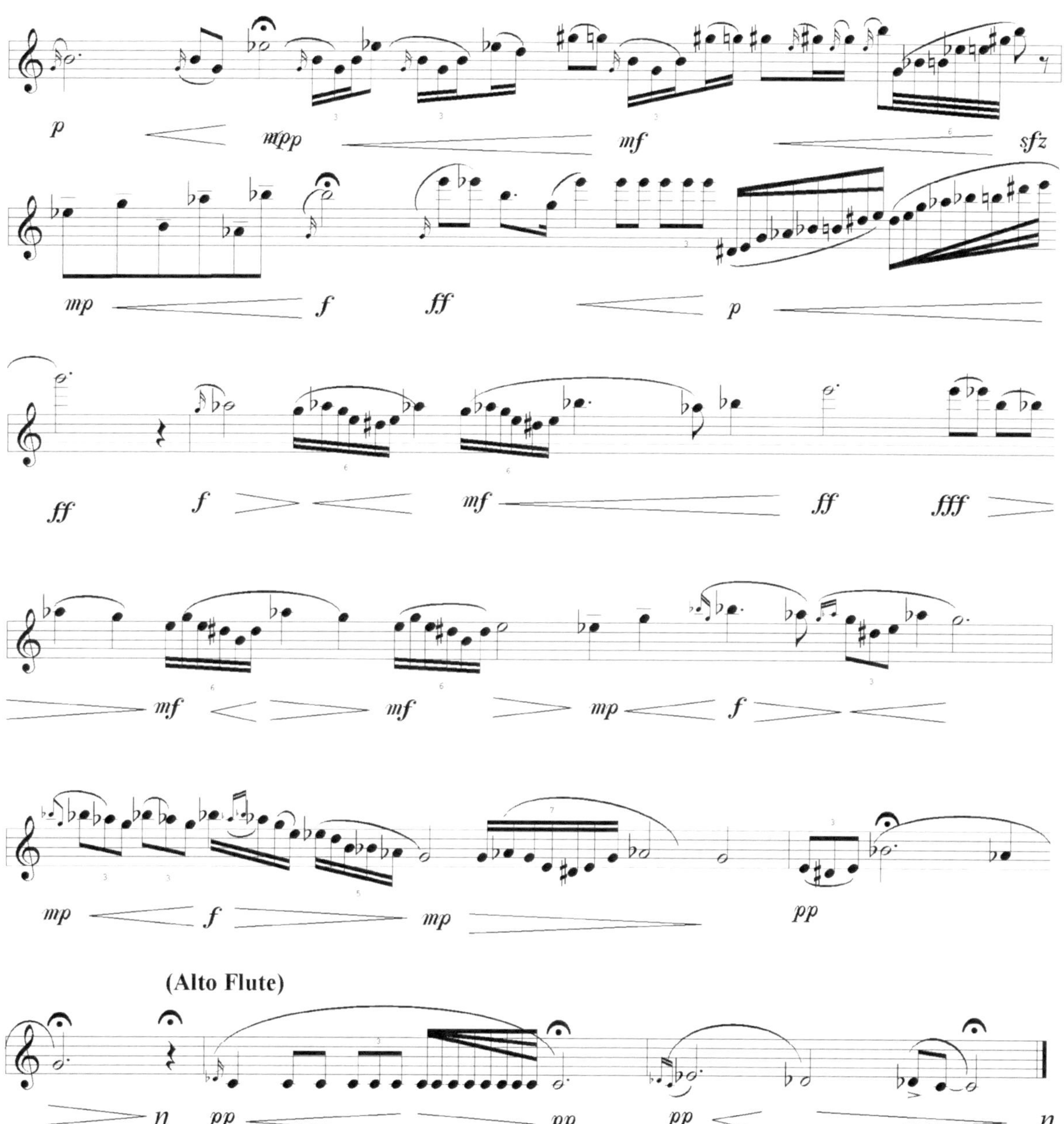
(Alto Flute)

Exercise

So far we have been doing deep breathing exercises and energetic walking. Let's add some stretching exercises to the breathing and walking, exercises that will help you loosen your muscles and limber up your joints. It would be most beneficial to do the deep breathing first, then follow with some of these stretches, and then interrupt your walk (at least thirty minutes now, right?) with some more stretches and breathing.

Complete between five and ten repetitions of each of these stretches.

1. Balance yourself on one foot, holding on to a pole or tree. Circle your raised foot five to ten times slowly. Circle in both directions. Change position and circle the other foot.

2. Stand with your knees loose and your hands out at a right angle from your elbow. Circle your hands from the wrist just as you did the ankles. Go five to ten times in both directions.

3. Stand with your feet positioned straight ahead and below your shoulders. Rise up as high as possible on your toes and count slowly to five before lowering yourself slowly. After doing the above five to ten times, stand in the same position and raise your toes as high as possible, balancing on your heels. Do this slowly, holding your position with the toes up as far as possible for a slow five-count.

4. Balance yourself with a tree or pole, and bring your right knee up to a 90 degree angle. Hold for five seconds and slowly lower your foot to the ground. After doing this five-ten times, repeat with your left knee.

5. Balance yourself again and lift your right foot backwards, forming a right angle with your thigh (both of your knees should be in the same upright position. Hold for five seconds and slowly return your foot to the ground. Repeat with the left foot.

6. Slightly flex your knees, pull in your stomach, and twist your shoulders and chest as far as you can to the right, keeping your hips, face, knees and feet facing forward. Hold for five seconds, feeling the abdominal stretch, and slowly rotate back. Do this rotating to the left too.

We'll add some more of these later. When you interrupt your walk with these stretches, pay attention to your body during walking and then choose from these stretches to loosen whichever part of your body seems to be tight or under duress.

Always, in exercise, pay attention to what your body is saying to you! Don't push certain exercises too far beyond your comfort zone -- you don't want to hurt yourself! Try to increase the energy and amount of each exercise every three to four days, and build up to a solid 30-45 minute walk with an additional 15 minutes of breathing and stretching. The consistency of daily exercise will pay huge dividends in health and mobility!

Recipes

Breakfast

So many of us don't take the time to eat breakfast (I'm guilty of this often...), so here is a recipe for a cold cereal easily made with whatever fruits you have on hand. It's delicious, fresh, helps lower cholesterol, and it isn't full of sugar.

Oatmeal Muesli

½ C 'quick' rolled oats
raisins, berries, dried fruit pieces to taste
chopped almonds or hazelnuts
cinnamon to taste
pinch of galangal
teaspoon of honey if desired
Mix together with cold milk, soy creamer, or goat's milk to a thick porridge consistency
(if you add too much liquid, it becomes breakfast cereal...)
Top with fresh berries of the season

Lunch

If you use the chapter one recipe for baked salmon, add an extra piece and then save it in the refrigerator for lunch.

Baked Salmon Capresi Salad

6-10 leaves of baby spinach or other fresh salad greens
1 ripe, organic heirloom (or other vine-ripened) tomato, cut in wedges
3 large leaves of basil, cut in thirds
2-3 small balls of fresh mozzarella, sliced in half or thirds
freshly ground sea salt and black pepper to taste
mix 3-4 tablespoons of olive or almond oil with 1-2 tablespoons of balsamic vinegar
1 piece of baked salmon, cut into bite-sized pieces or served whole over the salad
Toss all ingredients together and serve with hard breadsticks or crackers -- and a nice glass of cold pinot grigio!

Dinner

This recipe is for one person, but you can double and triple it and invite friends! It is very easy to do, does not take much time, and is delicious -- and healthy!

Whitefish with a White Wine Sauce

1 fish filet (trout, tilapia, catfish, perch, etc.)
spelt flour to coat the fish (maybe 3 Tbs.)
2-4 Tbs. coconut oil
Freshly ground sea salt and black pepper to taste
¼ C. dry white wine (how about some of the pinot grigio from lunch?!)
1 Tbs. heavy cream (the only 'sin', but it's small...)
a pinch of saffron
a pinch of galingal
chopped parsely and one green onion for garnish

Coat the fish with the spelt flour, season with salt and pepper and saute in a small pan for 4-5 minutes on each side. Be careful to not overcook or burn the fish! Remove the fish and set aside. Add the wine to the pan and thicken it with the cream, adding the saffron and galingale. Serve the sauce over the fish and garnish with the parsely and onion.

Serving this with cold, raw beet slices or a large, beautiful radish with some good real pumpernickel bread and blue cheese -- and a nice glass of white wine, will put a smile on your face!

IV.
Hildegard the Healer

So far we have learned about Hildegard's life, we have examined and prayed about four of her visions, and we've read a lot about and listened to some of her music. It becomes clearer and clearer as we learn and experience more of her life and work, that she lived her life to the fullest, using the gifts bestowed upon her at birth to their fullest, and that she made no distinction between those gifts. One was no greater or more important than another (except maybe music...😎...). Once she was 'freed' by command of the voice of the Living Light to write down all that she saw and heard...my goodness! The quantity and quality of her work from that time on was extraordinary. She was not following a chosen 'career path', focusing on one particular discipline. Not at all. Within the boundaries of God's command to write everything, she had total freedom to be the vessel through which amazing works of music, medicine, theology, art, and spirituality literally poured forth onto wax tablets and then vellum, all refined by her open heart and mind and her rather incredible creative abilities.

As a Benedictine, her work in the hospices and clinics of her monasteries was an important part of the life of those communities. In his 'Rule', St. Benedict specifies that:

> Care of the sick must rank above and before all else, so that they may truly be served as Christ, for he said: *I was sick and you visited me* (Matthew 25:36) and *What you did for one of these least brothers you did for me* (Matthew 25:40). Let the sick on their part bear in mind that they are served out of honor for God, and let them not by their excessive demands distress their brothers who serve them...[143]

Hildegard not only cared for the sick, she taught her sisters how to treat a multitude of illnesses and wounds and encapsulated those treatments within a spiritual discipline that served the whole 'microcosm'. And then she wrote all of it down, in the form of two books (which may at one time have been a single large medical resource). Those books are *Causae et Curae* and *Physica*.[144]

Before digging into Hildegard's medicine – and medieval medicine in general – some information about the Benedictine monasteries of the time is in order. The monasteries were constructed to contain everything necessary to carry out their mission. A good example is the St. Gall monastery in Switzerland (remember Tuotilo and Notker?? See pp. 44-46).

---

[143] *The Rule of St. Benedict,* ed. and tr. Timothy Fry, O.S.B. (Collegeville, MN: The Liturgical Press, 1981), p.235.

[144] Both books have been translated into English:
Palmquist, Mary and John Kulas, OSB, eds. *Holistic Healing* (Collegeville, MN: The Liturgical Press, 1994)
Throop, Priscilla, tr. *Hildegard von Bingen's Physica* (Rochester, VT: Healing Arts Press, 1998)

St. Gall was founded during the 7th and 8th centuries, and it is active still at the present time. This aerial photograph shows the central location of the monastery, surrounded by medieval, then Renaissance, Baroque and more contemporary circles of growth. The architectural plan of St. Gall today is understandably altered from that of its 8th Century beginnings, but it has maintained the centrality of the monastery church. A 'floor plan' of the monastery as it was during Hildegard's time is a further exhibit of the emphasis placed upon hospitality and care for the poor and sick.

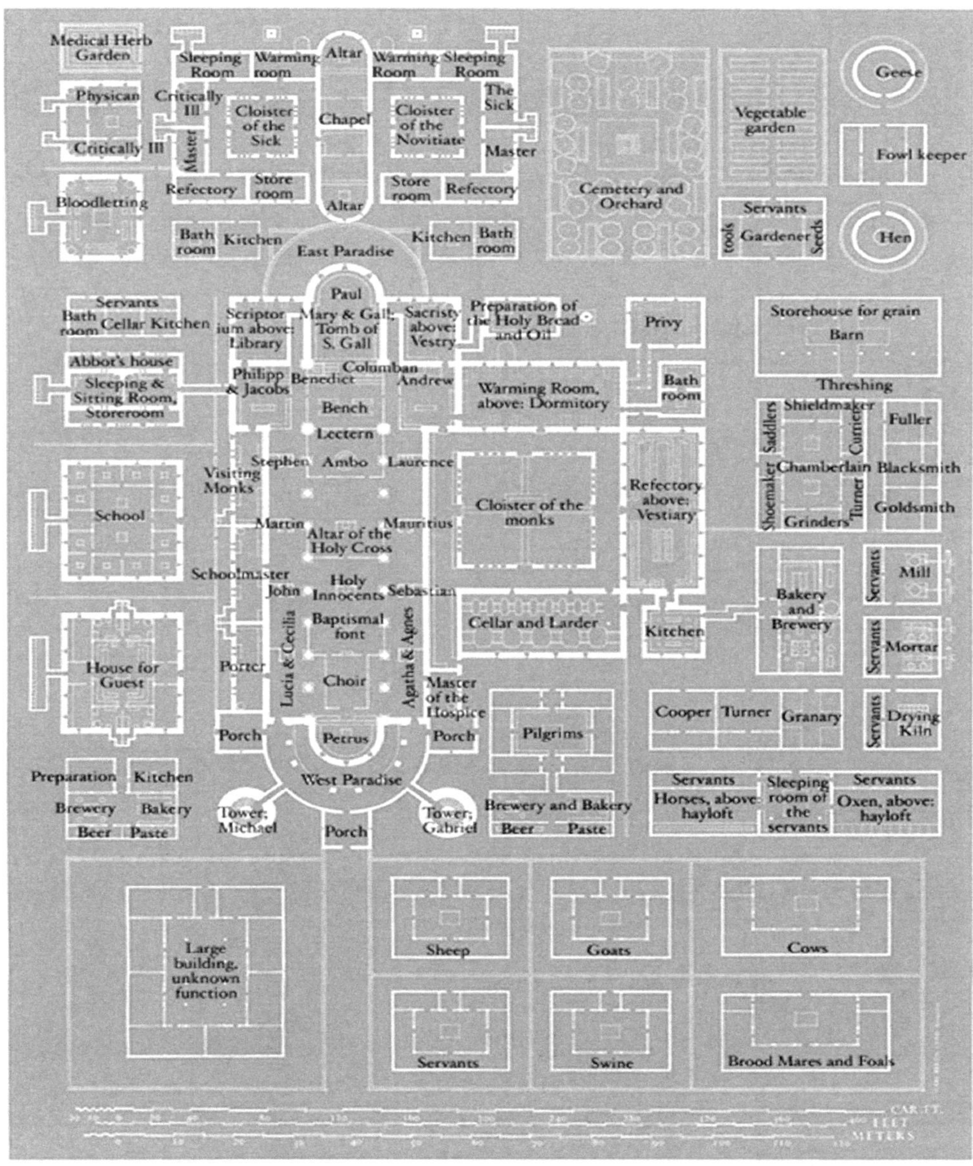

St. Gall as it was in the 11th – 12th centuries[145]

---

[145] http://www.stgallplan.org/en/index.html This site is a collaboration of UCLA and the University of Virginia, funded primarily by the Andrew Mellon Foundation. It is a fascinating site, yielding much more information about St.Gall.

This image is also from St. Gall[146], showing another very important structure in most monasteries – the library! Judging from the room decor, this image is from a period later than Hildegard's, but the size and import of the library was very probably quite close to this depiction. The Scriptorium at St. Gall is directly above the library. In the Scriptorium, monks prepared, copied, and repaired manuscripts which were then transferred to the library or sent to other monasteries or to persons who had requested them.

In the top right corner of the 'floor plan' is the indication of a medicinal herb garden. These gardens were the apothecaries for the monasteries, living pharmacies from which appropriate herbs were harvested to make the medicines to treat disease and illness.

When I was young, reading was one of my primary joys, and I remember reading many books about native Americans and early American pioneers. Included were stories of healing practices and of young boys or girls who were identified as healers, learning which plants or trees or animals, insects, mushrooms, lichens, etc. to use in treating different illnesses or wounds. The knowledge of the plants, animals, insects or other substances was, in these stories, handed down from an older master or shaman to the young person in an apprenticeship relationship. The medicinal herbs and other materials were always gathered from nature, and were indigenous to the area in which the community lived. The connection between humans and the earth was direct, respectful and co-dependent. If humans showed no respect for what the earth provided and abused the earth and its creatures, they had no means by which they could heal themselves.

In Europe, the monasteries enhanced the art of healing by cultivating gardens of plants that were used for healing purposes. This happened long before the 'discovery' of the new world and the beginnings of mass immigration. The Benedictine monasteries grew plants which were indigenous to their geographical areas, but since the Benedictines expanded and developed monasteries all over Europe, many plants that were particular to one area were 'imported' through the system of monasteries to other areas. By Hildegard's time, there was a rather large 'list' of plants that were known for particular diseases or wounds – with few if any side effects! And not only plants, but animal and mineral products too.

Monasteries continue the practice of growing medicinal herbs today. There are two 'Hildegarten' locations in Bingen, one along the Rhine attached to the Hildegard Museum, and another up on the Rochusberg near the Hildegard Forum, close to the St. Rochus-kapelle (for a long time Hildegard's memorial chapel and tomb). The gardens are carefully – and beautifully! – laid out, serving to comfort not only the diseases for which the plants are used but also the person who works in the

[146] http://commons.wikimedia.org/wiki/Commons:Reusing_content_outside_Wikimedia

garden or who visits the garden. The careful respect with which they are planned and tended is yet another acknowledgement of the co-dependent interconnection of earth, air, fire and water with humanity (the microcosm).

In the Bingen garden, each section of the garden is identified according to Hildegard's nomenclature in *Physica*. The image to the left shows one of the placards which explain the use of the plants in that section of the garden ("Of warm Blood and black Gall"). Further, as is the case in most herb gardens, each plant is identified.

The Hildegarten near the St. Rochus-kapelle was larger and 400 to 500 feet higher in elevation. Bingen and Eibingen are located on the Rhine near the confluence of the Main and the Nahe rivers. This part of Germany is a rich, fertile wine district, and the hills on either side of the rivers are a tapestry of vinyards. These photos were taken in July of 2009 during a visit to the Abtei St. Hildegard in Eibingen. Both of these gardens are centered around a fountain, the one in Bingen being a serpentine 'path' of water, and this one showing a more traditional fountain resting on a bed of rocks.

During the 18th and 19th centuries, medical practice began to grow into what is today our current employment of compounded drugs, antibiotics, and treatments used to alleviate the symptoms of diseases or to remove diseases from the human body. Herbal medicine was largely discarded in favor of the 'new' medical practices and discoveries. But recently there has been interest and movement toward rediscovering the values and natural healing properties of the earlier 'holistic' medicine. In combination with current practices, what a strong and healthy healing process that conjunction offers to our needy, ailing culture and society!

Hildegard's Medicine

Hildegard presents to us two parallel 'paths' for human existence. The first is the cosmic path of creation followed by the fall into sin and then salvation of the soul through Christ's redemption. The second is the 'earthly' path of birth, earthly life, and death:

1. Creation → The Fall into Sin → Salvation through Christ
2. Birth → Earthly Life → Death[147]

These two paths course their way throughout Hildegard's book *Causes and Cures*, infused with her vision and teaching that humans are a microcosm of the macrocosm. Everything in nature and in the cosmos is present in humanity as part of the divine image in which we were created.

Hildegard's approach to healing and the methods, techniques and medicines she used were not haphazardly learned or 'passed on' to her. They were not 'folk medicine' or shamanic, visionary medicine. Her treatments and writings were grounded firmly on the practice of medieval medicine as developed over the centuries from ancient Greek medical practice and theory. Medicine was part of the academic program of Medieval universities and schools and there were numerous books and other resources on the subject gathered and refined over at least two millennia. Hildegard's two books are part of that line of discovery and research.

A foundational precept of medieval medicine involved the 'Doctrine of the Humors'. This doctrine probably was initiated in ancient Egypt or Mesopotamia, but it was Hippocrates who formalized it into the basis for medical diagnosis and treatment. The humors were four different types of bodily fluid which had direct effects on the personality traits, or 'temperaments' of the human being.

---

[147] Margret Berger. *Hildegard of Bingen on Natural Philosophy and Medicine.* (D.S. Brewer, Cambridge, 1999) p.14

Manuscript Illustration, 14th Century

MS C. 54, Zentralbibliothek Zurich,
The Four Humors. The ancient doctrine of the Four Humors, as illustrated in this medieval manuscript, stated that there were four basic human temperaments (above, clockwise): phlegmatic, sanguine, melancholic, and choleric.

To these temperaments were added a number of other categories which aided in treatment of an imbalance of the humors– a practice which continued to the 17th century!

Temperament	**Melancholic**	**Sanguine**	**Choleric**	**Phlegmatic**
Humor	Black bile	Blood	Yellow bile	Phlegm
Element	Earth	Air	Fire	Water
Organ	Spleen	Heart	Liver	Brain
Season	Autumn	Spring	Summer	Winter
Cardinal point	West	East	South	North
Fever[148]	Quartan	Continuous	Tertian	Quotidian
Phase of life	Old age	Adolescence	Prime	Childhood
Quality	Cold and Dry	Warm and moist	Warm and dry	Cold and moist

An aside is proper here. To understand Hildegard's appropriation and use of this medical foundation, we must remember Hildegard's era...the twelfth century. Copernicus did not turn the world upside down, so to speak, until the publication of his book *De revolutionibus orbium*

---

148 **Fever:** Intermittent fever is present only for some hours in a day, remaining normal for the remaining hours. When fever occurs daily, it is quotidian, every alternate day, it is tertian and every third day, it is quartan.

coelestium (*On the Revolutions of the Celestial Spheres*) in 1543. That book initiated the scientific revolution and decentralized the position of the earth in the known universe. Up to that point, the earth was believed to be flat (with four corners), and the sun, moon, planets and stars were believed to revolve around the earth. Ancient astrology was based upon this belief, ancient wisdom and science were based on this belief, and ancient religious theology taught and presumed this to be true. It does bring into sharper focus Hildegard's microcosm/macrocosm and universal interconnectivity visions. The Divine Image, the microcosm, is at the center of the universe which is God.

The discovery by Copernicus does not, certainly, negate and disprove all of the knowledge and teaching that had been accomplished before his time. He did bring about an enormous change in the direction knowledge and understanding of the earth and the universe was to take (an understatement!), and as is the case with most revolutionary ideas much was rejected and lost in the furious energy of research and investigation of new discoveries resulting from his discovery and writings. But the universe is balanced! And the balance reasserts itself in so many ways – perhaps (hopefully) the resurgence in interest about natural means of treatment and healing will eventually bring a synthesis of scientific medicine with natural medicine. Well, back to the Doctrine of the Humors!

There were three categories of affects which 'affected' the humors. Those categories are:

1. Res naturales: seven natural affects.
    1) Elements,
    2) qualities,
    3) humors,
    4) parts of the body,
    5) faculties,
    6) spirits, and
    7) temperaments.
2. Res non naturales: six lifestyle effects.
    1) Air,
    2) food and drink,
    3) evacuation and repletion,
    4) sleep and waking,
    5) rest and motion, and
    6) the passions of the mind.
3. Res praeter naturam: three pathogenic effects.
    1) Disease,
    2) its causes, and
    3) its symptoms.

In Hildegard's practice of medicine the first category, Res naturales, played an especially crucial role in diagnosis and treatment. The four elements had been defined in the 5th century B.C. as the 'roots of all things' and the humors had been correlated to their organ of origin.[149] Already, in the study of her visions and illuminations, we have seen the prominent role of the elements and the cardinal points in the symbology of the visions. And the humors become equally symbolic and crucial.

---

[149] Berger, *Op. Cit.*, p. 16

The second category, Res non naturales, was also an important consideration in both diagnosis and treatment. And the third of course was fundamental to her suggestions for treatment. In all three categories, Hildegard included spirituality – no part of the human body or mind was in balance or was healthy if the soul was not healthy and in balance.

To carry this brief summary of Medieval medical practice further, the temperaments were affected by the state of a human's humoral balance. Hippocratic texts offered descriptions of different states of humoral balance:

Crasis – the proportional mixture of the humors *Eucrasia:*
correct humoral balance

Dyscrasia – systemic disorders in and among the humors
Dyscrasia – incorrect mixture of the humors
Abundantia – excess amounts of one or more humors
Corruptio – deterioration of one or more humors
Coagulatio – curdling of a humor
Putrefactio – degeneration or decomposition

For Hildegard, good health exhibited good balance in all of the categories shown in the table above, not just good humoral balance. If one humor or quality became dominant over another, the body would become out of balance and 'ill'. In addition, Hildegard taught that an illness indicated an imbalance of the whole person, not just the 'part' indicated by and producing the 'symptom'. So her approach to healing focused on more than treating a symptom – she searched for the underlying cause of the illness, a cause which could be imbalance in any of the categories, a physical injury, and/or a spiritual malady. Humoral rebalance was achieved through diet, medication, changes in lifestyle, elimination of waste matter through sweating, sneezing, tears, bloodletting, etc., and – first and foremost for Hildegard – spiritual renewal.

Surgical procedures were common during the time, but they were not for Hildegard. Though they could be beneficial, surgical procedures served primarily to 'cut out' the affected tissue with little or no focus on the determination of emotional, environmental, or spiritual causes for the illness or disease, and as a result surgery was not a primary tool for monastic healers, and certainly not for Hildegard.

With this brief review of the basis for medieval medical practice, we now turn to Hildegard's books. There is still some discussion about Hildegard's medical writing. A number of scholars propose that she did not write two books, but only one which included both of the current volumes. Others believe she was not the author of *Causes and Cures*, but that it was written by an admirer during the century following her death. And then, of course, there are many Hildegard scholars who believe she did write the two books which were combined into one after her death (when she was being considered for sainthood) and then separated again into the original two volumes. Regardless of whether the two became one or one became two, nothing has disproved the assertion that Hildegard was the author of all of it. Today, our resources come as two books. The contents of *Causes et Cures* include the following topics:

1. The creation of the world. The cosmos and its components.
   Macrocosm and microcosm.
2. Elements and humors
3. Adam
4. Embryology
5. Human Sexuality
6. Complexion and aptitude. Complexional differences

7. Sleep and dreams. Waking
8. Disorders and diseases
9. Menstruation. Conception and pregnancy. Childbirth and infancy
10. Regimen of health
11. Bloodletting
12. Bathing
13. Nutritional disorders. Digestive system disorders. Disorders of the skin. Fevers
14. Treatment
15. Diagnostic and prognostic signs
16. Lunar effects

The information offered on the topics listed above are written in prose, detailing information about each topic, various states of imbalance that can occur, diagnoses of effects that cause imbalance, and suggested remedies for the imbalances.

The second book, *Physica*, was named as such first in a manuscript dated 1533 by Johannes Schott in Strasbourg. Hildegard's title was "Subtleties of the Diverse Qualities of Created Things". There are at least six different manuscripts of the work.[150] Priscilla Throop's translation of the complete manuscript of *Physica* is from the *Patrologia Latina* (the writings of the fathers in Latin), a collection of 221volumes of writings compiled and edited by Jacques-Paul Migne (1844-1866) in two series:

Series prima, volumes 1-73 from Tertullian to Gregory the Great
Series secunda, volumes 74-217 from Gregory the Great to Pope Innocent the 3rd

The two series included writings in chronological sequence from c.200 A.D. to 1216 A.D. The veritable explosion of writings occurring during and after the thirteenth century rendered it impractical to continue any sort of comprehensive collection of even the most important texts.[151]

There were only a very few volumes in the *Patrologia Latina* that included writings by women. Hildegard's collection appears as Volume 197. As her writings were collected after her death in 1179 in preparation for the petition for canonization and the collection of works in the *Patrologia* ended with the year 1216, it can be assumed the work was reasonably accurate and probably not severely edited or altered, unless Fr. Migne's source was from a later edition.

The chart on the following page lists the nine books of *Physica*. Each entry identifies the resource, describes its nature, and suggests its uses in the healing process. The writing is a wonderful example of Hildegard's synthesis of the Doctrine of the Four Temperaments with the human condition and with spiritual/theological implications and suggested remedies. The nine books are:

1. Plants	2. Elements	3. Trees
4. Stones	5. Fish	6. Birds
7. Animals	8. Reptiles	9. Metals

---

150 See the footnote on p.4 of Priscilla Throop's translation of *Physica* (Rochester, Vermont: Healing Arts Press, 1998).

151 From the *Patrologia* Latina database at:
http://pld.chadwyck.com/helphtx/htxview?template=basic.htx&content=about.htx

None of the remedies are specific as to detailed preparation or amounts. The works of Dr. Gottfried Hertzka and Dr. Wighard Strehlow are suggested for current practice of Hildegard Medicine and practical application.[152] There are many resources and translations available in German, and they are slowly being translated to English and other languages. Considerable research on some of the plant and mineral applications has been done in Germany and are readily available at Apothecaries there.

The chart below lists the items in alphabetical order, not in the order in which Hildegard introduces them. There are 233 entries for plants (several are not plants, but they were listed in the book on plants so are included here), 14 elements, 63 trees, 25+ stones, 36 fish, 72 birds, 45 animals, 18 reptiles/insects, and 8 metals – over five hundred entries! This certainly was and is a significant work!

Plants	Elements	Trees	Stones	Fish	Birds (& Insects)	Animals	Reptiles (& Insects)	Metals
Agrimony	Air	Apple	Emerald	Whale	Griffin	Elephant	Dragon	Gold
Aloe	Water	Pear	Jacinth	Sturgeon	Ostrich	Camel	A Certain Serpent	Silver
Arnica	The Sea	Walnut	Onyx	Seal	Peacock	Lion	Slowworm	Lead
Arum	The Saar	Quince	Beryl	Turbot	Crane	Bear	Toad	Tin
Asafoetida	The Rhine	Peach	Sardonyx	Salmon	Swan	Unicorn	Frog	Copper
Asarum	The Main	Cherry	Sapphire	Sheatfish	Heron	Tiger	Tree Frog	Brass
Balsam	The Danube	Plum	Sard	Pike	Vulture	Panther	Harumna	Iron
Barley	The Moselle	Rowan	Topaz	Copprea	Eagle	Horse	Moll	Steel
Basil	The Nahe	Black Mulberry	Chrysolite	Northern Pike	Stork	Ass	Lizard	
Bearberry Plant	The Glan	Almond	Jasper	European Catfish	Goose	Deer	Spider	
Belladonna	Earth	Hazel	Prasine	Carp	Wild Goose	Roe Deer	Viper	
Bennet	Calamine	Chestnut	Chalcedony	Sea Bream	Domestic Duck	Ibex	Basilisk	
Betony	Chalk	Medlar	Chrysoprase	Elsua	Wild Duck	Bison	Scorpion	
Bilberry	Greenish Earth	Fig	Carbuncle	Plaice	Cock, Hen	Ox	Tarantula	
Bindweed		Laurel	Amethyst	Salmon Trout	Caperdaillie	Sheep	Tyriaca	
Birthwort or Aristolochia		Olive	Agate	Monuwa	Partridge	Goat	Scherzbedra	
Bitter Vetch		Date Palm	Diamond	Perch	Grouse	Pig	Earthworm	
Black Dock		Citron	Magnesian (Magnet)	Meysisch	Falcon	Hare	Snail or Slug	
Black Hellebore		Cedar	Ligure	Fish with Shell	Hawk	Wolf		
Black Nightshade		Cypress	Crystal	Grayling	Sparrow Hawk	Dog		
Blind Nettle		Savin	Pearls	Roach	Kite	Fox		
Bloodwort		Box	Mother-of-Pearl	Herring	Weho	Beaver		
Borage		Fir	Carnelian	Groundling	Raven	Otter		
Bramble		Oak	Alabaster	Chub	Crows and Jackdaws	Monkey		
Broad Beans		Beech	Limestone	Bleak	Carrion Crow	Marmoset		
Brooklime		Ash		Pafenduno	Hooded Crow	Cat		
Bryony		Aspen		Tench	Ordumel	Lynx		
Burdock		Alder		Grundula	Alkreya	Badger		

[152] Dr. Stehlow practices Hildegard Medicine at his clinic in Konstanz, Germany and has many publications available. Dr. Gottfried Hertzka was the first contemporary physician to apply Hildegard's medicine to current practice. Please see the listings in the bibliography for both of these persons.

Butter	Plane	Stechela	Seagull	Polecat
Butterbur	Yew	Loach	Dove	Hedgehog
Cabbage	White Birch	Rulheubt	Turtle Dove	Squirrel
Calendula	Sea Fir	Crawfish	Parrot	Hamster
Camphor	Spindle	Eel	Magpie	Marten
Catnip	English Elm	Cod	Nutcracker	Water Marten
Cattail	Willow	Punbelen	Screech Owl	Sable
Celandine	Sallow, or Goat Willow	Lamprey	Great Horned Owl	Ermine
Celery	Folbaum		Pelican	Mole
Charlock	Felbaum		Cuckoo	Weasel
Chervil	Cornel Cherry		Snipe	Mouse
Chickweed	Mascel		Woodpecker	Cormouse
Cinnamon	Myrtle		Sparrow	Shrew
Cinquefoil	Juniper		Titmouse	Flea
Clary Sage	Elder		Blackbird	Ant
Clover	Gall Oak		Thrush	Helim
Cloves	Hartbrogelbaum		Lark	Dromedary
Cockscomb or Yellow Rattle	Elm		Kingfisher	
Colchicum	Harbaum		Hoopoe	
Coltsfoot	Schulbaum		Quail	
Columbine	Tamarisk		Nightingale	
Comfrey	Agenbaum		Starling	
Cornflower, Centaury or Bachelor's Button	Rose Hip		Chaffinch	
Costmary	Blackthorn		Goldfinch	
Cress	Grapevine		Bunting	
Cumin	Gichtbaum		Pipit	
Danewort	Smoke		Speckled Magpie	
Dauwurtz	Moss		Blackbird	
Dill	Unguent of Hilarion		White Wagtail	
Dittany or Fraxinella	Sysemera		Yellow Wagtail	
Dorth	Scrofula		Swallow	
Duckweed	Palm		Gold-Crested Kinglet	
Dwarf Elder	Red Fir		Bat	
Eggs	Tribulus		Widderwalo	
Elecampane			Honey Bee	
Female Fern			House Fly	
Fennel			Tree Cricket	
Fenugreek			Grasshopper	
Fern			Gnat	
Feverfew or Pellitory			Bumblebees	
Ficaria, Lesser Celandine			Wasp	
Field Mint			Glowworm	
Flax			Meygelana	
Flaxseed			Wren	
Forget-me-not				
Frankincense				
Ganingale				
Garbanzo Beans				

Garden Spurge	**Plants, Continued**	**Plants, Continued**	**Plants, Continued**	**Plants, Continued**	**Plants, Continued**	**Plants, Continued**	**Plants, Continued**	**Plants, Continued**
Garlic	Hog's-Fennel	Licorice	Milk	Orach	Psaffo	Sorrel	Sysemera	Welsh Onion
Geranium or Cranesbill	Honey	Lilim	Millet	Oregano,Wild Marjoram	Psyllium	Southernwood	Tansy	Wheat
German Chamomile	Hops	Lily	Millet	Panic Grass	Purlane	Spearmint	Thistle	White Dock
Germander	Horehound	Lovage	Mountain Parsley	Parsely	Radish	Spelt	Thyme	Wild Lettuce
Ginger	Horesradish	Lungwort	Mouse-ear	Parsnip	Rose	Spike Lavender	Tithymal	Wild Strawberry
Gladiolus	Horsemint	Lupine	Mugwort	Peas	Rue	Spruce Pitch	Tormentil	Wild Thyme
Goatsbeard	Houseleek	Madder	Mullein	Pennyroyal	Rush	Spurge	Turnip	Winter Cherry
Goose Grass	Humela	Mallow	Musetha	Peony	Rye	Squashes	Ugera	Woad
Goutweed	Hyssop	Mandrake	Mushrooms	Pepper	Sage	St. John's Wort	Valerian	Wormwood or Absinthe
Ground Ivy	Indian Chickweed	Mare's-tail	Mustard	Pimpernel or Saxifrage	Salt	Storax	Vervain	Woundwort
Hart's-Tongue Fern	Ivy	Marshmallow or Althaea	Myrrh	Pine Resin	Savory	Stutgras	Vetch	Yarrow
Hazelwort	Java Pepper or Cubeb	Masterwort	Nettle	Plantain	Saxifrage	Sugar	Violet	Yellow Gentian
Hemlock	Lavender	Meadow Grasses	Nigella	Plionia	Shallot	Sulphur	Water Lily	Zedoary
Hemp	Leek	Menna	Nutmeg	Poppy	Silverweed	Summer Savory	Water Mint	Zugelnich
Henbane	Lentils	Meranda	Oats	Prickly Lettuce	Skirret	Sunnewirbel	Water Parsnip	
Herb Robert or Storksbill	Lettuce	Meygelana	Onion	Primrose	Smartweed		Watercress	

Seeing this list provides quite an insight into medieval life and thought, particularly for the region of Europe where Hildegard lived. By 1200 Northern Europe had a significant history of trade with southern Europe, the Orient, and the Mediterranean countries. The list above reflects that – I don't believe elephants, lions, and camels were indigenous to the Rhineland! Nor were tarantulas... Galangal and ginger, two of Hildegard's more commonly used and potent spices were from the East. But Spelt, or Dinkel, was grown in and around her territory.

Not all of the items included in her *Physica* are beneficial as medicinal treatments. She lists quite a few that are poisonous or of no benefit whatsoever, and in many of those instances provides advice for what one is to do if the poison is ingested or if one is bitten by a poisonous creature. All of the entries are described as to their hot/cold and dry/moist qualities, and those that are primary in treatment are further described as to their relationship to the Doctrine of the Humors.

As mentioned earlier, Hildegard's medicine is intrinsically enmeshed with her spirituality. She taught that as a result of original sin (i.e. Adam and Eve's sin) humans have become not only mortal, but weak and susceptible to imbalance, or ill health. Health involved the whole person – body, mind and spirit. So emotional and spiritual imbalances were just as much causes of illness and disease as anything physical. For Hildegard, 'holistic' medicine was the primary medieval practice, with sound theological basis.

Viriditas

Well, so what is this word? In the last quarter of a century it is a word which has become attributed to and associated with Hildegard. It's a pungent word, it is fun to say (it feels good on the tongue), and it does not have one specific definition. Hildegard did not 'make it up', and it is not included in her own secret language (the Lingua Ignota). In fact, she did not use it much in her early writings[153] and in her later works she uses it in different ways (as a metaphorical term, as a spiritual reference, and as a physiological term).

The general definition which would encompass all of the above meanings is the one presented most often by authors writing about Hildegard: the 'green' life-force or energy of growth, whether it be physical, spiritual, or fruitful. The term had been around for millennium before Hildegard, appearing at least once in the Vulgate bible, though not with the same intent as Hildegard's use of the term.[154] There is no use of it in the ancient botanical or medical texts. Hildegard must have become acquainted with it through the writings of the church, where viriditas appeared metaphorically to imply growth and fruitfulness of faith, good works, or belief.

It was in the growth of her use and understanding of the term that Hildegard offered a major contribution to medical practices of her time. For millennia the Four Humors served as the basis for diagnosis and treatment, but Hildegard adds a fifth humor, 'green sap' (viriditas) not just within plants, but within the human body. Dr. Victoria Sweet writes:

> In sum, while viriditas was a common concept in the botanical and theological literature, only Hildegard used it to mean something in the body. Although there are passages in her work that suggest that she sometimes used it simply as a metaphor for fertility, abundance, or life, on the whole she seems to have meant viriditas as an actual substance, a kind of fifth humor. Bodily viriditas came from plants and completed the physical cycle that connected plants with body and gardening with medicine. While Hildegard learned the concept of viriditas from the Church Fathers, its ancient *physical* meaning was revealed to her not in the chapel or in the library but in the garden, and she herself brought it to the infirmary.[155]

I would add one word to the above quote: "...its ancient *physical* meaning was revealed to her not {only} in the chapel or in the library...

So, Hildegard once again exhibits her foundational belief in the interconnectivity of all things and the codependence of all things in the universe – and on the right balance within all of those relationships. Health and healing involve not just what happens in the body, but the relationships of the body to the environment, to affects on the physical, mental and spiritual elements of the microcosm, to what we ingest, expel, process, prepare, and create with what is available to us in creation. And always, we must hear her admonition to do everything with discretion.[156]

---

[153] Dr. Victoria Sweet M.D., Ph.D spends a considerable and fascinating time discussing *viriditas*, its origins and its usage from ancient times, and, of course, particularly Hildegard's use in *Rooted in the Earth, Rooted in the Sky* (New York, Routledge, 2006) all of Chapter Five.

[154] *Op. cit.,* p.141ff

[155] *Op. Cit*., p.154

[156] Please see the bibliography for a listing of works about Hildegard's medicine.

Scivias

Book Three, Vision Nine

The Tower of the Church

The previous four chapters each introduced one of Hildegard's visions, chosen to trace her visionary theology and spirituality via the form of the creed (Nicene or Apostolic). The first vision, the "Egg of the Universe", presented us with the macrocosm of the created universe and the next three chapters the Trinity. I haven't outlined the credal form presented in this book yet, so here it is:

"I believe" (Credo):

1. in God the Father
2. in God the Son
3. in God the Holy Spirit
4. in the holy catholic church
5. in the communion of saints
6. in the forgiveness of sins
7. in life everlasting

How appropriate that this particular chapter introducing Hildegard as a Healer also brings us Hildegard's vision of "The Tower of the Church". She wrote about and had several visions pertaining to the church in *Scivias*. In Book One she introduced 'The Synagogue', and in Book Two 'The Church, Bride of Christ and Mother of the Faithful', 'The Three Orders in the Church', and 'Christ's Sacrifice and the Church. Book Three is titled "The History of Salvation Symbolized by a Building", and vision nine in that book is 'The Tower of the Church'.

I have chosen this particular vision of the church to present here because it is a vision of the strength and support the church offers to humanity in its struggles in the world—which of course includes care of the sick. The images and figures are, of course, medieval and representative of the time of the crusades in both dress and architectural design. All is symbolic and is the means through which Hildegard was told to teach/preach the vision as given to her by the 'Voice of the Living Light.

The vision shown below is accompanied once again by a neutral image with identifying numbers.[157]

---

[157] Descriptions are abstracted from: Hildegard, Saint. *Scivias*, tr. Columba Hart and Jane Bishop (New Jersey, Paulist Press 1990) pp.455ff.

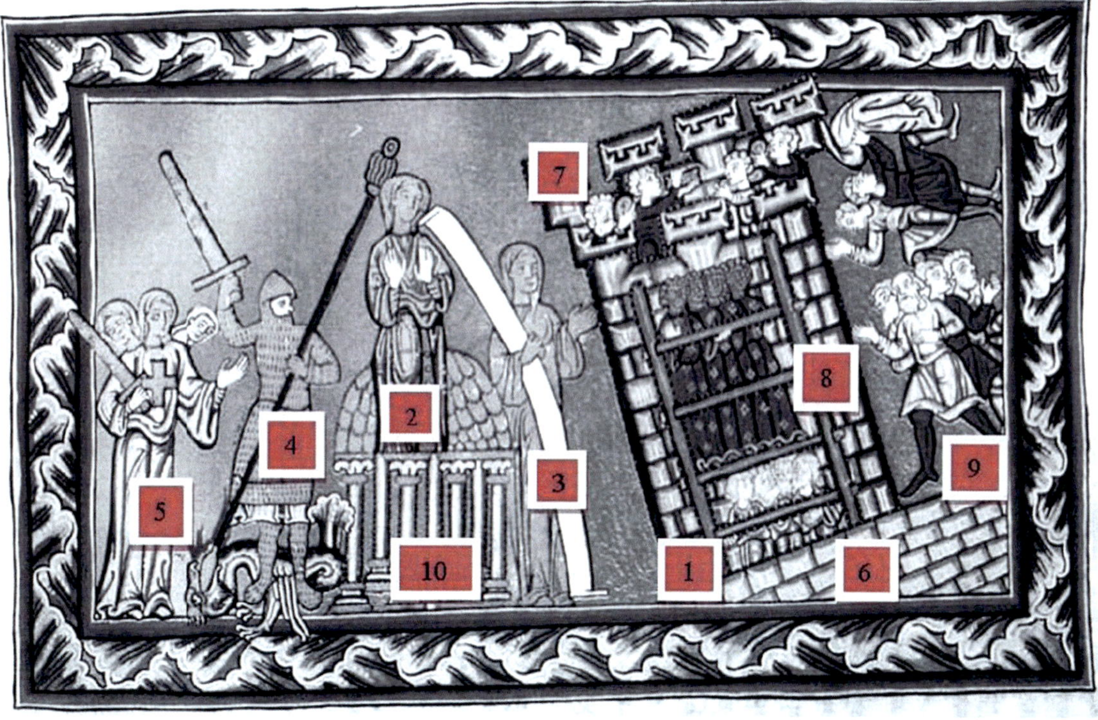
7
8
2
4
3
9
5
10
1
6

1. *The church is this tower...of brilliant splendor, set into the stone wall...so that it is visible both inside and outside the building.*

Hildegard uses the following descriptors for the tower:

a. it is illumined by the human nature of Christ.
b. it is built of living stones (humans) fired by the Holy Spirit.
c. the visibility of inside and outside refers to the inner understanding coming from knowledge of scripture and the outer foolishness of worldly affairs.
d. the church honors Christ by giving Him all inner thoughts and meditations inspired by the Holy Spirit and received through the five senses. The church also gives Him all virtues.
e. the height of the tower is so great to represent the height and depth of divine wisdom and knowledge experienced in the church.
f. the gap between the tower and the wall represents the knowledge of God and great praise that is not yet in 'full flower' in human hearts. The tower (church) is not yet finished but incessantly hastens toward her full beauty through swiftly *passing time and by means of her children.*

To complete the description of the tower, I am going to take the next items out of order:

6. a wall which is 'one cubit'[158] away from the tower, representing the firm foundation of the knowledge of God. It conceals from the church the praise the church will have, for the church is not yet perfected. But the gap is only one cubit, so people can know good and evil and are able to grasp from the knowledge of God what is useful, and they are also able to continue work on building the church.

7. *...around its summit seven bulwarks [are] built with wonderful strength. These bulwarks represent the seven gifts of the Holy Spirit that are so strong that no adversary can destroy them, or even lift his mind so far as to touch them.*[159]

8. a ladder which reaches to the summit of the tower.

a. the ladder represents the many stages of preparation and 'building' of the church. Each stage was part of God's plan, and completion of each stage strengthened and fortified the church.
b. the people standing on the rungs of the ladder are the *shining apostles [standing] on the rungs of God's commands...* They are the doctors of the Church, who bring back the errant (spiritually sick) to the church (to health).

---

[158] The cubit was not an exact measurement, most often being related to the distance between a person's longest fingertip and the elbow joint. The 'palm' was used too – the width of the fingers (not including the thumb), and 6, 7, 8, or 9 palms equaled one cubit. Generally, the cubit measured 18-23 inches.

[159] The seven gifts were first listed in the Old Testament book of Isaiah 11:2-3. The following list is from the *Summa Theologica* of Thomas Aquinas, showing the correspondence of each to the seven virtues. http://en.wikipedia.org/wiki/Seven_gifts_of_the_Holy_Spirit

- The gift of wisdom corresponds to the virtue of charity.
- The gift of understanding corresponds to the virtue of faith.
- The gift of counsel (right judgment) corresponds to the virtue of prudence.
- The gift of fortitude corresponds to the virtue of courage.
- The gift of knowledge corresponds to the virtue of faith.
- The gift of piety corresponds to the virtue of justice.
- The gift of fear of the Lord corresponds to the virtue of hope.

They wear resplendent robes, but their shoes are black from walking the paths of the unfaithful and sinful world.

9. Many different types of people come to the tower. Some enter clothed in a pure white garment, others take off the garment and throw it away, others return and reclaim the garment, some enter weighed down by the garment. And some invade the tower, hissing and blaspheming. Hildegard goes to some length describing these different peoples and the manner in which they enter the tower (church).

Hildegard also spends some time describing the offices of power in the church, and she firmly states that those who resist the power of the offices resist God, as God has set up the offices.

10. Everything to the left of the tower is inside the building containing the tower. There are seven marble pillars which are perfectly smooth and round – God the omnipotent Father with power in the perfect 'round' of eternity (Alpha and Omega). They represent the "seven modes of the purifying inspiration of the Holy Spirit" and are each seven cubits high. Being taller than a human, they are stronger and greater than human intellect, showing that God the Creator must be worshipped in pure faith. They support a dome made of iron, and in their perfection of height and straightness they support and protect those who, through the gifts of the Holy Spirit, have left behind the carnal pleasures of earth.

2. Standing on top of the pillars is a figure which represents the wisdom of God. Hildegard points out that Wisdom existed before all else, "giving counsel in the formation of all the creatures made in heaven and earth". She [wisdom] is also the portal for all other virtues that live in God. There is a beautiful description of this figure in *Scivias*, Book Three, Vision Nine.

3, 4, 5. There are three more figures, symbols of virtues, to the left of Wisdom – Justice, Fortitude and Sanctity. These three move the church toward eternity in the children of the church, nourishing them through teachers, fighting against the Devil, and rejecting the vices of sin. Justice (number 3) leans against the pillars supporting Wisdom. Fortitude (number 4) follows Justice, wearing the armor of God to repel all traps and advances of the Devil set for humans. She is standing on a horrible dragon, subjugating it to her power, and she has pierced its mouth, making it vomit all uncleanliness. She holds a sword used to slay idol-worship and other heresies and unbelief. And number 5 is Sanctity, wearing three heads. The center, larger head is "He who is the Judge of the good and the evil". The head to the right "is so honorable and sweet and full of heavenly grace that the depth of her mystery exceeds the human intellect". The head to the left, not so bright, is veiled, "sternly constraining itself for love of God". "And the middle looks at the other two, and they look at it, and they all consult together for their advantage; for they are strongly united in inner vision and in love, and none of them can last without the help of the others."[160]

As was true with the earlier visions presented, reading the entire text by Hildegard about this vision would be a good and valuable use of time! There is much to reflect on in this vision, and much to think about as it speaks to our own time, nearly a millenium later. What enormous changes in the structure of the 'church' have occurred, but also how much has been retained and serves still a foundational purpose for our lives. Hildegard's 'Tower' continues to grow, and the essential truths serving as its foundation remain and nourish.

---

[160] *Op. Cit.,* p. 469

The church is a community, described in so many different ways all through scripture (Old Testament and New Testament). Here on earth, strength and nourishment and love and order are gifts of grace that come through community. Hildegard's communities were very specifically ordered; our communities are perhaps less specific, but they are very important to our spiritual, moral, and physical health and well-being. As indicated earlier, Hildegard's community, a Benedictine monastery, was a source of care and healing for the physically and spiritually ill, so part of her responsibilities in those communities involved medical and spiritual practices. Her study of medieval medicine and her practice of it were part of her vocation, and what she wrote about it was written as part of her response to the command she received to write all that she received and experienced. She has given us a healthy legacy!

Hildegard's Chant and the Question of Rhythm

Nunc gaudeant
(for the dedication of a church)

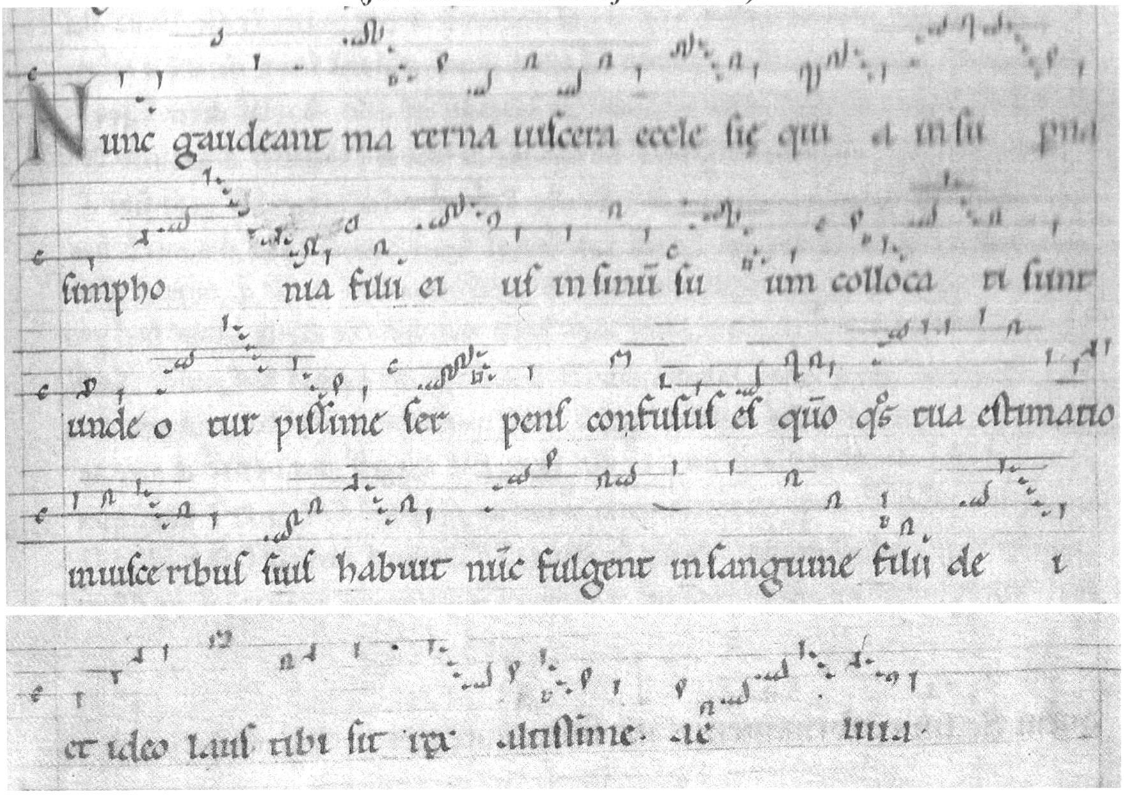

Now let rejoice the motherly heart of the Church,
for in supernal symphony
her children into her bosom are gathered.
And so O shameful serpent you are confused
and those your jealousy held in your bowels
now shine in the blood of the Son of God
and therefore praise to you most high King Alleluia.

Hildegard's votive antiphon, Nunc gaudeant appears in the Dendermonde manuscript as the last chant, a joyful chant written for the dedication of a church. Because of its place in the manuscript, perhaps it also reflects the joy and relief of the lifting of the interdict on her community[161] or the end of schism in the church caused by Arnold of Brescia in the 1150's. Using the Dendermonde notation, the following is my transcription of the chant with neumes slurred:

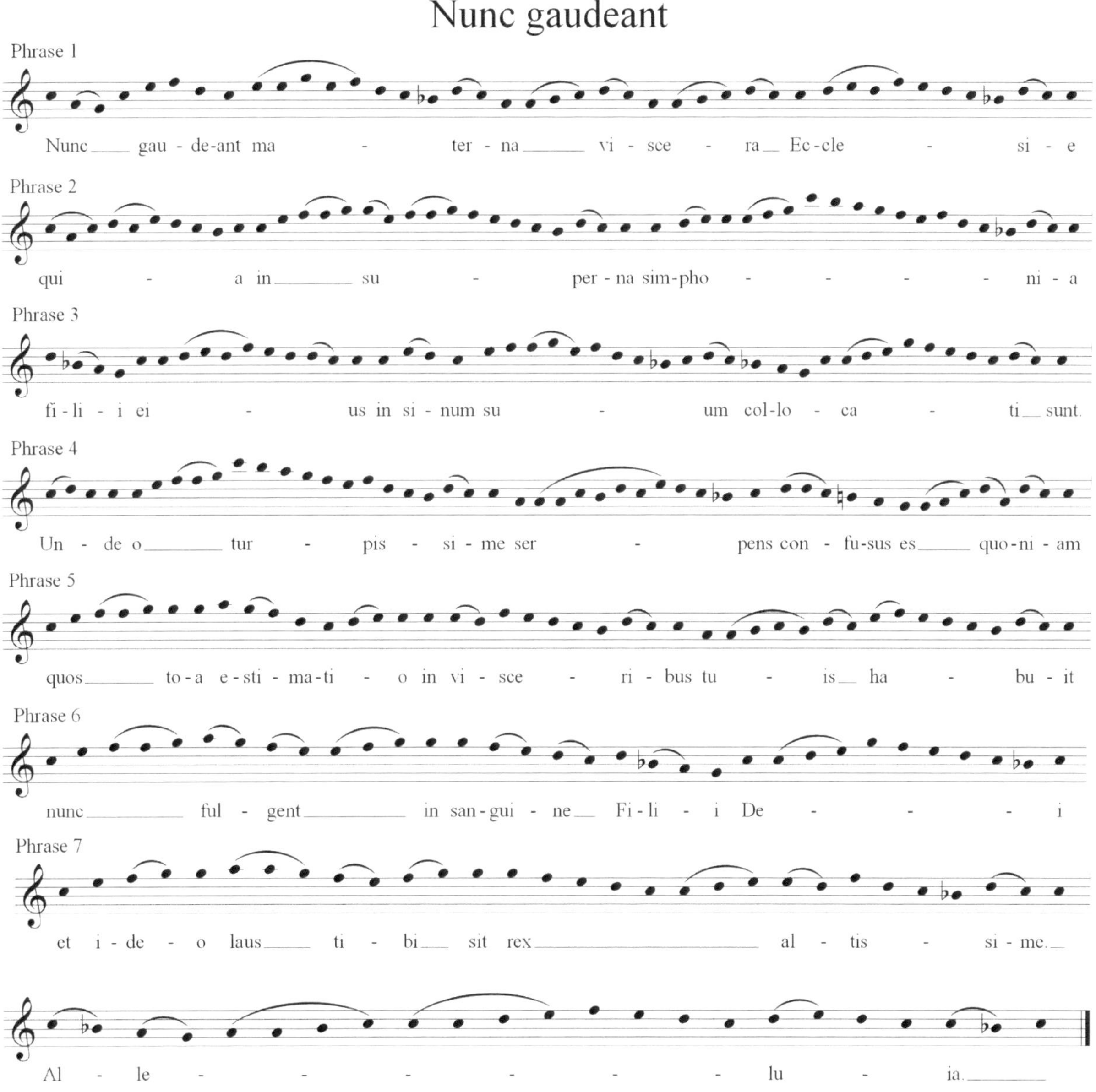

---

161 Newman, Barbara. *Hildegard of Bingen: Symphonia*. (Ithaca, New York. Cornell University Press 1998). pp. 315-316

The chant is in C Mixolydian with Ionian implied in the fourth phrase. All of the terminatio patterns are identical with the exception of that of Phrase 6 and the final "Alleluia", where Hildegard decorates the arrival on the final pitch with the insertion/ornamentation of a clivis marked with the musica ficta B^b. There are numerous syllables ornamented in neumatic and melismatic patterns, and some rather obvious text painting on the words 'simphonia', 'serpent' and 'confused'. She also shouts at the Devil on the word "turpissime"!

The Rhythm of Chant

With some trepidation I address this difficult and disputed topic! The rhythm, or flow, of chant is not notated in such a way that there are 'absolute' interpretations. Chant has never been contained by a system of regular beats, meter, or durational patterns. I am speaking here specifically about Gregorian chant which developed out of the Hebrew practice in existence during the time of Christ. That chant became a foundation for the development of Western music over the last two millennia.

Willi Apel, a pre-eminent musicologist who has written one of the most exhaustive and highly respected works about chant, *Gregorian Chant,*[162] says:

> ...I cannot help feeling that the importance of the rhythmic problem has been somewhat exaggerated. The numerous efforts made in this direction appear to me like so many answers to a question that was never raised. This does not mean to say that Gregorian chant had no rhythm. Music without rhythm is obviously a contradiction in itself. However, rhythm is not the same as a fixed rhythmic system, that is, a clearly formulated and consistently applied set of rules governing the duration of the notes and other matters pertaining to rhythm in the most general sense of the word. It is toward the discovery of some such system that the efforts of so many scholars have been directed—without any incontestable or generally accepted result. Could it be that they were chasing a phantom, that they were trying to find something that never existed? I believe so, for at least two reasons. One is that the melodies of the chant, in their specific melodic design, lend themselves to a rhythmic (or better, a-rhythmic?) rendition of the greatest flexibility and variability, similar to what we find in so many folk melodies (e.g. American Indian) of a "rhapsodic" character...
>
> The other reason is, that I am convinced there would be some tangible evidence of systematic rhythm either in the musical sources or in the medieval treatises if there ever had been a stable tradition in this field comparable to that which we find in the purely melodic aspect of the chant.[163]

Dr. Apel goes on to explain that those who have researched and written about rhythm in Gregorian chant fall into one of two categories, equalists who believe there is only one basic time value and mensuralists who believe there are several time values for each note. Chant as we hear it performed today usually follows the equalist theorem proposed by Dom Andre' Mocquereau at the Abbey of Solesmes in the late 1800s. His work was adopted by the Abbey

[162] Apel, Willi. *Gregorian Chant.* (Bloomington: Indiana University Press. 1958)

[163] *Op. Cit.* p126

and has been published as a guide for performance of chant in all publications of the *Liber Usualis* since that time.

The chant as notated and performed today is the result of a restoration process initiated in the 1830's. From the medieval times it had undergone numerous revisions and notational innovations, resulting in so much 'paring down' (today we would call it 'dumbing down') and imposition of individual tastes that it fell from its place of primacy in Catholic worship as a means to praise and worship God in a voice of unity and purity. The restoration began in the 1830's at the Abbey, aided by photography, as the Abbey was able to collect photographic copies of many old medieval manuscripts.

Chant was originally passed from generation to generation as an oral tradition, though with more notated indications than chant of other cultures. Initially these notations occurred above the written text and indicated only contoural changes without specificity of pitch. By Hildegard's time, those notations had been classified and developed into a system of neumes placed on a framework of ledger lines to indicate pitch, but duration of the neumes was still the result of declaiming the text. The few indications for duration emphasis as indicated below are, therefore, significant.

So much has changed since medieval times in the development of music and particularly in the notation of rhythm and the use of meter and durational patterns. How difficult, and speculative, for trained musicians to retrace performance practice back to an age where rhythm as we experience it today did not yet exist. The clues are few, so in a near-vacuum of notated indications of anything rhythmical, we have primarily a reliance on text rhythm.

And what are the 'few' clues? They would include some implied 'performance practice' accents as well. The list is short, reading from the most common and explicit to conjecture. They imply what we now call 'agogic' accents, or accents of duration – pitches sounded longer than those preceding or following. The first four types found in *nunc gaudeant* are indicated on the score according to the following table.

Rhythmic Indication	Definition	Color	Number of Instances
repeated punctae, single or within a neume		Green	19
rhythmic letters[164]	t – *trahere* vel *tenere* (to drag, to hold) x – *expectare* (to await, to retard) m – *mediocriter* moderari melodiam (moderation, retard?)	Purple	4
	c – ut *cito* vel *celeriter* dicatur (should be sung quickly)	Blue	2
Episema	a horizontal line over a syllable – two of these may be small corrections by a scribe of letters omitted from the word: *sinum* and *nunc* (the first and third red boxes)	Red	1 (possibly two more)
terminatio patterns, especially the final note	In *Nunc gaudeant*, d-c-c + embellishiment		12
text accents	In multisyllabic words		30
first pitch of a multi-note neume	Accented if they correspond to a text accent		15
contoural accents, textual and in melismatic and neumatic passages			12

164 *Op. Cit.*, p.117 Apel explains that Notker (St. Gall monastery, d.912) wrote a letter in which he offered a table "in which practically every letter of the alphabet is explained as the abbreviation of some significant word".

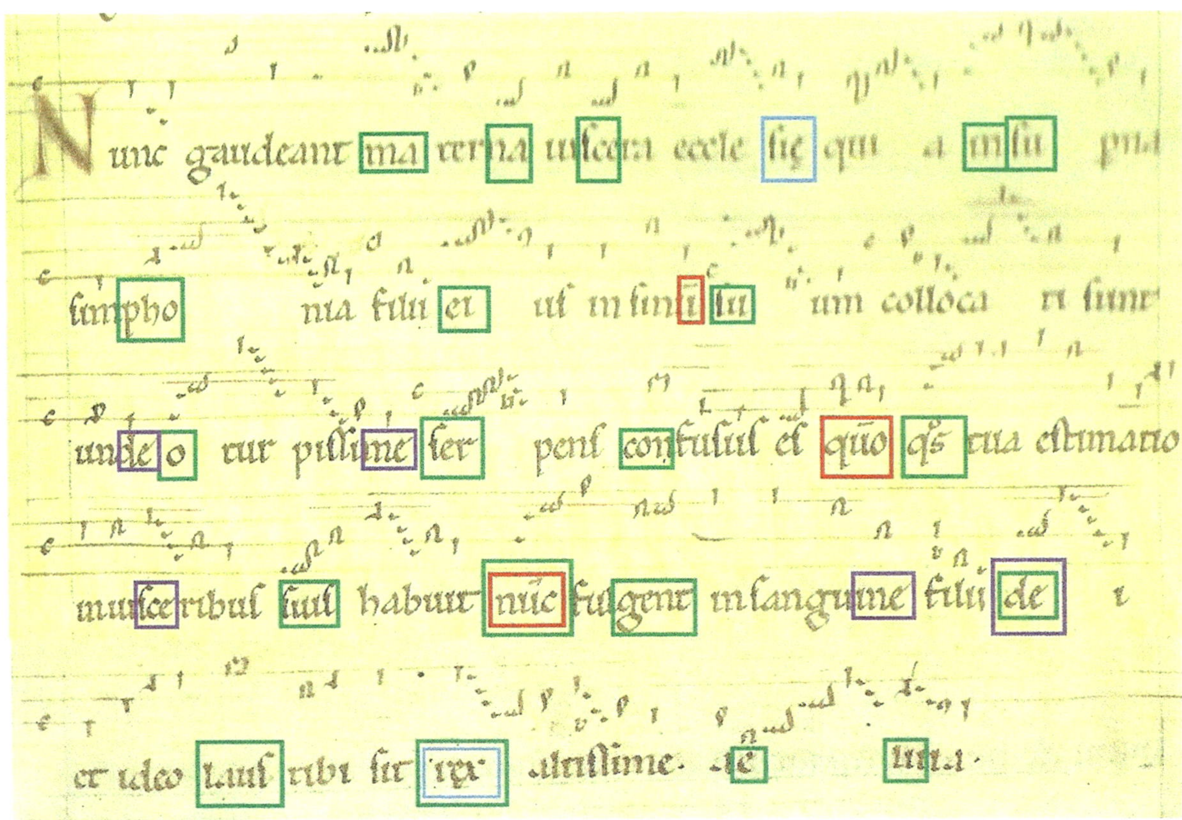

The textual accents (in red) are more of an articulation rather than duration accent, performed with more 'weight' rather than more duration:

Nunc gaud-e-ant ma-ter-na vi-scer-a Ec-cle-si-e,
qui-a in su-per-na sim-phon-i-a
fi-li-i e-ius in si-num su-um col-lo-ca-ti sunt.
Un-de, o tur-pis-si-me ser-pens con-fus-us es,
quo-ni-am quos tu-a es-ti-ma-ti-o in vi-scer-i-bus su-is ha-bu-it
nunc ful-gent in san-gui-ne Fi-li-i De-i,
et i-de-o laus ti-bi sit, rex al-tis-si-me,
Al-le-lu-i-a.

When combined with one of the durational accents they are particularly noteworthy in performance, becoming primary in emphasis of the word being sung and in their point of arrival in the meaning of the text.

From the above information, some conclusions may be drawn about Hildegard's rhythmic 'style', though all is speculation, even if based upon actual indications in the manuscript.

1. Text accents are the most common means of creating rhythmic groupings in Hildegard's chants.
   a. they often are further emphasized with either a neumatic accent or a contoural accent (a change of direction)
   b. they may be emphasized with an agogic accent:
      -- repeated note neume (10 times)
      -- episema (1 on 'quo', possibly a second on 'nunc').
2. Stretching with the terminatio figure d-c-c (12 times) creates ceasura.
3. Elongations using the crossbar of the letter 't' (4 times) create agogic accents.
4. Multi-note neumes or combinations of neumes with the letter 'c' below a syllable of text, indicate a faster performance of the neume (2 times).
5. Slight durational extension of contoural high notes or the notes leading to the apex of a line (especially if it is an extreme high point such as the 'high Cs' in this chant) may be expected. The pitches/neumes following such an apex are often increased in speed.

Well. I'm not going to offer another transcription of *Nunc gaudeant* indicating durational rhythm. Marianne Richert Pfau has done so showing proportional rhythm[165], and there must be at least two other transcriptions showing some durational notation – I have been listening to two different performances of the chant that vary considerably from each other in rhythm (and in pitch!). One is not 'more correct' than the other. Neither is Ms. Pfau's transcription the 'definitive' transcription. Chant is a means of musically expressing free prose which contains no rhymed meter. If sung by a group, it requires practice so the multiple voices might be united into a single voice, following the directions of the director...a metaphor for the church, don't you think? It is the textually-shaped rhythm of the chant which allows the melody to soar, to bend, to rise and fall without the restriction of beat and bar line, allowing it to be the musical expression of the soul linking heaven and earth, elevating praise and prayer beyond the restrictions and control and busyness of our lives on earth. Hildegard's chants soar a bit more than traditional Gregorian chants... Let's meditate.

---

[165] Marianne Richert Pfau, ed. and tr. *Hildegard von Bingen: Symphonia armonie celestium revelationum.* Vol. VIII, Chants for Ecclesia. (Hildegard Publishing Company: Theodore Presser Company, Pennsylvania, 1997). pp.6-7

Meditation[166]

...in supernal symphony her children into her bosom are gathered...

[166] Artist's impression of a quasar located in a primeval galaxy (or protogalaxy) a few hundred million years after the Big Bang. Astronomers used the NASA/ESA Hubble Space Telescope to discover substantial amount of iron in three such quasars. This is the first time that anyone has found elements believed to have been created exclusively by the first generation of stars. Information about the very first generation of stars has been one of the Universe's best-kept secrets. When the first stars ended their lives as supernovae, the explosions expelled gas into space. These 'ashes' contained heavier elements such as oxygen, carbon, silicon, and iron created in the nuclear furnaces within the centers of stars. This new discovery allows astronomers to construct a revised timescale for the history of the Universe. About 13.7 thousand million years ago, the Universe is created in the Big Bang. In this cataclysmic hot explosion, hydrogen and helium are almost the only substances present. As the gases cool, the Universe becomes transparent and the gases start to gather. After 200 million years, the first generation of stars form. About 500 to 800 million years later, these first stars explode as supernovae, dispersing elements like iron and other elements into the surroundings. The new observations suggest that the first stars formed before the super massive black holes that power the quasar engines in the centers of galaxies. The light from the quasars has travelled for 12.8 thousand million years before reaching Hubble and had left the quasars only 900 million years after the Big Bang. **Credit:** European Space Agency and Wolfram Freudling (Space Telescope-European Coordinating Facility/European Southern Observatory, Germany)

What is my tower? Its strength?

Each day for a week, meditate on one of the gifts of the Spirit and its corresponding virtue (fruit).

How is the gift manifested in you as a fruit?

The gift of wisdom corresponds to the virtue of charity.
The gift of understanding corresponds to the virtue of faith.
The gift of counsel (right judgment) corresponds to the virtue of prudence.
The gift of fortitude corresponds to the virtue of courage.
The gift of knowledge corresponds to the virtue of faith.
The gift of piety corresponds to the virtue of justice.
The gift of fear of the Lord corresponds to the virtue of hope.

A work for solo flute is offered for this meditation.

a gradual accelerando to m. 22 (free, non-metric)
mp
mf
f
mp
f
mf
ff
mf
ff
f
mp
mf
f
ff
mp
f
mf
p
mp
mf
p
p
pp
p
mf
f
mp
p

Exercise

Walking, stretching and doing deep breathing exercises three or four times a week has hopefully brought you much more energy – viriditas! – and acquainted you with some trails around your home that offer beauty and joy. Well, how about expanding your horizons on the other three or four days of the week?! Get a bike! Riding for 20-30 minutes a day (wearing a helmet...) will take you farther away from home and bring back lots of childhood memories. Riding in your neighborhood, or taking your bike to parks is much more fun than sitting on a bike machine in a gym, although those are excellent for rainy day backups.

If you haven't been on a bicycle for a long time, begin close to home and in 15-20 minute increments, building up to 30 minutes or more. I hadn't been on a bike for 25 years when I was gifted with one (accompanied by stern looks of 'why aren't you doing this?'), and the first few times were humbling! Jellyfish thighs, a funny sensation walking afterwards for a few minutes, and a bit of embarrassment! But it came back quickly, thanks in large part to the walking I had been doing for several months. And what delight! I felt like a 'kid' again, with that initial sense of freedom and speed. We didn't wear helmets then, but please do now – especially if you haven't ridden a bike for awhile. They are light, letting the wind blow in, and they certainly offer a measure of safety if you fall.

Many cities have bike trails and provide special lanes on city streets for bicycles, and state and national parks are 'bike-friendly'. Take a bike on vacation, or rent one when you arrive at your destination. It is amazing how quickly you can develop your stamina! After two or three weeks, I rode for five miles on the seawall in Galveston, and a couple of months later a 12-mile ride for a benefit for breast cancer research. Be sure to pack water on your bike!

Recipes

Breakfast – Soft Scrambled Eggs

Protein for breakfast is good, and eggs are a great source of protein – just don't fix them every day! Once or twice a week make them a special treat. Here is a delicious way to enjoy them with some vegetables too.

3 eggs
1½ T Vegenaise (a non-dairy soy 'mayonaise')
1½ T light sour cream
½ onion, chopped
2 T sun dried tomatoes or chopped tomatoes
2 cloves garlic, chopped
1 T coconut oil or olive oil

Melt the oil in a skillet, add the onion and garlic and sauté until opaque. Add the tomato.

In a separate bowl, mix the eggs, Vegenaise and sour cream together. If preferred, whisk them until perfectly smooth – I prefer a light mixing, leaving 'lumps' of sour cream and Vegenaise.

Pour the egg mixture into the skillet and cook, stirring intermittently. Cook only until liquid has congealed – serve soft with toast or a spelt muffin, tea or coffee.

Lunch – Fresh Vegetable Soup

Around 10:30 in the morning, begin to cook vegetables to prepare a soup. This recipe will prepare several dishes for you, so have some freezer bags ready!

1C sliced carrots
1C celery cut into small pieces
1 chopped onion
2 small broccoli flowerettes, cut into small pieces
½ a cauliflower head, cut into small pieces
salt and pepper to taste (use Himalayan salt or sea salt)

Add 24 oz. of chicken stock to a pot with all of the above. Bring to a boil and then simmer for one hour.

Remove all solid materials from the broth, reserving them for dinner.

In a small pan, pour an amount of the broth for soup for lunch. Freeze the rest of the broth to use later.

Bring the broth to a boil. Add:

2 leaves of baby bock choy, cut into small pieces
3 fresh small mushrooms
3 small cherry tomatoes, whole

Immediately remove from heat and pour into a deep, small serving bowl. When it has cooled enough to eat, enjoy with pita chips and hummus as a side, water or a light white wine to drink, and a piece of fruit for dessert.

Dinner – Shrimp and Vegetable Pasta

4T olive or coconut oil
½ onion, chopped
6 cloves of garlic, chopped
2 chopped medium tomatoes
8 leaves of chopped basil
½ lb fresh shrimp, peeled and headed
4T dry red wine
cooked vegetables reserved from lunch soup

6 C boiling water
2 T kosher salt
2 C spelt pasta

In a medium pot, bring the water and salt to a boil. Add the pasta and cook for about 8 minutes.

In a pan, pour the oil and sauté the onions and garlic until opaque. Add the wine, tomato and basil, cooking for 2 minutes. Add the cooked vegetables and heat to a simmer. When simmering, add the shrimp and cook until it is bright pink.

Drain the spelt pasta, serve with the mixture of vegetables and shrimp. Freshly grated parmesan cheese may be added to taste.

V.
Hildegard the Artist

Hildegard's five senses (to say nothing of the sixth!) must have been extremely acute. The work she has left for us to study and from which to learn speaks loudly to – and from – those five senses.

Certainly Hildegard's music is representative of an acute sense of hearing, both 'inner' hearing and 'outer hearing. To notate melodies on wax tablets requires a highly developed 'inner' ear – the ability to imagine and hear music in the mind. And the medieval conventions of composing chant (modes, neumes, formulaic patterns, etc.) were elements she heard and assimilated into her own compositional style. The acute sense of hearing she possessed was certainly a gift, but it was also developed through years of experience and practice. It became part of her being. But beyond any 'normal' realization of her sense of inner or outer hearing, Hildegard taught that her chants were 'given' to her, that she was the transcriber of music from the spiritual realm. The picture above is from a church window in Bingen, showing Hildegard notating music played on a harp or psaltery by an angel. Hildegard believed that through music, she was in direct communion with the heavenly realm. The music was not of her earthly effort or making, but was a gift from God.

Her sense of touch also was acute, revealing itself primarily in her healing practices. Wet and dry, hot and cold were added to her medical practice of diagnosis and treatment, and with her emphasis on the 'veriditas' of living things, I wouldn't be surprised if that also indicated an ability to sense energy levels through touch, also aiding in diagnosis and treatment of areas of the body where energy flow was blocked or not what it should be at a healthy level. The picture to the left shows Hildegard healing a young blind boy in Rudesheim. (The oar boat in which she travelled back and forth from Rupertsburg (Bingen) to Rüdesheim-Eibingen is on the right.) Who knows, because of a heightened sense of touch, maybe Hildegard was a 'Reiki' healer, or a human MRI scanner!

Taste? She speaks of bitter, sweet, pleasant, sharp, and uses other descriptive words for foods and medicines. She did nothing without intention – or intensity – and that surely would include eating and cooking. There are many recipes attributed to her, usually with commentary as to the benefits or healing properties of the dish, but it is legitimate to assume that she took pleasure in what she cooked and ate too. And she would probably prefer to prescribe medicinal food to her patients that would be 'edible'. OK, this is just speculation…

And so too with the sense of smell. It is another sense she employed in her practice of medicine, describing different odors that indicated certain types of diseases or infections and also the nature of different plants which she used in healing.

But like her sense of hearing, her sense of sight manifested itself in both her inner spiritual world (her visions) and her world of reality in ways we can observe today. She was a 'seer', a woman who 'saw' visions from another realm and brought them into her present (and our present) through text and visual representations. Some writers have proposed the idea that her 'visions' were the result of severe migraine headaches, an idea supported by her emphasis on the presence of the "Living Light. She also suffered from debilitating and frequent illness and weakness. Whether or not her visions were from migraine headaches will never be known or proved. I do not believe that something so well-organized, specifically visual, or deeply spiritual and theological as her three primary books could be the result of migraine headaches…

Furthermore, her own 'self portraits' show her receiving the visions sitting at a desk with a wax tablet with Volmar and sometimes also Richardis present. She also writes that the visions were given to her in a waking state, not through pain-induced hallucinations or dreams. This image is a portion of the first vision in her *Book of Divine Works*. Many of the illuminations carry a similar 'signature' image, emphasizing her assertion that the visions were given to her, and were not products of her own imagination.

Hildegard's visions included both a visual illumination and a textual explanation of the vision. During the middle ages, even the early middle ages, illuminated manuscripts were crafted. The illuminations were not considered to be works of art in the same sense we use the term today. They were illustrations, following in the tradition of early Byzantine icons. They were not 'decorative' either. A comparison of illuminations in books with sculpture, friezes, and painting in cathedrals and other holy places can be drawn, where the images were intended to tell the stories of scripture visually. They were educational tools, and were considered to be spiritually as influential as the written word. In fact, in a society that was largely illiterate, they were very important for teaching people biblical stories and theological truths. The example to the left is a page from Hildegard's own prayerbook.[167]

[167] Hildegard-Gebetbuch Codex Latinus Monacensis 935. Wiesbaden: L.Reichert, 1982 BX4700.H5 A3 1982 Special collections

Another illumination of a Medieval Bible serves as a foil for comparison with Hildegard's illuminations. This is a page from the Carinthian codex (one of the earliest examples of a manuscript in German) dated from around 1150.[168] A brief background of bookmaking and the use of illumination is helpful to place Hildegard in that historical practice.

Books have a long history of evolution, beginning with clay tablets that were impressed with a stylus. Such tablets were used by the ancient Sumerians and Babylonians as well as other tribes and nations in ancient Mesopotamia.

The earliest known illuminated manuscripts were Egyptian, including the oldest example dating from around 2000 BCE. The following examples are found on a papyrus from the Egyptian "Book of the Dead".[169] Papyrus was made from a pounded pith of reeds which grew in the Nile delta. The material was then formed into continuous strips that, after drying, were still pliable and were rolled around a wooden stick. The manuscript was unrolled as it was read. The longest existing papyrus scroll is an Egyptian papyrus now housed in the British Museum in London, measuring 133 feet long.

These early scrolls were copied and illuminated by professional scribes, often a number of times. There were three primary centers for copying such scrolls, ancient Fedex-Kinko establishments! Those centers were in Athens, Alexandria and Rome. (We have learned of another more recent [i.e. CE] center located in Quran, where most of the Dead Sea Scrolls were copied.) The three ancient centers produced and exported scrolls throughout the ancient world, where, because of their cost, they were purchased by or gifted to temples, rulers, and a few wealthy individuals.

The Egyptian example above shows one of the three styles of illumination, in which the text wraps around the images. Other styles included columns of text alternating with columns of images, and a style in which a strip of images appears at either the top or the bottom of the scroll with text filling the remainder of the script.[170]

---

168 The codex comes from the southern area of Bavaria. It is currently held in the Kärntner Landesarchiv, Klagenfurt, Austria.

169 http://www.maasberg.ch/eLuccaCodex_Ani.html

170 Examples also from the *Egyptian Book of the Dead*. http://www.maasberg.ch/eLuccaCodex_Ani.html

Very little remains of ancient Greek illumination. It is thought that the scientific treatises and certainly the epic poetry scrolls included illuminations. Due to the fragile nature of papyrus (its 'shelf life' was normally less than 100 years before it disintegrated) there are very few original artifacts left. There is a Greek astronomical text dating from the second century BCE in the Louvre which contains illuminations.

Gradually parchment replaced papyrus as the primary material for codices, also replacing scrolls with 'books' (*codex* is the Latin word for *book*). The codex was rectangular and was first used by the Greeks and Romans for business records. They were small notebooks made of parchment leaves between covers made of wood. The initial writings were inscribed with a stylus on tablets of wood covered with wax. The wax could be smoothed over and replenished to be reused over and over. The writing or figures were transferred from the wax tablet to a sheet of parchment by scribes. (This is the method used by Hildegard to record her visions and write her other manuscripts.) The image is a picture of a wax tablet similar to those used by Hildegard, part of the exhibit in the Hildegard museum in Bingen. She may have sketched the outline of her visions on these tablets too, and then carefully supervised the transcription of the wax imprints to the parchment by scribes in her abbey scriptorium. Hmmm. Had our western civilization progressed so far in teaching and learning by the early 19th and the 20th centuries when students – and teachers – used slate tablets marked with chalk in exactly the same manner?

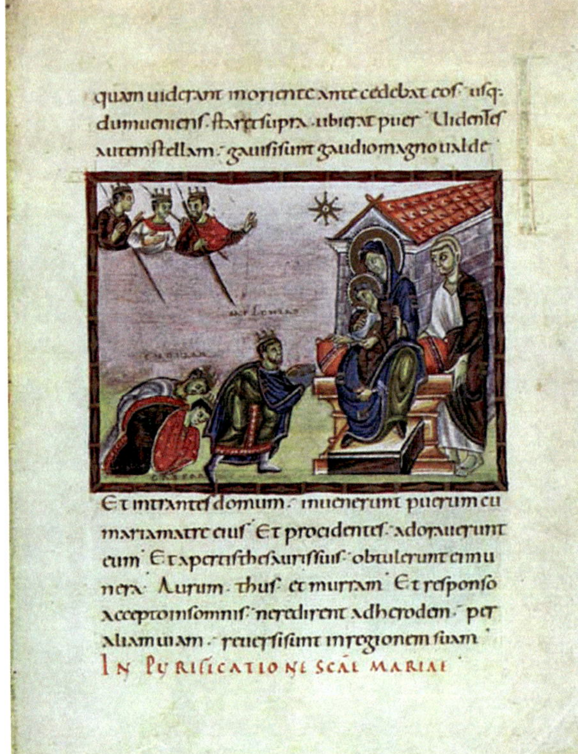

The following two examples are from manuscripts more closely related to Hildegard in time and manner. The first illumination is from the Codex Egberti, now housed in the Stadtbibliothek in Trier, Germany (Hildegard preached in Trier on one of her preaching tours). The illumination dates from the 10th or

11th century during the Ottoman Empire, immediately preceding Hildegard's time. The illuminations during these centuries show very expressive figures that are clearly outlined and were often set against brilliant gold backgrounds. In addition to the illuminations, often the initial letter of the text was drawn in brilliant gold and was highly decorated in a manner reminiscent of Celtic designs.

The next example is from the famous St. Albans Psalter, created in Hildesheim, Germany during the same period of time as Hildegard's work. The Psalter was written around 1120 by a monastic scribe and illuminated by a lay artist. A number of lay illuminators became active during this time, leading to gradual growth in non-religious bookmaking and publishing in the 13th century.

Parchment was difficult and time-consuming to make, and the scribes and illuminators were necessarily very careful in their work – there were no erasers! The image to the left shows an animal skin which has been soaked in a lime solution to remove the fur and then stretched tightly on a frame. While it was still wet, it was scraped, and the ties were continually tightened as it dried to keep it taut. That process continued for several days until the skin was a proper thickness, and it had dried. The skin of newborn or stillborn goats or sheep were specially prized for their smooth texture.

Individual leaves of parchment were folded and then combined into groups of leaves called 'gatherings'. After transcriptions and illuminations were complete, the gatherings were placed in proper sequence and then sewn together on a cords\ or thong that served as the vertical support for the gathering. Then the gatherings were combined by lacing the thongs or cords into channels that had been carved into the boards creating the covers, after which a leather or fabric cover was glued to the boards.

So how were the illuminations transcribed on the parchment vellum? The illuminator first made an outline drawing with leadpoint or with a quill and ink. If gold was used in the illumination, it would be gold leaf, which was extremely thin and fragile. It had to be flexible in order to withstand the turning of the leaves without cracking or flaking away. To do this, the illuminator spread a special glue (a flexible gilding gesso), traditionally made during that century from fish eyes and jaws which were naturally flexible and moisture-sensitive. Then the gold leaf was laid on the 'glue' and burnished to a high gloss. The color media was usually tempera.

Making books was very complicated and involved a number of different types of artisans:

- a parchmenter to prepare the vellum
- a scribe to copy the text
- a rubricator and an illuminator to create the illuminations
- a bookbinder to bind the sections together and prepare the cover

The following image shows the top cover of the Riesencodex, a manuscript that includes Hildegard's books and music. The metal embellishments on the corners and in the center were protectors for the cover, which is wood covered with embellished leather.

It is not known whether Hildegard crafted any of her visions as illuminations herself, but she most probably maintained close supervision and direction of the nuns or monks who did draw them, certainly insisting on accurate representations of the inner visions given to her. The process was exacting and time consuming, and two manuscripts remain for our study and observation. The Dendermonde manuscript has been dated sometime shortly after Hildegard's death, though recent research has indicated it might have been copied during the last three to four years of Hildegard's life (1175-1180). This manuscript contains all three of Hildegard's visionary books and, as a result, the illuminations with which we have become familiar today. The manuscript was originally housed in Rupertsburg and then in Wiesbaden, where it was copied during the early 20th century by nuns from the Eibingen Abbey. The original was then sent to Dresden for safekeeping during the second world war and was lost or destroyed during the firebombing of the city toward the end of the war. The Riesencodex also contains Hildegard's works, but not the illuminations.

Hildegard's illuminations are, as we have seen in earlier chapters, highly detailed and very symbolic. Very little represents the clothing, lifestyle, or mannerisms of Hildegard's time. There is some indication of architecture, and certainly in her medical books there are many representations of plants, animals, fish, trees, and other natural elements current during her lifetime. But her visions are distinct from worldly influence, and bear messages from the supernatural, 'heavenly' realm to mortals on earth.

In comparison with the other examples from the same time period, Hildegard's illuminations (sometimes called 'miniatures') leap off the page with vibrant colors. The nuns who faithfully copied the Dendermonde codex in the 20th century may have enhanced the intensity of the colors, and the intensity of color in the two other examples may have faded with time, but there is no question about Hildegard's use of color in the symbology of the visions! The *Lucca Codex*, housed in the library of Lucca, Tuscany, contains a copy of Hildegard's book, *Liber divinorum operum*, or *Book of Divine Works*. There are copies of eight of the full page illuminations in that book, and also copies of the small 'self portraits' attached to each of the illuminations.[171] The image to the left (now familiar!) is the first from this work, and the illumination of Hildegard receiving the vision with Volmar and Richardis is attached to the bottom of this illumination.

All of her illuminations are framed, a practice which became traditional during Medieval times. The design of the borders are repetitive and symmetrical, and the color is always complimentary to the colors used in the illumination. For those illuminations with attached or included 'self portraits', the borders are crossed, or in many instances contain doors or gates through which God's word and will is passed to Hildegard. So her borders also serve to show that the visions were communicated from the spiritual realm to her earthly habitation.

Hildegard's Vision

Scivias, Book One, Vision Six

The Choirs of Angels

Angels! The sixth vision in Book One of Hildegard's *Scivias* is about angels. Nine different choirs of angels! And she must have heard them singing too! What was their music like? Could she even hear their music? As I was made to realize from the movie "What the Bleep Do We Know?", we see what we have been trained to see, and cannot see what we do not know. That must be true for our sense of hearing too, that we hear what we have been conditioned to hear, and anything beyond our learned and developed physical reality of sound frequencies and 'organization' is incomprehensible and indeed inaudible to us. But she must have heard something!

---

171 http://www.maasberg.ch/eLuccaCodex_Ani.html

172

Wow! What a beautiful, symbolic illumination! But before initiating a discussion of the symbols in this illumination, there are some words we must put into a 12th century context – text and its myriad difficulties as well as beauty and usefulness. We used to think the human species was superior and more blessed by our Creator because we could speak. Well, science and anthropology and research into the life and habits of animals, birds, and sea creatures has changed that "fact"! Perhaps botanists and arborists will be next with news of plant and tree 'speech'! And, where there is speech, there is interpretation and the potential for difficulties in communication! Words mean different things to different people, and over time, the primary meaning of a word may change significantly, particularly if it has been translated from one language to another.

Apropo for this discussion, let's look at the word 'angel'. The etymology of the word begins with the Greek "aggelos/aggelois" which means to bear a message, to announce, or to bring news – a messenger. The Romans 'Latinized' the word to "angelus/angeli", still referring to a spiritual

---

172 "Vision of the Angelic Hierarchy" from "Liber Scivias," 1150-1175 CE, http://albertis-window.com/?s=scivias. *"Vision of the Angelic Hierarchy" image courtesy of Wikipedia.*

being, a messenger of God. The English word 'angel' is an obvious derivation from the Latin, refined and adapted through medieval French and German ('engel) and English (angel).[173]

The reference – and source! – of angelology (the study of angels) begins, in the Christian tradition, with Hebrew tradition through the Old Testament. The following discussion of angels derives from the Hebrew Old Testament followed by references in the New Testament, as that is the source of Hildegard's experience and learning.

There are two hundred and twenty-seven mentions of angels in the Catholic Bible, beginning in Genesis and continuing to and through the book of Revelations in the New Testament. And there are references to specific categories of angels too, with Angels, Seraphim and Cherubim being presented in the Old Testament, and six more being added through Paul's books and letters in the New Testament (Archangels, Principalities, Powers, Virtues, Dominations, and Thrones).

The term "choirs" brings us to another misperception. Today we think of a choir as being a group of musicians gathered to sing or to play instruments. The word derives from the Greek 'choros', which did not specifically refer to a musical group, but more often to a 'ring' of speakers/actors or dancers. For understanding Hildegard's vision, the interpretation of a ring is most beneficial, as is the implication of a 'group' that performs a certain role (speaking, acting or dancing).

Thomas Aquinas, in his *Summa Theologica,* details the hierarchy of the nine groups of angels and their specific duties. His interpretation is what is currently taught in the Roman Catholic tradition. He arranges the nine choirs into a hierarchy of three groups of three, and that arrangement remains to this day. The three groups of the choirs are:[174]

The innermost group of three: contemplate and praise the glory of God
- Seraphim
- Cherubim
- Thrones

The middle group of three: governing and ordering the laws of the created universe
- Dominations
- Virtues
- Powers

And the outer group of three, messengers to creation
- Principalities
- Archangels
- Angels

But Aquinas lived in the 13th Century (1225-1279), after Hildegard. In her vision, Hildegard refers to these nine groups as 'armies', not choirs! And her 'armies' have specific duties, resulting in a different hierarchical ordering than that proposed by Aquinas a century later.

Let's take a look at Hildegard's vision.[175]

In the illumination, there are nine rings – armies of angels, each different from all other rings. Moving from the outermost to the center she groups them and describes their appearances:

---

173 http://www.raphael.net/Scripture/angels.htm

174 http://www.rosaryworkshop.com/HISTORY-9-Choirs-Angels.html

175 The following material is a synopsis of the information included in *Scivias*, Book One, Vision Six, pp. 139-143, Tr. Mother Columba Hart and Jane Bishop (New York, Paulist Press, 1990).

-- two armies grouped together
    -- the first with wings on their breasts and human forms in front of them as if mirrored in water
    -- the second also with wings on their breasts, but with human forms that mirrored the image of the human Christ
--then five armies appear within the circles of the first two:
    -- the first ring had human forms which shone with splendor from the shoulders down
    -- the second army was so resplendent and bright, Hildegard could not look at them
    -- the third had human heads with torches above them, and looked like white marble "surrounded by an iron-gray cloud"
    -- the fourth also resembled humans, wearing helmets and marble tunics, and they had what appeared to be human feet
    -- the fifth army did not resemble humans, "and shone red like the dawn"
-- the innermost two rings of armies are:
    -- full of eyes which had mirrored images of human forms, and wings that were' "raised to a celestial height"
    -- and the innermost circle had wings that reflected all the church ranks in order, and burned like fire

Then Hildegard states "And all these armies were singing with marvelous voices all kinds of music about the wonders that God works in blessed souls, and by this God was magnificently glorified."[176]

She continues, "He [God] also set in place the blessed angels, both for human salvation and for the honor of His name. How? By assigning some to help humans in their need, and others to manifest to people the judgements of His secrets."[177] She explains the hierarchy and roles of the armies in a mystical, theologically interpretive manner.

The outer two rings represent the body and soul, celebrating how humans ought to be servants of God. The outermost celebrates the "beauty of rationality" with wings symbolizing "the intellectual powers that emanate from God to humans" (Aquinas' later circle of 'Angels'). The second army reveals the mystery of the Incarnation (Aquinas' 'Archangels').

The next five rings stand for the five senses, and those senses are regulated by the outer two rings (the body and soul). The first of these (third ring) represents the virtues which lead humans to the fourth ring, brightness where no weakness, not death or sin, can "apprehend the serenity and beauty of the power of God". The fifth ring represents principalities, or persons who exist as leaders and who must learn to "put on the sincere strength[s] of justice…and fairness". The sixth choir exhorts humans to imitate God and God's son through developing a desire for doing good works. The last of this group of five rings, the seventh ring, are Thrones that "in their red-ness, are so immersed in the very many mysteries of heavenly secrets which human weakness is not able to comprehend. They are the color of the dawn because they represent the coming of the Holy spirit over Mary."[178]

The eighth circle is the army of cherubim, signifying the knowledge of God, and the ninth is

---

176 *Op. Cit.*, p.139

177 Ibid., pp. 139-140

178 Ibid.

the army of the seraphim, "burning in the love of god and having the greatest desire for His vision".[179]

The innermost circle is empty. It is the 'full emptiness', the *via negative*, a hole that represents the "path of transcendence". It is all things and no thing, containing full potentiality, the source of all creativity, the mystery of the 'not-yet-created' – the center where beauty is born. Traditionally the number ten (this is the tenth circle) symbolizes the return to unity and the beginning of new creation. It also indicates the totality of the universe.

There are no little, pudgy, sweet-faced 'cherubs' in these celestial armies! Our current culture has diminished the nature of angels to the status of 'cute' or 'precious' imaginary little figurines used for decoration in various ways. We have lost the power and beauty and purpose inherent in the angels of Hildegard's vision. Something rich to think about the next time you hear or see the word 'angel'!

Hildegard's Chant

O vos Angeli

O Angels

O vos angeli qui custoditis populos, quorum forma fulget in facie vestra,	O angels that guard the peoples, whose form gleams in your faces;
et o vos archangeli qui suscipitis animas iustorum,	and O archangels, that receive the souls of the just;
et vos virtutes, potestates, principatus,dominationes et troni, qui estis computati in quintum secretum numerum,	and you virtues, powers, princedoms, dominions and thrones, who are reckoned in the mystical number of five;
et o vos cherubim et seraphim, sigillum secretorum Dei:	and O you cherubim and seraphim, seal upon the secret things of God:
Sit laus vobis, qui loculum antiqui cordis in fonte asspicitis.	Praise to you, who behold in the fountain the little place of the ancient heart.
Videtis enim interiorem vim Patris, que de corde illius spirat quasi facies.	For you see the inmost strength of the Father, which breathes from his heart like a face.
Sit laus vobis, qui loculum antiqui cordis in fonte asspicitis.	Praise to you, who behold in the fountain the little place of the ancient heart.

[179] Ibid.

Hildegard's text is crafted as a responsory, or a text which has a "respond" that is repeated after different versicles. Psalms 118 and 136 are examples with Psalm 136 being a Litany where the respond occurs after every line of text.[180] Most Gregorian responsories begin with two or more versicles before the respond appears for the first time. Then one more versicle, usually a versicle of praise, leads to the final respond. The most common format then, is:

Versicle, Versicle, Respond, Versicle, Respond.

Traditionally today, a responsory chant begins with the cantor intoning a versicle and the respond, followed by a repetition of the respond by the entire choir. The respond is often sung to one of the traditional tones. Then the cantor (or a small group) sings a versicle followed by the entire choir singing the respond. The majority of the sixty-five responsoria in the current *Liber Usualis* follow this pattern as do responsories and psalms used in other liturgical traditions (i.e. Lutherans and Episcopalians). Several also include the 'short' Gloria after the respond; "Glory be to the Father and to the Son and to the Holy Spirit".

All of Hildegard's responsories follow this pattern. None of the responsories for Patron Saints include the short Gloria, nor does *O Vos Angeli*, but her other responsories do. There are five versicles in *O Vos Angeli*, four which identify groups of the nine choirs of angels and briefly describe their roles, followed by the versicle which becomes the respond of praise for the cherubim and seraphim. Then one more versicle further describes the cherubim and seraphim, followed by a final repetition of the respond.

Versicle, versicle, versicle, versicle, Respond, versicle, Respond.

Textually the four versicles prior to the intonation of the respond clearly name the groups of angels described so vividly in her vision. She follows these descriptive versicles with a respond of praise especially for the cherubim and seraphim who are closest to and serve the infinite center of the image, the place, or fountain, wherein resides the ancient heart. A final versicle is offered, further explaining the special status of the cherubim and seraphim followed by the repetition of the respond.

The first two versicles refer to choirs of angels who have direct contact or responsibilities with human beings. They are the 'messenger' angels, including what are commonly referred to today as 'guardian angels'. They also include the named messenger angels of the Old and New Testament:

Gabriel: Daniel 9:21 Delivering explanations of Daniel's visions
Luke 1: 10-20 Announcing John the Baptist's birth to Zacharias
Luke 1: 21-25 (Ave Maria) Announcing Christ's coming to Mary
Michael: Jude 1:9, Daniel, Revelation
Raphael: Enoch, Tobit – a healing archangel

The third versicle refers to five choirs who are reflections of the hierarchy of the heavenly kingdom, and the fourth versicle completes the circle by referring to choirs of angels whose focus and contact is with the Father.

The end of the responsory is a three-part reflection on the last two choirs of angels and their relationship to the Father, who is described in a cosmic, subconscious – or maybe superconscious – manner. In the versicle which becomes the respond we are invited to a glimpse of the innermost place of God, his visionary ancient heart, residing in a holy fountain. What a cosmic view of all creation! Angels bring us, singing!, into and through the spiritual realm to the

---

[180] Psalm 136 is recited at the Passover meal and is called 'the Great Hallel'. The refrain, "for his faithfulness endures forever" is stated after each of the twenty-six single-phrase verses of the Psalm.

fountain that is fed by – that is – the eternal (ancient) heart (life source, viriditas) of the creator Father.

Oh, Hildegard! Your words are just words written on wax tablets and transferred to parchment until they are envigorated by "the voice of the Living Light" in prayer and meditation – with help from your images and music!

According to Hildegard's chant and vision, it is the cherubim and seraphim who see the "vim", of the Father. Do you remember, or have you used the phrase "vim, vigor and vitality"? It is very much in use today, especially in promotion of vitamin supplements... It was at one point an advertising signature for Dr. Pepper – with a 'Leo' gaining his strength from the drink. Now, there is a subject for all kinds of contemporary as well as ancient symbology! But that's not the topic here...

What does the word "vim" mean? Vim comes from the Latin/Greek 'vis', referring to physical or mental strength, force, vigor, power, energy, and virtue. Obviously, "vim" encompasses – and surpasses – vigor and vitality. "Vim" is all of them plus much more. It is interior, incredible strength and energy which breathes from this interior center of unconditional love (heart) through the face of God, emanating from the holy fountain, spreading as water, feeding, nourishing, bringing life to all creation.

Hmm. According to Bernard of Clairveaux, music must serve the text. He was closely acquainted with Hildegard's writing, and she with his. So... how does she set a text like this? Like no other...In an unearthly manner! In so many of her chants, Hildegard flings her praise and petitions into the heavens with extended ranges and dramatic, leaping melodic lines. This responsory chant far surpasses all others, and it is the only chant of Hildegard's to reach such extremes.

Responsories are primarily used during the office of Matins, part of the daily order of prayer practiced by monastic communities (more on that in a later chapter). Matins (also called the 'Night Office' or 'Vigils') was usually observed around 2:00 AM in anticipation of the coming day, It is one of the longer Offices, and contains most (twelve) of the responsories chanted in the Daily Office.

In Germany, 2 AM is one of the darkest times of the night, so we can transport ourselves to a medieval stone chapel, lit only by candles carried by the nuns, and probably very cold and somewhat damp, being right on the Rhine river. The nuns were called to prayer by the monastery bells, and they gathered in silence. During the 12th century, there was obviously no ground light, so the stars must have hung brightly and low in the sky, setting a dramatic environment of silence marked only by the wind and the quiet footsteps of twenty or more nuns moving quickly to the doors of the chapel. They had in their heads and hearts the music of the texts they were about to pray, so their focus was on the meaning of the texts and how they prefaced the new day they were about to experience living in God's creation as God's children.

A transcription of *O Vos Angeli* as notated in the Dendermonde Manuscript follows.[181]

O vos angeli

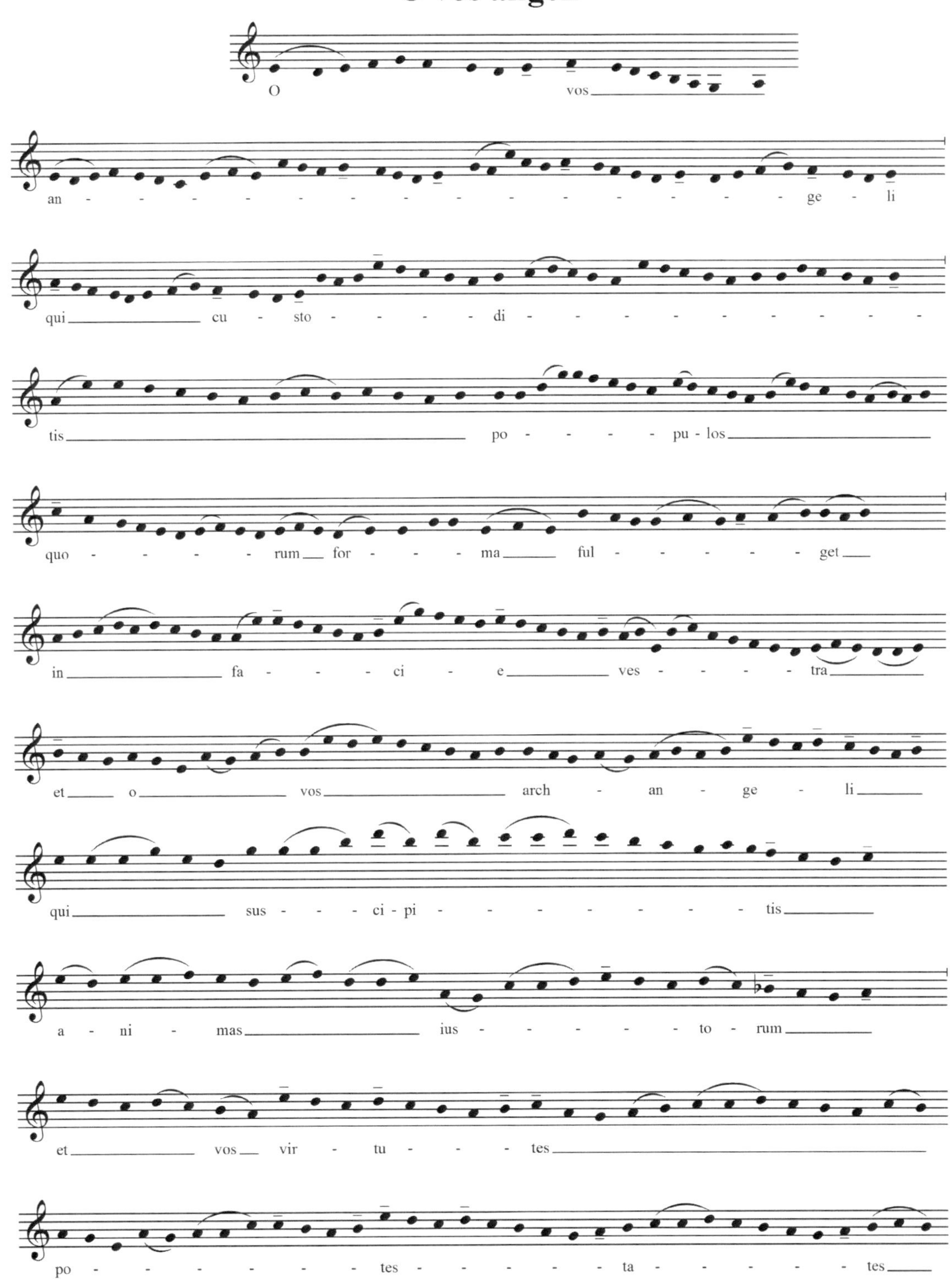

---

[181] The transcription was made from Hufnagelschrift notation from folios 159-160 of the Dendermonde Manuscript: *Hildegard of Bingen: Symphonia Harmoniae Celestium Revelationum. Dendermpnde St.-Pieters & Paulusabdij Ms. Cod.9* . (Alamire, Belgium. 1991).

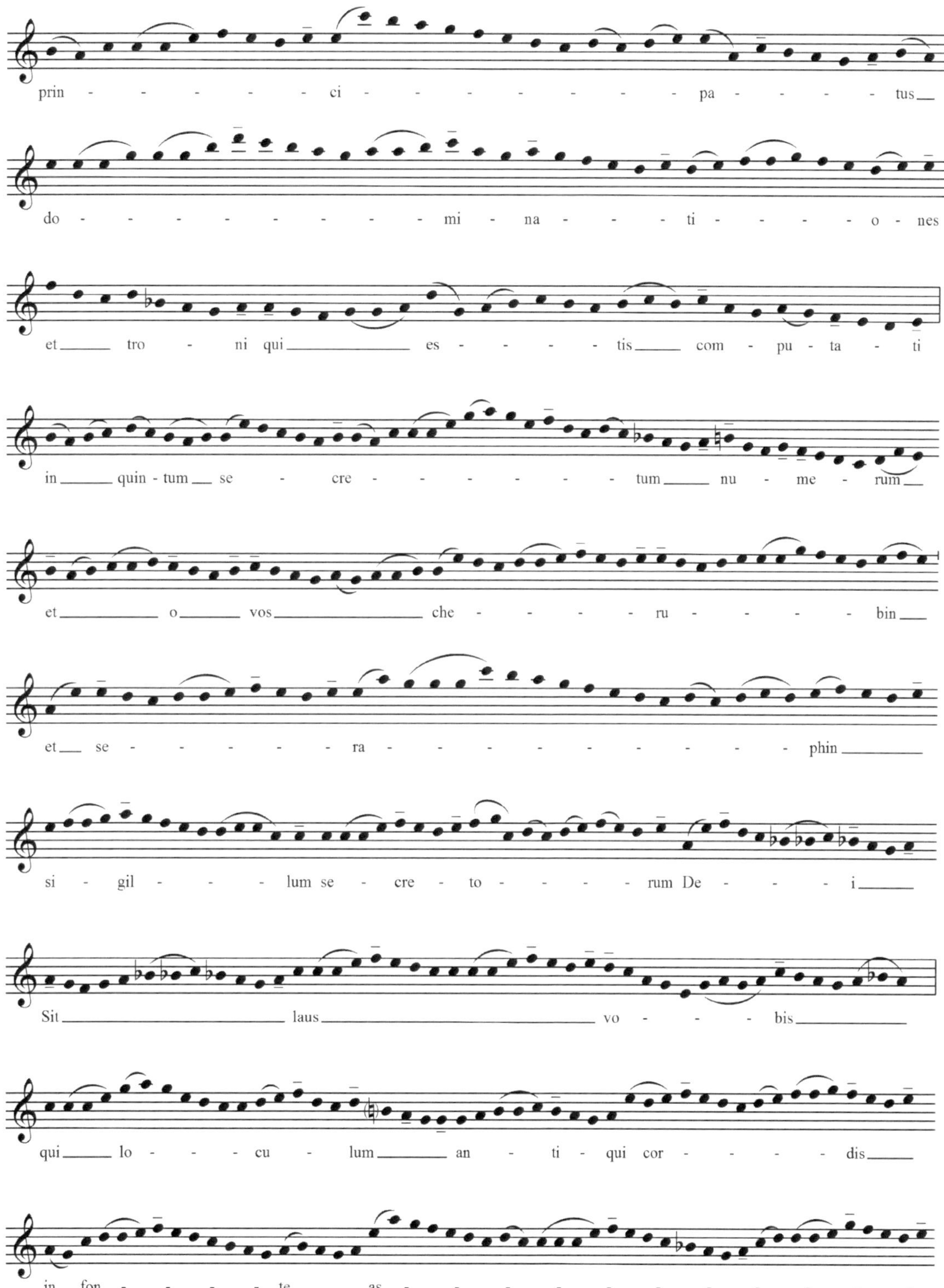
prin - - - - - - ci - - - - - - - - - - pa - - - - - tus
do - - - - - - - - - - mi - na - - - - ti - - - - - o - nes
et tro - ni qui es - - - - - tis com - pu - ta - ti
in quin - tum se - cre - - - - - - - - - tum nu - me - rum
et o vos che - - - - - ru - - - - - bin
et se - - - - - - ra - - - - - - - - - - - - phin
si - gil - - - - lum se - cre - to - - - - rum De - - - - i
Sit laus vo - - - bis
qui lo - - - - cu - lum an - ti - qui cor - - - - - dis
in fon - - - - te as - - - - - - - - - - - - - -

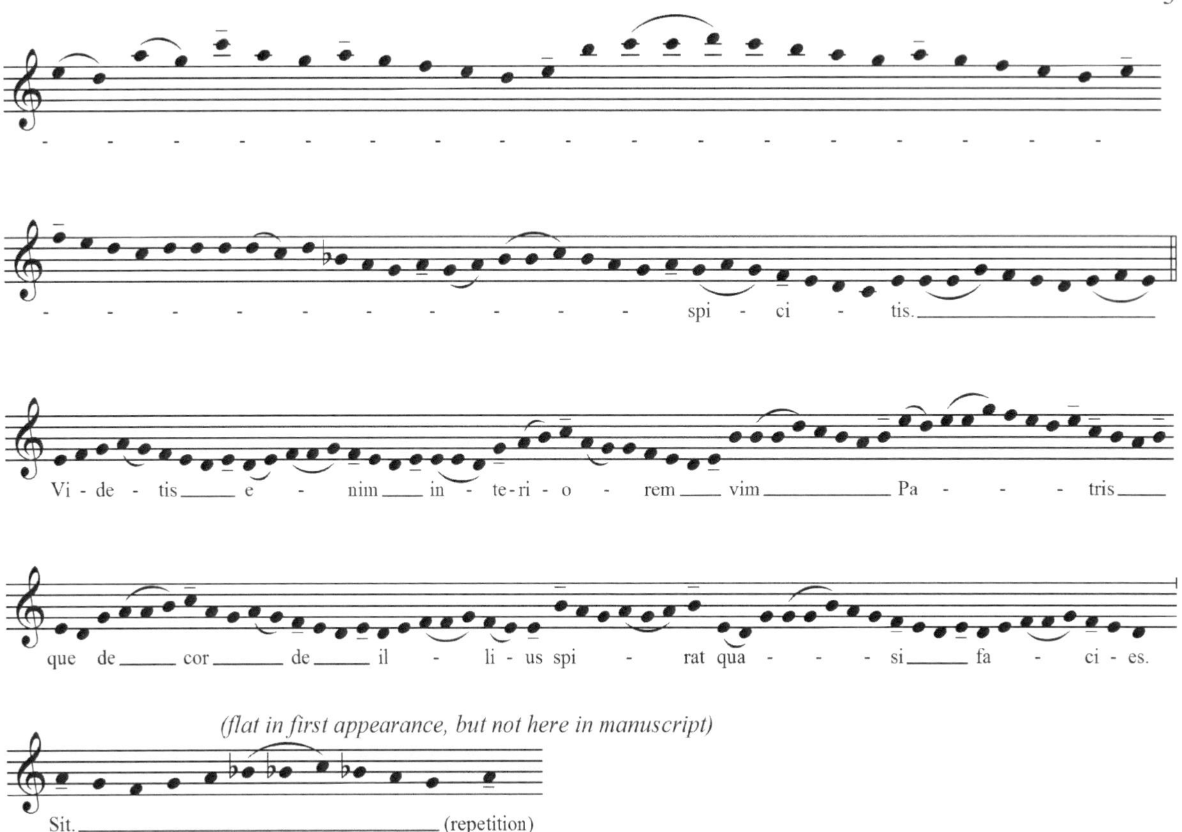

Well! That is Hildegard's chant for the angels! It is one of a kind! It is easy to imagine Hildegard and her nuns standing outside the chapel, above the Rhine valley with grapevine covered hills marching down to the river around quiet, sleeping villages and farmhouses, singing this chant to the star-laden sky, joining with all of the angels in their praise of the unbounded love and energy flowing from the ancient heart.

Let's take a look at what she does to make it so unusual. And we'll look at it from a perspective of what was identified as being characteristic for plainchant during her time. There was considerable activity going on during Hildegard's time in liturgical reform. Bernard of Clairvaux was one of the leaders of liturgical reform, and produced (with the assistance of Guido d'Eu and Richard of Vauclair) a Cistercian theory to correct past errors in liturgical material – both textual and musical.[182] Hildegard was well acquainted with Bernard of Clairvaux, and it would be reasonable to assume that she was also acquainted with his work with liturgical reform.

The resources for Cistercian reform of the liturgy during Hildegard's time are scant, though Bernard's *Tonale* of 1147, "a work which indicates the unique theory used to correct problems of the first attempt at the Cistercian liturgical reform",[183] was available to Hildegard for over thirty years. It is not the purpose here to investigate Cistercian liturgy or liturgical reform, though it is quite interesting. Suffice it to say, the basic tenets of the reform were for the purpose of 'cleansing' the 12th Century liturgical texts and music, returning the composition of liturgical

---

182 McGuire, Kent C. *Symphonia Caritatis: The Cistercian Chants of Hildegard von Bingen*. Unpublished Master's Thesis, University of Minnesota, 2007. pp.40-63.

183 *Op. Cit.*

music to earlier practice that would keep it distinctly separate from secular music and poetic literature. As is the case today, there were intense discussions and disagreements. Included in the disagreements during Hildegard's time were the use of rhythmic poetic texts, more than one melodic line at a time (polyphony), and repetitive texts.

As a brief reminder of the basic characteristics of Gregorian chant, the following table is offered, including the basic reforms tendered by Bernard of Clairvaux and the Cistercians during Hildegard's time.

Musical Element	**Gregorian Practice**	**Cistercian Reform (12th C.)**
Ambitus (range)	Lowest and highest pitches of all eight modes.	Ranges were not to exceed an octave plus a third.
Contour	Primarily arch forms, with some ascending or descending lines.	
Cadences (Terminatio)	Terminatio figures approach the final pitch by step from above or below, or occasionally by third from above.	
Accents	Dynamic, agogic and contoural accents are common.	
Modal Usage	Frequent or occasional commixture of modes, but infrequent 'modulation', even within long chants. Musica ficta involved both the use of b^b and $f^\#$ to avoid tritones.	Only one mode was to be used; no modulation. There was to be no modal mixture of authentic and plagal modes, much less modes with differing finalis pitches. The alteration of the pitch <u>b</u> to <u>b^b</u> was to be avoided (no musica ficta).
Repetition	Immediate and sequential repetitions of melodic motives is common. Also reiteration of a melodic idea occurs frequently.	Any repetition of text or music was to be avoided.
Reiterative Style	Reiteration of a melodic idea with interpolated neumes or 'decorative' pitches is common.	
Melismas	Short (6-10 pitches) to very long (50 or more pitches) melismae are used.	Long melismae were not to be used as they distracted from the text.

And now, to Hildegard's *O vos angeli*!

Ambitus

The range of *O vos angeli* is, in itself, enough to set this chant apart from literally any other chant written in the 12th century. Or before. Or after! Hildegard had her nuns soaring from the depths of earth (G3) to the heights of heaven (D6), two and a half octaves! According to normal Gregorian practice, she extends the range on both ends, and if she was aware of the Cistercian reforms, she extended far beyond that recommendation of only an octave and a third above the finalis of the mode being employed (in this case, E Phrygian).

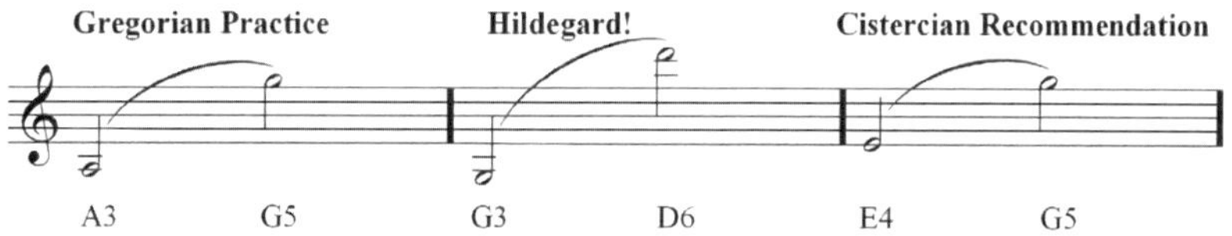

Hildegard's angels cannot be contained by human academic rules!

Contour

Any discussion of contour must also include observations about the ambitus of each versicle. After all, music serves the text in all chant. The first versicle of Hildegard's prayer/poem addresses the choir of 'Angels', those who work with humanity on earth. Guardian angels, angels of conscience, guidance, protection, synchronicity, etc. The first line of text is set 'on earth', as it uses the lowest register of the chant. In fact, this first verse does have an ambitus of two octaves (she breaks the rules from the start!), allowing the angels room to surround and guard humans on earth.

The contours of all four lines are, naturally, wave forms, with the highest pitches reserved for "peoples" and "faces". The lowest are found in the neumatic and melismatic settings of the words "you", "guard", "whose form", and "your". A visual image of beginning, high-low and ending pitches for all phrases is more useful than tracing each line individually, showing a 'purposeful' placement of each line in accordance with the hierarchical purpose of the angels addressed in each verse.

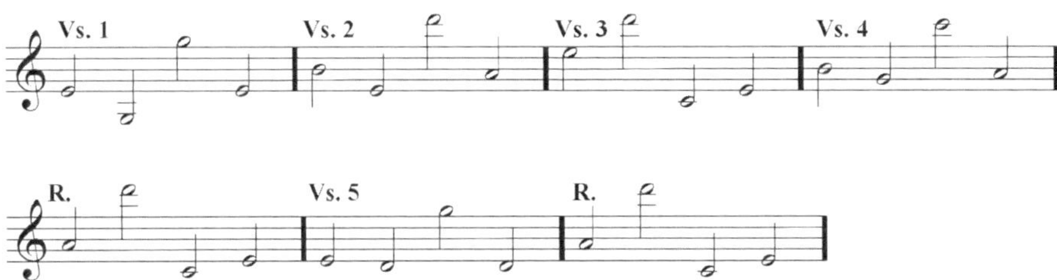

Versicle 1: the closest relationship to earth.
Versicle 2: the messengers to earth from heaven
Versicle 3: the heavenly hierarchy
Versicle 4: the closest relationship to God
Respond: praise of the cherubim and seraphim
Versicle 5: vision of what is in the fountain – the holy of holies

The ambitus of nearly all verses is close to or exceeds two octaves. The two exceptions are the verses referring to the cherubim and seraphim, whose purpose is to serve the Creator, and who circle the inner fountain. Versicle 4 maintains the most consistent register, ascending to G5 for the cherubim and to the apex, C6, for the cherubim, and then descending to surround the secret things of God.

So Hildegard presents us with four levels of angelic activity, spanning the universe and beyond – a cosmic ring of angelic choirs subsuming and serving the heavens and the earth.

Cadences (Terminatio)

Hildegard does not depart from common practice in the terminatio patterns in the chant. All final pitches are E, B, or A, with one exception. Versicle 5 terminates on D, preparing for the final respond. She is consistent in the direction of the terminatio patterns too, approching the final pitch from below in Versicles 1 and 2, from above four times in Versicle 3 (and two times from below), and from both directions in Versicles 4 and 5. The Respond approaches in alternation from above and below, twice each. Again, her choices would appear to be made according to the position of the choirs in the hierarchy.

Accents

The accents (-) indicated in the transcription of *O vos angeli* have been added to identify where Hildegard uses a virga instead of a simple punctum. They always coincide with a final pitch of a clause or phrase of text or with the initial syllable of a clause or phrase. They are not dynamic accents, but agogic accents, receiving, as the virga intends, a slight lengthening of duration.

Modal Usage

Hildegard freely mixes modes in this chant. E Phrygian is the 'mother mode', with A Aeolian being second in importance. But Hildegard isn't satisfied with only two modes. In Versicles 2, 3, 4 and the Respond she employs the musica ficta B^b, mutating the A Aeolian mode to A Phrygian. There are momentary glimpses of G Mixolydian, C Ionian and D Dorian too. The only mode not clearly implied is F Lydian, which contains the tritone F-B. But in the final melisma of the respond, there is momentary emphasis and an agogic accent on F, softened by the following music ficta B^b.

Repetition, Reiteration

Obviously Hildegard uses repetition with the Respond, but that is usual in Responsories. There is no obvious or patterned repetition here, but individual neumatic gestures are repeated, especially the rising P5 noted in each previous chapter of this book. Worthy of note is the absence of Hildegard's 'signature', the rising P5-P4 that marks so many of her chants. The only place in this chant that comes close to that figure is in the Respond, at the beginning of the word 'asspicitis', 'see', or better, 'behold'. But the first pitch of the rising A4-E5-A5 figure is the final pitch of the preceding word 'fonte', or 'fountain'.

Melisma

Well, here we go. This is one of the most melismatic chants in all chantdom! Hildegard is aurally weaving ribbons of melody through the heavens, around the earth, and into the very center of the cosmos! Every choir of angels floats – with purpose! – freely within its own realm. This is far from the more common syllabic and/or neumatic responsories. In fact, the only places in this chant that are syllabic or neumatic (2-5 pitches per syllable) are, with rare exceptions, on short, unaccented syllables of text or on conjunctions or participles. The melismae rule! A brief chart follows, showing the number of occurrences of melismae which use specific numbers of pitches:

Pitches (in the melisma)	Occurrences	Pitches (in the melisma)	Occurrences
6 -	6	13 -	2
7 -	7	14 -	1
8 -	7	15 -	1
9 -	11	16 -	2
10 -	7	18 -	2
11 -	4	37 -	1
12 -	4	81 -	1

Wow. Fifty-six melismae in this chant. And two extremely long melismae, one at the beginning (37 pitches) and one at the end (81 pitches). Guess what words they gild? Angels (AN-geli) and asscipitis (AS-scipitis). 'Angels' and 'BEHOLD'!! The entire word 'angeli' uses 41 pitches, and 'asscipitis' uses 98!

So she invites us to behold her vision of angels in this remarkable chant/prayer. This is truly a vision of the Creator's caretakers and messengers on a level and in a manner not approached in any other chant or song before or since. Yes, that's my personal opinion. So be it!

Meditation

I think we shall stay earthbound for this meditation, gazing into the eternity of space and experiencing our own vision of the myriads of angels active on so many levels of different realities. Here is a photo to peruse, preferably in a darkened room with one candle, quietly and gently seated in a comfortable chair or on the floor. Look at the image, examining all parts of it, and center on the place which draws you back time and again.

Now close your eyes and breathe deeply several times, holding each breath to a slow count of ten and then exhaling slowly. Let all of your concerns and tension exit your body as you exhale.

Now visualize in your mind the place in the image that kept drawing you back. As you move to that place in your imagination, see the beauty and clarity of the sky, feel a slight, comforting breeze, and return your gaze to the place of concentration.

Move slowly into the light of that place. Sense the light surrounding you, comforting you, and filling you with love and peace.

Experience the light and the love fully. Listen. Lift up your inner voice in love and praise. Sense the security and peace surrounding you.

When you begin to return from that place, ask your guardian angel to accompany you.

As you slowly open your eyes to the present, you continue to experience the love and security and peace of that place and a sense of the presence of your guardian angel.

Meditation: A Prayer for Jacob

It's impossible to write another work that is an 'adequate' contemplation of Hildegard's O vos angeli. But a prayer to that Ancient Heart, carried by the breath of a flute, without words, for the healing, comfort, and peace to be found in that place -- and for the answer of life, healing, and health is offered here. God did send his holy angels to watch over him (Jacob), and they did hide him in the shadow of their wings. And he is whole again.

A Prayer for Jacob

For a full and complete recovery for my nephew and Godson, Jacob John-Robert Gebuhr, March 2011

And for my friend and superb flutist Teresa Grawunder.

14 March 2011
Houston, Texas

Exercise

OK. It's time for some angelic exercise! Let's pull together everything we've done so far, if possible. And add a bit more!

Do some deep breathing and stretching before you leave your home. Then climb on your bike and ride to a park that is at least ten minutes of steady pumping away. The park should have some children's exercise equipment or a building or some sports field stands – something with at least five stairsteps.

First, walk at a steady pace around the park for ten minutes. Then walk to the steps and, without pulling yourself up, climb the first five steps without pause. Turn and go down the steps. Then climb them again, repeating the pattern three times (for a total of twenty steps up and twenty steps down). Stop to catch your breath, and then do it again. And again, And again. And again. That's the equivalent of five flights of stairs (100 steps). Rest until your heart rate and breathing return to normal, and then bike home.

This might seem strenuous, but if you do it three times a week, it will become easier – and you might begin extending the number of steps in the pattern! One summer I lived in Munich for a month (studying German), and my room was in a flat on the fifth floor of an older building, a ten minute walk – uphill – from the U-Bahn station. No lift. I learned the value of this exercise the hard way – sudden immersion! But I returned to the US much more fit than when I left! It's a normal part of life in Europe, and the people there are more fit, walking, riding bikes, and climbing stairs! I also learned to quickly count to one hundred ten in a week...

Recipes

Breakfast

Once or twice a week eggs are beneficial and delicious. A good way to begin the day with protein! This is my own personal recipe for fluffy, delicious scrambled eggs to have with a piece of toast with sugarless fruit topping and tea or coffee.

Scrambled Eggs

2 eggs
2 Tbs Mayonnaise or Lite Sour Cream
1 Tb chopped chives or finely chopped onions
1 Tb melted butter or almond oil
Himalayan salt or seasalt and pepper to taste.

Mix the eggs and mayo or sour cream together lightly, leaving some small 'chunks' of the mayo or sour cream.

Heat the butter or oil in a small pan, lightly saute the chives or onions, and pour in the egg mixture. Cook until barely done, leaving the scrambled eggs soft.

Lunch

Soup for lunch, especially a hearty soup with crackers and fruit, is always a healthy and delicious way to refuel for an active afternoon. This soup is a favorite, very tasty, colorful to serve, and healthy!

Butternut Squash, Coconut, and Lentil Stew

1 C yellow split pigeon peas (Toor Dal)
1 lb. butternut squash, peeled, cut into ½-inch cubes (about 2½ C)
1 Roma tomato, diced, or 8 cherry tomatoes, halved
½ C shredded coconut
½ tsp. turmeric
½ tsp. ground cumin
4 C stock or water to cover (I use organic chicken stock)

Tempering:

2 Tbs canola or almond oil
1 tsp. brown or black mustard seeds
½ tsp. crushed red pepper flakes
1 clove garlic, minced
1½ tsp. kosher salt
1 Tbs honey or agave syrup
1 lime, juiced
½ C fresh minced cilantro leaves

Rinse the pigeon peas in a couple of changes of water.

In a large soup pot, combine the squash, drained pigeon peas, tomato, coconut, turmeric, cumin, and stock to cover. Bring to a boil, then simmer covered for 20 minutes. Remove the cover and simmer another 10 minutes.

To temper:

In a small pot with a cover, warm the oil until shimmering. Add the mustard seeds and cover immediately.

When the seeds stop popping (10-12 seconds), add the pepper flakes, garlic and salt. Swirl the pot so the ingredients cook evenly for another 10 seconds.

Pour the contents of the pot into the soup. Spoon a ladleful of soup into the pot (be careful, it will sizzle and pop), and pour it back into the soup.

Finish with the honey, lime juice and cilantro.

Dinner

This is one of my favorite, quick dinners. A local really fine restaurant spurred me on to try and duplicate their pork chop and spinach (just mentioning it makes me salivate...). They served a thick, very sweet plum sauce with the chop (which I am leaving out!), and a side of polenta or garlic mashed potatoes. I substitute here a side of baked sweet potato. The entire dinner takes 15-20 minutes to prepare!

Pork Chop

Thoroughly coat a nice, boneless pork chop on both sides with seasalt and pepper. Cook in almond oil over medium-high heat for six minutes on each side.

Fresh, cooked spinach

One-Half a regular sized bag of organic baby spinach
2 Tb Olive or almond oil
1 Tb chopped garlic
2 Tb freshly squeezed lemon juice

While the chop is frying, heat the oil and lightly saute the garlic.
Add the spinach when you turn the chop over.
Cover and steam for 1½ - 2 minutes, stirring occasionally.
Add the lemon juice, stir, and serve with the chop.

Baked Sweet Potato

Wash and cut a large sweet potato in half.
Cook on high in a microwave for five minutes.
Test to see if it is soft throughout. Cook another minute if not.
Remove and cut in half, then mash slightly and add butter, salt and pepper to taste.

A capuccino or latte with sugar-free biscotti is a nice cap to the meal!

VI.
Hildegard: A Poet of Mysticism

Mysticism

What in the world is a 'poet of mysticism"? We know what it means to be a poet, so that leaves mysticism as the enigmatic term here. More specifically, we must approach the question of what might have been Hildegard's 12th Century mysticism.

We bandy the term 'mysticism' about a good bit, often with the implication that we might know what we are talking about! But what are we talking about? The dictionary isn't much help, defining 'mystic' as "relating to religious mysteries or occult rites or practices. Of or relating to mysticism or mystics. Inspiring a sense of wonder and mystery. One who practices or believes in mysticism or a specified form of mysticism."[184] Well, that clears that right up, doesn't it?

The term 'mystical' isn't any more hopeful, defined as "mysterious, bizarre, puzzling, obscure".[185] But finding the term 'mysticism', we are helped a bit more: "a spiritual discipline aiming at direct union or communion with God or with ultimate reality through trancelike contemplation or deep meditation. The experience of such communion as described by mystics. A belief in the existence of realities beyond intellectual or perceptual apprehension that are central to being and directly accessible by subjective experience, as by intuition. Vague and unsupportable speculation."[186]

Hmmm. Yes, a bit more helpful, but let's go to a more specific source, Brother Bruno Borchert, a Carmelite brother and senior researcher on art and mysticism at the Titus Brandsma Institute in Holland. He offers a description of mysticism as "a phenomenon that seems to occur in all religions and cultures; it is different in external form, but in essence everywhere it is the same: *it is the experimental knowledge that, in one way or another, everything is interconnected, that all things have a single source."*[187]

He continues, saying that mystical experience is much like being in love. But being in love with the all-embracing reality (i.e. God) that suffuses, permeates, and surpasses our every-day (mundane) existence. Mysticism is experience and what grows out of that experience, and a mystic is someone whose life is shaped and ordered by that experience.

OK. Now we deal with the word 'experience' as it is used here. I've seen the word 'theophany' applied to sudden experiences, though a theophany is a single event. Vision, waking dream, 'mountaintop experience' are also more contemporary terms. But the depth of the experience and the response to the experience for one who is or becomes a 'mystic' raises a deeper level of reality to the level of the conscious mind. It is a reality that has always been there, but has not often been perceived. Sometimes, as in Hildegard's experience, it rises out of

---

[184] Webster's 7th Collegiate Dictionary. p.781

[185] Ibid.

[186] Ibid.

[187] Borchert, Bruno. *Mysticism: Its History and challenge.* York beach, Maine: Samuel Weiser, Inc. 1994. ISBN 0-87728-772-4. p.3

the subconscious in the form of images (visions). Most often though, the most fundamental level of reality is inexpressible and indescribable except in vague terms (or music?) – light, darkness, love, infinity, nothingness, presence, Father, the ocean, etc.[188] Persons experiencing the reality of another world are for that specific moment united with that 'other' world; the inner and the outer become one.

Brother Borchert goes on to point out that mystical experience and religious experience are often very different. Religious experience is an experience of dependence upon God. Mystical experience is an experience of love – an experience of God – not God's love or love for God, but the experience of God, who is Love. It is an experience of knowing that "all things are one, a universe, an organic whole into which everything fits…and everything seems to be good – the whole is not divided into good and evil, I and Thou, or body and mind…"[189]

Well, my purpose here is not to 'prove' that Hildegard was a mystic, or to thoroughly discuss the 'nature' of mysticism as it could be applied to Hildegard's life and work. Evidence is plentiful, including three of her visions already discussed at some length in this book. Three of the points made by Brother Bruno about the nature of mysticism are amply illustrated by Hildegard:

-- Chapter One – the vision of the Egg of the Universe: "in one way or another, everything is interconnected, that all things have a single source."

-- Chapter Two – Vision One from *Liber divinorum operum*: the mystical experience "raises a deeper level of reality to the level of the conscious mind…and it rises out of the subconscious most often in the form of pictures, or images".

-- Chapter Five – the vision of the heavenly choirs of angels – "all creation is a symphony of joy and jubilation".

In the Medieval world, experiencing a mystical event led to the question "Is this of the devil, or does it come from God?" Hildegard was aided by Bernard of Clairvaux, who was impressed and moved by her writing – and probably also her music, in receiving the approval of the Pope. Pope Eugenius, who commanded her to continue recording her visions, opened the way for her to write, compose, teach, preach, and heal. This was very unusual for a woman of the time, and she did all of these things in response to her mystical experience of God. Of unconditional love. Isn't it amazing that today, 833 years after her death, the power and truth of her mystical experience and the applications of the experience to this worldly reality have grown and led to her church, through Pope Benedict, officially entering her into the book of Saints (10 May, 2012) and naming her a Doctor of the Church (the 35th in history, the 4th woman) on 7 October 2012? Hildegard lives, and her work lives through her mystical experience of Love.

Well. That should answer once and for all the question "Is this of the devil, or does it come from God?"! But what of the devil? This chapter approaches the sixth statement of belief in the creed, "…the forgiveness of sins…", and the devil surely has something to do with that! And what is sin? Well, this is not the place to embark upon a theological or philosophical discussion on the nature or definition of 'sin'. To say nothing of my lack of qualification to do so – except as a simple human being who tries to live without committing any major – or minor – sins knowingly. My own simple understanding of sin is any thought or act committed without the presence of God (i.e. Love). That simple definition can become very complex immediately.

---

[188] Ibid., p.7

[189] Ibid., p.11

So, is the 'devil' involved? And does the Devil cause us to sin, or is he hanging around waiting for us to sin (thanks to God's gift of free will) so he can jump in and recruit us to his legions and purpose? And just who-what is the devil? In a binary universe, the devil is the personification of evil, the opposite of good. The name even appears to be derived from the word evil… The devil has been given names—Lucifer, Satan—and is portrayed in the New Testament as the ultimate tempter. The lesson is that the devil does not make us sin, he tempts us to sin, and we sin because we choose to do so. Hmmm. That apparently makes us responsible for our own sins – we can't push them off on the devil!

This all goes back of course to the teachings about 'original sin'. Human beings were created with the gift of free will, making them (the microcosm) as much like God (the macrocosm) at least in this reality (on this planet, in this galaxy). This reality is bounded by birth – life – death, which is not part of the macrocosm. And the 'first' humans chose to know everything, including the 'fruits' of good and evil. As a result of temptation by the devil – in this case a serpent. In an interconnected universe, evil, the devil, is part and parcel of everything, just as is good, God, love. Whether or not we yield to the temptation of evil thoughts, acts, or situations is our choice. And the results of our choices are our own responsibility.

Well. The devil. Our culture has done all kinds of things to the nature and understanding of evil through different personifications of evil. Halloween is only one example – dressing up our children in costumes representing a little horned demon, filling TV ads and video games with dancing, 'cute' little devils that are always tempting us to do something 'naughty'. Enormous evil creatures representing alien life (which may exist, after all) that seeks only to destroy or dominate. Oof dah. to say nothing of an increasingly dominant emphasis on TV series focused on evil.

The devil – in any guise – is not cute. And Hildegard's vision of the devil in *Scivias* (Book 2, Vision 7) is not cute.

Book 2, Vision 7 (Scivias)

We will look only at the devil in this vision. What an ugly, horrible creature chained to a stone, spewing and defecating and struggling against its chains! Hildegard presents the devil to us as a worm, -- a 'hybrid' worm. Its body is a worm, but its nose, mouth and feet are those of a viper. Its hands are human. It is lying down because Christ wounded it and destroyed so much of its health (strength) that it cannot stand. But it still arouses horror and rage because we mortal humans do not have the ability to understand its limitless variations of poisonous temptations, fury, or maliciousness.

The worm "is black and bristly, covered with ulcers and pustules".[190] The color black has been from ancient times a symbol of darkness and evil – here Hildegard intends the color to symbolize betrayal. The bristles, ulcers, and pustules represent deception, pollution, and repressed fury, respectively.

There are five stripes from head to feet on the worm, representing his corruption of the five senses of humans: green = worldly melancholy, white = improper irreverence, red = deceptive glory, yellow = biting envy, and black = shameful deceit. These and "all other perversities bring death to the souls of those who consent to them."[191]

Its eyes are bloody and burning, representing his vicious, harmful intent and wounding of souls with fiery darts. Its bristly ears pierce humans, looking for anything within a person that is the devil's. Its nose and mouth are shaped like a viper's representing "unbridled and vile behavior" used to transfix humans with vices so it might kill them.

"Its hands are human, for he practices his arts in human deeds; its feet a viper's feet, because he ceaselessly ambushes people when they are journeying and inflicts devilish lacerations on them; and its tail short and horrible, for it signifies his power in the short but most evil time of the son of perdition, whose desire to run wild exceeds his power to do it."[192]

In addition to what is portrayed in the illumination, Hildegard describes other 'attributes' of this hideous beast that appeared to her in the vision.

> And I saw sharp arrows whistling loudly from its mouth, and black smoke exhaling from its breast, and a burning fluid boiling up from its loins, and a hot whirlwind blowing from its navel, and the uncleanness of frogs issuing from its bowels; all of which affected human beings with grave disquiet. And the hideous and foul-smelling vapor that came out of it infected many people with its own perversity…And I heard again the voice from Heaven, saying to me: God strengthens the faithful so that the Devil cannot conquer them."[193]

Hildegard gives us the image of the devil as the great tempter, offering vices, viciousness, power, anger, envy, gluttony, lust, greed, pride, and all other temptations. But the devil can act only when humans succumb to the temptations, when they buy into them. Turning the back, keeping eyes, hearts, and hopes on the good (God) keeps the devil in the chains created by Christ and his victory over death and the devil.

There is much more in this vision regarding the human relationships with the devil and with the celestial sphere. If you haven't yet purchased a copy of *Scivias*, I highly recommend doing so! But now it is time to move to Hildegard's music. She actually did write one chant about the devil. And it is also full of symbols and secondary meanings! It is even a little 'bristly'…

---

[190] Hildegard von Bingen. *Scivias*. Tr. by Mother Columba Hart and Jane Bishop. (1990 by the Abbey of Regina Laudis: Benedictine Congregation Regina Laudis of the Strict Observance, Inc. Pub. by Paulist Press, New Jersey) p.296

[191] *Ibid.*

[192] *Ibid.*

[193] *Ibid.* p. 294

Sed Diabolus

-- from a collection of Antiphons for St. Ursula

We must have a brief history lesson before looking at this chant, which is so appropriate for the vision from *Scivias* discussed earlier. Who was St. Ursula, and why would Hildegard write nine antiphons, arranged into a liturgy, in veneration of her?

The image of St. Ursula is by Carlo Cravelli, a 15th century Italian who lived probably 1,000 years after the event creating the legend of St. Ursula and 11,000 virgins supposedly occurred. The legend of St. Ursula is no longer part of official Roman Catholic tradition, as there have been many, many variations of the story and none can be proved. According to the most common version, St. Ursula was a British princess who was promised to a pagan prince in marriage, probably for political reasons. She resisted, and asked to make a pilgrimage to Rome instead, accompanied by eleven companions. The route took them from Britain to the Rhine, past Köln (Cologne), Germany. After reaching Rome and spending some time there, they returned to Britain, but on the way back their ship was attacked at Köln, and all of them were killed by the Huns.

In the intervening centuries a number of variations of the legend have expanded the number martyred to 11,000 virgins. This exaggeration was possibly either a 'clerical' error or a misreading of one of the companion's names (Undecimillia) as the number 11.000. It might also be a misinterpretation of the abbreviation XI.M.V. (eleven martyred virgins) as the Roman numeral XIM (11,000). However the legend expanded in scope, the reasons for Ursula's travels have been enhanced and offered as cause for canonization and veneration.

Pozzi Escot, a noted musician and Hildegard scholar, gave the following speculation about Hildegard's attraction to St. Ursula in a preface to the edition of her transcription of the Ursula Antiphons:[194]

> Hildegard was exquisitely attracted to Ursula because of the many ways in which Ursula personified her. Ursula was an admirable leader. She had the power of wisdom. She had fought the hierarchy and the laws of her origins. She had served Christianity and stood by her pure principles of faith and submission to One beyond the pagan forces. She had commanded and led her legions from a distant land to Rome, the seat of the apostles of Jesus…Ursula was Church, Faith, Wisdom, all in one.

The first eight antiphons are full of peace, beauty, God's grace, laudatory comments about following God's will and the gifts of grace which accompany doing God's will. In the first eight antiphons, Hildegard celebrates the purity, vision and leadership of Ursula, emphasizing the call

---

[194] Hildegard von Bingen. *The Ursula Antiphons*. Ed. and transcribed by Pozzi Escot. (1994 Hildegard Publishing Company, PA), pp. 3-4

and vision from God, the care and nurturing of the Holy Spirit, and the obedience of Ursula and her companions. It is only in the final antiphon, *Sed diabolus*, that the darkness of evil enters the picture, tainting all that preceded it and telling the final tale, the end of the legend allegorically. The final antiphon is a sudden 'shock', bringing into the liturgy the ultimate action of the devil, observing that the devil leaves nothing in God's creation untouched. Perhaps the implication here is that the holier, purer and more innocent a person or creation is, the more severely the devil attacks and destroys. Or that even the utmost purity and innocence might be used for or transformed into evil.

The Chant

Sed diabolus	*But the devil*
Sed diabolus in invidia sua istud irrisit	But the devil mocked in his envy,
qua nullum opus Dei intactum dimisit.	leaving no work of God untouched.

Hildegard's score as found in the Dendermonde manuscript (Number 53):

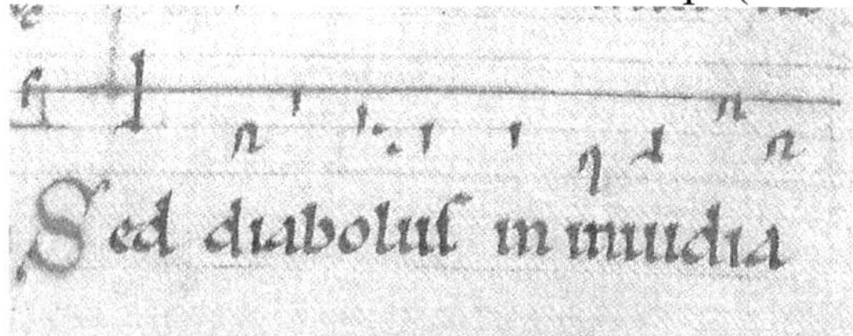

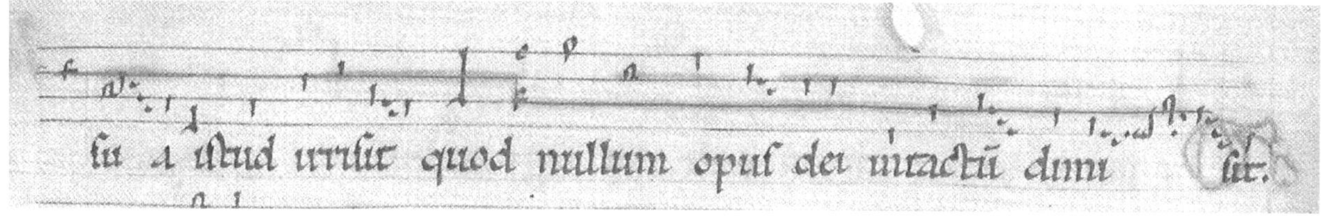

I offer a transcription of the Hufnagelschrift, with slurs grouping the neumes as notated.

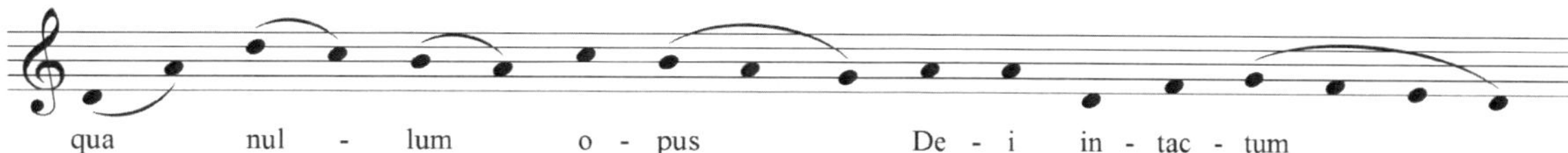

This chant is the shortest of all of Hildegard's seventy-plus chants. But in its brevity it is a concise summation of many characteristic practices that identify it as particularly Hildegard's. Perhaps also, in a mystical manner, it is representative of the beauty, symmetry, and order that is fundamental to creation and the order of the cosmos. Wow. But it is about the devil! Who is present in everything and everyone… It is organic, using only sixty-six (66) pitches to create an amazing, complex, highly organized entity. Thus, we may use this short chant to summarize many of the things we have seen in the other chants presented in earlier chapters.

First, Hildegard employs a combination of syllabic, neumatic and melismatic settings of the text, prompting a question: was Hildegard intending to present a subtext here? The only two words bearing melismae are "sua" (his) and "dimisit" (dismissed, or 'leaving'). The other two words with the most tones are "irrisit" (mockery) and "intactum" (touched). So Hildegard emphasizes the words "his… mockery… touched…leaving". A lesson resides here – no matter that the devil (sin) mocks and touches everyone and everything in this world, ultimately he/it/sin and all of its mockery, pain, and evil is left behind. Evil can only survive and work and mock in this worldly existence. When we leave and go to another realm – heaven – the devil and all of his/its reality/mockery/evil is left behind. Well. She not only gives us a definition of the devil in her short poetic text, she gives us the ultimate victory – the basic foundation of the Christian faith. The victory over death – freedom from evil. We go on in love and freedom; the devil is left behind. The lesson is offered here as the result of the union of text and music – inseparable and whole. If observed separately, the subtext is lost.

There is no mode mixture in this chant, other than switching from Hypodorian to Dorian. Hildegard uses the lower register (Hypodorian) to set the text introducing the devil and his mockery. The chant moves between the pitches A3 and A4, with contoural emphasis on the confinalis F4. The phrase begins and ends on the finalis D4, with the cadence circling the finalis using the supertonic and subtonic pitches – a common termination figure in chant.

She moves to the higher register (Dorian) when speaking of the works of God. With only two small exceptions, the second phrase moves within the octave D4-D5 with considerable emphasis on the confinalis A4 in the first half of the phrase. The phrase ends with the same cadential figure as the first.

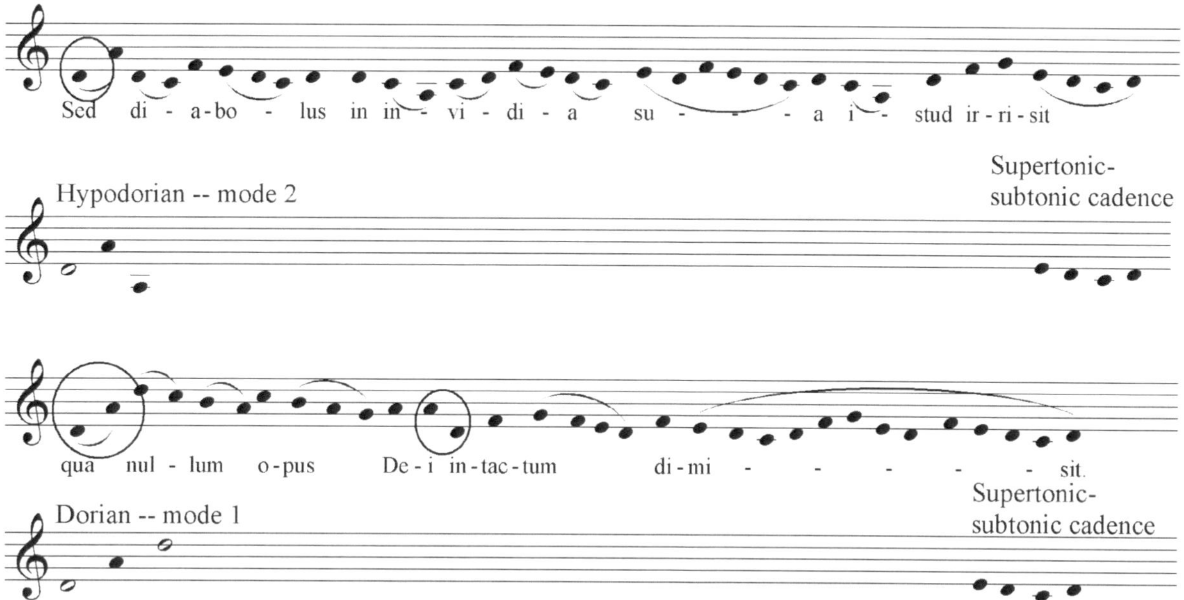

There are some circled figures in the example above. They identify this chant in an even more significant manner as a 'Hildegard' chant. The leaping P5 of D4-A4 begins both phrases, and it is used in a descending direction at the point in the text where the devil 'touches' the works of God. We also see the extension of the rising P5 with an additional P4 at the beginning of the second phrase – Hildegard's signature motive. And hmmm, that point also happens to be the Golden Section of the chant. More on that in a bit.

In addition to the P5 motives, Hildegard's craftsmanship in unifying the chant is evident through juxtaposition of neumes that create reiterated motives larger than the individual neumes. Some of these more complex figurations correspond to the syllables of text, but others do not. In examining the motives, we move to a 'deeper' level of the structure of the chant, away from the surface materials. In this second layer, we find further evidence of unity – more organic material – that binds the melodic line into a beautiful whole. It is rather like examining an orange – first seeing the pebbled patterns on the outer skin, then removing the rind and seeing the wonderfully symmetrical individual pieces of the fruit. I offer the following motivic graphing for further examination:

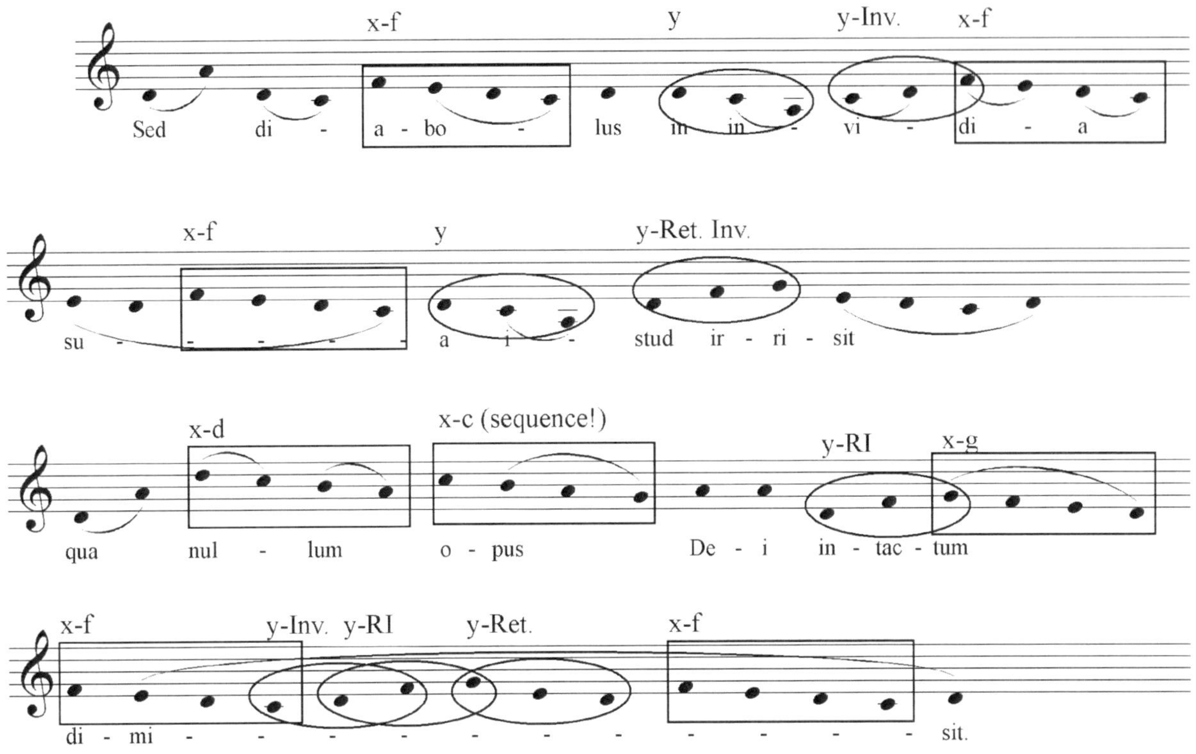

Hildegard uses two distinct motives in systematic ways:

x – a descending step motive of four pitches

y – a trichordal (3pitches) motive containing M2 and m3 in ascending or descending motion

1. The 'x' motive appears always in descending motion, beginning on one of four pitches:
   - f – the confinalis of the Hypodorian mode
   - d – the finalis
   - c – in sequence
   - g – leading to the finalis

   Tracing this motive throughout the chant yields a certain symmetry:

Phrase 1, Hypodorian	x-f, x-f, x-f
Phrase 2, Dorian	x-d (Golden section), x-c (sequence)
	x-g, x-f (sequence, beginning final melisma),
	x-f (at the end)

   Even though she never returns to the Hypodorian mode (the lower register) at the end, the return of the x-f motives emphasize the confinalis of the Hypodorian mode as in the first phrase.

2. When adding the 'y' motive into the mix, even more structural unity becomes apparent. The first 'y' appears immediately after the word 'diabolus', connecting the words 'in invidia' (in mockery) and descends from the finalis D4 to the lower 'dominant', A3. That exact motive is reiterated to connect the words 'sua'

(devil – 'his') and 'istud' (stood). So the devil stood in mockery in the lowest register…

Then Hildegard becomes a 20th century composer…she operates (twists? mocks?) on the motive in three other ways:

- -- she immediately turns it upside down (y-Inversion) on the syllables "in invi-"
- -- after the first reiteration, she immediately presents it upside down and backward (y-Retrograde Inversion) on the syllables "-stud ir-ri-"
- -- she reiterates the y-RI after the Golden Section ("qua nullum opus Dei) on 'touch' ("intactum")
- -- and in the final melisma, 'dismisses' the motive's twists and turns with interlocked reiterations of the y-I, y-RI, and y-R,surrounded by the x-f.

Is this imposing too much, or implying too much, on or about an early Medieval chant? Did Hildegard think about these methods of organizing melodic materials? Is it appropriate or 'academically sound' to apply current analytical methods and speculations to a nearly one thousand year old chant?

Yes, yes, yes. Yes. We have been doing this for centuries. We are a curious species, wishing to understand and learn about our world, i.e. our God who created all of this. And the more we learn, the deeper is our appreciation of the magnificent, complex, beautifully organized cosmos in which we live and breathe. The discoveries and theorems proposed by curious investigators in centuries and millennia past have been proven and reproven in their truth throughout history. And they have been enhanced and probed more deeply – unpeeled, you might say – by modern methods of speculation and investigation, much to our benefit. We discover ourselves through our discoveries, and as we learn, we grow and live. When this process stops, if we believe we know all that there is to know, when we tell ourselves we can rest and quell our curiosity, we begin to die. Furthermore, we can't hear or examine Hildegard's chants like a Medieval perceiver. There has been a millennium of growth, learning and understanding since they were first notated. And the more we learn and discover in these works or anything and everything else created in earlier times using contemporary techniques and methods of analysis, the more wondrous and beautiful and amazing they become. The big lesson here, I believe, is that we cannot – must not – try to go back. To do so is to begin to die. We must move ahead. And that goes for our attempts to understand the 'diabolus' too!

Hildegard was a mystic. She received visions. And she recorded them as best as she was able. Her music and visions and prayers and life within the Benedictine rule were all one, not fractured separate parts of daily duties. Her purpose for life was to love and give praise to her Lord through everything that was given to her, including things which were not so pleasant! She was not a 'fractured' person either – she was not a composer. A medical practitioner. A poet. An abbess. An artist. A CEO. A spiritual director. A preacher. A nun. She was all of these things. She was Hildegard, serving God in all of the best ways she was able to serve. We can look at each one of her gifts individually and in great detail, applying all of our known techniques and methods of investigation, and we don't begin to understand or comprehend the whole person, the microcosm that was Hildegard. But we are the richer for our efforts.

I think it is time to meditate…

Meditation

For this meditation, I offer another image from the Hubble Space Telescope. It is titled "Mystic Mountain" by NASA! So, science and exploration offer an image from the cosmos, a reality other than the one we inhabit for us to explore and experience with open hearts and minds The guided meditation is based upon one I experienced many years ago. From the Psalms: "Be still, and know that I am God."

[195]

---

[195] This turbulent cosmic pinnacle lies within a tempestuous stellar nursery called the Carina Nebula, located 7,500 light-years away in the southern constellation Carina. The image celebrates the 20th anniversary of Hubble's launch and deployment into an orbit around Earth.

Scorching radiation and fast winds (streams of charged particles) from super-hot newborn stars in the nebula are shaping and compressing the pillar, causing new stars to form within it. Streamers of hot ionized gas can be seen flowing off the ridges of the structure, and wispy veils of gas and dust, illuminated by starlight, float around its towering peaks. The denser parts of the pillar are resisting being eroded by radiation much like a towering butte in Utah's Monument Valley withstands erosion by water and wind.

Nestled inside this dense mountain are fledgling stars. Long streamers of gas can be seen shooting in opposite directions off the pedestal at the top of the image. Another pair of jets is visible at another peak near the center of the image. These jets (known as HH 901 and HH 902, respectively) are the signpost for new star birth. The jets are launched by swirling disks around the young stars, which allow material to slowly accrete onto the stars' surfaces.

Hubble's Wide Field Camera 3 observed the pillar on Feb. 1-2, 2010. The colors in this composite image correspond to the glow of oxygen (blue), hydrogen and nitrogen (green), and sulfur (red).

Object Names: HH 901, HH 902

Look at the picture, examining every detail. Pick a favorite place in the picture.

In your imagination:

Pick up a large, black trash bag sitting on the floor next to you. Place into the bag several things that have weighed on you, some for years. Things you did that you wished you hadn't done, things you have said, hurts you have received or given. Then tie the top of the bag into a knot, lift it over your shoulder, and move your concentration to the favorite place in the image.

In your imagination, slowly move toward that place. Memorize what it looks like, remembering every detail.

Close your eyes as you move closer to the place, seeing in your imagination details that were not in the original image.

As you move into that place, you see a brilliant but not glaring warm Light in the distance.

Slowly you approach the Light, gradually being surrounded and embraced by the light. Quietly experience this for some time.

The Light gently takes your bag off your shoulder and opens it. Each thing you placed in the bag is brought out for you to examine and accept. Then it is placed back into the bag.

When all has been examined, the Light takes the bag and places it into one of the streams of hot gas, destroying it and flinging its ashes into the cosmos.

Sit and experience unconditional love and forgiveness.

Slowly return to this reality, remembering the experience and noting the thoughts you have as a result of the experience.

I offer a new work for this meditation: Offertorium.

Image Type: Astronomical
Credit: NASA, ESA, and M. Livio and the Hubble 20th Anniversary Team (STScI)

Solo Flute

Offertorium

Exercise

Because of the 'mystical' nature of this chapter, perhaps an exercise that is both mental and physical is in order. This exercise is a good one to use when trying to fall asleep, preparing the body and mind for true rest.

Lie comfortably on your back or on your tummy, with the room dark and all electronics turned off.

In your mind, go to a favorite quiet place – even back to the place of the meditation above.

Beginning with the top of your head, relax all muscles. FEEL them relax. Gradually move down to your face, starting with the forehead. Also the back of your head. Then your neck.

Go back to the top of your head and repeat the relaxation of all muscles in your head and neck until they are relaxed. Breathe deeply and slowly three times, keeping your head and neck relaxed.

Move to your shoulders and upper back. Repeat, including your head and neck in the repetition. Breathe deeply and slowly three times.

Then move to your chest and arms. Don't forget your hands and fingers – each one! Repeat from the beginning, following with the three slow, deep breaths.

Relax your abdomen and lower back (with repetition!), then your pelvic area, then your buttocks, then thighs, knees and lower legs, and finally (if you are still awake), your feet.

Take time with all of these areas – don't rush! That just sets up tension again.

With the deep breathing times, return in your mind to the favorite place, still being aware of the relaxation of muscles. Notice if there are any areas of your body that don't want to relax, that are always tense when you revisit them. Ask your body why, and try to figure out a remedy.

Recipes

Breakfast

Spelt Buttermilk Biscuits

- 2 C Spelt flour
- 1 Tbs baking powder
- ¼ tsp. sea salt
- 1 C buttermilk

Preheat your oven to 425°F and lightly grease a baking sheet. Combine all of the ingredients, adding the buttermilk slowly until it is barely blended. Drop the batter in heaping spoonfuls on the baking sheet, leaving space between so they don't touch each other.

Bake for 12-15 minutes, until lightly browned.

This makes about 12 biscuits.Serve with butter and organic honey or other non-sugar topping.

Lunch

Fig and Goat Cheese Pizza

1 slice of small whole wheat pita bread
Olive Oil
2-3 fresh Mission figs, quartered
2 slices of cooked bacon (pancetta is wonderful if you want to pay for it…), crumbled
Crumbled goat cheese
Fresh diced basil

Preheat the oven to 400°F. Spit the pita bread in halves. Rub the smooth side of each half with olive oil, and bake in the oven until lightly brown. Remove from the oven and place the quartered figs, goat cheese, and basil evenly over each half. Then add the crumbled bacon and return to the oven until thoroughly heated (4-5 minutes). Serve with a cool glass of white wine.

Dinner

Stuffed Pork Loin with Sweet Red Cabbage

1 small pork loin (4-6 inches long)	1 large head of red cabbage
1 pkg of dried apricots	¼ lb butter
1 pkg of dried pitted prunes	¼ C red wine vinegar
Sea salt, black pepper	2 Tb xylitol or Splenda
	¼ C water
	1 tsp sea salt
	3 apples, cored and chopped

Clean and chop the head of red cabbage. In a large pot, melt the butter and add the cabbage. Add the xylitol (or Splenda) and stir well. After cooking gently for a few minutes, add the water, vinegar and salt and pepper, cooking it slowly for 1 ½ hours. Core and chop the apples, adding them to the cabbage for another ½ hour.

While the cabbage is cooking, preheat the oven to 350°F. Wash and pat dry the small loin. Slice it lengthwise nearly through, leaving at least ½ inch on one side. line the center portion with apricots and prunes, and then tie the loin closed with baker's twine. Salt and pepper and then sear the loin on all sides until medium brown. Place in a greased baking dish in the oven for 1 hour or until done.

Enjoy with a glass of white wine and fresh fruit for dessert.

VII.
Hildegard the Benedictine Abbess

Hildegard, a Benedictine Abbess. What does this mean? Hildegard lived the Benedictine life from age eight on, a life which certainly would have enormous influence on her work, her actions, and her way of life. So what is it to be a Benedictine?

Around 530 AD Benedict of Nursia founded a monastery in Italy, followed relatively quickly by another half dozen monasteries. These monasteries were intended to be autonomous communities and were not governed by the church or by a single Abbot. The brothers (and eventually sisters) who became part of any of these communities were bound by vow only to the single community which they joined. The vow required three things: 1) that the person remain with that particular community for life, 2) that the person convert to the proscribed way of life of the community, 3) and that the person be obedient to the abbot or abbess of the community. The way of life of the community is known as "The Benedictine Rule". Since the beginnings of formations of Benedictine communities, several other orders and churches have adopted the 'Rule' and have 'Benedictine' communities – the Cistercians, the Trappists, and the Protestant Anglicans and Lutherans.

The Rule of St. Benedict has been the cornerstone of thousands of monastic communities for well over a millennium. It has been translated into hundreds of languages. Even Hildegard herself wrote an *Explanation of the Rule of Benedict*[196] at the request of a small community of brothers in Germany. Rev. Timothy Fry, OSB, offers the following introduction to a more current translation of the rule:

Benedict calls his Rule "a little rule for beginners." It contains directions for all aspects of the monastic life, from establishing the abbot as superior, the arrangement of psalms for prayers, measures for correction of faults, to details [197] of clothing and the amount of food and drink... St. Benedict taught that if the monk seeks to answer the call of God – "If you hear his voice today, do not harden your heart" – then he must put all else aside and follow the teaching of Christ in obedience. To this end St. Benedict established a "school for the Lord's service," a place where monks learn to serve the Lord in obedience to their abbot, who "is believed to hold the place of Christ." His spirituality is

---

[196] Hildegard von Bingen. *Explanation of The Rule of Benedict*. Tr. Hugh Feiss, O.S.B. (Toronto, Ontario. Peregrina Publishing Co. 1990)

[197] Image of an 8th century *Rule*, from the Bodley Library in Oxford.

Christocentric: "the love of Christ must come before all else." After a year of trial, the novice promises stability, fidelity to monastic life, and obedience. St. Benedict expected his monks to advance on the "path of God's commandments, [their] hearts overflowing with the inexpressible delight of love."[198]

Daily life in a Benedictine monastery is centered on prayer, work, and meditative reading ('Lectio divina'). Prayer is organized around the 'Divine Office', or 'liturgical hours' during which all 150 Psalms are prayed every week. Mass is also celebrated daily, immediately after the fourth canonical hour, Terce. The day was organized according to a twenty-four hour clock. Below on the left is a diagram showing the times for the eight 'office hours', and on the right a 12th century twenty-four hour clock[199] with the sun and the moon showing daylight and night hours on its face. The third image is a current twenty-four hour clock with day and night reversed from the 12th century time. Twenty-four hour clocks and time-keeping are very common today.

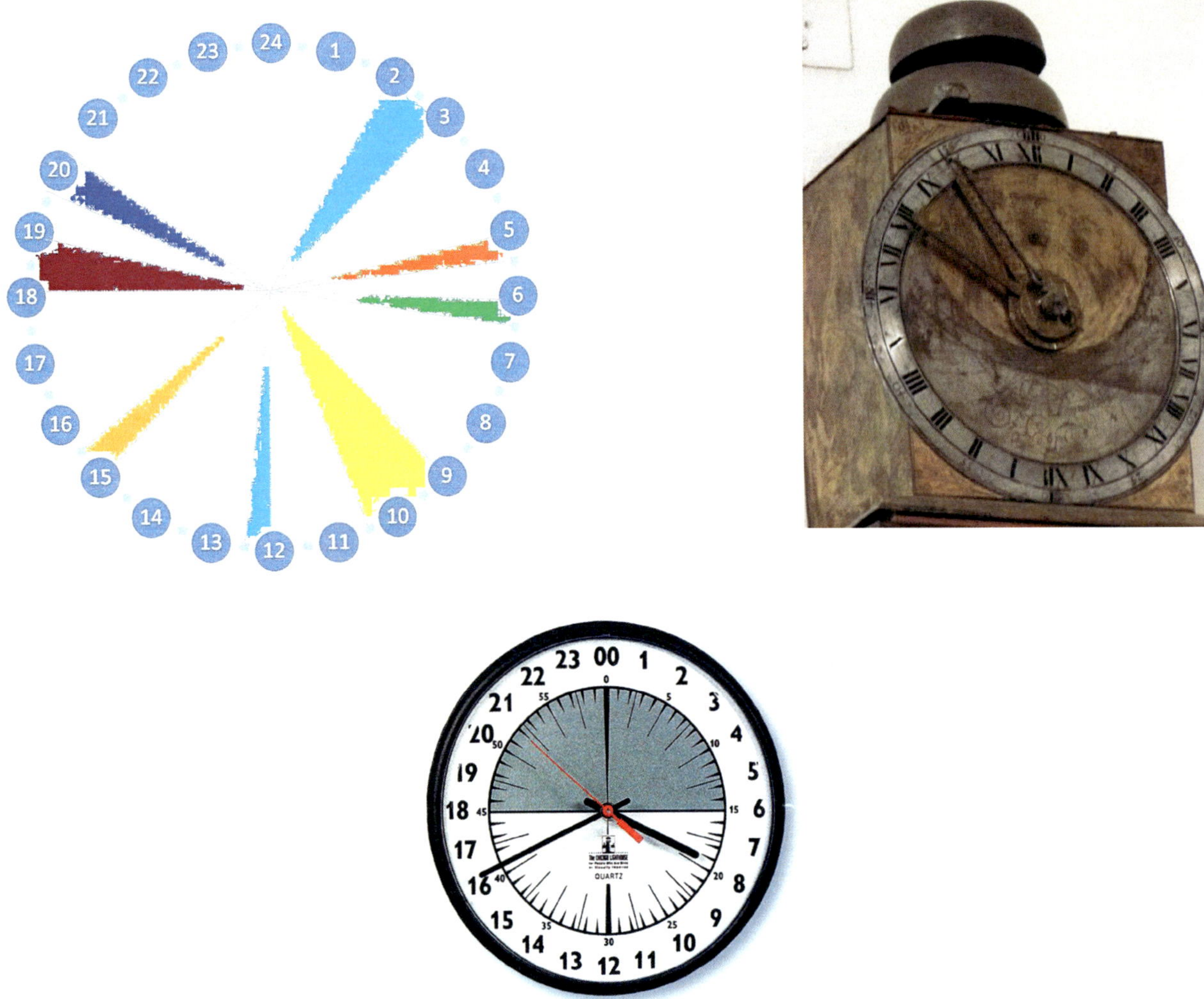

198 Benedict of Nursia. *The Rule of St. Benedict in English.* Ed. Timothy Fry, O.S.B. (Collegeville, Minnesota. The Liturgical Press, 1982) pp. 11-12

199 The clock is in the Harburg Castle near Rothenburg, Germany. The photo was taken in June 2012 during a visit there.

So, what did/does a Benedictine day look like? There are seventy-three 'rules' in the Rule, and numbers 8-19 refer to praying the Psalter within the Divine Office. The Divine Office developed out of the Jewish practice of regular times of prayer throughout the day, and the Psalter is, of course, the Jewish songbook/prayerbook of their tradition too. The Psalms govern the flow and the meditation of the day. St. Chrysostom (c.347-407, who predated St. Benedict) writes:[200]

> When the faithful keep the vigil in the church during night, David is first, middle, and last. When hymns are sung at dawn, David is first, middle, and last. At the funeral processions and burials, David is first, middle, and last. In the holy monasteries, among the ranks of the heavenly hosts, David is first, middle, and last. In the monasteries of the virgins, imitators of St. Mary, David is first, middle, and last.
>
> By Benedict's time, the 'office' hours had been organized into night vigils, hymns at dawn, and daily prayers, with each office serving a certain spiritual purpose containing specific songs and readings. Why the terms 'office' and 'office hours'? In liturgical 'speak' an 'office' is a beneficial act performed for others. It is usually a ceremony or rite celebrated for a special purpose. The 'office hours' are prayer services held for the individual, community and the world specified for certain hours of the twenty-four hour day.

You can see from the graphic above, that they do order the entire waking day, from 2AM until 8:30PM! They are, in order with their content:

Matins – before daybreak, usually around 2AM

Invitatory (Psalm 94), followed by an antiphon
Hymn, Versiculum (a short verse)
Nocturn I – Antiphon, 3 Psalms, 3 Lectio (readings), 3 Great Responsories
Nocturn II – Antiphon, 3 Psalms, 3 Lectio (readings), 3 Great Responsories
Nocturn III – Antiphon, 3 Psalms, 3 Lectio (readings), 3 Great Responsories

Lauds – at sunrise

3 Psalms with Antiphons
1st Lesser Canticle with Antiphon

Sunday: Canticle of Daniel, Benedicite omnia opera (Daniel 3:56-58) Canticle of the Three Children, Deus partum (Daniel 3:52-57)
Monday: Canticle of David, *Benedictus ex, Domine Deus Israel* (I Chr. 29) Canticle of Isaiah, *Confiteor tibi Domine* (Isaiah 12:1-6)
Tuesday: Canticle of Tobias (Tobit), *Magnus es Domine* (Tobit 13:1-10) Camticle of Ezechias, *Ego dixi* (Isaiah 38:10-20
Wednesday: Canticle of Judith, *Hymneum cantemus Domino* (Judith 16:15-21) Canticle of Anna, *Exultavit cor meum* (I Sam. 2:1-10)
Thursday: Canticle of Jeremiah, *Audite verbum* (Jer. 31:10-14) Canticle of Moses, *Cantemus Domino* (Exodus 15:1-9)
Friday: Canticle of Isaiah, *Ver tu es* (Isaiah 45:15-26) Canticle of Habakkuk, *Domine audivi* (Hab. 3:1-16)
Saturday: Canticle of Ecclesiastes, *Miserere nostri* (Eccl. 36:1-16) Canticle of Moses, *Audite coeli* (Deuteronomy 32:1-43)

[200] From the Typicon of the Orthodox Church, Chapter Two.

1 Chapter
Hymn, Versiculum
2nd Lesser Canticle with Antiphon
Major Canticle, *Benedictus Dominus*

Prime – around 6 AM
Hymn, Versiculum
Group of three Psalms, followed by one Antiphon
Chapter, Short Responsory and Versicle

Terce – around 9 AM
Hymn, Versiculum
Group of three Psalms, followed by one Antiphon
Chapter, Short Responsory and Versicle

MASS – following Terce

Sext – around noon
Hymn, Versiculum
Group of three Psalms, followed by one Antiphon
Chapter, Short Responsory and Versicle

None – around 3 PM
Hymn, Versiculum
Group of three Psalms, followed by one Antiphon
Chapter, Short Responsory and Versicle

Vespers – at sunset
5 Psalms with antiphons preceding and following each Psalm
Chapter
Hymn and Versicle
The Major Canticle, *Magnificat*, with antiphon

Compline – at the end of the day
Group of three Psalms, followed by one Antiphon
Hymn
Chapter with Short Responsory
The Canticle of Simeon, *Nunc dimittis,* with Antiphon
One of the four 'Marian' antiphons, based upon the season of the church year
Advent to Feb. 1: *Alma Redemptoris Mater* (Sweet Mother of the Redeemer)
Feb. 2-Wed. of Holy Week: *Ave Regina caelorum* (Hail, Queen of Heaven)
Easter to Trinity Sunday: *Regina caeli laetare* (Rejoice, Queen of Heaven)
Trinity Sunday to Advent: *Salve Regina* (Hail, O Queen)

So, during one week – Hildegard and her nuns would sing:

Psalms – 34 each day, 238 each week, plus those sung at Mass
Antiphons – 28 each day, 196 each week, plus those sung at Mass
Hymns – 8 each day, 56 each week, plus those sung at Mass
Responsories – 5 Short and 9 Great each day, 35 Short and 63 Great (plus those...)
Canticles – 3 Major and 2 Lesser each day, all 3 Major and 14 Lesser each week

Additionally, during Mass each day another form of song was used, the "Sequence" (which grew out of the Great Responsory). Sequences have evolved into hymns in today's liturgical practice.

We have dealt rather extensively with Antiphons, Hymns, Responsories and Sequences. The other liturgical components listed here deserve a brief explanation:

Canticles: songs/chants based upon scriptural texts. There were two types:

Major Canticles are based upon New Testament texts. There are three.

The Canticle of Zachary, *Benedictus Dominus* (Luke 1:68-79), sung at the conclusion of Lauds.

The Canticle of Mary, *Magnificat* (Luke 1:46-55), sung during Vespers.

The Canticle of Simeon, *Nunc dimittis* (Luke 2:29-32), sung during Compline.

Lesser Canticles are based upon Old Testament texts. There are fourteen, all sung during Lauds, between the third and fourth Psalm. (See p.193)

Readings during the Divine Office were of two types:

Lectio, or lessons: lengthy portions of scripture.

The Great Responsories followed lessons and were themselves of considerable length and elaboration.

Capitulum, or Chapters: single verses of scripture.

The Short Responsories followed chapters and were brief and simple.

The Versiculum was a short sentence with a response, and followed hymns.

Well. Hildegard had ample opportunity to compose for the Divine Office and for the Mass. Given the fullness of her daily schedule and all that she was involved in as Abbess, it is amazing that she found the time to compose texts and music for the seventy-seven chants of the *Symphonia*!

Hildegard's day consisted of:

6 hours – work
6 ½ hours – worship and prayer
2 ½ hours – reading and meditation
1 hour – meals (there were only two, breakfast around 5:30AM and dinner around 3:30 PM)
8 hours – rest and sleep (8:30PM-1:30AM, 1-3PM)

Hmmm. How does this compare to our daily schedules??? Hildegard's work periods must have been something to observe! During those six hours each day she must do the work of an administrator, a musician, a spiritual director, and author, a prophetess, a healer... The times of prayer, reading and meditation must have been true life savers for her. Her visions and writing might have been generated during times of reading and meditation, and their dictation to Volmar and Richardis during work periods.

Her travels were arduous, probably accomplished partially by boat, partially on horseback or in a wagon, or by plain old walking. Prayer life most likely did not stop during those trips either. The rhythm of the Divine Office throughout the day was a 'bio-rhythm', part of the flow of viriditas which connects all things.

All but eight hours of her day (the time allotted for sleep or rest) were spent in community with her nuns. The vows taken by each member of the community bound them to that place and to the group for life. No divorce here. No running away. Before taking final vows there was a period of training and learning how to live under the 'Rule'. First one became a postulant, declaring the intention and desire to join. Then followed a two-year period as a novice, living with the community, learning the way of life, spiritually as well as a lifestyle. At the end of that period, before taking final vows, the novice was rigorously evaluated by the Abbess and the community, and a determination was made as to the validity of 'the call' to monastic life, to the ability to live within a particular community, and to the ultimate fulfillment and purpose for the individual's life. The final vows were exactly that – final. Very, very seldom did people leave the community, and then only with great spiritual and personal difficulty, often including excommunication.

So the sisters must live in harmony with each other. A greater part of Benedict's Rule prescribes rigorous guidelines for members of the community in order to create and maintain that harmony. And it was the responsibility of the Abbess or Abbot to enforce those 'rules'. That was not always an easy task...

"Ora et labora" – Prayer and Work, the motto for Benedictines everywhere. The work was assigned to each nun or monk according to their gifts or what was needed. That is true today as well. The Abtei St. Hildegard in Eibingen, Germany continues the tradition of prayer and work centered around the Divine Office and the Rule of St. Benedict. This wonderful abbey sits on a hill overlooking town of Rudesheim, immediately above the church located on the site of Hildegard's third monastery.

The interior of the renovated church standing where Hildegard's Eibingen Abbey stood in Rudesheim, Germany holds the shrine containing her remains, placed behind the altar. A wonderful mosaic of the "Man in Sapphire Blue" vision hangs above her shrine. The church is not part of the current abbey, which was rebuilt in the early 1900s after being abandoned and destroyed during the period of secularization in Germany[201].

---

[201] Following the end of the Holy Roman Empire and the victory of French armies in 1794, there was a vast redistribution of land to compensate German kings who had lost land to the French. The redistribution secularized church-held properties and stripped the church of its governing powers. The church was nearly destroyed in Germany, and most Catholic universities closed and monasteries shut down. It no longer had governmental rights in Germany.

The Abtei St. Hildegard is impressive, standing in and above the rich vineyards rising from the village of Rüdesheim.[202] The sisters are fully engaged in a variety of work – kitchen, laundry, building and grounds upkeep and repair certainly. But they also garden, growing fruits and vegetables, work in their infirmary, caring for the sick, and maintain a very busy guesthouse for visitors. Hospitality and the welcoming of all who seek either refuge or rest is an important part of the Benedictine Rule.

The sisters also work in pastoral care in the surrounding communities, there is a goldsmith, a ceramic artist, sisters who restore old manuscripts, they operate their own winery (they grow over six hectares of Riesling and Spätburgunder vines), and they have a shop which sells their own wine and liquor, art, books, recordings, religious art, and spelt products. They ship internationally too! There are currently between fifty-five and sixty nuns, eight employees, and they host, on the average, twenty guests each day, providing a room with bath and three meals to each.

[202] All images of the Abtei St. Hildegard were taken during a visit there in July 2010.

As a Benedictine Abbey, they must be self-supportive, as neither the church nor the state contribute to the upkeep or operation of the abbey. Their day of prayer and work is very much in the Benedictine tradition, and they invite their guests to five of the daily office hours. Upon arrival at the Abbey, the following was resting on the desk in the room I was assigned (parentheses mine):

EIN TAG IN DER ABTEI ST.HILDEGARD
ORA ET LABORA

Unser Chorgebet,
zu dem Sie herzlich eingeladen sind:

5.30 Uhr Laudes **(So.: 6.00Uhr)**	danach stille Zeit	(Lauds)
7.30 Uhr Terz / Eucharistiefeier*	danach Frühstück (8.30Uhr)	(Terce/Mass)
(So.: 8.15 Uhr)	**(So.: Frühstück : 7.15-8.00Uhr !)**	(Breakfast)
	ab 9.00Uhr Zeit zur freien Gestaltung oder	Gespräch
*12.00 Uhr Mittagshore** **(So.: 12.00Uhr)**	danach Mittagstisch: 12.15 Uhr (Lunch)	(Sext)
*An Sonn- und Feiertagen:13.20 Uhr Non**	(None)	
danach Ruhezeit	Zeit zur freien Gestaltung oder	Gespräch
17.30 Uhr Vesper	danach Abendtisch: 18.10 Uhr (Dinner)	(Vespers)
19.20 Uhr Komplet/Vigilien	(Compline)	

* kurze Gebetszeit

So guests may observe six of the eight Office Hours! I say observe, as the hours are chanted (chorgebet, "sung prayer) in Latin. We are provided with the texts (in German and Latin) so may follow along, but the nuns sing the chant. Part of their mission is the preservation of Gregorian Chant. The sisters are called to prayer in the morning by the chapel bells ringing out over the hills and Rhine valley, beginning each day with a call to prayer and thanksgiving.

The Abbey is also on the pilgrimage path to Compostela[203], and many people walk by and stop to visit the church or the Klosterladen (shop) every day.

There were hikers, nordic walkers, cyclists, tour busses, and individual cars, all climbing the rather steep road from Rudesheim.

During the time for work between dinner and Vespers, the lovely sounds of the Abbess practicing cello in her quarters above the road were a giveaway as to how she was spending that work period. Practice is work! The current Abbess, Sr. Clementia Killewald, is the thirty-ninth successor of St. Hildegard.

This is an appropriate place to bring some excellent news. In December 2011, Pope Benedict XVI announced that Hildegard would be canonized and named a Doctor of the Church! After

[203] The image is a mosaic on the wall next to a path through the Abtei. The small circular stone has engraved on it "2795 km Santiago de Compostela"

900 years! She was canonized on 10 May 2012 and will be named Doctor of the Church on 7 October 2012. She is the fourth woman and only thirty-fourth person to be so honored.[204] The title is given to a saint who has been canonized, and whose writings have offered a great deal to the whole Church. They exhibit 'eminent learning' and sanctity, and they and their work have been proclaimed truthful and holy by a Pope or an ecumenical council. When Hildegard is named on October 7, 2012, she will become the earliest women in the history of the Roman Catholic Church to be so titled.

Certainly all of her works were considered in the decision to canonize her and name her Doctor of the Church. Probably her theological works weighed the most heavily, including letters, sermons, and other writings. In her letters, there is one which presents a remarkable 'theology' of music, written when music was taken from her and from her abbey during the lengthy interdict imposed toward the end of her life. To refresh memory, she had accepted a wounded man for care and treatment in the abbey, a man who had been excommunicated and who was running from the authorities. While under her care, he confessed and received absolution just before dying. Hildegard buried him on the Abbey grounds, and when the Archbishop of Mainz ordered her to dig him up and throw him out in the wild, she refused. The Abbey was put under interdict because of her action, meaning there was no Mass, the Divine Office was only spoken individually by each nun, and there certainly was no chanting or other music. After a rather substantial period of time under the interdict, Hildegard wrote to the Archbishop. The letter is not a fragile plea for mercy or an admission of 'guilt'. It is strong and warns the Archbishop of the consequences of silencing praise and worship of God.

In the letter to the Archbishop, Hildegard calls on the image of Adam, who lost his voice as a result of the fall – his voice that had "blended fully with the voices of the angels in their praise of God".[205] Later in the same letter, she offers the following:

> ...the canticle of praise, reflecting celestial harmony, is rooted in the Church through the Holy Spirit. The body is the vestment of the spirit, which has a living voice, and so it is proper for the body, in harmony with the soul, to use its voice to sing praises to God. Whence, in metaphor, the prophetic spirit commands us to praise God with clashing cymbals and cymbals of jubilation [cf. Ps 150.5], as well as other musical instruments which men of wisdom and zeal have invented, because all arts pertaining to things useful and necessary for mankind have been created by the breath that God sent into man's body. For this reason it is proper that God be praised in all things.
>
> And because sometimes a person sighs and groans at the sound of singing, remembering, as it were, the nature of celestial harmony, the prophet, aware that the soul is symphonic and thoughtfully reflecting on the profound nature of the spirit, urges us in the psalm [cf. Ps 32.2, 91.4] to confess to the Lord with the harp and to sing a psalm to Him with the ten-stringed psaltery. His meaning is that the harp, which is plucked from below, relates to the discipline of the body; the psaltery, which is plucked from above, pertains to the exertion of the spirit; the ten chords, to the fulfillment of the law.[206]

---

[204] The three women named in order of their naming are St. Teresa of Avila (1515-1582) in 1970, St. Catherine of Siena (1347-1380) in 1970, and St. Therese of Lisieux (1873-1897) in 1997.

[205] Hildegard. *The Letters of Hildegard of Bingen, Vol. I.* Tr. Joseph L. Baird and Radd K. Ehrman. (New York, Oxford University Press), p. 77

[206] *Ibid.* p.79

Hildegard's theology of music is mystical, but it was not far removed from the thoughts and understanding of her times. When Hildegard states that the soul is 'symphonic', she refers to an ancient belief (Pythagoras and Boethius) that the body and soul are united by musical harmony.

Beyond the very strong and beautiful letter cited above, the final vision in *Scivias* offers an amazing and wonderful 'cantus' to the place of music in the cosmos, the great unifier and voice of the inner spirit and knowledge – that which brings all together in praise of the Living Light.

Hildegard begins the description of this illumination saying:

> Then I saw the lucent sky, in which I heard different kinds of music, marvelously embodying all the meanings I had heard before. I heard the praises of the joyous citizens of Heaven, steadfastly persevering in the ways of Truth; and laments calling people back to those praises and joys; and the exhortations of the virtues, spurring one another on to secure the salvation of the peoples ensnared by the Devil. And the virtues destroyed his snares, so that the faithful at last through repentance passed out of their sins and into Heaven.
>
> And their song, like the voice of a multitude, making music in harmony praising the ranks of Heaven, had these words...[207]

She continues with poetry, the texts of songs sung by or to each of the groups represented in the seven circles of the vision. From the top they are:

Songs to holy Mary
Songs to the nine orders of heavenly spirits
Songs to the patriarchs and prophets
Songs to the apostles
Songs to the martyrs
Songs to the confessors
Songs to the virgins

The vision continues with a lament for "the ones to be recalled", ending with a victorious exclamation of the victory of the Living Light over the serpent, restoring the lost to grace. The vision concludes with a portion of the text of her *Ordo virtutem*, the work of the virtues in protecting and strengthening an innocent soul from the wiles of the devil. (So, the first morality play (opera) was given in a vision, partially offered as a conclusion to Hildegard's first major work, *Scivias*).

Hildegard is independent in her presentation of virtues in *Ordo virtutem*. Since the fifth century, the church had classified seven holy virtues that countered seven deadly sins – the basic plot of *Ordo*! But Hildegard begins with this plot and expands upon it, moving her beyond tradition, or interpretation of a long-held formula. The table below[208] identifies the traditional seven holy virtues and their opposite seven deadly sins.

Virtue	Latin	Gloss	(Vice)	(Latin)	Virtue's Meaning
Charity	*Caritas*	Will, benevolence, generosity, sacrifice	Greed	*Avaritia*	Generosity, charity, self-sacrifice; the term should not be confused with the more restricted modern use of the word charity to mean benevolent giving. In Christian theology, charity—or love (agäpé) -- is the greatest of the three theological virtues. Love, in the sense of an unlimited loving kindness towards all others, is held to be the ultimate perfection of the human spirit, because it is said to both glorify and reflect the nature of God. Such love is self-sacrificial. Confusion can arise from the multiple meanings of the English word "love". The love that is "caritas" is distinguished by its origin – being divinely infused into the soul – and by its residing in the will rather than emotions, regardless of

207 Hildegard. *Scivias*. Tr. Mother Columba Hart and Jane Bishop. (New York: Paulist Press, 1990) p.525

208 http://en.wikipedia.org/wiki/Seven_Virtues, 6 July 2012

Virtue	Latin	Gloss	(Vice)	(Latin)	Virtue's Meaning
					what emotions it stirs up. This love is necessary for salvation, and with it no one can be lost.
Chastity	*Castitas*	Purity, knowledge, honesty, wisdom	Lust	*Luxuria*	Abstaining from sexual conduct according to one's state in life; the practice of courtly love and romantic friendship. Cleanliness through cultivated good health and hygiene, and maintained by refraining from intoxicants. To be honest with oneself, one's family, one's friends, and to all of humanity. Embracing of moral wholesomeness and achieving purity of thought-through education and betterment. The ability to refrain from being distracted and influenced by hostility, temptation or corruption.
Diligence	*Industria*	Persistence, effort, ethics, rectitude	Sloth	*Acedia*	A zealous and careful nature in one's actions and work; decisive work ethic, steadfastness in belief, fortitude, and the capability of not giving up. Budgeting one's time; monitoring one's own activities to guard against laziness. Upholding one's convictions at all times, especially when no one else is watching (integrity). (The vice "acedia" is more commonly known as "sloth".)
Humility	*Humilitas*	Bravery, modesty, reverence, altruism	Pride	*Superbia*	Modest behavior, selflessness, and the giving of respect. Humility is not thinking less of yourself, it is thinking of yourself less. It is a spirit of self-examination; a hermeneutic of suspicion toward yourself and charity toward people you disagree with. The courage of the heart necessary to undertake tasks which are difficult, tedious or unglamorous, and to graciously accept the sacrifices involved. Reverence for those who have wisdom and those who selflessly teach in love. Giving credit where credit is due; not unfairly glorifying one's own self. Being faithful to promises, no matter how big or small they may be. Refraining from despair and the ability to confront fear and uncertainty, or intimidation.
Kindness	*Humanitas*	Satisfaction, loyalty, compassion, integrity	Envy	*Invidia*	Charity, compassion and friendship for its own sake. Empathy and trust without prejudice or resentment. Unselfish love and voluntary kindness without bias or spite. Having positive outlooks and cheerful demeanor; to inspire kindness in others.
Patience	*Patientia*	Peace, mercy, ahimsa, sufferance	Wrath	*Ira*	Forbearance and endurance through moderation. Resolving conflicts and injustice peacefully, as opposed to resorting to violence. Accepting the grace to forgive;[2] to show mercy to sinners. Creating a sense of peaceful stability and community rather than suffering, hostility, and antagonism.
Temperance	*Temperantia*	Self control, justice, honour, abstention	Gluttony	*Gula*	Restraint, temperance, justice. Constant mindfulness of others and one's surroundings; practicing self-control, abstention, moderation, zero-sum and deferred gratification. Prudence to judge between actions with regard to appropriate actions at a given time. Proper moderation between self-interest, versus public-interest, and against the rights and needs of others.

Hildegard's virtues in the *Ordo virtutem* are:[209]

Knowledge of God	Humility (Humilitas)
Charity (Caritas)	Fear of God
Obedience	Faith
Hope	Chastity (Castitas)
Innocence	Contempt of the World
Heavenly Love	Discipline
Modesty	Mercy
Victory	Discretion
Patience (Patientia)	

She introduces seventeen virtues in her epic battle of good versus evil, of the earthbound battle between good and evil for the soul. And good does win the victory, binding evil (the devil) and throwing him 'out'.

She ends this final vision with a strong admonition:

> And whoever tastes this prophecy and fixes it in his memory will become the mountain of myrrh, and of frankincense, and of all aromatical spices, and the diffusion of many blessings; he will ascend like Abraham from blessing to blessing. And the new spouse, the Bride of the Lamb, will take him to herself, for he is a pillar in the sight of God. And the shadow of the hand of the Lord will protect him.
>
> But whoever rashly conceals these words written by the finger of God, madly abridging them, or for any human reason taking them to a strange place and scoffing at them, let him be reprobate; and the finger of God shall crush him.
>
> Praise, therefore, praise God, ye blessed hearts, for the miracles God has wrought in the frail earthly reflection of the beauty of the Most High; as He Himself foreshadowed when He first made Woman from the rib of the man He had created.
>
> But let the one who has ears sharp to hear inner meanings ardently love My reflection and pant after My words, and inscribe them in his soul and conscience. Amen.[210]

Matthew Fox ends his discussion of this vision with a beautiful and probably very true statement:

"One suspects that Hildegard is singing somewhere still. And is eager to make music with her sisters and brothers on earth."[211]

For the final look at one of Hildegard's chants, we meet yet another virtue, here personified as the Sapientia.

---

[209] Sheingom, Pamela. "The Virtues of Hildegard's *Ordo Virtutum;* or, It *Was* a Woman's World" in *The Ordo Virtutum of Hildegard of Bingen: Critical Studies*, Audrey Ekdahl Davidson, Ed. (Kalamazoo, MI, Medieval Institute Publications, 1992) p.48.

[210] *Ibid.* p.536

[211] Fox, Matthew. *Illuminations of Hildegard of Bingen.* (Santa Fe. Bear and Company, 1985) p. 117

Hildegard's Chant

O virtus Sapientiae
O virtue of Wisdom

O virtus Sapientiae,	O virtue of Wisdom,
que circuiens circuisti,	who circles circling,
comprehendendo omnia	encompassing everything
in una via que habet vitam,	possessing life in one path,
tres alas habens,	you have three wings,
quarum una in altum volat	of which one on high flies
et altera de terra sudat	and another sweats on the earth
et tercia undique volat.	and the third all around flies.
Laus tibi sit,	Praise be to you,
sicut te decet, O Sapientiae.	as is befitting, O Wisdom.

This antiphon is the second chant in the Riesenkodex (Rupertsburg Codex of 1180-1190) currently held in the Landesbibliothek in Wiesbaden, Germany.[212] The Riesenkodex was prepared after Hildegard's death, probably as preparation for canonization, and it contains her collected works including the *Symphonia*. An earlier codex was prepared at the Rupertsberg scriptorium in 1175, most likely under Hildegard's supervision, but it was sent to a monastery at Villers and only fragments remain.[213] The image is of folio 466 from the Riesenkodex, containing the chant, *O virtus Sapientiae* (the fourth "O" antiphon on the page).

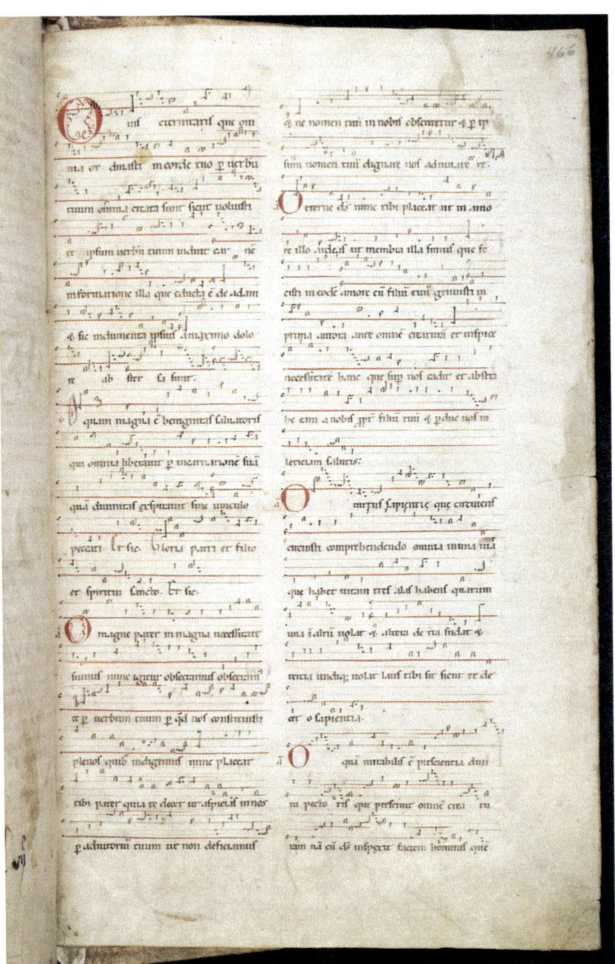

O Virtus Sapientiae most likely was a Psalm antiphon. Wisdom literature in scripture presents an interesting phenomenon – and question. Is wisdom a human achievement which leads to good relationships, health and well-being? Or is wisdom something which is given by God (grace) that helps to understand God and the divine plan for all creation? "Wisdom literature" in scripture is found primarily in Proverbs, Ecclesiastes, and Job. There are eight Psalms which are categorized as "Wisdom Psalms" (Ps. 1, 37, 49, 73, 112, 127, 128, and 133), a categorization offered much later than Hildegard's time. Hildegard's antiphon most closely resembles Psalm 36 (especially the bold text below).[214]

---

212 Newman, Barbara. *Symphonia.* (Cornell University, 1988). pp. 64-65.

213 *Ibid.* pp. 53-54.

214 Wansbrough, Henry, Gen. Ed. *The New Jerusalem Bible.* (Doubleday, 1985), pp. 848-849.

Sin is the oracle of the wicked in the depths of his heart,
there is no fear of God before his eyes.
He sees himself with too flattering an eye to detect and detest his guilt,
all he says is malicious and deceitful, he has turned his back on wisdom.
To get his way he hatches malicious plots even in his bed,
once set on his evil course no wickedness is too much for him.
Yahweh, your faithful love is in the heavens, your constancy reaches to the clouds,
your saving justice is like towering mountains, your judgments like the mighty deep.
Yahweh, you support both man and beast; how precious, God, is your faithful love.
So the children of Adam take refuge in the shadow of your wings.
They feast on the bounty of your house, you let them drink from your delicious streams;
in you is the source of life, by your light we see the light.
Maintain your faithful love to those who acknowledge you, and your saving justice to the honest of heart.
Do not let the foot of the arrogant overtake me or wicked hands drive me away.
There they have fallen, the evil-doers, flung down, never to rise again.

The similarity of this Psalm with Hildegard's text is readily apparent, even to similarities in language. The likelihood of her antiphon being used before and after the recitation of this Psalm when it occurred during the Divine Office or during Mass is very possible! It might also have been used during Lauds on Thursday, in conjunction with the Canticle of Jeremiah (Jer. 31:10-14), or during Mass with readings from the Book of Wisdom, from Proverbs, Ecclesiasticus, or from Job.

Hildegard's vision of wisdom here presents an abstract form which has three wings. Its circling is a strong and oft-used symbol in her writing with the circle implying wholeness, life, and loving care (among many others!). The three wings 'cover' the cosmos, earth and everything else, and may have their source in Isaiah 6 (the six-winged seraph). The wings might also symbolize the Trinity, the first representing God the Father, the second God the Son, and the third the Holy Spirit.

Hildegard sets her text in ten musical phrases of unequal length, using the Phrygian mode (Mode 3, the 'Deuterus authenticus' or 'Tertius tonus'), clearly establishing the pitch e as the finalis. The chant opens with her 'signature' 1-5-8 (final, confinal, upper final) gesture. And the initial pitch of all of the musical phrases is either the final (e) or the confinal (b) with only two exceptions (phrases 2 and 10). Furthermore, the terminatio for all phrases except phrase 8 is also either the final (e) or confinal (b).

O Virtus Sapientiae

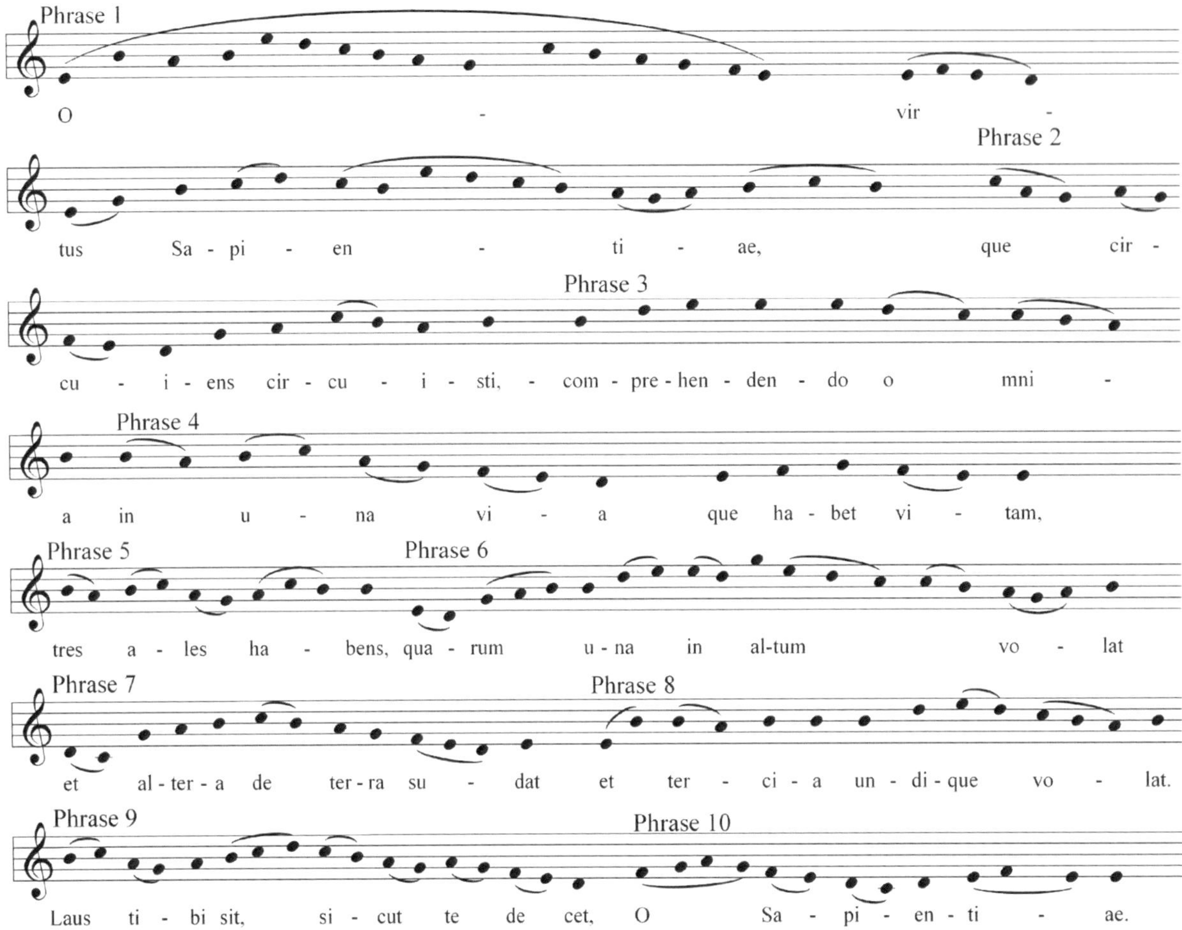

Phrases 2, 3, 9 and 10 show some emphasis other than that on the final or confinal, and in those phrases the momentary secondary emphases are on the subfinalis, d. The plurality of emphases on the final and confinal certainly support and confirm mode 3, e Phrygian, as the pitch resource for the chant.

The range of the antiphon is not as exaggerated as in the last chant, *O Vos Angelis*, but it is wider than that found in most Gregorian chant. It extends from C^4 to G^5 with the highest pitch occurring in the phrase "of which one on high flies". The lowest pitch occurs in phrase 7 ("another sweats on the earth") and in the closing phrase. Six of the ten phrases employ a range of at least an octave.

Hildegard is very consistent in the use of terminatio figures to help mark her style. Phrases 2, 3 and 8 use identical formulae leading to a pause on the confinal. Phrase 7 uses the same formula, but ends on the final. And phrase 9 is nearly identical, but does not complete the formula, ending on the subfinalis. Phrases 1 and 10 are also related, each using a lower neighbor/upper neighbor (porrectus-torculus) figuration, phrase 1 to the confinal and phrase 10 to the final. Phrases 5 and 6 are related in their use of an elaborated approach to the confinal from the pitch below (phrase 5 uses an appoggiatura [torculus] and phrase 6 a neighbor figure [porrectus] to move from 4 to 5). Phrase 4 stands alone, but bears a resemblance in approach to the final using a clivis followed by a repeated final pitch. The cadential formula types may be shown in the following manner (with the letters A, B, and C used to signify the different types):

Type		**Modal Degrees**	**Phrase**	**Signifier**
Type I	Initial formula	4-3-4/5-6-5	Phrase 1	A
	Variants	7-6-7/1-2-1	Phrase 10	A'
		2-1-1	Phrase 4	A"
Type II	Most common:	6-5-4-5	Phrases 2, 3, 8	B
	Variants	2-1-7-1	Phrase 7	B'
		2-1-7	Phrase 9	B"
Type III	Secondary formula	4-6-5	Phrase 5	C
	Variant	4-3-4-5	Phrase 6	C'

Using the signifying letter for each of the three types of cadence formulae, the following cadential pattern appears:

A B B A" C C' B' B B" A'

Several things can be noted about this pattern. First, it is more common to identify initiating gestures in determining form than looking at cadential figures, but there is a remarkable symmetry in the use of cadential formulae in this antiphon. There are only three terminal cadences in the antiphon, ending phrases 4, 7 and 10. Phrase 4 is the simplest formula, phrase 7 is a bit more elaborate, and the final phrase is the most elaborate. Additionally, the first (phrase 4) occurs at the end of the first textual phrase of the antiphon, the second in the middle of the second textual phrase, and of course, the last at the end. So even though Hildegard has extended the original three-phrase text into ten musical phrases, her use of terminal cadential structures preserves most of the original textual form.

Secondly, the 'variants' are either simple transpositions (changing the species or the emphasis from the final to the confinal or vice versa) or simple elaborations (using different neumes in the approaches to the final or confinal). She usually introduces the simplest formula first, then elaborates or transposes it in subsequent phrases. As an example, looking at the most common formula (Type II, B), she uses exactly the same formula to cadence on the dominant in phrases 2, 3, and 8. Phrase 7 uses a simple transposition of the pattern to the final. And phrase 9 is an incomplete terminal cadence, a repetition of Phrase 7 but without ending on the final – a very active progressive cadence which is so active because of the earlier formulae that create the anticipation of closure on the final. When that terminatio does not happen, the final phrase serves an even more important closural role than would have been the case had phrase 9 ended on the final.

In the following diagram, the three textual phrases are given showing Hildegard's musical subdivision into ten phrases. The initial and terminal pitches for each phrase are shown, the final as a whole note and the confinal as a lighter whole note. The highest and lowest pitches for each musical phrase appear as black notes, as do important structural melodic pitches other than the final or confinal.

After a cursory glance at the diagram it is obvious that the final and confinal play the most important roles as background structural pitches (they offer 24 of 43 indicated structural pitches).

The subfinalis offers the only 'deviation' from emphasis on e as a focus, emphasized first in phrase 4 and then particularly in phrase 9 and at the beginning of phrase 10 (supported by the confinal of d, the pitch a). A 'mono-modal' focus is certainly characteristic of medieval chant, but Hildegard does not in this antiphon employ as strict a usage of the authentic/plagal relationship through adherence to or us of the species of 4ths and 5ths as is most often the case in Gregorian chant. Instead, she moves to an emphasis on another mode – Dorian in d – toward the end, waiting until the last two syllables of text to return to the Phrygian e.

Structural Pitches in O virtus Sapientiae

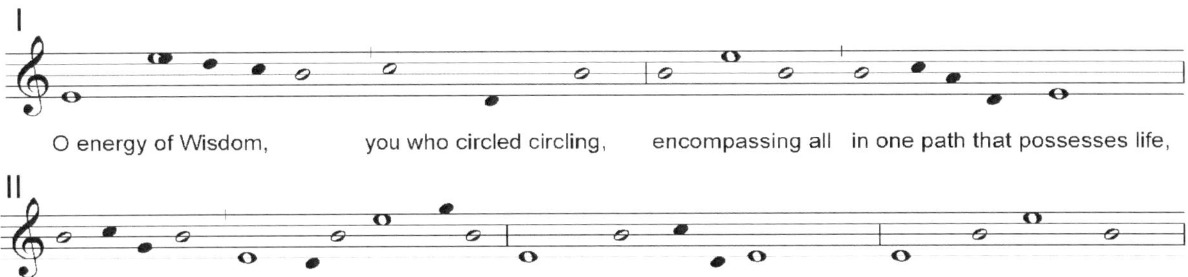

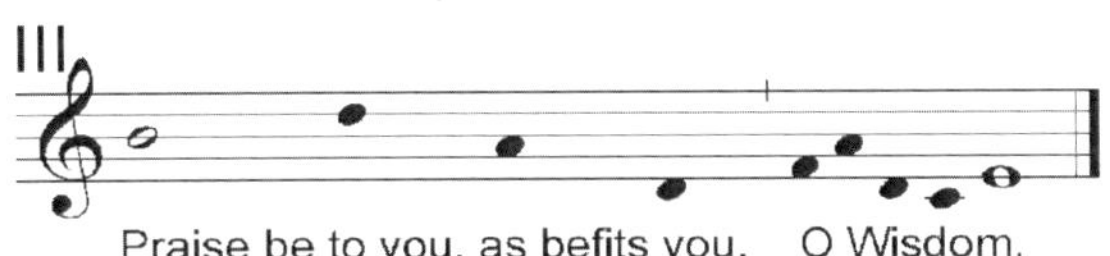

The most characteristic feature of the Phrygian mode is the minor second motion between the final and the second pitch of the mode. Hildegard emphasizes this modal characteristic in the first phrase (firtus), the cadence to phrase 4 (vitam), and at the end in the final cadence of phrase 10. Other uses of the f-e motion are within melodic gestures, and the only place she uses the f in an ascending line is in the final phrase, where the modal emphasis is Dorian rather than Phrygian (O Sapientiae).

Even though Hildegard does not employ the species in a strict manner, there is evidence of their use in a somewhat 'loose' fashion. The Modes and Species used in this antiphon are:

Species of 4ths – 1 (IV/I) Mode 2, Hypodorian
Mode 1, Dorian **D** e f g [a] b c **D**
Species of 5ths – I (V/1)
Species of 4ths – 2 (IV/2) Mode 4, Hypophrygian
Mode 3, Phrygian **E** f g a [b] c d **E**
Species of 5ths – 2 (V/2)

These pentachords (species of fifths) and tetrachords (species of fourths) have differing series of whole steps and half steps, creating different successive emphases which are characteristic of the different modes. The following diagram shows the use of the species and a good deal of commixture.

It is obvious that the emphasis throughout the antiphon is on species from the Phrygian and Hypophrygian modes. But it is also apparent that there is symmetry in Hildegard's departures from the Phrygian emphases. First, in phrase 2 she clearly outlines pitches from the Dorian mode, the one to which she will later turn for her longest and most profound departure from the Phrygian mode. Phrase 4, which ultimately ends with a termination on the final (as does phrase 10), contains a distinct emphasis on the Dorian pentachord (una via, or 'one path'). This passage ends the first portion of the textual form, a parallel with the end of the antiphon (phrase 10).

So Hildegard prepares the digression to Dorian with use of the fifth species 1, cadencing on the confinal, and then re-emphasizes the Dorian prior to the first terminal cadence in the antiphon (phrase 4). The parallel in phrases 9 and 10 thus fulfils the earlier prediction and shows evidence certainly of intentional and knowledgeable craftsmanship!

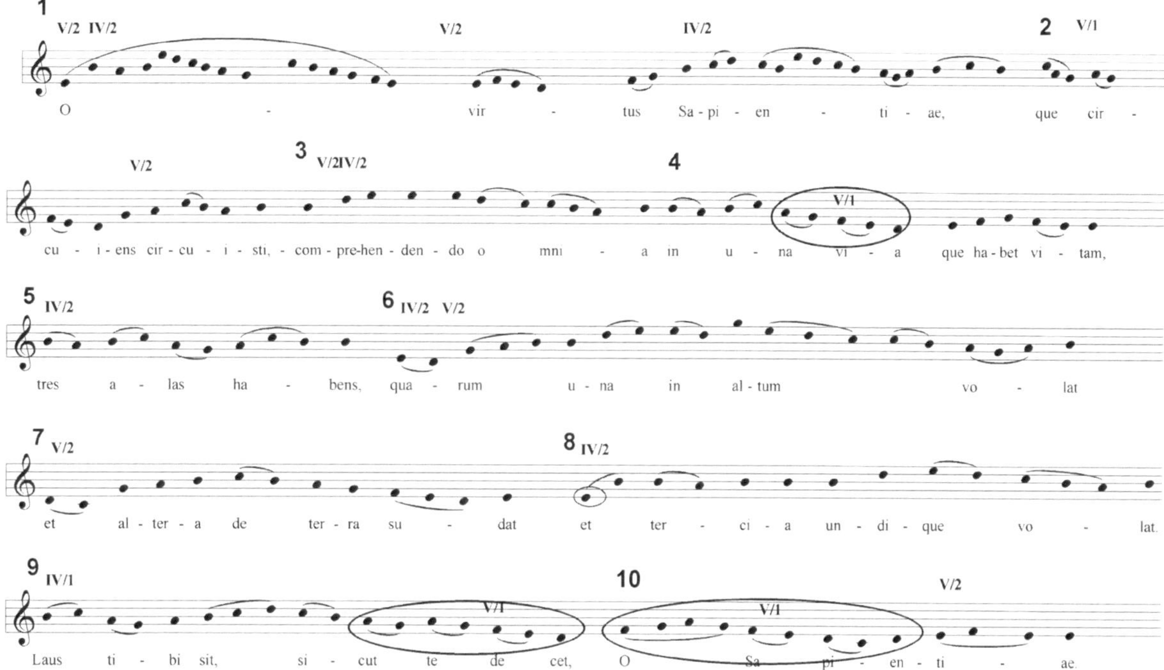

Melody

An identification of neumes used in the antiphon is provided in the next example. The work is clearly 'neumatic' in its style, containing only two melismae and infrequent syllabic settings. The neumes appearing in this antiphon, and their frequency of occurrence are:

1. Clivis (flexa) 23
2. Podatus (pes) 7
3. Climacus 5
4. Scandicus 2
5. Porrectus (flexus resupinus) 2
6. Torculus (pes flexus) 1
7. Scandicus flexus 1
8. Torculus flexus 1
9. Epiphonus 1

10 Porrectus liquescens 1

Only three of the neumes used contain more than three pitches, so the overall character of the antiphon leans decidedly toward a more syllabic style than a melismatic style. This is very characteristic of antiphons. Additionally, 30 of the total 44 neumes used contain only two pitches.

O Virtus Sapientiae

Other than the use of neumes, very little can be said about melodic 'motives'. There are, however, two gestures used in the antiphon which make perfect sense to identify as 'characteristic' gestures. The ascending fifth (labeled as 'A') from the final to the confinal is characteristically found in most works by Hildegard. These two pitches also encompass the species of fifth. A second gesture (labeled 'B') is introduced and then reappears in a slightly elaborated form (B'). It is an inverted form of A. There is a 'near' return in phrase 8, with the reappearance of gesture A followed quickly by the elaborated form of gesture B'.

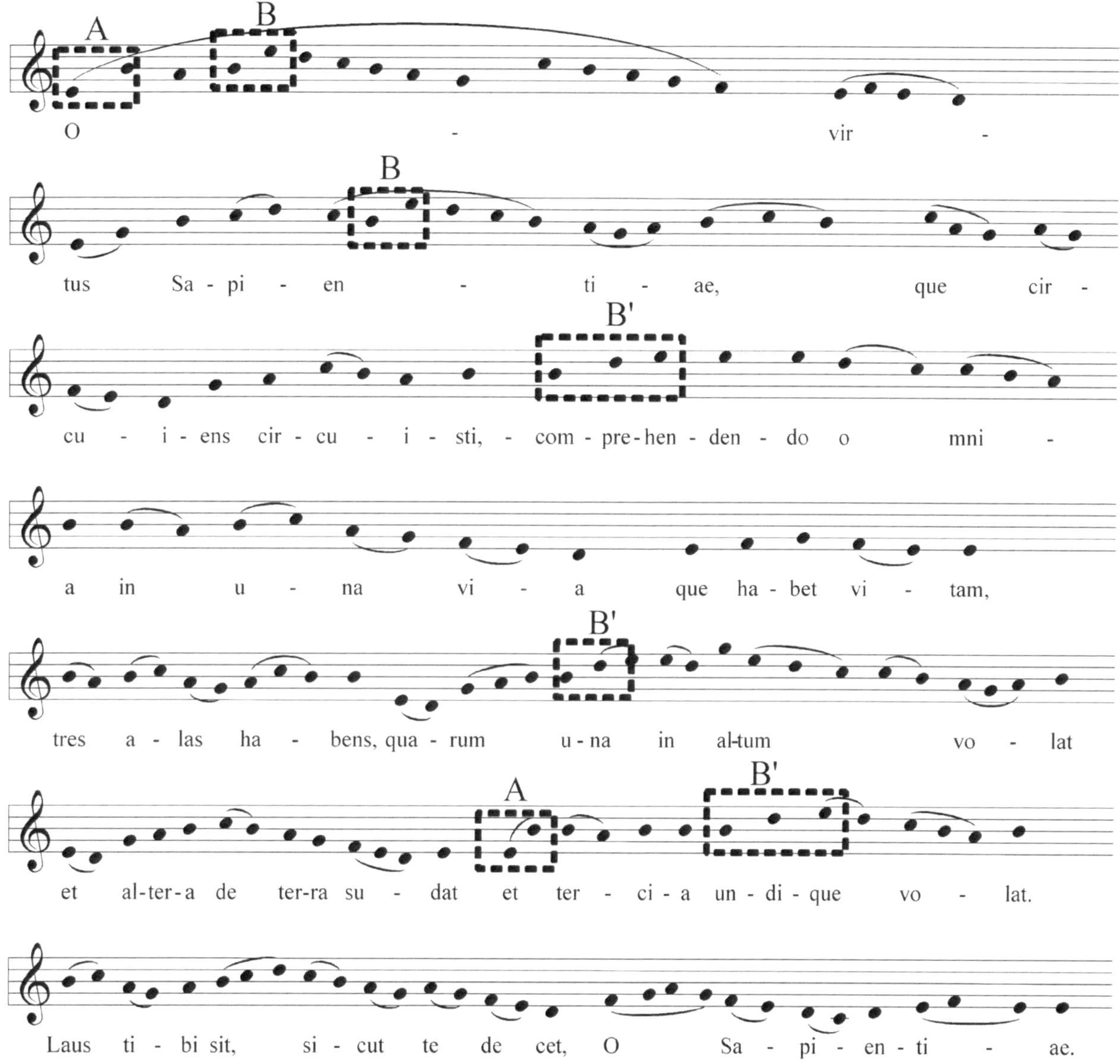

This appearance of intervallic gestures is not to be understood as being the same as use of melodic motives in later music, but it certainly is a predecessor of such compositional technique, and it serves here to unify the character and flow of this antiphon.

Rhythmic Groupings and Flow

Speaking of the flow of this antiphon, it might be instructive to flow a bit back to and then beyond the discussion of rhythm in chant offered in chapter four. To recapitulate: Willi Apel, in *Gregorian Chant*,[215] offers the following points which help to cast some light on the subject of rhythmic practice in the performance of chant as proposed by two different schools of thought – the mensuralists and the equalists.

---

215 Apel. *Op. Cit.* pp. 127ff

The equalists were not dogmatic about every note receiving an absolutely equal time value. The best-known equalists, Pothier and Mocquereau, spoke about longer and shorter notes, and Pothier even spoke of 'free musical rhythm. Mocquereau, in his "Solesmes system" allowed for some durational lengthening in specific instances:

1. the episema — a horizontal line over a note to indicate slight lengthening
2. punctum-mora — a dot after a punctum indicating approximate doubling of length
3. pressus, distropha, and tristropha — repercussive neumes which lengthen a tone
4. vertical episema — a vertical line below a note indicating a slight stress

Pothier and Mocquereau differ considerably as regards accentuation in chant. Pothier believed that the textual accentuation should govern the accentuation of the musical line – text determines musical accent. Mocquereau felt that rhythm was a "purely musical phenomenon, as a motion consisting of *élan* and *repos* (*arsis* and *thesis*; up-beat and down-beat)."[216] The neumes themselves, those containing groups of two or three notes, form patterns of irregular groupings They are controlled by a basic, constant impulse called the "ictus", which is indicated in the score by means of a small vertical line (the vertical episema) below the note to be stressed. These small patterns are mapped onto a larger hierarchical system of grouping into "incises, members, phrases and periods."[217]

On the other hand, the mensuralists attempted to offer strict modern interpretation of chant using rhythmic notation. The punctum was notated as either a quarter-note or an eighth-note, and the virga became a half-note or a quarter-note. The podatus and clivis became eighth-notes, and the climacus and scandicus were triplets, etc. There were numerous theories and attempts to regulate chant in this manner. And today, both sides are still actively debated.

Being primarily neumatic, *O virtus Sapientiae* offers an opportunity to 'play' with both sides of the rhythmic argument in order to discover a suitable performance interpretation. First, the opening melisma (the word "O") is composed of three neumes and a bistropha. If one were an 'equalist', all pitches would receive equal value with a light elongation on the virgas. The bistropha would serve to elongate the g, and the repeated e at the beginning of the word "virtus" would also serve as a temporal emphasis. This would also be true for the second syllable of "virtus" where a punctum e is followed by a podatus beginning on e. Hildegard also provides a 'built-in' positura at the end of the phrase using two punctae interpolated with a bistropha. This positura (cadence) is a 'metrum', ending on the confinal b.

If one were a mensuralist, the following rhythmic solution might emerge, assigning to the punctum the value of a quarter note. Most mensuralists would also couch this solution within the confines of a simple duple meter as well.

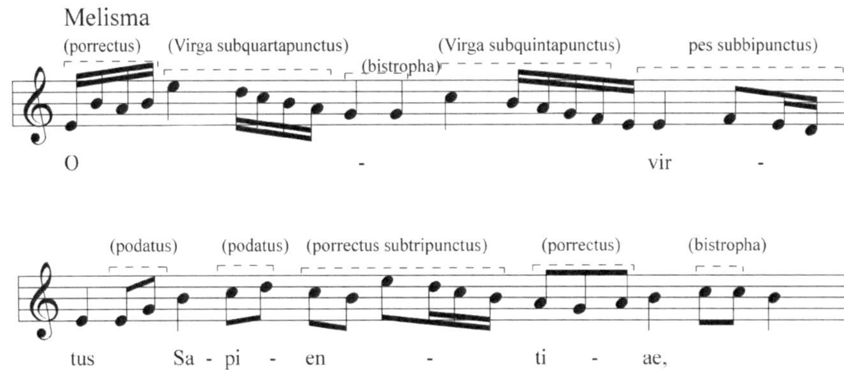

---

[216] *Ibid.* p.128

[217] Ibid.

Taking the 'equalist' point of view espoused by Pothier, Hildegard's rhythm (created by the use of neumes interspersed with punctae in occasional syllabic settings) does basically reflect the accentuation of the Latin texts. The accentuation for this text is given here, with accented syllables underlined.

O vir-tus Sa-pi-en-ti-ae, que cir-cu-i-ens cir-cu-i-sti, com-pre-hen-den-do
om-ni-a in u-na vi-a que ha-bet vi-tam,
tres a-las ha-bens, qua-rum u-na in al-tum vo-lat et al-ter-a de ter-a su-dat
et ter-ci-a un-di-que vo-lat.
Laus ti-bi sit, si-cut te de-cet, O Sa-pi-en-ti-ae.

Hildegard accents syllables through the use of neumes and longer notes as well as with contoural changes. Her musical accentuation parallels textual accentuation for the most part. The only instances where Hildegard does not emphasize the textually accented syllables are:

1. circuisti more emphasis is placed on the syllable 'cu' than on the 'i'. This possibly was to replicate the emphasis of the preceding word, 'circuiens', for poetic and rhythmic purposes.

2. omnia a climacus is used on the second syllable, containing three notes. If one follows the 'equalist' trend, the second syllable would receive more time, though interpreting the passage freely, the climacus would naturally be performed at a slightly increased speed.

3. quarum the same is true here as in no. 2. The scandicus on 'rum' would naturally be performed at a slightly faster tempo.

4. una the emphasis on the second syllable here is a musical phenomenon, with the ascent to the highest point of the antiphon.

5. altum the first syllable receives considerable attention and would probably be sustained slightly as it is the highest pitch of the chant. It also shows a bit of what must have been intentional word painting.

6. undique again, a purely musical phenomenon here, with the e of the last syllable serving as a contoural accent.

7. Sapientiae the accented syllable 'en' does receive a slight stress because of the recurrence of the subfinalis (which has been emphasized as a focal point) and by its presentation as a virga. The following positura figure duplicates that used on the first 'Sapientiae', but now as a full stop.

The only remarkable 'emergent' pattern of rhythmic flow here is Hildegard's use of longer neumes on accented syllables (with the exceptions noted above). The neumes chosen for these accented syllables do not form a specific pattern, though the descending clivis is certainly predominant. Also, at positurae Hildegard often repeats notes (bistropha), creating a natural slowing of the motion.

As a personal observation, it would seem that either a strict mensural approach or an equally strict equalist approach would inhibit the natural flow of the neumatic setting of the text.

Another manner in which Hildegard shapes time and motion in this antiphon is through the use of the registers used in successive phrases. The following table shows the registers for each phrase.

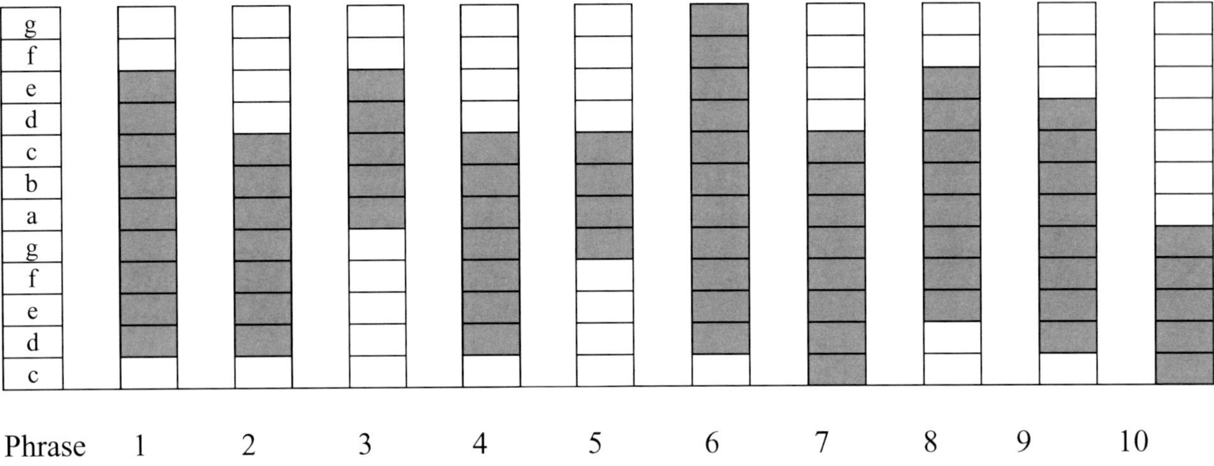

Hildegard first establishes the basic range in phrase 1 and then creates motion through time by contrasting registers within successive phrases. The greatest range is saved for phrase 6 (the Golden Section phrase), and the phrases following serve to gradually lower the register to the final cadence. Phrase 8 shows a return to the basic range of the opening phrase, and it also begins with the same initial melodic pattern – the ascending fifth . In fact, the contour of phrase 8 is quite similar to the initial gesture in phrase 1 (through the first ten pitches).

Two more observations can be drawn from the graph. First, there is a considerable use of the pitches d and c as the lowest pitches of all but three phrases, and as the highest pitches of five phrases. The pitch c is the subfinalis of the Dorian mode, and, of course, d is the finalis. Hildegard's digression to an emphasis on that mode has been marked previously.

Second, the range of a twelfth is larger than what is normally found in chant, but it is not unusual for Hildegard.

Well. This is not a traditional antiphon in that it is not a refrain extracted from a Psalm – it is a setting of an original text by Hildegard. This practice was not at all unusual during Hildegard's time as there was a plethora of antiphonal composition and poetic creativity. But most of that activity has been lost or at least 'not rediscovered', yet here we have a complete collection of works attributed to a single composer by name, for the first time in Western History. Hildegard's antiphon is allegorical and visionary rather than being a commentary or poetic reflection on a specific scriptural verse of Psalm. And her composition is artistic and creative to a degree not seen in liturgical composition until her work became known. Let's meditate.

Meditation

218

---

[218] This image of a pair of interacting galaxies called Arp 273 was released to celebrate the 21st anniversary of the launch of the NASA/ESA Hubble Space Telescope. The distorted shape of the larger of the two galaxies shows signs of tidal interactions with the smaller of the two. It is thought that the smaller galaxy has actually passed through the larger one.

Credit: NASA, ESA and the Hubble Heritage Team (STScI/AURA)

Sit quietly and comfortably in a peaceful place and quietly play one of the following as background:

Barber: *Adagio for Strings* (orchestral version)
Pärt: *Fratres* (any version)

Pärt: *Spiegel im Spiegel* (violin and piano version)
Gebuhr: *2.73* and *Offertorium*

Take time to fall into the image, becoming part of it. Choose one of the following texts from Hildegard[219] and follow the practice of *Lectio divina* while remaining in the image. Read the excerpt through completely, then return to the beginning and read slowly, stopping with words that capture you, letting your mind and soul follow their path of 'greenness'. Gently return to the text and continue until the next word gives you pause. After completing the text in this manner, read it through again and revisit some of the images and thoughts you received while reading slowly (Lectio divina).

End your meditation by reciting the short doxology or other meaningful prayer of praise prayerfully.

From Vision Four, *De Operatione Dei*
The firmament has a revolving orbit in imitation of the power of God which has neither beginning nor end, just as no one can see where the encircling wheel begins or ends. For the throne of God is God's eternity in which God alone sits, and all the living sparks are rays of God's splendor, just as the rays of the sun proceed from the sun itself. And how could God be known to be life, except through the living things which glorify God, since the creatures which praise God's glory have come from God.

From Vision Four, *De Operatione Dei*
There is nothing in creation which does not have some radiance, either greenness or seeds or flowers or beauty – otherwise it would not be part of creation.

From Vision Eight, *De Operatione Dei*
Everything that God has effected has been perfected in Love, Humility and Peace. Human beings, therefore, should esteem Love, embrace Humility and grasp Peace.

Glory be to the Father,
to the Son,
and to the Holy Spirit.
As it was in the beginning is now,
And shall be Forever.

---

[219] Bowie, Fiona, Ed. *The Wisdom of Hildegard of Bingen*. (Grand Rapids, William B. Eerdmans Publishing Company), pp. 12, 13, 18.

A musical response to meditation on Hildegard's antiphon is offered.

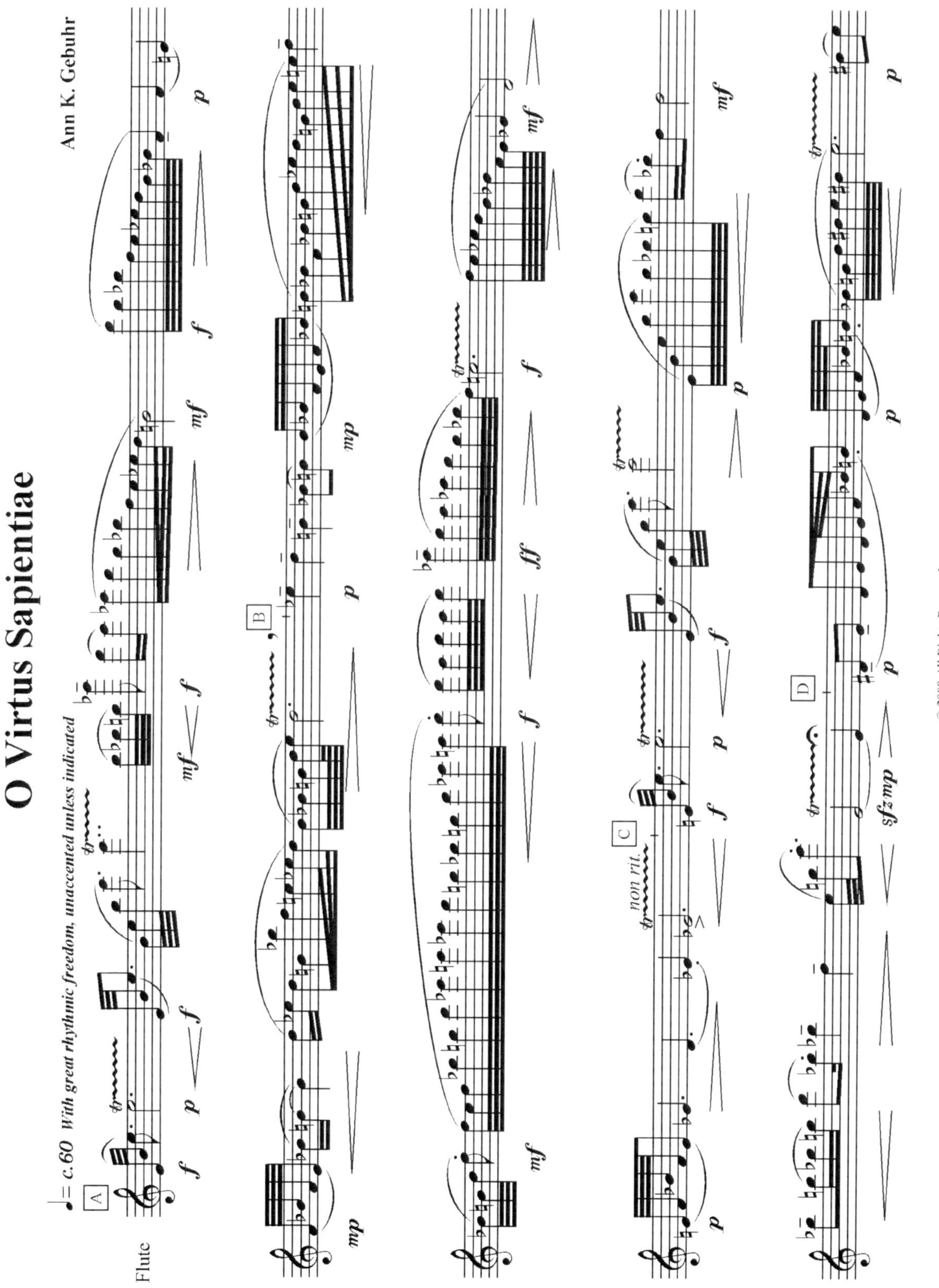

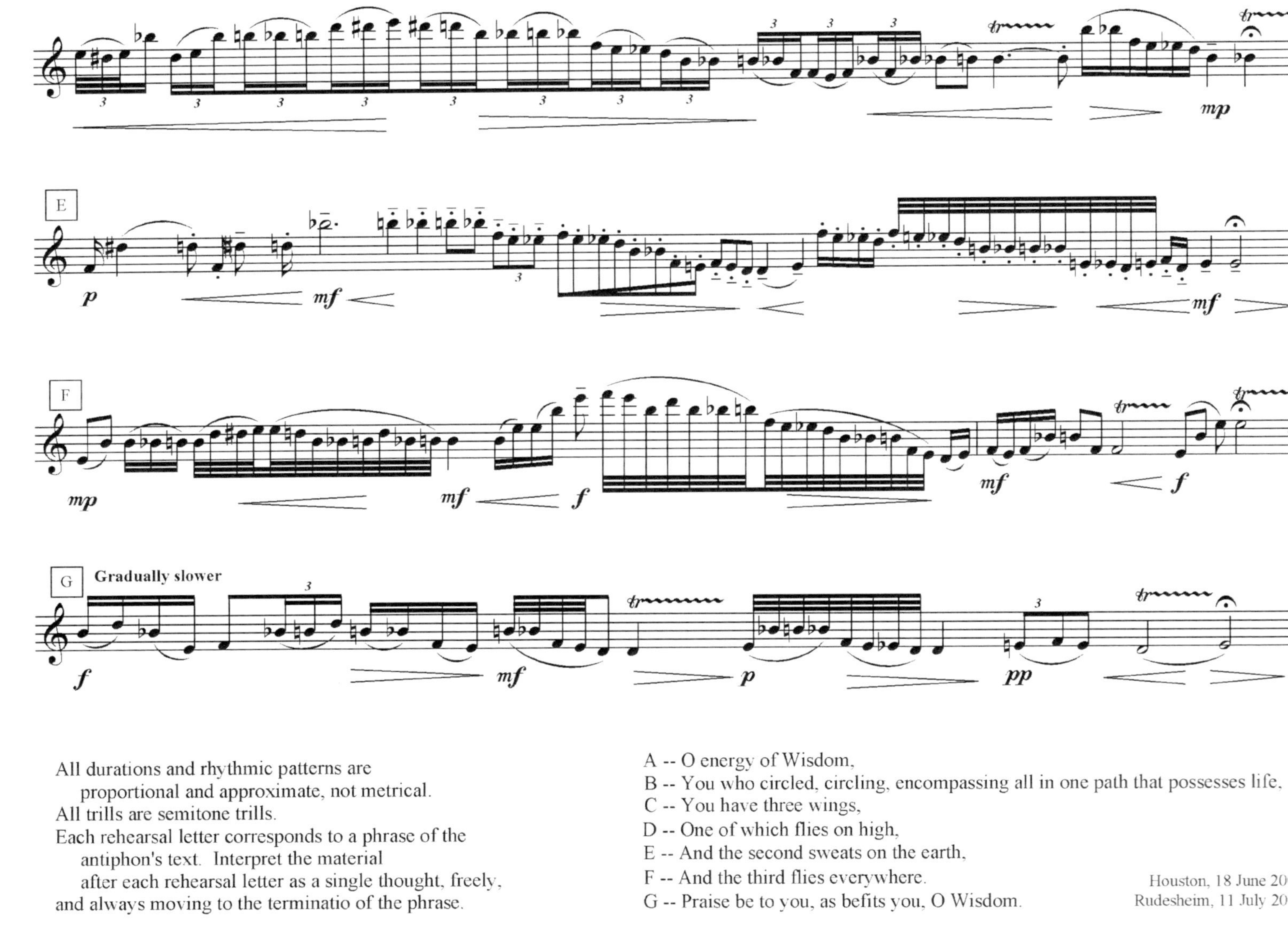
2
E
F
G
Gradually slower
All durations and rhythmic patterns are
proportional and approximate, not metrical.
All trills are semitone trills.
Each rehearsal letter corresponds to a phrase of the
antiphon's text. Interpret the material
after each rehearsal letter as a single thought, freely,
and always moving to the terminatio of the phrase.
A -- O energy of Wisdom,
B -- You who circled, circling, encompassing all in one path that possesses life,
C -- You have three wings,
D -- One of which flies on high,
E -- And the second sweats on the earth,
F -- And the third flies everywhere.
G -- Praise be to you, as befits you, O Wisdom.
Houston, 18 June 2007
Rudesheim, 11 July 2009

Exercise

Find a location either in your home or nearby where you have access to at least one set of 18-24 stairs with a hand rail or banister. Wear good athletic shoes (do not do this barefoot or in leather-soled shoes).

Begin the exercise with three stretching deep breaths. Then at a regular pace, not too slow or too fast, climb at least ten steps without holding on to the banister. Stop on the tenth step and release all tension in your body, breathe deeply twice and then climb ten more steps. Stop, release tension, breathe deeply and return to the bottom of the stairs.

Repeat this two more times (three times total) for two weeks, then add an additional repetition every two weeks until you are climbing the equivalent of five flights of stairs each time. As you increase the number of flights, you may want to use the banister to help 'pull' you up – this adds some upper body exercise to the process!

If you continue with all of the exercises offered in this book, you might order them into a weekly pattern with a different exercise each day. That would give variety, inside and outside experiences, and the opportunity to re-energize your body and mind and soul every day.

Recipes

This is an offering of a recipe for healthy living, based on a Benedictine 'rule'!

6 AM — Wake up! Stay in bed for five minutes of slow stretching and deep breathing, thanking God for the new day and for the peace and refreshing night's sleep.

Complete your morning ablution and dressing.

6:30 — Break your fast with a good meal. Hildegard's habermus is an excellent idea! Include protein and fruit. And, of course, coffee. Make a ceremony out of it, taking time to sit down to eat. You can think through your day quietly while having your breakfast. If you are in the habit or grabbing something on the run or during through a fast food shop, break the habit! It is harmful to your health and to your soul!

7-10 — Work

10 AM — Take a fifteen minute break for a cup of coffee or piece of fruit (stay away from breads or sweets!). But most important, take the break from work to be quiet, to meditate or to pray.

10:15-noon — Work

Noon — Break for lunch. Enjoy a meal with friends – but don't talk about work issues! Let the time be a true break from work. Enjoy your food, be grateful for it, pay attention to it! Try to eat fresh food.

1-2 — Rest. Be quiet. Read, nap, pray. Or exercise.

2-4 — Work

4 PM — Go home and have tea and quiet in your favorite place in your home.

4:30-6 — Community time! Enjoy family and friends. Or exercise with them.

6-7:30 — Prepare and enjoy dinner. Plan your meal with discretion!

7:30-9:45 — Enjoy your evening. NO WORK!

9:45 — Evening prayer time, alone or with your family.

10 PM — Go to bed, use the relaxing meditation to quiet your body and mind, and sleep well!

This is a suggestion, not a rule – any kind of pattern that offers you a chance to eat, live and pray in a less driven, stressful manner is healthy and good!

Bibliographic Resources in English

Primary Sources

Book of Divine Works, with Letters and Songs. Fox, Matthew, Ed.
Bear & Company, Santa Fe, 1987. ISBN 0-939680-35-1

Explanatio Regulae S. Benedicti (Commentary on the Rule of St. Benedict)
Feiss, H., O.S.B. (tr.) *Explanation of the rule of Benedict by Hildegard of Bingen.*
Toronto, Peregrina Publishing Co., 1990. ISBN 0-920669-15

Hildegard's Healing Plants. Bruce Hozeski, Tr. Beacon Press, Boston, 2001 ISBN 0-8070-2109-1
Liber compositae medicinae/Causae et curae. (Book of Compound Medicine or Causes and Cures)
Pawlik, M. (translation of Latin, Patrick Madigan, S.J. (translation of German), John Kulas, O.S.B. (translation of Forward), Mary Palmquist and John Kulas, O.S.B., eds., published as *Holistic Healing.*
The Liturgical Press, Collegeville, Minnesota, 1994. ISBN 0-8146-2224-0

Physica, Priscilla Throop, Tr. The Healing Arts Press, Vermont, 1998. ISBN 0-89281-661-9

Scivias. Bruce Hozeski, Tr. Bear & Company, Santa Fe, 1986. ISBN 0-9396-80-22-X

Scivias. Mother Columba Hart and Jane Bishop, Tr. Paulist Press, New York, 1990. ISBN 0-8091-3130-7

Symphonia Harmoniae Caelestium Revelationum. Dendermonde St.-Pieters & Paulusabdij. Ms. Cod. 9.
Alamire, Belgium, 1991. ISBN 90-6853-051-8

The Life of the Holy Hildegard, by the monks Gottfried and Theoderic
Translated from Latin to German by Adelgundis Führkötter
Translated from German to English by James McGrath
Edited by Mary Palmquist with the assistance of John Kulas, O.S.B.
The Liturgical Press, Collegeville, Minnesota. 1995 ISBN 0-8146-2244-5

The Letters of Hildegard of Bingen, Volumes I, II and III
Translated by Joseph L. Baird and Radd K. Ehrman
Oxford University Press, Oxford and New York, 1994, 1998 and 2004
ISBN 0-19-512117-1, 0-19-512010-8 and 0-19-516837-2

Secondary Sources

Berger, Margret. *Hildegard of Bingen: On Natural Philosophy and Medicine.*
Cambridge, D.S. Brewer, 1999. ISBN 0-85991-551-4

Bobko, Jane, ed. *Vision: The Life and Music of Hildegard von Bingen.*
New York, Penguin Books, 1995. ISBN 0-670-86405-6

Bowie, Fiona. *The Wisdom of Hildegard of Bingen.*
Grand Rapids, Michigan, Eerdmans Publishing Company, 1987. ISBN 0-8028-3851-0

Bowie, Fiona and Oliver Davies, eds. New Translations by Robert Carver, *Mystical Writings*
Spiritual Classics: Crossroad, New York, 1992. ISBN 0-8245-1027-5

Boyce-Tillman, June. *The Creative Spirit.* Morehouse Publishing, Pennsylvania, 2001. ISBN 0-8192-1882-0

Butcher, Carmen. *Hildegard of Bingen, A Spiritual Reader.*
Paraclete Press, Massachusetts, 2007. ISBN 978-1-55725-490-0

Chervin, Ronda De Sola. *Prayers of the Women Mystics.*
Ann Arbor, Michigan, Servant Publications, 1992. ISBN 0-89283-750-0

Crain, Renata. *Hildegard: Prophet of the Cosmic Christ.*
The Crossroad Publishing Company, New York, 1997. ISBN 0-8245-2510-8

Davidson, Audrey Ekdahl, ed. *The Ordo Virtutum of Hildegard of Bingen.*
Kalamazoo, Michigan, Western Michigan University, 1992. ISBN 1-879288-17-6

Dreyer, Elizabeth. *Passionate Women: Two Medieval Mystics.*
Paulist Press, New York. ISBN 0-89-0913-082-3

Passionate Spirituality, Hildegard of Bingen and Hadewijch of Brabant.
Paulist Press, New York, 2005. ISBN 0-8091-4304-6

Durka, Gloria. *Praying with Hildegard of Bingen.*
Winona, MN, Saint Mary's Press, 1991. ISBN 0-884849-254-9

Fierro, Nancy. *Hildegard of Bingen and Her Vision of the Feminine.*
Sheed and Ward, Kansas City, Missouri, 1994. ISBN 1-55612-733-7

Flanagan, Sabina. *Hildegard of Bingen: A Visionary Life.*
London and New York, Routledge, 1989. ISBN 0-7607-1361-8

Hildegard von Bingen, in "German Writers and Works of the Early Middle Ages: 800- 1170," *Dictionary of Literary Biography*, vol. 148. New York:, Gale, 1995.

Secrets of God: Writings of Hildegard of Bingen
Shambala Publications, Boston, 1996. ISBN 1-57062-164-0

Fox. Matthew, ed. *Illuminations of Hildegard of Bingen*
Bear & Company, Santa Fe, 1985. ISBN 0-939680-21-1

Hart, Mother Columba and Jane Bishop, Tr. *Creation and Christ, The Wisdom of Hildegard of Bingen.*
Paulist Press, New York, 1996. ISBN 0-8891-3674-0

Hildegard of Bingen, Selections from Her Writings.
Harper, San Francisco, 1990. ISBN 0-06-075-66-9

Higley, Sarah, Tr., Ed. *Hildegard of Bingen's Unknown Language.*
Palgrave MacMillan, New York, 2007. ISBN 1-4039-7673-2

Hutchinson, Gloria. *A Retreat with Gerard Manley Hopkins and Hildegard of Bingen: Turning Pain IntoPower.*
Cincinnati, st. Anthony Messenger Press, 1995. ISBN 0867162511

King-Lenzmeier, Anne. *Hildegard of Bingen, An Integrated Vision.*
The Liturgical Press, Minnesota, 2001. ISBN 0-8146-5842-3

Kirvan, John. *Let Ther Be Light: based on the visionary spirituality of Hildegard von Bingen.*
Notre Dame, IN, Ave Maria Press, 1997.

Kraft, Kent Thomas. *The Eye Sees More than the Heart Knows: The Visionary Cosmology of Hildegard of Bingen.* Ann Arbor, University Microfilms International, 1978.

Lauter, Dr. Werner. *The Parish and Pilgrim Church St. Hildegard.* The Catholic Parish Office, Rüdesheim-Eibingen, 2008

Maddocks, Fiona. *Hildegard of Bingen, The Woman of Her Age.* Doubleday, New York, 2001. ISBN 0-325-49867-5

McInerny, Maud, Ed. *Hildegard of Bingen, A Book of Essays.* Garland Publishing, Inc., New York, 1998. ISBN 0-8153-2588-6

Meehan, Bridget. *Praying with Visionary Women.* Sheed & Ward, Wisconsin, 1999. ISBN 1-58051-063-9

Newman, Barbara. *Sister of Wisdom: St. Hildegard's Theology of the Feminine.* Berkeley, University of california Press, 1987.

Saint Hildegard of Bingen: symphonia: A Critical Edition of the "Symphonia armonie celestium revelationum." Cornell University Press, 1988. ISBN 0-8014-9514-8

Voice of the Living Light: Hildegard of Bingen and Her World. Berkeley, University of California Press, 1998 ISBN 0-520-21758-6

Pernoud, Régine. *Hildegard of Bingen.* New York, Marlowe and Company, 1998. ISBN 1-56924-727-7

Powers, John. *Holy Human: Mystics for Our Time.* Mystic, Connecticut, Twenty-Third Publications, 1989. ISBN 0896223981

Rath, Sr. Philippa. *Benedictine Abbey of St. Hildegard, Rüdesheim-Eibingen.* Michael Imhof Verlag, Petersberg, Germany, 2003. ISBN 3-935590-76-8

Reed-Jones, Carol. *Hildegard of Bingen, Woman of Vision.* Paper Crane Press, Washington, 2004. ISBN 0-9650833-1-4

Sacks, O. "The Visions of Hildegard": *The Man who Mistook his Wife for a Hat.* London, Picador/Pan, 1986.

Schipperges, Heinrich. *Hildegard von Bingen.* New York, Philosophical Library, 1989. ISBN 0802225330

Hildegard of Bingen: Healing and the Nature of the cosmos. Princeton, M. Weiner, 1997. ISBN 1558761381

The World of Hildegard of Bingen: Her Life, Times and Visions. Collegeville, MN, The Liturgical Press, 1998. ISBN 0-8146-2543-6

Schleissner, Margaret, Ed. *Manuscript Sources of Medieval Medicine, A Book of Essays.* Garland Publishing, Inc., New York, 1995. ISBN 0-8153-0815-9

Schmitt, Miriam. "Blessed Jutta of Disibodenberg: Hildegard of Bingen's Magistra and Abbess" in *American Benedictine Review* 40:2, June 1989.

Silvas, Anna, tr. *Jutta & Hildegard: The Biographical Sources.* State College, Penn State University Press, 1999. ISBN 0-271-01954-9

Storch, Walburga, Ed. *Prayers of Hildegard of Bingen.*
St. Anthony Messenger Press, Cincinnati, Ohio, 1989. ISBN 0-87160-491-3

Strehlow, W., and Hertzka, G. *Hildegard of Bingen's Medicine.*
Bear & Company, Santa Fe, 1988. ISBN 0-939680-44-0

Strehlow, Wighard. *Hildegard of Bingen's Spiritual Remedies.*
Healing Arts Press, Vermont, 2002. ISBN 0-89281-985-5

St. Hildegard of Bingen's Nutrition: Spelt – The Superfood.
Available as a Kindle Edition, Amazon Digital Services, Strehlow Verlag, 2012. ASIN B008FF6K8I

Sweet, Dr. Victoria. *Rooted in the Earth, Rooted in the Sky, Hildegard of Bingen and Premodern Medicine.*
Routledge, New York, 2006. ISBN 0-415-97634-0

Uhlein, Gabriele. *Meditations with Hildegard of Bingen.*
Bear & Company, Santa Fe, 1983. ISBN 0939680122

Ulrich, Ingeborg. *Hildegard of Bingen, Mystic, Healer, Companion of the Angels.*
The Liturgical Press, Minnesota, 1993. ISBN 0-3146-2132-5

Van de Weyer, Robert. *Hildegard in a Nutshell.*
London, Hodder and Stoughton, Ltd, 1997. ISBN 0-340-69404-5

Wiethaus, Ulrike. "Cathar Influences in Hildegard of Bingen's Play 'Ordo virtutum'"
in *American Benedictine Review* 38:2, June 1987.

Unpublished Master's Theses and Doctoral Dissertations

Collingridge, Lorna. Music as Evocative Power: The Intersection of Music with Images of the Divine in the Songs of Hildegard of Bingen.
Unpublished Dissertation for the Doctor of Philosophy Degree, Griffith University, Australia, 2003

Lomer, Beverly. Music, Rhetoric and the Creation of Feminist Consciousness in the Marian Songs of Hildegard of Bingen (1098-1179).
Unpublished Dissertation for the Doctor of Philosophy Degree, Florida Atlantic University, 2006

Jeffreys, Catherine. Melodia et rhetorica: The Devotional-Song Repertory of Hildegard of Bingen.
Unpublished Dissertation for the Doctor of Philosophy Degree, University of Melbourne, 2000

McGuire, Kent. Symphonia Caritatis: The Cistercian Chants of Hildegard von Bingen.
Unpublished Thesis for the Master of Arts Degree, University of Minnesota. 2007

Historical Fiction

Lachman, Barbara. *The Journal of Hildegard of Bingen.*
New York, Bell Tower, 1993. ISBN 0517591693

Hildegard, the Last Year. Boston, Shambhala, 1997. ISBN 1-57062-315-5

Ohanneson, Joan. *Scarlet Music: Hildegard of Bingen, A Novel.*
New York, Crossroad Publishing, 1997. ISBN 082451646X

Video Resources

VHS

Hildegard. VHS, Color/52 minutes. Gateway Films/Vision Video, 1994. ISBN 1-56364-107-0

Hildegard of Bingen. VHS, Color/60 minutes. Washington National Cathedral by Morehouse Publishing, 1989.
Pioneers of the Spirit: Hildegard of Bingen. VHS, Color, 24 minutes. Gateway Films/Vision Video, 1998ISBN 1-56364-265-4

Ordo virtutum: Hildegard of Bingen. VHS Color, 70 minutes, English subtitles. Petri Visser Productions, 1997.
Radiant Life: Meditations and Visions of Hildegard of Bingen. VHS, Color/40 minutes. Wellspring Media, Inc., 1996 ISBN 1-885538-28-6

DVD

Hildegard von Bingen in Portrait. A double DVD including the first, third and fourth VHS listings above with two additional interviews with Matthew Fox. Opus Arte 0875D
In the Symphony of the World. 50 minutes. Flare Productions, Inc. 2004.
Vision. A film by Margarethe von Trotta, 110 minutes. Zeitgeist Films, 2010.

Discography

The following is a listing of all of Hildegard's chants and a discography which offers performances of most of her music (the number of the recording is given on the list). This list contains all chants from both sources, the Dendermonde , St.-Pieters-&-Paulusabdij, Codex 9; and the Wiesbaden, Landesbibliothek, Hs. 2 ("Riesenkodex"). The discography is not complete.

Title (Latin	Type of Chant	Recording(s)
Father and Son		
O vis eternitatis	Responsory	7, 10, 34
O virtus Sapientiae	Antiphon	6, 10, 11, 13, 28
O quam mirabilis	Antiphon	6, 10, 11, 16, 30, 31, 32, 34
O pastor animarum	Antiphon	8, 12, 25, 26
O cruor sanguinis	Antiphon	7
O magne Pater	Antiphon	10, 22, 34
O eterne Deus	Antiphon	7, 10, 17, 32, 34
Mother and Son		
Ave Maria	Responsory	8, 10, 17, 28
O clarissima mater	Responsory	6, 11, 16, 17, 26
O spendidissima gemma	Antiphon	17
Hodie aperuit	Antiphon	11, 13, 17, 26, 29
Quia ergo femina	Antiphon	8, 13, 26, 28
Cum processit factura	Antiphon	8, 12, 28
Cum erubuerint	Antiphon	9, 12
O frondens virga	Antiphon-Dendermonde only, not Riesenkodex	9, 10, 11, 12, 13, 26(x2), 28, 31, 33

O quam magnum miraculum	Antiphon	9, 28
Ave generosa	Hymn	1, 9, 10, 12, 13, 17, 21, 25, 28, 31
O virga mediatrix	Alleluia-verse	8, 11, 25
O viridissima virga	Song	1, 8, 13, 25, 29, 30, 31
O virga ac diadema	Sequence	6, 12, 21, 25, 28
O tu suavissima virga	Responsory	8
O quam preciosa	Responsory	9, 12, 28
O tu illustrata	Antiphon	9, 13, 16, 27, 30
The Holy Spirit		
Spiritus sanctus vivificans vita	Antiphon	8, 13, 34
Karitas habundat	Antiphon	8, 11, 12, 13, 17, 26, 28, 30, 31, 32, 33, 34
Laus Trinitati	Antiphon-Dendermonde only, not Riesenkodex	7, 25
O ignee Spiritus	Hymn	9, 27, 32
O ignis Spiritus Paracliti	Sequence	1, 8, 25, 32, 34
The Celestial Hierarchy		
O gloriosissimi lux vivens angeli	Antiphon	2, 13, 27
O vos angeli	Responsory	2, 27
O spectabiles viri	Antiphon	30
O vos felices radices	Responsory	6, 29
O cohors milicie floris	Antiphon	29
O lucidissima apostolorum turba	Responsory	6, 30
O speculum columbe	Antiphon	29

O dulcis electe	Responsory	
O victoriosissimi triumphatores	Antiphon	
Vos flores rosarum	Responsory	6
O vos imitatores	Responsory	
O successores	Antiphon	6, 29
Patron Saints		
O mirum admirandum	Antiphon	22, 29
O viriditas digiti Dei	Responsory	22, 31
O felix anima	Responsory	10, 22, 26, 32
O beata infantia	Antiphon	22, 29
O presul vere civitatis	Sequence	1, 22, 25, 29, 34
O felix apparicio	Antiphon	9
O beatissime Ruperte	Antiphon	9
Quia felix puericia	Antiphon	9
O Ierusalem	Sequence	1, 9, 24, 34
Mathias sanctus	Hymn	22, 29
O Bonifaci	Antiphon	22, 29
O Euchari columba	Responsory	22
O Euchari in leta via	Sequence	1, 18, 22, 25, 31, 33
Columba aspexit	Sequence	1, 22, 29, 31, 33
Virgins, Widows, Innocents		
O pulchra facies	Antiphon	6, 13, 26
O nobilissima viriditas	Responsory	8, 26, 29, 31

O dulcissime amator	Symphony of Virgins	7, 28
O Pater omnium	Symphony of Widows	22, 28
Rex noster promptus	Responsory	7, 17, 27
St. Ursula and Companions		
Spiritui sancto	Responsory	6, 17, 22, 26, 28, 31
O rubor sanguinis	Antiphon	7, 26, 27
Favus distillans	Responsory	7, 13, 17, 23, 26, 27
O Ecclesia	Sequence	7, 13, 22, 23
In matutinus laudibus	Antiphon	7, 33
Cum vox sanguinis	Hymn	7, 15
Antiphons for Matins		
Studium divinitatis	Antiphon	15 , 26, 27, 33
Unde quocumque	Antiphon	15, 26, 27, 33
De patria	Antiphon	15, 26, 27, 33
Deus enim in prima	Antiphon	15, 26, 27
Aer enim volat	Antiphon	15, 26
Et ideo puelle	Antiphon	26, 27, 33
Deus enim rorem	Antiphon	15, 26, 28
Sed diabolus	Antiphon	15, 26, 27
Ecclesia		
O virgo Ecclesia	Antiphon	7
Nunc gaudeant	Antiphon	7, 27, 30
O orzchis Ecclesia	Antiphon	7, 27

O coruscans lux stellarum	Antiphon	8, 13, 26
Other Liturgical Songs		
Kyrie		12, 13, 25, 26
Nunc aperuit nobis	Antiphon	8
Four Songs without Music		
O Verbum Patris	Song	
O Fili diectissime	Song	
O factura Dei	Song	
O magna res	Song	

Compact Disc Recordings

1 - *A Feather on the Breath of God: Sequences and Hymns by Abbess Hjildegard of Bingen.* Gothic Voices. Hyperion A/KA/CDA 66039 (1981)

2 - *Angeli: Music of Angels.* Ensemble P.A.N. with guest ensemble Tapestry. CD TELARC 80448 (1996)

3 -*Geistliche Musik des Mittelalters und der Ranissance.* Instrumentalkreise Helga Weber. TELDEC LP 66.22387 (1980).

4 - *Gesänger der hl. Hildegard von Bingen.* Schola der Benediktinerinnenabtei St. Hildegard in Eibingen. LP/MC: Psallite 242.040479/242 (1979).

5 - *Hildegard von Bingen: Ordo virtutum.* Sequentia, Deutsch Harmonia Mundi CDS 7492498. (1982) With an English translation by Peter Dronke.

6 - *Hildegard von Bingen: Symphoniae.* Sequentia, Deutsch Harmonia Mundi CDC 7492512 (1983).

7 - *Hildegard von Bingen: Voice of the Blood.* Sequentia, Deutsch Harmonia Mundi CD 05472 77345 2 (1995).

8 - *Hildegard von Bingen: Canticles of Ecstasy.* Sequentia, Deutsch Harmonia Mundi CD 05472 77320 2 (1994).

9 - *Hildegard von Bingen: O Jerusalem.* Sequentia, Deutsch Harmonia Mundi CDC 05472-77353-2 (1997).

10 - *Hildegard von Bingen und ihre Zeit.* (Songs by Hildegard and Abelard). Ensemble für frühe Musik Augsburg. Christophorus CD 74584 (1990).

11 - *Hildegard von Bingen (1098-1179): Lieder und Antiphonen* (Also works of Dunstable, Dufay, and Brassart). Instrumentalkreise Helga Weber. Christophorus CD CHE 0041-2 (1980/1993).

12 -*Hildegard von Bingen.* Schola der Benediktinerinnenabtei St. Hildegard in Eibingen. CD 100-116 Bayer Records (1994)

13 - *Hildegard of Bingen: The Harmony of Heaven.* Ellen Oak. CD Bison Tales 0001.

14 - *Jouissance: Hildegard and Abelard.* Viriditas. CD Spectrum Publications, Richmond, Victoria, Australia 3121 (1994).

15 - *The Lauds of Saint Ursula.* Early Music Institute, Indiana University. CD: Focus 911 (1991).

16 - *The Monk and the Abbess.* Music by Hildegard von Bingen and Meredith Monk. Musica Sacra, Richard Westenburg, Conductor. CD Catalyst 09026-68329-2 (1996).

17 - *Unfurling Love's Creation:* Chants by Hildegard von Bingen. Lyrichord Discs Inc. LEMS 8027 (1997)

18 - *Renaissance of Humanity:* Music of Hildegard of Bingen, Arvo Pärt, and Jan Jirásek. CD 09026-68331-2 Catalyst (1996).

19 - *Vision*: The Music of Hildegard von Bingen. Contemporary arrangements. Angel CDC 7243 5 55246 2 1 (1994).

20 - *Illumination:* Hildegard von Bingen: The Fire of the Spirit. Contemporary arrangements. Sony SK 62853

21 - *Zum Fest der Heiligen Hildegard.* Deutsch Harmonia Mundi. HM942-2 (1990)

22 - *Hildegard von Bingen: Saints.* Sequentia, Deutsch Harmonia Mundi CDC 05472-77378-2 (1998).

23 - *Musik der Kloester: Saint Martial, Aquitanian Monasteries, Rupertsberg, Santiago de Compostela.* Sequentia, Schola Cantorum Basiliensis. Deutsche Harmonia Mundi. CD 05472 77606 2

24 - *Hildegard von Bingen, Perotin, Otto von Wolkenstein.* Sequentia, Deller Consort et al. Deutsche Harmonia Mundi. CD 05472 77600 2

25 - *Hildegard von Bingen: Heavenly Revelations.* Oxford Camerata, Jeremy Summerly, Director. Naxos 8.550998 (1995)

26 - *Music of the Angels: Hildegard von Bingen.* The Hildegard von Bingen Choir. Fine classics, 4427-2. (2000)

27 – *Sinfonye,* Volume 1. Celestial Harmonies 13127-2. (1996)

28 – *Sinfonye,* Volume 2. Celestial Harmonies 13128-2. (1999)

29 – *Sinfonye,* Volume 3. Celestial Harmonies 13129-2. (2004)

30 – *Celestial Stairs, Hildegard von Bingen.* Christophorus CD 77205. (1997)

31 – *Hildegard von Bingen.* Alba, The International Music Company AG, Hamburg, Germany. 220536 (2002)

32 – *The origin of Fire.* Anonymous 4, Harmoni Mundi. HMU 907327 (2004)

33 – *Sapphire Night.* Tapestry, MDG Gold, Germany MDG 344 1193-2 (2003)

34 – *O Vis Aeternitatis.* Schola, Abbey of St. Hildegard, Rüdesheim-Eibingen, Germany. AHM 270002 (2007)

About the author...

Author Ann K. Gebuhr is a composer, music theorist, author and teacher. Her orchestral music has been performed by symphonies throughout the United States and in Germany and Romania. She is a MacDowell Colony Fellow, a Rockefeller Scholar in Residence in Bellagio, and the first woman to be awarded the Creative Artist Award in Composition by the Cultural Arts Council of Houston/Harris County in 1998 and again in 2009. She currently teaches, learns, writes and lives in Houston, Texas.

About the flutist...

In addition to solo performances, flutist Teresa Grawunder has performed professionally with the Houston Ballet Orchestra, Theater Under the Stars and as a substitute in the Houston Symphony. Ms. Grawunder set out to explore more creative aspects of playing and teaching while continuing her classical freelance work. She has been a Teaching Artist for Texas Institute for Arts in Education and has been part of many collaborative performances with artists in various media, including dance and film. She developed a style of free improvisation on the flute that eventually led to the recording of a CD, *Mysterium*, and she was a founding member of the classical chamber ensemble “MOSAIC,” which rediscovered and performed beautiful but rarely heard repertoire with unusual combinations of voice and instruments.